West Sales Associates will get you additional copies fast or answer your questions.
Just call **1-800-328-9352**

Do more in less time on your PC with *Black's Electronic Editions!*

Over 30,000 up-to-date legal terms and expressions—works stand-alone or pops up within WordPerfect® or any other word processor. Powerful WESTLAW®-like search capabilities go beyond simple word look-ups to find legal *ideas* or even find a word based on how it *sounds.*

Check the spelling of important legal terms *and* common words in a single pass. Over 20,000 legal terms from *Black's Law Dictionary®, 6th Edition* integrate directly into your WordPerfect Speller Main Dictionary.

Electronic Editions are easy to install and use!

- *Black's Law Dictionary* includes a User's Guide, plus on-screen help in a simple pull-down menu.
- 3½" or 5¼" disks (network versions available).
- *Black's Law Dictionary* works with any IBM® PC or compatible with 640K RAM. *Black's Legal Speller* works with WordPerfect only.

INTRODUCTORY DISCOUNT!
Order your *Black's Electronic Editions* today and save!
Contact your local West representative, or call
1-800-328-9352.

© 1993 West Publishing Company

LAW OFFICE PRACTICE TOOLS FROM WEST

LAW OFFICE SERIES
 How to Use WordPerfect® 5.0/5.1 in the Law Office
 Guy Wiggins and Dave Greenwald

BLACK'S LAW DICTIONARY®—ELECTRONIC EDITION
BLACK'S™ LEGAL SPELLER—ELECTRONIC EDITION

WEST'S® DESKTOP PRACTICE SYSTEMS   *Computer Disks*
 Bankruptcy Code, Rules and Forms\FAST
 Bankruptcy Practice Forms and Commentary\FAST
 Federal Civil Judicial Procedure and Rules\FAST
 Federal Criminal Code and Rules\FAST
 Federal Jury Instructions

WEST'S® EXPRESS FORMS   *Computer Disks*
 Bankruptcy
 California Litigation
 Massachusetts Criminal Defense

WESTLAW®   *Legal Practice Databases*
 COMPCOUN   Computer Counsel
 LAWPC   The Lawyer's PC
 LPMGMT   Law Practice Management
 LS-ABAEO   ABA Ethics Opinions
 LS-MRPC   Model Rules of Professional Conduct
 OGE   Office of Government Ethics
 PERFLAW   The Perfect Lawyer
 PH-LWH   Lawyer Hiring and Training Report
 PRACLAW   The Practical Lawyer
 WLD   West's Legal Directory
 WLD-CORPCO   West's Legal Directory—Corporate Counsel
 WLD-LFM   West's Legal Directory—Law Firm Marketing

WIN™
WESTfax™
WESTCheck® and WESTMATE®
West's CD-ROM Libraries®

WESTLAW® and WEST BOOKS
 The Ultimate Research System

TO ORDER ANY OF THESE LAW OFFICE PRACTICE TOOLS,
CALL YOUR WEST REPRESENTATIVE OR 800-328-9352

NEED A NEW CASE TODAY?
 You can get copies of new court cases faxed to you
 today—introducing WESTfax™ at **800-562-2329**

How to Use WordPerfect® 5.0/5.1 in the Law Office

GUY S. WIGGINS
President
LegalTek Research

DAVID GREENWALD
Head of Desktop Publishing and Computer Graphics Department
Shea & Gould

WEST PUBLISHING COMPANY
St. Paul, Minnesota

WEST'S COMMITMENT TO THE ENVIRONMENT

In 1906, West Publishing Company began recycling materials left over from the production of books. This began a tradition of efficient and responsible use of resources. Today, more than 95% of our legal books and 70% of our college texts are printed on acid-free, recycled paper consisting of 50% new paper pulp and 50% paper that has undergone a de-inking process. We also use soy-based inks to print many of our books. West recycles nearly 22,650,000 pounds of scrap paper annually—the equivalent of 187,500 trees. Since the 1960s, West has devised ways to capture and recycle waste inks, solvents, oils, and vapors created in the printing process. We also recycle plastics of all kinds, wood, glass, corrugated cardboard, and batteries, and have eliminated the use of styrofoam book packaging. We at West are proud of the longevity and the scope of our commitment to the environment.

West pocket parts are printed on recyclable paper and can be collected and recycled with newspapers. Staples do not have to be removed because recycling companies use magnets to extract staples during the recycling process.

Production, Prepress, Printing and Binding by West Publishing Company

Project Management	Lisa M. Labrecque
Interior Design	Seventeenth Street Studios
Copy Editing	Mark Woodworth
Page Makeup	Curtis Philips
Proofreading	Christopher Bernard

WordPerfect®
WordPerfect is a registered trademark of WordPerfect Corporation.

WordPerfect v.5.0, ©WordPerfect Corporation 1988. Reprinted with permission from WordPerfect Corporation.

WordPerfect v.5.1, ©WordPerfect Corporation 1989. Reprinted with permission from WordPerfect Corporation.

Lithographs reprinted with permission from The Metropolitan Museum of Art, bequest of Edwin de T. Bechtel, 1957: 57.650.211 (p. 2), 57.650.217 (p. 46), 57.650.214 (p. 113), 57.650.134 (p. 156), 57.650.196 (p. 185), and 57.650.223 (p. 259).

Cover image:
Frje Echeverria. Franklin County Courthouse, Iowa. West Art and the Law, 1981.
Copyright © 1981 West Publishing Company, Eagan, Minnesota.

COPYRIGHT ©1993 by   West Publishing Company
                       610 Opperman Drive
                       P.O. Box 64526
                       St. Paul, MN 55164-0526
                       (800) 328-9352

All rights reserved
Printed in the United States of America
00 99 98 97 96 95 94 93   8 7 6 5 4 3 2 1

Library of Congress Cataloging-in-Publication Data

Wiggins, Guy S.
  How to use WordPerfect 5.0/5.1 in the law office / Guy S. Wiggins, David Greenwald.
      p.   cm. --
  Includes index.
  ISBN 0-314-01850-6
  1. WordPerfect (Computer file) 2. Law offices--United States--Automation.
3. Word processing--Computer programs.   I. Greenwald, David, 1953-
II. Title.
KF320.A9W49   1993   92-43186
340'.0285'5369--dc20   CIP

CONTENTS SUMMARY

Preface	xv
Acknowledgments	xxv
About the Authors	xxvi
Chapter 1: Getting Started with WordPerfect— A Tutorial	1
Chapter 2: Using WordPerfect for Legal Correspondence	44
Chapter 3: Assembling Contracts and Standard Legal Forms	111
Chapter 4: Assembling Pleadings and Court-Related Documents	154
Chapter 5: Writing and Assembling the Brief	183
Chapter 6: Desktop Publishing Corporate Documents in WordPerfect	257
Appendix A: Configuring WordPerfect for the Legal Office	301
Appendix B: Document Management Techniques	312
Appendix C: Creating Macros for an Advanced Keyboard Layout	326
Appendix D: Supplemental Disk Contents	361
Appendix E: Product Information	366
Index	369

CONTENTS

Preface	xv
WordPerfect 5.x In the Legal Office	xv
Who Should Read This Book	xvi
Goal of the Book	xvii
Ordering the Supplementary Disks	xviii
Using This Book	xviii
Conventions Used	xx
Major Function	xx
Keystrokes	xx
Using the WordPerfect Template	xx
Book Narrative: The Mythical Firm of Marshall, Cardozo, Hand, Holmes & Blackstone	xxii
System Requirements	xxiii
Contacting the Authors	xxiv
Acknowledgments	xxv
About the Authors	xxvi
Chapter 1: Getting Started with WordPerfect—A Tutorial	1
1.1 Some WordPerfect Preliminaries	4
1.1.1 The Status Line	4
1.1.2 Reveal Codes	5
1.1.3 The Basics of Entering Text	7
1.2 Exercise 1: Copying and Printing Text, and Navigating Around a Document	7
1.2.1 Using the Copy Page and Hard Page Functions	7
1.2.2 Printing Your Document	9
1.2.3 Saving Your Document	10
1.2.4 Learning to Navigate	11
1.3 Exercise 2: The Block Function	13
1.3.1 Deleting and Undeleting Text	13
1.3.2 Cutting, Pasting, and Copying	15

1.4 Exercise 3: Using List Files to Retrieve Files, Plus Basic Formatting	17
1.4.1 Finding and Retrieving Files Using List Files	17
1.4.2 Basic Formatting Techniques	19
1.4.3 Changing the Margins	19
1.4.4 Centering Text	19
1.4.5 Changing Text Justification	20
1.4.6 Changing Line Spacing	21
1.4.7 Adding Tabs and Indents	23
1.4.8 Changing Tab Settings	24
1.4.9 Underlining, Bolding, and Italicizing Text and Viewing the Document	25
1.4.10 Underlining Existing Text	26
1.4.11 Bolding Existing Text	26
1.4.12 Italicizing Existing Text	26
1.4.13 Using View Document to See How Your Work Will Look When Printed	27
1.4.14 Deleting Codes in a Document	28
1.5 Exercise 4: Page Numbering; Headers, Footers, and Footnotes; Using the Spell Checker and Thesaurus	29
1.5.1 Adding Page Numbers in WP 5.1	29
1.5.2 Adding Page Numbers in WP 5.0	30
1.5.3 Suppressing Page Numbers	30
1.5.4 Headers, Footers, and Footnotes	31
1.5.5 Using the Spell Check and Thesaurus	34
1.6 Some "Power User" Techniques	37
1.6.1 Using the [Esc] Key's Repeat Value	37
1.6.2 Moving Text Between Document Screens	37
1.6.3 Restoring a Split Screen	38
1.7 Command Review	39
Chapter 2: Using WordPerfect for Legal Correspondence	**44**
2.1 Legal Correspondence—Basic Skills	48
2.1.1 Introduction	48
2.1.2 Margins and Tabs	49
2.1.3 Adding Text Attributes to the Re: Line	51
2.1.4 Centering a Letter Vertically	53
2.1.5 Using Headers and Footers	53
2.1.6 Positioning and Automatically Inserting the Date	56
2.1.7 Using the Automatic Date Feature	57

2.2   Intermediate WordPerfect Letter Writing Skills   58
   2.2.1   Using WordPerfect Styles to Insert Formatting Commands   58
   2.2.2   Types of Styles   60
   2.2.3   Using Named Macros to Insert Client Names and Addresses   64
   Exercise: Creating a Named Macro Using the Pause Feature   68
   2.2.4   Editing a WordPerfect Macro   68
2.3   Advanced WordPerfect Letter Writing Skills   70
   2.3.1   Using Simple Keyboard Merges to Create Reusable Boilerplate Letters (Templates)   70
   2.3.2   Using Merge Templates   74
   2.3.3   Editing a Template   75
   2.3.4   Printing a Letter Address Block on Envelopes   76
   2.3.5   Using Merge to Automate Mass Mailings   77
   2.3.6   Creating a WordPerfect Secondary File—Overview   78
   2.3.7   Creating a Secondary Merge File in WordPerfect 5.1   79
   2.3.8   Creating a WordPerfect 5.1 Primary Merge File   81
   2.3.9   Creating a Secondary Merge File in WordPerfect 5.0   83
   2.3.10   Creating a WordPerfect 5.0 Primary Merge File   83
   Exercise: Creating an Envelope Primary Merge Document   85
   2.3.11   Eliminating Blank Lines During a Merge   86
   2.3.12   Sorting a Secondary Merge File Before Merging   88
   2.3.13   Using Sort to Alphabetize Records by Last Name   90
   2.3.14   Sorting a Secondary Merge File by Zip Code   92
   2.3.15   Using Select to Sort Specific Records Only   94
   2.3.16   Merging Primary and Secondary Merge Files   96
   2.3.17   Using WordPerfect Notebook as a Secondary Merge File (For WordPerfect Office Users Only)   97
   2.3.18   Printing Addresses on Labels   99
   2.3.19   Using Labels (WP5.1)   100
2.4   Command Review   105

Chapter 3: Assembling Contracts and Standard Legal Forms — 111

   3.1 Basic WordPerfect Contract Assembly Skills — 114
      3.1.1 Basic Clause Preparation Tips — 114
      3.1.2 Automatic Paragraph Numbering — 115
      3.1.3 Paragraph and Outline Numbering Options — 117
      3.1.4 Using Paragraph Numbering — 118
      Exercise: Creating a User-Defined Legal Paragraph Numbering Style — 119
      3.1.5 The Outline Style Feature — 121
      3.1.6 How to Keep Text Together: Block Protect, Widow/Orphan Protection, and Conditional End of Page — 125
   3.2 Intermediate WordPerfect Contract Assembly Skills — 127
      3.2.1 Using the Master Document Feature — 127
      3.2.2 Creating a Contract as a Master Document — 129
      3.2.3 Using Redlining and Strikeout (Blacklining) — 134
      3.2.4 Creating a Simple Document Assembly System Using the Merge Template Feature — 136
      Exercise: Creating an Advanced Template Using {Variable} and {Text} Codes — 139
      3.2.5 Using Merge Templates (Executing the Merge) — 142
      3.2.6 Editing a Template — 143
      3.2.7 Creating a Table of Contents — 144
   3.3 Command Review — 151

Chapter 4: Assembling Pleadings and Court-Related Documents — 154

   4.1 Beginning WordPerfect Pleading Creation Skills — 157
      4.1.1 Case Captions — 157
      4.1.2 Creating Case Captions Using WordPerfect 5.1's Tables Feature — 158
      4.1.3 Creating a Case Caption Using Newspaper Columns and Line Draw — 162
      4.1.4 Using the Caption Macros — 166
   4.2 Intermediate WordPerfect Pleading Creation Skills — 166
      4.2.1 Using Merge Templates to Automate Pleadings — 167
      4.2.2 Nesting and Chaining — 168
      4.2.3 Creating a Pleading Merge Template that Includes a Case Caption and a Pleading Cover — 169
      4.2.4 How to Create Pleading Paper — 176
   4.3 Command Review — 180

Chapter 5: Writing and Assembling the Brief	183
5.1 WordPerfect Brief Writing Skills—The Basics	187
5.1.1 Basic WordPerfect Features	187
5.2 Intermediate WordPerfect Brief Writing Skills	189
5.2.1 Using the Outline Feature to Structure Ideas	189
Exercise: Using the Outline Feature	191
5.2.2 Using Footnotes	193
Exercise: Creating a Footnote from Previously Entered Text	196
5.2.3 Exploring Footnote Options	197
5.2.4 Using the Endnote Feature to Number Exhibits and Create an Exhibits List	201
5.2.5 The Comment Feature	203
5.2.6 The Search, Extended Search, and Search and Replace Features	205
5.2.7 Using Search and Replace to Clean Up Downloaded Text	207
5.2.8 Using the Compose Feature to Insert Special Characters	209
5.2.9 Techniques for Keeping Lines of Text Together	210
5.2.10 Using Hyphenation to Improve the Appearance of Your Document	212
5.3 Advanced WordPerfect Brief Writing Skills	214
5.3.1 Using Macros to Automate Frequently Performed Tasks	214
Exercise: Creating an [Alt][Z] Macro to Change Line Spacing for Quotes	217
5.3.2 WordPerfect Keyboard Macros	218
Exercise: Creating a Temporary Macro for Fed. R. Civ. P.	219
Exercise: Creating a Keyboard Macro	224
5.3.3 Using the Parallel Columns and Tables Features	225
5.3.4 WP5.1—Using the Tables Feature	228
Exercise: Creating a Table	231
5.3.5 Table Formatting Options	230
5.3.6 Creating the Table of Contents and the Table of Authorities—Overview	233
5.3.7 Creating a Table of Authorities	234
5.3.8 Putting a Generated Table of Authorities in Alphabetical Order	241
5.3.9 Creating a Table of Contents	243
5.4 Command Review	252

Chapter 6: Desktop Publishing Corporate Documents in WordPerfect — 257

- 6.1 The Basic Principles of Typography — 261
  - 6.1.1 Typefaces vs. Fonts — 262
  - 6.1.2 The "Color" of Type and Body vs. Display Text — 263
  - 6.1.3 Style — 264
  - 6.1.4 Measuring Type — 265
  - 6.1.5 Baseline — 266
  - 6.1.6 Leading — 266
  - 6.1.7 Kerning — 267
  - 6.1.8 Portrait vs. Landscape Paper Orientation — 268
  - 6.1.9 Some Basic Typesetting Do's and Dont's — 269
  - 6.1.10 Scalable Typefaces — 273
  - 6.1.11 Some Practical Buying Tips — 274
- 6.2 Creating a Prospectus Cover Page Using WordPerfect's Desktop Publishing Features — 276
  - 6.2.1 Choose a Proportionally Spaced Serif Base Font — 276
  - 6.2.2 Adding Graphic Lines — 277
  - 6.2.3 Inserting Graphics into Text Using a Figure Box — 279
  - 6.2.4 Rotating Text Using a User Box — 283
  - 6.2.5 Changing the Size of Text — 286
  - 6.2.6 Using Paired Styles to Format Text — 287
  - 6.2.7 Using WordPerfect 5.1's Tables Feature — 293
  - 6.2.8 Placing a Border on a Page — 294
  - 6.2.9 Creating Check Boxes — 296
- 6.3 Command Review — 297

Appendix A: Configuring WordPerfect for the Legal Office — 301

- A.1 The Essentials of Installing WordPerfect 5.1 on a Network — 302
  - A.1.1 Understanding Personal and Master Setup Files — 302
  - A.1.2 Changing the Master Settings — 303
  - A.1.3 Running NWPSETUP.EXE to Update Personal Setup Files — 303
  - A.1.4 The WP{WP}.ENV File — 304
  - A.1.5 The AUTOEXEC.BAT File — 305
  - A.1.6 Installing Network Printers — 305
- A.2 Installing Additional Printers — 306
- A.3 Properly Configuring WordPerfect for Macros — 307
- A.4 Editing the Master Setup File to Create a Global Macros Subdirectory — 308
- A.5 Initial Codes — 309

  A.6 Document Summary/Management Options 309
  A.7 Document Backup Options 311

Appendix B: Document Management Techniques 312
  B.1 Using List Files to Understand DOS Functions 313
    B.1.1 Basic DOS Concepts 313
    B.1.2 How to Get the Most Out of the List Files Feature 318
  B.2 File Management Suggestions and Techniques—Install a Network 321
    B.2.1 Peer-to-Peer vs. Dedicated Networks 321
    B.2.2 File Management Tips and Techniques—Create a Directory Structure that Matches Your Practice 322
    B.2.3 File Management Tips and Techniques—Management Must Get Involved 323
    B.2.4 Computers Can Give Your Firm a Competitive Edge 323
  B.3 WESTMATE Downloading Format Options 324

Appendix C: Creating Macros for an Advanced Keyboard Layout 326
  C.1 Writing and Editing Advanced Macros 327
  C.2 Using the Macro Editor 327
  C.3 Macro Keyboards 330
  C.4 Dissecting the [Ctrl][M] Macro 332
  C.5 Sample Macros 335
  C.6 Named Macros to be Called From the [Ctrl][M] Main Menu Macro 352

Appendix D: Supplemental Disk Contents 361
  D.1 A Few Words About Shareware 361
  D.2 Disk Contents 362
    D.2.1 Disk 1: Book and Shareware WordPerfect Macros and WordPerfect-Related Shareware 362
    D.2.2 Disk 2: Legal Shareware and Demos 365

Appendix E: Product Information 366

Index 369

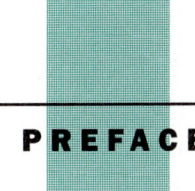

PREFACE

WORDPERFECT 5.X IN THE LEGAL OFFICE

WordPerfect is the most popular word processing software package for the MS-DOS, IBM compatible computer environment. The program is loaded with features that allow users to prepare anything from simple memos to full-fledged, desktop published documents. The popularity of WordPerfect is especially evident in the legal profession, where the vast majority of firms—both large and small—now use it as their word processing software of choice. Why? Because, from the program's inception, WordPerfect Corporation wanted WordPerfect to be used by lawyers. To this end, they have added such features as a table-of-authorities generator and line numbering that are especially helpful to lawyers. Legal professionals like its clean and uncluttered user interface (the "blank page" approach) that makes the transition from yellow pad to electronic tabula rosa a more natural one.

To retain its pride of place in the Darwinian world of software development, the WordPerfect Corporation has constantly sought to improve, refine, and supplement the features of its flagship program. WordPerfect 5.1 is the most recent DOS version of the WordPerfect program and benefits from some important enhancements over its predecessor, version 5.0. Some of the improvements that law offices will find particularly helpful include:

> - **Long Document Name feature**: Allows users to attach a 26-letter description to their files (R.I.P. cryptic DOS file names!).
> - **Tables feature**: Allows users to create and format tables for a variety of functions, including the creation of forms and the arrangement of text or numbers into rows and columns (this feature is ideal for presenting graphically clear and compelling indices or worksheets for the review of documents).

An incompetent attorney can delay a trial for months or years. A competent attorney can delay one even longer.
— Evelle J. Younger

- **Improved macro and merge features**: WordPerfect 5.1 has greatly expanded the merge functions of the program, which allow for sophisticated, reusable templates for forms, boilerplates, and letters.

- **Improvements to the Outlining feature**: "Families" within an outline can be moved up or down the hierarchy; the outlining feature can be toggled on or off.

While this book covers both versions 5.0 and 5.1, if you don't have WordPerfect 5.1 yet, allow us to be blunt. Don't be penny wise and pound foolish. The WordPerfect Corporation spends millions of dollars to have top-notch developers improve the program. These individuals have but two jobs: to enhance existing features and to incorporate new ones. It costs the individual user less than $100 to benefit from the programming expertise of this resourceful corporation when you upgrade from a previous version of the program. After all, lawyers are wordsmiths: a good measure of their success hinges on their ability to commit language and textual presentations to paper, and to do so efficiently. Lawyers owe it to themselves, to their support staff, and to their clients to have the finest productivity tools available—especially when it can save time and help your bottom line. To order an upgrade, you can reach WordPerfect Corporation at (800) 321-5906, or go to your nearest authorized WordPerfect dealer.

WHO SHOULD READ THIS BOOK

This book is written to assist anyone who processes text in a legal environment, including legal secretaries, paralegals, *and* lawyers. We have assumed that readers of this text have already acquired a basic set of skills (e.g., that you know how to initiate procedures from a menu, that you know your away around the keyboard, that you have some acquaintance with WordPerfect's DOS-based file organization, etc.) Many of the legal functions covered in this guide require intermediate to advanced skills, and, while we have strived to make this guide as clear as possible, some of what we describe may well be confusing to the beginner. If you have never used WordPerfect before, or if you are coming to WordPerfect from another word processing program, you may wish to start with Chapter 1.

If you are an attorney who already owns and uses a computer, the following message does not apply to you. If, on the other hand, you

Lawyers and tarts are the two oldest professions in the world. And we always aim to please.
Horace Rumpole
(John Mortimer)

belong to the legion of lawyers who refuse to type and who fail to see the sense of cluttering your desktop with yet another costly piece of equipment, we urge you to reconsider the issue. Not only can PC's dramatically increase your productivity, but in competent hands personal computers make possible the creative management and marshaling of information. In a legal office, this can mean everything from the latest case law to the billing history of a specific client. Computers are changing the world as we speak. With the information revolution exploding all around us, it will simply not do to banish them outside of your office.

A final argument should convince even the most recalcitrant skeptic that at least some level of computer literacy is essential. Given the tremendous influx of computers into the work environment, as well as the likelihood that this trend will continue, lawyers confront the choice of remaining dependent on legal and computer-support staff *or* of achieving self-sufficiency. If you are like most attorneys, you may often be working late hours and weekends when your normal support staff is not readily available. A basic knowledge of the PC and word processing software such as WordPerfect 5.X makes it possible to retrieve, revise, and create documents at *your* convenience—not at theirs. Once you get a taste of the organizational freedom that a PC allows, you will wonder how you ever did without one.

GOAL OF THE BOOK

Ius est ars boni et aequi [Legal justice is the art of the good and the fair].
Anonymous (Latin saying)

The goal of this book is to focus exclusively on the many WordPerfect features that can prove useful to law firms. It is meant as a hands-on reference tool to be kept near the computer, with a description of each function and an example of its possible use in a typical law office. To help the user get the most out of each function, we have also included tips and macro suggestions, as well as simple exercises for some of the less intuitive functions. (Macros are a group of keystrokes that have been combined for quick and easy access. They can greatly speed up and facilitate the use of the program. The keystrokes for the macros in this book are found in Appendix C. If you do not wish to key in these macros, you can order them on disk—plus hundreds of others; see the section below.) Our greatest hope is that this book will reveal to the legal professional or office worker the many beneficial features of the program.

ORDERING THE SUPPLEMENTARY DISKS

Two supplementary disks are available as a special service to the purchasers of this book. They include sample documents and all of the macros described in this book plus hundreds of the finest "shareware" WordPerfect macros on the market. Shareware, as opposed to commercial software, can be tried out first before you purchase to see if you like it. If you do like and use the shareware, you pay a small registration fee for recieving updates and technical support. Besides WordPerfect macro shareware, the disks also include some of the most popular shareware utilities, such as PKZIP for compressing files. At $24.95 plus shipping and handling, we think you'll find it the smartest computer investment you can make—besides buying this book, that is! The order form is at the back of the book.

USING THIS BOOK

Summum ius summa iniuria [Extreme justice is extreme injustice].
Anonymous, Latin legal maxim cited by Cicero in De Officiis, I, 10, 33

As stated, the goal of this book is to answer most of the questions that users will have about the use of WordPerfect 5.X in a law office and to help them understand the many possibilities of the program in automating standard legal tasks. Most reference guides group functions alphabetically or by level of difficulty, and not by how they would actually be used in a typical office environment. The problem with this approach is that it does not alert the user to the possibility of using a certain function to perform a legally related task. For example, it is not clear from most reference books that the Tables feature of WordPerfect 5.1 is excellent for creating case captions for pleadings. And because the Tables feature is useful for arranging information in columns, it can also be used for creating exhibits and exhibits lists. For this reason, the table function is discussed in both Chapters 4 and 5.

Hence, our organizational approach has been to base each chapter on one of the most common types of documents produced in a legal office. These are:

- ➤ Writing letters and correspondence
- ➤ Writing a brief or memo
- ➤ Writing and assembling a contract

- Putting together a pleading
- Assembling a corporate document such as a 10K

Generally, within each chapter, the different WordPerfect functions have been broken down into Basic, Intermediate, and Advanced skills—although we recognize that these categories are sometimes arbitrary.

There are also five appendices and a pull-out quick-reference card that contains short-hand versions of many of the procedures we describe throughout the book. Appendices A and B discuss how to configure WordPerfect—including network tips; using the List Files feature to perform DOS file functions; and tips on how to organize the files on your computer. Appendix C is devoted to creating advanced macros and includes the code for the macros discussed throughout the book. Appendix D lists the contents of the supplementary disks that you can purchase. Appendix E contains the addresses and telephone numbers for the vendors mentioned in the book, as well as a list of legal BBSs (electronic bulletin boards) for those who have a modem.

To none will we sell, to none deny or delay, right or justice.
Magna Carta
Clause 40

Tutorial for WordPerfect beginners

Besides the above chapters, we have also included Chapter 1 for the neophyte WordPerfect user, entitled "Getting Started with WordPerfect: A Tutorial." This chapter is different in style from the others. For example, it is meant to be a guided tutorial that should be read from beginning to end. It covers the basics of creating and formatting a document in WordPerfect, as well as cutting and pasting and printing. Another difference in style concerns its narrative tone. To make it less threatening to the beginner, we have written it in a more conversational manner. It is comprised of six parts, each of which takes about a half hour to work through.

CONVENTIONS USED

The following points will help you understand the conventions used in this training guide.

A major function is identified by the following heading:

MAJOR FUNCTION

The various ways of using that function are identified by the following subheading:

Ways of using that function

The use of each function is explained first, followed by the steps necessary to use the function. Notes are designated by use of the ■ symbol. Any relevant tips or macros will be found in the margins.

> **TIP**
> Any relevant tips or macros will be found in the margins, like this.

KEYSTROKES

Using the function keys

This book provides instructions for use of the function keys only. We have left out the use of the WordPerfect 5.1 menu for two reasons: first, this manual is for both 5.0 and 5.1 versions, so the description of the 5.1 menu system could confuse 5.0 users; second, in our experience, law offices do not use the menu bar because it is less efficient than using the function keys and the accompanying keyboard template.

> *A man may see how this world goes with no eyes. Look with thine ears: see how yond justice rails upon yon simple thief. Hark, in thine ear: change places; and, handy-dandy, which is the justice, which is the thief?*
>
> William Shakespeare
> King Lear
> [1605-1606]

USING THE WORDPERFECT TEMPLATE

WordPerfect makes extensive use of the function keys to issue commands. Because it is difficult to memorize all these combinations, a template is provided with the program that lists the commands generated by the associated function keys. See Figure P-1.

FIGURE P-1

This figure shows a WordPerfect template for enhanced keyboards, broken to fit the page.

	WordPerfect® for IBM Personal Computers	Shell Thesaurus Setup Cancel F1	Spell Replace ♦Search ♦Search F2	Screen Reveal Codes Switch Help F3	Move Block ♦Indent♦ ♦Indent F4	Ctrl Alt Shift	Text In/Out Mark Text Date/Outline List Files F5

Tab Align	Footnote	Font	Ctrl	Merge/Sort	Macro Define		
Flush Right	Math/Columns	Style	Alt	Graphics	Macro		
Center	Print	Format	Shift	Merge Codes	Retrieve		
Bold	Exit	Underline		Merge R	Save	Reveal Codes	Block
F6	F7	F8		F9	F10	F11	F12

Note: The Extended Keyboard (with 12 function keys on top) uses the [F11] and [F12] keys to duplicate the Reveal Codes and Block functions, respectively.

Black commands, listed in the fourth and bottom row of the template, are issued by pressing only the specified function. Example: [F3] (Help).

Green commands, listed in the third row of the template, are issued by holding down the [Shift] key and pressing the corresponding function key. Example: [Shift][F7] (Print).

Blue commands, listed in the second row of the template, are issued by holding down the [Alt] key and then pressing the function key. Example: [Alt][F1] (Thesaurus).

Red commands, listed in the first and top row of the template, are issued by holding down the [Ctrl] key and then pressing the function key. Example: [Ctrl][F4] (Move).

To make the keystrokes stand out in this book, the function key commands are printed with a special keycap typeface.

Example: the [F1] keycap in an instruction tells you to press the F1 key. The [Enter] keycap tells you to press the Enter or Return key. (On some older keyboards, the Enter key is unlabeled except for a crooked arrow.)

Example: an instruction such as [Shift][F8] tells you to first press the Shift key and, *while holding down that key*, quickly press the F8 function key. When keys are separated by a comma, they are to be pressed one after the other.

WordPerfect commands appear in this training guide as they appear on the template. They are in parentheses immediately to the right of the keys used to execute the WordPerfect commands.

TIP

When using the function keys, hold down the booster key first (i.e., [Ctrl], [Shift], or [Alt]) and, while holding it down, quickly tap the function key. The function key should only be held for a fraction of a second.

TIP

If you press the wrong function key by mistake or choose the wrong command, press the Cancel ([F1]) key. The [Esc] key will also often work.

Preface xxi

It is not, what a lawyer tells me I may do; but what humanity, reason, and justice, tell me I ought to do.

Edmund Burke
Second Speech on
Conciliation with
America
[March 22, 1775]

Example: [Shift][F7] (Print) tells you to press F7 while holding down Shift to access the Print menu.

Choices from the WordPerfect menus will show the number in a keycap (as it appears on the keyboard) and the letter choice in boldface.

Example: Press [1] for **L**ine.

Reveal Codes

WordPerfect functions place hidden codes in a document, which are revealed by pressing the Reveal Codes function, [Alt][F3] or [F11]. Because knowing how to manipulate these codes is crucial to an understanding of WordPerfect, we have frequently illustrated these codes throughout the manual. They are set off in a separate Reveal Codes section. Example:

▬▬▬▬▬▬▬▬▬▬▬▬▬▬▬▬▬▬▬▬▬▬▬▬▬▬

A [Par Num:Auto] code has been inserted.

WordPerfect 5.1 and 5.0 differences

Differences between the features and commands of the two programs, both large and small, will be noted graphically by the use of the short form "WP5.1" and "WP5.0" in headlines or the use of **WP5.1** and **WP5.0** in the text, in numbered steps, and in the Command Review section that concludes each chapter.

BOOK NARRATIVE: THE MYTHICAL FIRM OF MARSHALL, CARDOZO, HAND, HOLMES & BLACKSTONE

Let's face it—computer manuals, no matter how attractively presented, make for dull reading. Realizing this, we've worked in a narrative to spice things up a bit. At the beginning of most of the sections of this book is a short scenario that we have used to "set the scene," highlighting how the various functions in the guide can come in handy. In each chapter, the reader is placed in the shoes of one of five young attorneys: Tom Marshall, Linda Cardozo, Steve Hand, Sarah Holmes, or Larry Blackstone. These five law school buddies have just decided to start their own firm and are determined (with varying degrees of enthusiasm) to become WordPerfect "power users." Some of the sample templates and macros that come with this book will use the address of this mythical firm. However, any similarity between this firm and an actual firm is completely coincidental!

THE narrative section throughout the book begins with an enlarged capital letter, as in this paragraph.

Also, to make reading this book more fun to read, we've included quotes from famous cases and eminent jurists over the centuries, as well as lithographs from the great nineteenth century French caricaturist Honoré Daumier. We hope these make the admittedly tedious process of learning the software a bit more fun and at times intellectually rewarding.

SYSTEM REQUIREMENTS

To run WordPerfect 5.x, your DOS compatible system should include the following components:

God grants liberty only to those who love it, and are always ready to guard and defend it.
Daniel Webster
Speech
[June 3, 1834]

- A computer with at least 512K RAM memory (640K or more is highly recommended) and a hard disk. While WordPerfect 5.1 will operate on an XT class machine, it is strongly recommended that you use an AT class machine or better. An AT class computer has an 80286 chip, if that makes it any clearer!

- A keyboard. (It can be either the regular or extended keyboard. The extended keyboard has 12 function keys and separate keys for the cursor movement arrows.)

- A monitor, either color or monochrome, with a graphics card. For monchrome monitors, you will need a Hercules compatible graphics card. For color monitors, it is highly recommended that you use an EGA or VGA graphics card.

- A printer. (A laser printer is highly recommended.)

- A CONFIG.SYS file that specifies a FILES=20 or greater command. CONFIG.SYS needs to be in the root directory of your hard disk. (Don't worry about this if WordPerfect works fine. However, if you get an "INSUFFICIENT FILE HANDLES" error message, you'll have to summon up all your courage and plunge into the mysteries of your DOS manual, or better yet, ask the office computer guru.)

CONTACTING THE AUTHORS

This is the first in a series of books that we hope to write for West. Therefore, we'd appreciate any constructive criticisms and suggested improvements (we'll gladly settle for praise) for subsequent books. Please address all correspondence to:

> *In order to enjoy the inestimable benefits that the liberty of the press ensures, it is necessary to submit to the inevitable evils that it creates.*
> — Alexis Charles Henri Maurice Clerel de Tocqueville
> *Democracy in America* [1835]

Guy Wiggins and David Greenwald
c/o CIDEX Computer Systems
2 Willow Terrace
Hoboken, NJ 07030
Fax: (201) 653-8507

We hope to hear from you!

G. W. and D. G.
January 1, 1993

ACKNOWLEDGMENTS

To John McEnany, Esq., who made us appreciate the value of personal computers in the legal workplace; to Larry and the good folks at CIDEX, whose hardware, software, and forbearance enabled us to complete this book; to those at the law firm of Shea & Gould, especially Alan I. Annex, Esq., who were always forthcoming with advice and helpful suggestions; and last, but certainly not least, to our parents, whose support was critical in seeing this project through to completion.

TRADEMARKS

Throughout this book trademarked names are used. Rather than put a trademark symbol in every occurrence of a trademarked name, we state that we are using the names only in an editorial fashion and to the benefit of the trademark owner with no intention of infringement of the trademark.

ABOUT THE AUTHORS

Guy S. Wiggins is the President of Legaltek Research (a subsidiary of CIDEX Corporation), a consulting firm that specializes in computer training and installations for the New York/New Jersey legal market. Before founding the company, he served as a senior paralegal for the Securities Fraud Unit of the U.S. Attorney's office for the Southern District of New York. He also worked as a paralegal for Shearman & Sterling and Fried, Frank, Harris, Shriver & Jacobson in New York.

David Greenwald currently works in the MIS department of Shea & Gould in New York, where he is in charge of the desktop publishing and computer graphics department. Previously, he worked as an editorial assistant for a New York-based legal publishing company.

Getting Started with WordPerfect— A Tutorial

FUNCTIONS USED

- Understanding the status line §1.1.1
- An introduction to Reveal Codes §1.1.2
- Printing and saving a document §1.2.2–1.2.3
- Getting around a document §1.2.4
- Deleting and undeleting text §1.3.1
- Cutting, pasting, and copying text §1.3.2
- Finding and retrieving a document using List Files §1.4.1
- Basic formatting, e.g., bolding, italicizing, line spacing §1.4.2–1.4.12
- Deleting codes §1.4.14
- Page numbering §1.5
- Headers, footers, and footnotes §1.5.4
- Using Spell Check and the Thesaurus §1.5.5
- Power-user techniques §1.6

"It's funny, isn't it, that you are about to give me the same argument that I gave you in the same kind of case only three weeks ago ... ha ha ha!"

"And I'm about to answer you the same way you answered me ... hi hi hi!"

OVERVIEW

We understand. You've been avoiding computers for reasons like, "I'm not ever going to let myself become dependent on a &}%!#@ machine" or "I've gotten along just fine without one all these years." But recently you've caught yourself gazing with envy and longing (disguised as disdain) at those people at social gatherings boasting about the sophistication of their WordPerfect macros, bandying about terms like "RAM" or "Megabytes," or trumpeting the clock speed of their new laptops. You've begun to feel left out. Let's face it, just about everyone is using one.

Well, welcome to the 90s. What's that—a computer on your office desk? A laptop on your kitchen table? How did that happen? You say you were coerced—you had no choice in the matter? For expedience's sake we'll believe you. So, let's get you through this introductory chapter as painlessly as possible so that you can get to the good stuff. Before long you too will have your mastery of the most sophisticated DOS-based word processing program in the world to flaunt at parties.

By the way, you can disregard that entire diatribe if you're simply making the switch from another word processing package to Word-Perfect. What took you so long anyway?

> They [the makers of the Constitution] conferred, as against the Government, the right to be let alone—the most comprehensive of rights and the right most valued by civilized men.
>
> Justice Louis Dembitz Brandeis, dissenting, Olmstead v. United States, 277 U.S. 438, 478 [1928]

The exercises used in this chapter involve the following skills:

Exercise 1

- Using the hard page and copy page functions
- Printing
- Using the help feature
- Saving and naming a document
- Navigating through a document

Exercise 2

Fear of serious injury cannot alone justify suppression of free speech and assembly. Men feared witches and burned women. It is the function of speech to free men from the bondage of irrational fears.
Justice Louis Dembitz Brandeis, concurring, Whitney v. California, 274 U.S. 357, 376 [1927]

- Deleting and restoring deleted text
- Cutting, pasting, and copying text
- Storing and retrieving text in temporary memory
- Clearing the screen

Exercise 3

- Finding and retrieving files using List Files
- Basic formatting
- Using and changing tab settings
- Adding text attributes, e.g., underlining and italics
- Using the View Document feature
- Deleting codes in Reveal Codes

Exercise 4

- Adding page numbers
- Using headers and footers
- Adding footnotes
- Using Spell Check and the Thesaurus
- "Power user" techniques

1.1 SOME WORDPERFECT PRELIMINARIES

1.1.1 THE STATUS LINE

Type wp at the DOS prompt (C>) or select Word Perfect 5.1 or 5.0 from your menu if that's how you're set up. You'll note that your screen—aside from the "status line" in the bottom right-hand corner, which we will get to in a moment—is blank (and blue if you have a color monitor), just waiting for you to electronically inscribe your prose.

When you enter WordPerfect, you are presented with a blank screen—with the exception of the status line at the bottom right portion of the screen. Although it may look straightforward, the status line can convey a great deal more information about your document than is apparent at first blush. Get used to looking at it while you're creating or editing a document.

"Doc" on the status line indicates which document you're working in. It should read "1." You can actually have two documents open simultaneously. Try pressing [Shift][F3] (Switch). The status line tells you you're in Document 2 (Doc 2). Press [Shift][F3] again and you're back in the original document. The Switch function is a *toggle* function—in other words, the same keystrokes are used to switch back and forth from one state to another. We'll use this term frequently, because many of WordPerfect's commands are toggles.

The ability to have two document screens open at once allows you to easily copy or move text from one document to another. This is a feature many lawyers and their staff will find useful, especially when copying language from boilerplate documents and forms. We'll show you an example or two of that later in the chapter.

The "Pg" indicator on the status line tells you what page you're on in the document. "Ln" indicates how far down the page your cursor is, in inches or lines. (You'll get 54 lines on a page with the default top and bottom margins of 1" each, if your lines are single-spaced.) "Pos" indicates (in characters, centimeters, or inches, as well as several other more esoteric units of measurement from the left margin) where your cursor is on any particular line.

Notice that the default unit of measure for WordPerfect is inches. Although you can use other units of measure, we recommend staying with inches. That way you can use a ruler to quickly measure the page if you want to change your margins, and so on.

> **TIP**
>
> When using the function keys, hold down the *booster* key first (i.e., [Ctrl], [Shift], or [Alt]) and, while holding it down, quickly tap the function key. The function key should only be held for a fraction of a second.

> **TIP**
>
> If you pressed the wrong function key by mistake or chose the wrong command, press the [F1] key. The [Esc] key will also often work.

■ *If you want to change the default unit of measure, refer to Appendix A.*

Using the status line to find attribute codes

One of the key functions of the status line is to tell you about different text attributes (actually, hidden codes) found in your document. For example, press [F8] to turn on underlining. Note that the "Pos" number is now displayed differently. (This will depend on the monitor you are using). Press [F8] to turn off underlining. ("Aha!" you say, "another toggle.") Try this with the [F6] (Bold) key as well. Also, watch what happens to the "Pos" indicator when you press the [Caps Lock] key on and off.

Remember, when navigating through your document, to glance occasionally at the status line. It can alert you to hidden codes you may not have been aware of. Later on in this chapter, we'll show you how to use the Reveal Codes function ([Alt][F3] or [F11]) to find and edit these hidden codes.

There is no such thing as justice—in or out of court.
Clarence Seward Darrow
Interview at Chicago
[April 1936]

1.1.2 REVEAL CODES

This is an ideal time to introduce you to the concept of Reveal Codes. Anytime you do any formatting—from simply underlining a word, to positioning complex graphics on a page—WordPerfect places formatting codes in your document that are not visible in the normal editing screen. You can ignore the presence of these codes while creating a document, but you'll want to perform almost all editing procedures with Reveal Codes turned on ([Alt][F3] or [F11]).

1. Make your line spacing double by pressing [Shift][F8], [1] for Line, [6] for Line Spacing, then type [2].

2. Press [F7] (Exit) twice to return to the editing screen.

3. Type the following and press [Enter] once after you finish:

```
Now is the time for all potential WordPerfect users
to learn about Reveal Codes. If you don't edit your
documents with Reveal Codes turned on, you may,
sooner or later, come to grief.
```

4. Now change the line spacing back to single spacing by pressing [Shift][F8], [1] for Line, [6] for Line Spacing, then typing [1]. Press [F7] (Exit) to return to the editing screen.

FIGURE 1-1

Pressing [Alt][F3] or [F11] reveals codes. In this instance we can see the line-spacing codes indicating single and double spacing. The rule separates the two screens and shows tab stops and margin settings.

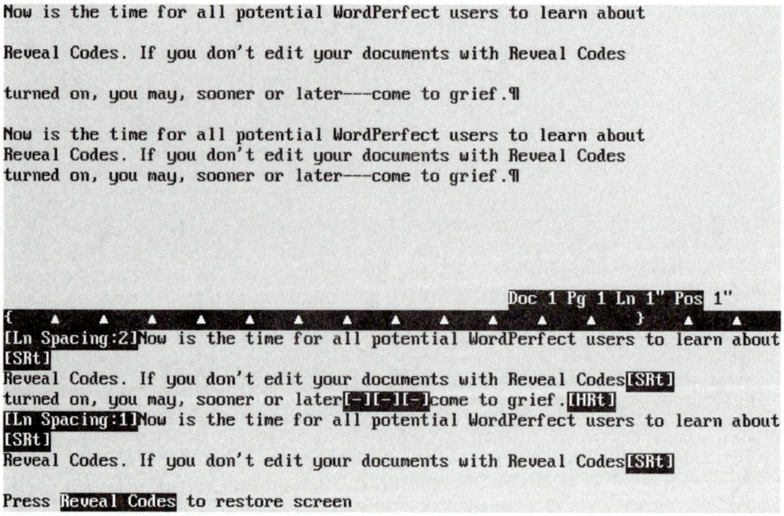

```
Now is the time for all potential WordPerfect users to learn about
Reveal Codes. If you don't edit your documents with Reveal Codes
turned on, you may, sooner or later---come to grief.¶

Now is the time for all potential WordPerfect users to learn about
Reveal Codes. If you don't edit your documents with Reveal Codes
turned on, you may, sooner or later---come to grief.¶




                                                     Doc 1 Pg 1 Ln 1" Pos 1"
{    ▲    ▲    ▲    ▲    ▲    ▲    ▲    ▲    ▲    }    ▲    ▲
[Ln Spacing:2]Now is the time for all potential WordPerfect users to learn about
[SRt]
Reveal Codes. If you don't edit your documents with Reveal Codes[SRt]
turned on, you may, sooner or later[-][-][-]come to grief.[HRt]
[Ln Spacing:1]Now is the time for all potential WordPerfect users to learn about
[SRt]
Reveal Codes. If you don't edit your documents with Reveal Codes[SRt]

Press Reveal Codes to restore screen
```

5. Type the same paragraph again.

6. Turn on Reveal Codes ([Alt][F3] or [F11]) and press [↑] until you see the [Ln Spacing:1] and [Ln Spacing:2] codes indicating single and double spacing prior to the text in both paragraphs. The [SRt] and [HRt] codes indicate soft and hard returns; these are discussed under the next subheading. (See Figure 1-1.)

A brief explanation of this initially confusing screen: the top half of the screen shows the actual document edit mode. The bottom half of the screen shows the *same* document with the hidden codes revealed. The two are separated by a ruler, which reveals the current tab stops and margins. The trick to using Reveal Codes is to track the movement of the cursor in the bottom half of the screen when editing. You'll see many examples of this in the chapters to come.

It's very important that you learn to recognize and identify the many codes WordPerfect places in your documents, in all kinds of editing circumstances. To help you get familiar with WordPerfect's many codes, we have used the following symbol to designate them throughout the book:

▲▲▲▲▲▲▲▲▲▲▲▲▲▲▲▲▲▲▲▲▲▲▲▲▲▲▲▲

This symbol is usually followed by a code or two, to illustrate the point.

You will be reading more about Reveal Codes in this chapter and throughout the book, and you'll soon become comfortable working with the formatting codes you'll encounter. We can assure you of that.

> **TIP**
>
> To help distinguish between hard and soft returns on the screen, WordPerfect gives you the option of using a Hard Return Display character. Some of the screen captures in this book use the hard return symbol ¶ for this character. To use a hard return display character, press [Shift][F1], [2] for **D**isplay, [6] for **E**dit Screen Options, [4] for **H**ard Return Display Character.

1.1.3 THE BASICS OF ENTERING TEXT

The key to entering text in WordPerfect and all other word processors is to understand the difference between a "hard return" and a "soft return." Unlike on a typewriter, when you enter text in WordPerfect you don't have to press the [Enter] key at the end of each line; in fact you *shouldn't* do so unless you wish to start a new paragraph. WordPerfect will automatically "wrap" the text to the next line when it reaches the right margin. This is also known as a "soft return." To properly use WordPerfect, you must let it word wrap. Otherwise, WordPerfect will be unable to reformat your text properly when you edit your document.

By contrast, pressing [Enter] puts in a "hard return," which should only be used at the end of a paragraph or when you wish to insert a new line.

1.2 EXERCISE 1: COPYING AND PRINTING TEXT, AND NAVIGATING AROUND A DOCUMENT

> *Injustice is relatively easy to bear; what stings is justice.*
>
> Henry Louis Mencken
> Prejudices [1922]

For your first exercise, we'll have you type a paragraph, copy it several times, insert "hard page" breaks to make your document several pages in length, then print it. Then we'll show you the basics of navigating through a document. As with a ship, learning to navigate might seem somewhat tedious, but these skills will keep you from going on the rocks and save you a lot of time in the long run. The ability to sail through a document as efficiently as possible is critical in law offices, which often deal with long, complex documents.

1.2.1 USING THE COPY PAGE AND HARD PAGE FUNCTIONS

1. On a blank screen, type the two paragraphs from a hypothetical First Amendment memo. Remember, use the [Enter] key only when finishing a paragraph.

```
In Lemon v. Kurtzman, 403 U.S. 602 (1971), the
Supreme Court adopted the following three prong
approach ("Lemon test") to determine whether
```

government has impermissibly involved itself in matters of religion:

First, the statute must have a secular legislative purpose; second, its principal or primary effect must be one that neither advances nor inhibits religion...finally, the statute must not foster "an excessive government entanglement with religion." (Emphasis added)

> ■ *The insert mode is WordPerfect's default when you are typing. If you want to type over text (or numbers) already on your screen, press the [Ins] key. The word "Typeover" will appear in the bottom left-hand corner of your screen and you will be in typeover mode until you press the [Ins] key again (a toggle).*

Conscience is the inner voice that warns us somebody may be looking.
Henry Louis Mencken
A Mencken Chrestomathy [1949]

2. Because we want you to work with a multipage document and we want to spare you the tedium of doing all the typing, we're going to show you how to quickly copy the text you just entered, as well as add a few extra pages. Press [Enter] twice at the end of the second paragraph, then press [Ctrl][F4] (Move), [3] for **Page**, [2] for **Copy**. Don't worry, we'll be going into more detail later about the various methods of moving text around in a document. Just follow these instructions for now.

3. Notice that you are prompted in the bottom left-hand corner of the screen to "Move cursor, press **Enter** to retrieve." You don't have to move the cursor; just press [Enter].

4. Press [Home], [Home], [↓] (go to end of document) and perform steps 2 and 3 twice more. Then press [↓] to move towards the bottom of the page. As you move downwards, you should see a dashed line (WordPerfect's indicator of a new page) across your screen. When you cross that line, you'll see on your status line that you are now on page 2 of the document.

5. When you've cursored to the end of the document, copy the page twice more, using the method we described in steps 2 and 3.

6. We'll create one more page so we'll have a four-page document for this exercise. Make sure your cursor is at the very end of the document by pressing [Home], [Home], [↓], then hold down the [Ctrl] key and press [Enter]. A double dashed line will appear on your screen and your status line will tell you you're on page 4. See Figure 1.2.

You've just created a *hard page break* that will remain in place no matter what other changes you make in your document unless you delete it. The single dashed line is a *soft page break* that the program

FIGURE 1-2

A hard page break is represented by a double dashed line, a single page break by a single dashed line.

```
First, the statute must have secular legislative purpose; second,
its principal or primary effect must be one that neither advances
nor inhibits religion . . . finally, the statute must not foster
"an excessive government entanglement with religion." (Emphasis
added)

In Lemon v. Kurtzman, 403 U.S. 602 (1971), the Supreme Court
adopted the following three prong approach ("Lemon test") to
determine whether government has impermissibly involved itself in
matters of religion:

First, the statute must have secular legislative purpose; second,
its principal or primary effect must be one that neither advances
nor inhibits religion . . . finally, the statute must not foster
"an excessive government entanglement with religion." (Emphasis
added)
================================================================================
In Lemon v. Kurtzman, 403 U.S. 602 (1971), the Supreme Court
adopted the following three prong approach ("Lemon test") to
determine whether government has impermissibly involved itself in
added)

D:\MANUAL\INTRO\1STAMEND.MEM                        Doc 1 Pg 4 Ln 1.5" Pos 1"
```

inserts automatically when a page has been filled with text. The concept is similar to "hard" vs. "soft" returns as discussed above.

7. Type or copy another paragraph or two of text on the fourth page and we're ready to go.

1.2.2 PRINTING YOUR DOCUMENT

To commit those electronic lines of type to paper, follow these two easy steps.

1. Press [Shift][F7] (Print).
2. Now press [1] for **F**ull document. If your hardware has been configured correctly and is turned on and loaded with paper, you'll see your work on bond pretty quickly.

NOTE: To print only the page on which the cursor appears on the screen, choose [2] for **P**age from the Print menu. To print multiple pages choose [5] for **M**ultiple pages and type the desired pages at the "Page(s):" prompt. For instance, to print pages 3 through 7 of a document, type 3-7; to print 3, 5, and 8, type 3,5,8 or 3 5 8; to print from a certain point in the document to the end, type the page number followed by a dash, e.g., 7- will print from page 7 to the end of the document. If you enter 3, 5, 7-15, pages 3 and 5 and 7 through 15 will print. (See either Chapters 3 or 4 for an explanation of how to print pages of a document that has been divided into renumbered sections.)

For information on configuring your printer on a network, see Appendix A.

TIP

To print a document directly from a diskette without retrieving it, choose option [3], **D**ocument on Disk. In response to the prompt "Document name," type the drive letter first, followed by a colon and the document name (e.g., a:Bob.let). In response to the prompt "Page(s): (All)," press [Enter] if you want to print the entire document, or type the page numbers of the pages you wish to print.

MACRO

If you bought the supplementary disks, use the [Alt][P] macro to print. The code for the macro is found in Appendix C.

Using Help to explain print options

At this point, we could go into a long and detailed exegesis of all of the different options available on the Print screen. But we figured this would be a perfect opportunity to introduce you to WordPerfect's built-in help system. As with all sophisticated software, using WordPerfect will only become second nature after many months of constant use. By that time, you will probably have forgotten many of the tricks and techniques we've outlined in this book. However, on-line help is only a keystroke away. We're going to show you how to use Help to find explanations of the many different options on the Print screen, but it's the same principle for all other functions as well. Remember: the Help feature is the quickest way for you to get help when you're stumped.

1. Press [F3] (Help).
2. Press [Shift][F7] (Print) to bring up the Print screen. You'll be presented with an almost identical screen, except that each menu option is now an explanation. For example, press [3] for **Document on Disk** to get a full explanation of this function.
3. To exit help, press [Enter] or the [Spacebar].

1.2.3 SAVING YOUR DOCUMENT

All right, let's save the sample document. By this, we mean to inscribe it permanently on either your hard or floppy disk. *Key point to remember when using computers:* What you see on the screen will not really exist, except in RAM (your computer's temporary memory), until you give it a name and save it to disk. You could print it without saving it, but as soon as you exited WordPerfect it would be gone forever—lost in cyberspace.

There are two ways to save a newly-created document.

MACRO

Use the [Alt][S] macro to quickly save your document.

Method 1

Press [F10] (Save). In answer to the prompt "Document to be saved'" type the name of the document. You will immediately see that name appear in the lower left-hand corner of your screen at the end of the current path. (A path is the route a program must go to find files on a disk—say, through the root directory and a subdirectory.) You can give each document a name of up to eight letters with a three-letter extension, e.g., 1STAMEND.MEM. See Appendix B for more information about DOS naming conventions.

> *One of the nice features of WordPerfect 5.1 is the Long Document Name feature. This allows you to give a document a regular English description of up to 26 characters, as well as the more cryptic DOS file name. For example, a document could be called* First Amendment Memo *as well as* 1STAMEND.MEM. *For more information on using the Long Document Name feature, see Appendix A.*

Method 2

Press [F7] (Exit). You will be prompted "Save Document?" Press [Y] for Yes and then type the name of the document in answer to the prompt "Document to be saved:," and press [Enter]. After typing the name you will be asked if you want to exit WordPerfect. Type the appropriate response. If you answer [N] for No you will remain in WordPerfect with a brand new blank screen. Not to worry, your document has been saved with the name you gave it, and you will be able to retrieve it easily using the List Files feature ([F5]).

WARNING: Don't use Method 2 as the only method for saving your work. If you press [N] instead of [Y] by mistake, you'll lose all your work. Get used to saving your work frequently by using the [F10] key described above.

> *If you want to save the document to a floppy disk, type an* a: *or* b: *in front of the document name, depending on which disk drive the disk is in.*

You'll find a much more extensive discussion in Appendix B that details document management techniques about DOS (your PC's operating system) and such arcana as *paths*, *directories*, *subdirectories*, and *file naming conventions*.

OK, press [F10] and type 1STAMEND.MEM. It doesn't matter what case you type the name in, it will henceforth always appear in capital letters. As we mentioned, you will see that name (1STAMEND.MEM) at the end of the DOS path in the lower left-hand corner of your screen. (See Figure 1-2.)

> *The path and file name appear at the bottom left of the screen only after the document has been saved at least once.*

1.2.4 LEARNING TO NAVIGATE

Now that we've got a multipage document to work with, the next step is to learn the numerous techniques for navigating around a document. Because legal documents are often long and complex, this

---

TIP

Save your document frequently. Don't wait until you've completely finished your document—if something goes wrong, you'll lose all your work! We sincerely hope you don't learn this lesson the hard way—many do.

TIP

Use the three-letter extension consistently for different types of document. For example, file names for correspondence could end with an .LET extension, file names for memos and briefs with an .MEM extension. This makes it easier to find and identify documents when using the List Files feature.

is an important skill for anyone using WordPerfect in a legal environment. WordPerfect offers a wealth of different navigating shortcuts. Here are some of the most important ones:

[Ctrl] **key**: Place your cursor on any word, at any point in that word. The [Ctrl] key in combination with the right or left cursor keys will move you from word to word. Try it. Note that the cursor leaps to the beginning of the next word, or to the beginning of the word you're in if you press [Ctrl][←] cursor while in the middle of that word.

WP5.1 (The notes in this paragraph apply *only* to WordPerfect version 5.1.) [Ctrl][↑] and [Ctrl][↓] move you from paragraph to paragraph. If you're in the middle of a paragraph and press [Ctrl][↑], you will find yourself at the beginning of that paragraph. [Ctrl][↓] will take you to the first word in the next paragraph.

Moving around on the same line: Place your cursor in the middle of a line. Press the [End] key. Surprise, you're at the end of the line. ([Home], [→] achieves the same effect.) To return to the beginning of the line press [Home], [←]. There may be circumstances, discussed later, where the entire line will not be visible on the screen. If that's the case [Home], [Home], [←] or [Home], [Home], [→] will take you to the beginning or the end of the line.

Moving to the beginning or end of a document: Press [Home], [Home], [↑]. You'll find yourself at the beginning of the document. [Home], [Home], [↓] takes you to the end. [Home], [Home], [Home], [↑] will take you to the *very* beginning of the document before all the codes. We'll be discussing codes throughout this chapter—suffice it to say now, there will be times when you'll want to be at the very beginning of the document.

Moving to the beginning or end of a page: [PgUp] takes you to the first line of the previous page. [PgDn] takes you to the first line of the next page.

Pressing [Ctrl][Home], [↑] brings you to the first line of the page you're on, [Ctrl][Home], [↓] brings you to the last line of that page, while [Home], [↑] brings you to the top of the visible *screen* and [Home], [↓] takes you to the bottom of that screen.

Finally, [Ctrl], [Home] (the Go To page function) followed by a particular page number will take you to the beginning of that page. Try it. Put your cursor somewhere on page 1 and press [Ctrl], [Home] (Go To Page). Type 3 and press [Enter]. Voilà, you're at the top of page 3.

All right, we know this might seem like quite a lot to digest for your first lesson. But it won't be long before moving around Word-

> *Man's capacity for justice makes democracy possible, but man's inclination to injustice makes democracy necessary.*
> Reinhold Niebuhr
> The Children of Light and the Children of Darkness [1944]

Perfect documents becomes second nature to you, as familiar as the positions of the keys on the keyboard are to an experienced typist.

Congratulations, you've just finished the first exercise! Now it's on to the mysteries of the block function and cutting, pasting, and deleting text.

1.3 EXERCISE 2: THE BLOCK FUNCTION

1.3.1 DELETING AND UNDELETING TEXT

MACRO

Use the [Alt][D] macro to quickly delete blocks of text.

Since this exercise will involve deleting and moving around chunks of text, let's clear the 1STAMEND.MEM document from the screen for the time being. We'll return to it in the next exercise.

1. Press [F7] (Exit) and type [N] for No and [N] in answer to the "Exit WordPerfect?" prompt. Don't panic; a copy has been saved on your disk, which we'll retrieve later.

2. On this blank screen type the following three sentences, making sure you let WordPerfect wordwrap the text:

```
I'm well on my way to learning sufficient
WordPerfect skills to create and edit any type of
legal document. This hasn't been nearly as difficult
as I imagined thanks to the lucid and captivating
instruction of the authors, Wiggins and Greenwald.
But I've still got a ways to go before I become a
power user.
```

TIP

You can restore up to the last three deletions. To view them, press [F1] and then the [↑] or [↓] cursor arrow. The previous deletions will appear, one by one, highlighted on your screen. Pressing [1] for **R**estore can restore the one shown.

Deleting words and undeleting text using the Undelete function

Let's delete a couple of words, just for the fun of it. Needless to say, you can use the [Del] key to delete text one character at a time, but we're going to show you much more efficient methods.

1. Place your cursor anywhere in the word "captivating." Press the [Ctrl][Backspace] keys. Do it once again.

2. Now watch closely: press the [F1] (Cancel) key and [1] for **R**estore. The text you deleted reappears at the point of the cursor. This is the undelete function and it comes in very handy if you change your

mind about eliminating text or a code, or if you want a quick and easy way of cutting and pasting text.

- [Ctrl][Del] *does the same thing as* [Ctrl][Backspace].

- *Aside from the cancel key's ability to restore text that's been deleted—as we described earlier—you can also use it to cancel most operations.* [Esc] *also functions in that capacity quite frequently.*

Injustice anywhere is a threat to justice everywhere.
Martin Luther King, Jr.
Letter from the Birmingham jail. In the Atlantic Monthly [August 1963]

The [Backspace] key works in the same manner as the delete key, eliminating text one character at a time in the opposite direction. To delete an entire word, use the [Home], [Backspace] key combination, but not at the same time. Press [Home], then [Backspace]. (Notice the direction in which text is being deleted: it's the opposite of [Ctrl][Del] and [Ctrl][Backspace].)

Deleting a line of text

Place your cursor anywhere in the third line. Now press [Ctrl][End] (delete to end of line). That's right, you've just erased all the text from the point of your cursor to the end of the line. Press [F1] to restore (undelete) the text.

Deleting to the end of a page of text

Press [Ctrl][PgDn] (delete to end of page). You're prompted "Delete Remainder of Page?" Press [Y] for yes and all the text to the bottom of the page is deleted. Restore it using [F1]. By prompting you, WordPerfect gives you a chance to reconsider deleting such a large block of text.

TIP

With block on, pressing any character key highlights the text up to the first instance of that key after the cursor. For example, if you want to delete text in a sentence up to the first comma, turn on block ([F12] or [Ctrl][F4]) and type , (a comma). The text is highlighted automatically and can be deleted by pressing the [Del] or [Backspace] key.

Using the block function to delete text

The block function is a basic WordPerfect function that is used to perform many editing commands including copying, deleting, moving, underlining, bolding, and more. Understanding the block function is essential to using WordPerfect efficiently.

1. Place your cursor anywhere in the word "learning."
2. Now press [F12] or [Alt][F4], depending on what kind of keyboard you have. Note the flashing "Block on" prompt at the bottom left-hand side of your screen.
3. Type . (a period). The text from the point of your cursor to the end of the sentence is highlighted.

4. Pressing [Del] will give you the prompt "Delete Block?" Pressing [Y] deletes the text.

We'll discuss the block function in more detail a little later on.

You can also delete much larger chunks of text in this manner. Pressing [PgUp] with block on will highlight all the text from the cursor point to the top of the previous page. [PgDn] will do the same thing in the opposite direction. [Home], [Home], [↑] with block on will highlight everything from that point to the beginning of the document. [Home], [Home], [↓] will do the same to the end of the document. Once again, WordPerfect will prompt you with "Delete Block?" if you press the [Del] or [Backspace] key.

1.3.2 CUTTING, PASTING, AND COPYING

The larger part of editing will involve moving text around. Let's go back to our paragraph and do just that.

> It is better that ten guilty persons escape than one innocent suffer.
>
> Sir William Blackstone
> *Commentaries*
> [1765–1769]

Moving a sentence

1. Place your cursor anywhere in the first sentence and press [Ctrl][F4].

2. Choose [1] for **S**entence.

3. Choose [1] for **M**ove. The sentence disappears for a moment and the prompt "Move cursor; press **Enter** to retrieve" appears. Place your cursor on the "B" in "But" and press [Enter]. The sentence is repositioned.

Copying a paragraph

1. Go to the very end of the paragraph (remember, [Ctrl][↓] is the quickest way to move to the end of the paragraph, *but only if you're a WP 5.1 user*) and press the [Enter] key twice so that there are two returns after the paragraph. Now type a sentence or two.

2. Place your cursor anywhere in the initial paragraph and press [Ctrl][F4].

3. Choose [2] for **P**aragraph (the entire paragraph is highlighted), then [2] for **C**opy. The paragraph remains on the screen and the same prompt appears. Move your cursor to the beginning of the second paragraph and press [Enter]. The result should not surprise you.

Copying/moving/deleting a page

Pressing `Ctrl`-`F4` and `3` highlights the entire page automatically, which you can move, copy, and delete by choosing option 3.

Storing and retrieving text in memory

This is bit more esoteric, but probably useful to lawyers sweating out the language of a legal document.

1. Place your cursor in the second paragraph and press `Ctrl`-`F4`, `2` for **P**aragraph, `1` for **M**ove.

2. Suppose that you're not sure where you want this paragraph to go just yet; you want to perform some other editing tasks before you decide. Press `F1`, the cancel key. We'll talk about the cancel key a little later; suffice it to say that in this instance it simply turns off the prompt and allows you to go about your business.

3. Use your imagination now. You've done whatever you've wanted to do and now you want to paste that paragraph back into the document. Go to the end of the document (`Home`, `Home`, `↓`). Press `Ctrl`-`F4` and choose `4` for **R**etrieve and `1` for **B**lock. That text remained in memory (the computer's) just waiting to be removed from limbo and allowed to live again somewhere on your page.

> ■ *This is not a bad way to store blocks of text if you remember that, once you replace this text with a different block in a similar fashion, your original text disappears. In other words, you can only store one block of text in memory at a time. And, of course, once you exit WordPerfect, any text in memory will disappear.*

Moving, copying, and deleting text with the block function

Suppose, however, that the text you want to move, copy, or delete is not in a conveniently discrete sentence, paragraph, or page format. Let's say we want to move part of a paragraph.

1. Place your cursor on the "T" in "This" and turn on Block `F12` or `Alt`-`F4`.

2. We'll move the first part of the sentence up to "difficult" and place it after "imagined." Press `Ctrl`-`→` 6 times.

3. Press `Ctrl`-`F4`, `1` for **B**lock and `1` for **M**ove.

4. Place the cursor after the word "imagined" and press `Enter`. There's the text block.

WP5.1 A shortcut for moving text is to block it and press `Ctrl`-`Del`. You'll be prompted to "Move cursor; press **Enter** to retrieve." To

---

TIP

You can use the retrieve function to retrieve the same block of text throughout a document. An example might be a contract that has repeating instances of a long corporate name and address.

MACRO

Use the `Alt`-`M` macro to move text, the `Alt`-`C` macro to copy, and the `Alt`-`D` macro to delete text.

copy, block the text, press [Ctrl][Ins] and respond to the prompt "Move cursor; press **Enter** to retrieve."

Clearing the screen

1. Press [F7] (Exit) and type [N].
2. Type [N] for No to the prompt "Exit WordPerfect?"

■ *If you make revisions to your document and exit it without saying "Yes" to "Save document?" those changes will be not be saved; you will be left with the last saved version of the document.*

You should now have a blank screen.
Congratulations, you've just finished Exercise 2!

The people's good is the highest law.
Marcus Tullius Cicero
De Legibus

1.4 EXERCISE 3: USING LIST FILES TO RETRIEVE FILES, PLUS BASIC FORMATTING

1.4.1 FINDING AND RETRIEVING FILES USING LIST FILES

The List Files feature is one of the most important functions of the WordPerfect program. It lists all the files in a particular directory (think of a *directory* as a folder in which files are stored), and it allows you to perform many of the most fundamental file maintenance tasks such as retrieving, copying, renaming, and deleting files. It also gives you essential information on your files, including their names, size in bytes, and the date and time last saved. For now, we'll just titillate you by explaining how to find and retrieve files using the List Files function. Appendix B has a detailed explanation of how to use all of the powerful features of this function. And, believe us, there is a lot more to the List Files function than first meets the eye.

TIP

Pressing [F5] twice will return you to your former place (last logged directory) in List Files. This is ideal if you are several subdirectories deep and want to return there quickly.

We're going to use List Files to retrieve the 1STAMEND.MEM file created in Exercise 1. See Figures 1-3 and 1-4.

1. At a blank screen, press [F5] and press [Enter] or [F5] twice. Your screen will look much like Figure 1-3.

2. Press [N] for **N**ame Search and type the first two or three letters of the document name. There's your document with the reverse video bar highlighting it. You can, of course, move that bar around manu-

FIGURE 1-3

This is the all-important List Document menu with the 1STAMEND.MEM highlighted and ready to be retrieved.

```
11-07-92  07:46p              Directory C:\WP51\MEMO\*.*
Document size:        0  Free:  9,412,608  Used:    17,335  Files:     11

.    Current    <Dir>              ..   Parent     <Dir>
1STAMEND.MEM    3,125  11-01-92 10:10p  INTROCOM.LEX  6,938  10-27-92 08:19p
INTRODUC.CAP    1,339  09-11-92 06:37a  INTRODUC.CHP  2,879  10-30-92 06:59p
INTRODUC.VGR      128  09-11-92 06:37a  OLDBRIEF.MEM    128  10-27-92 08:19p
PREFACE .CAP       26  10-19-92 01:23p  PREFACE .CHP  1,610  10-20-92 08:54p
PREFACE .CIF      128  10-20-92 09:07p  RESEARCH.WL     906  10-27-92 08:19p
SMITH   .LET      128  10-31-92 07:07p






1 Retrieve; 2 Delete; 3 Move/Rename; 4 Print; 5 Short/Long Display;
6 Look; 7 Other Directory; 8 Copy; 9 Find; N Name Search: 6
```

ally by using your cursor keys, but if you have a great many files in a directory and you know the name of the file, the smart (and fast) way to find it is with the Name Search function.

3. With 1STAMEND.MEM highlighted, press [Enter] to clear Name Search, then press [1] for Retrieve. Voilà, your document has just been retrieved, ready to do your bidding.

■ *You can also retrieve documents using* [Shift][F10] *(Retrieve). At the "Document to be retrieved:" prompt, type the exact file name, including the path name if the document is stored in another directory (e.g., C:\WP51\RESEARCH\1STAMEND.MEM). If you forget the file name or the directory where it was stored, you can always use* [F5] *(List Files) instead.*

FIGURE 1-4

WordPerfect 5.1 offers a Long Document Name feature, which allows an English description of a file name of up to 26 characters. Refer to Appendix A for more information about this feature.

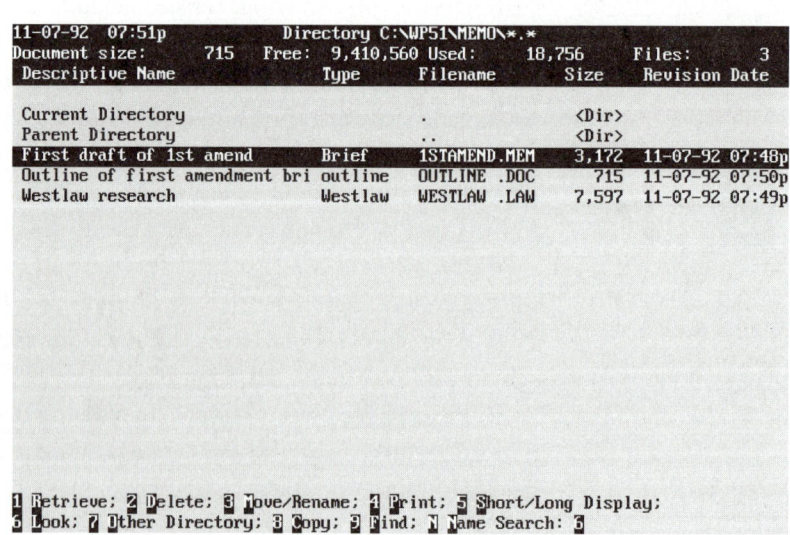

1.4.2 BASIC FORMATTING TECHNIQUES

Now that the text from our sample First Amendment brief is on the screen, we're going to have fun with it. To begin, let's change the left and right margins to 1.25" inches. Then we'll add a centered title.

1.4.3 CHANGING THE MARGINS

Earlier in the chapter, we mentioned the fact that the default top and bottom margins for WordPerfect documents are 1" and 1", respectively. In other words, those are the margins WordPerfect will automatically provide unless you change them. The same holds true for the left and right margins of your page.

There will probably be many more occasions when you want to change the default for the margins, but it's easy to do both. The options are in the Format menu ([Shift][F8]), where almost all of WordPerfect's important formatting functions are located.

1. Press [Shift][F8] (Format).
2. Choose [1] for **Line** and [7] for **Margins**.
3. Type 1.25, press [Enter] and repeat. You needn't follow the number with the inch symbol; it will automatically be placed there after you type the value if inches are your default unit of measurement. Again, in all likelihood inches will be the unit of measurement, unless you're more comfortable with the metric system and you can relate to centimeters. The authors confess to having no such ability.
4. Press [F7] to return to the document. Note that "Pos" on the status line now reads 1.25".

▪ *To change the top/bottom margins, it's* [Shift][F8] *again,* [2] *for* **Page**, [5] *for* **Margins**.

> **TIP**
>
> WESTLAW gives you the option of downloading documents to disk in WordPerfect 5.0/5.1 format, so that your documents are ready to use without converting from text. Just follow these simple steps:
> 1. Type options at any WESTLAW screen.
> 2. Type 14 to bring up the Downloaded Format menu.
> 3. Choose either [1] for WordPerfect 5.0/5.1 format or [2] for WordPerfect 5.0/5.1 format with search terms highlighted. WESTLAW will retain this download format for all of your subsequent downloads. See Appendix B.3 for more information.

1.4.4 CENTERING TEXT

1. With your cursor at the beginning of the document (line 1", position 1.25" on the status line) press [Enter] twice to put in two hard returns, then move the cursor back to the top of the document.

2. Press [Shift][F6] (Center). Type FIRST AMENDMENT MEMORANDUM. Your text centers itself automatically. Press [Enter] and you're back at the left margin.

■ *To center more than one line of text at a time, block out the text you want centered ([Alt][F4] or [F12], press [Shift][F6], and answer [Y] to the "[Just:Center]? No (Yes)" prompt).*

1.4.5 CHANGING TEXT JUSTIFICATION

Justification refers to how the margins of your text are aligned. WordPerfect's default is full justification. This means that the text you type in a document will align itself *both* with the left margin (no problem there) *and* the right margin as in the first of the four examples below.

This is sometimes, though not very often, a desirable state of affairs in legal documents. Full justification inserts extra spaces between words, which can often make a page harder to read. For that reason, we advise that you use left justification.

MACRO

Use the [Alt][J] macro to quickly change justification.

This is merely sample text for the purpose of demonstration. It is fully justified, which means that the text is flush with the left and right margins

As you can see, this text aligns with the right margin and is "ragged left." You may use this for whatever perverse purposes you wish.

This is merely sample text for the purpose of demonstration. This is an example of left-justified text. It is commonly called "ragged right."

This is merely sample text for the purpose of demonstration. The text here is centered.

WP5.1

1. Press [Shift][F8] and choose [1] for **Line**.
2. Choose [3] for **Justification** and you'll see a minimenu at the bottom of the screen.
3. Choose [1] for **Left** and press [F7] (Exit). A [Just:left] code will be placed in your document and any text you type from that point on, no matter how many times you press return, will be left-justified.

WP5.0

1. Press [Shift][F8] and choose [1] for **Line**.
2. Choose [3] for **Justification** and type [N] to indicate no justification.

TIP

By putting a [Just:Left] code in the Initial Codes screen under Setup (**WP5.1**: [Shift][F1], [4], [5]), all of your documents will automatically begin left-justified. See Appendix A.

FIGURE 1-5

WordPerfect 5.0 uses the [Just Off] code to turn off full justification. You must place it at the beginning of your document (before any text) if you want to override the default of Full Justification.

```
              In Lemon v. Kurtzman, 403 U.S. 602 (1971), the Supreme
Court adopted the following three prong approach ("Lemon test")
to determine whether government has impermissibly involved itself
in matters of religion:
          First, the statute must have secular
          legislative purpose; second, its principal or
C:\WP50\MEMO\1STAMEND.MEM                            Doc 1 Pg 1 Ln 1.17" Pos 1"
 ▲    ▲    ▲    ▲    ▲    ▲    ▲    ▲    ▲    }    ▲    ▲    ▲    ▲    ▲    ▲
[Just Off][Cntr]FIRST AMENDMENT MEMORANDUM[C/A/Flrt][HRt]
[HRt]
[Ln Spacing:2][Tab][Tab]In Lemon v. Kurtzman, 403 U.S. 602 (1971), the Supreme[S
Rt]
Court adopted the following three prong approach ("Lemon test")[SRt]
to determine whether government has impermissibly involved itself[SRt]
in matters of religion:[HRt]
[Ln Spacing:1][→Indent←][→Indent←]First, the statute must have secular[SRt]
legislative purpose; second, its principal or[SRt]
primary

Press Reveal Codes to restore screen
```

3. A [Just off] code will be inserted in your document and all your text from that point on will be left-justified. See Figure 1-5.

All right. You have to have your curiosity satisfied about the Right Justification option. Give it a try. . . .

1.4.6 CHANGING LINE SPACING

Let's make the line spacing in our sample document double-spaced so that it's easier to read.

1. With the cursor at the beginning of the first paragraph, press [Shift][F8] (Format).

2. Press [1] for Line.

3. Press [6] for Line Spacing, then type 2 and press [Enter].

4. Press [F7] (Exit) to get back to the document. The spacing should now look double-spaced on the screen.

MACRO

Use the [Alt][L] macro to change line spacing.

"What does WordPerfect do to perform that magic?" you ask. Well, the keystrokes described above told WordPerfect to insert a double-spacing code. It's not visible from the document editing screen, but if you press [F11] or [Alt][F3] Reveal Codes (depending on your keyboard type) you will see, at the bottom of your screen below the bar with the triangles, the following code: [Ln Spacing:2]. The "2" indicates double spacing. A "3" in this position would indicate triple spacing (ideal for first drafts where plenty of room is needed between lines for comments). Also note both the [HRt] and [SRt] codes, for hard and soft returns, respectively. Press [F11] or [Alt][F3] again to toggle Reveal Codes off. See Figure 1-6 for some typical codes.

FIGURE 1-6

Reveal Codes (below the graphical representation of your tab sets) show you the codes hidden in your text.

Now, suppose you wanted the second paragraph—which is a quote from the *Lemon* case—to be single-spaced. (For those who have not gone through the tortures of a first year law school legal writing course, briefs and legal memos are normally double-spaced, but long quotes are single-spaced.)

1. Press [Ctrl][↓] to move the cursor to the beginning of the second paragraph.

2. Change your line spacing back to single-spaced. That's right: [Shift][F8], [1], [6], type 1, and press [Enter].

3. Press [F7] to return to the editing screen.

[Freedom of expression] is the matrix, the indispensable condition, of nearly every other form of freedom.

Justice Benjamin Nathan Cardozo, Palko v. Connecticut, 302 U.S. 319, 327 [1937]

If you go into Reveal Codes mode, you'll see that a [Ln Spacing:1] code has been inserted.

"Great," you say. "The second paragraph is now single-spaced—but so is the rest of the document, and I only wanted to single space the second paragraph." This exercise illustrates an essential point about WordPerfect's design. WordPerfect works in a linear fashion, starting from the top of the document down. This means that the single-line-spacing code at the beginning of the second paragraph, which is further down the page, takes precedence over the double-line-spacing code at the beginning of the first paragraph.

Another key point: WordPerfect inserts codes at the exact position of the cursor. For example, if you are in the middle of a paragraph and you change the line spacing from single to double, the first half of the paragraph will be single-spaced, and the second half will be double-spaced. Therefore, always pay attention to the position of the cursor

> *Every idea is an incitement . . . If in the long run the beliefs expressed in proletarian dictatorship are destined to be accepted by the dominant forces of the community, the only meaning of free speech is that they should be given their chance and have their way.*
>
> Justice Oliver Wendell Holmes, Jr., dissenting, Gitlow v. People of the State of New York, 268 U.S. 652, 673 [1925]

before inserting a formatting code. A general rule is to put your format codes at the beginning of a paragraph.

The upshot to all of this is simple: *understanding WordPerfect's linear nature is essential to mastering the program.*

4. That said, press [Ctrl][↓] to move to the beginning of the third paragraph, and change line spacing back to double-spaced. From the beginning of the third paragraph until the next Line Spacing code is encountered, double spacing will take effect.

■ *WordPerfect's linear design underscores the importance of the Reveal Codes feature. If a document does not seem to be "behaving" properly, be sure to check the Reveal Codes screen to see if there are any unexpected codes that are interfering with your formatting.*

1.4.7 ADDING TABS AND INDENTS

Now that our document is starting to take shape, let's add some tabs and indents. By default, there is a tab stop every .5", which applies to both tabs and indents. This measure is the distance from the left WordPerfect margin, *not* the distance from the left edge of the page. You can, of course, change the tab stops to suit your needs, which we'll show you shortly. For now, we'll stick with defaults.

Before we perform this exercise, let's remove the L/R Margin code we placed in the document earlier. With Reveal Codes on, press [Home], [Home], [↑], and place your cursor on the [L/R Mar: 1.25", 1.25"] code. Now delete it. Your document's margins will revert to the default of 1" left and right.

1. Press [Ctrl][↓] until the cursor is at the beginning of the first paragraph.

2. Pressing the [Tab] key once takes you to the first tab location in your document. (Note that the position on the status line is 1.5" because the default left and right margins for WordPerfect are 1" and 1", respectively.)

3. Press [Ctrl][↓] to move to the beginning of the second paragraph. Now press [F4] (left indent). The entire paragraph is indented to the first tab position. Press [F4] again. The text is indented to the next tab position.

4. However, since quotes are left/right indented, [Backspace] twice to delete the indent codes and this time press [Shift][F4] (left/right indent). The block of text is indented .5" from both the left and right margins. Your document should look something like Figure 1-7.

FIGURE 1-7

The second paragraph has been block-indented (left and right) by pressing [Shift][F4].

```
                    FIRST AMENDMENT MEMORANDUM

In Lemon v. Kurtzman, 403 U.S. 602 (1971), the Supreme Court
adopted the following three prong approach ("Lemon test") to
determine whether government has impermissibly involved itself in
matters of religion:
          First, the statute must have secular
          legislative purpose; second, its principal or
          primary effect must be one that neither
          advances nor inhibits religion . . . finally,
          the statute must not foster "an excessive
          government entanglement with religion."
          (Emphasis added)
In Lemon v. Kurtzman, 403 U.S. 602 (1971), the Supreme Court
adopted the following three prong approach ("Lemon test") to
determine whether government has impermissibly involved itself in
matters of religion:
C:\WP51\MEMO\1STAMEND.MEM                    Doc 1 Pg 1 Ln 1" Pos 5.25"
```

■ *Press* [F11] *or* [Alt][F4] *and you'll find that the triangles on the bar dividing the screen represent the location of the tabs. The curly braces { and } represent the left and right margins of your document; these can also be adjusted. (We'll get to that at the end of the chapter.)*

1.4.8 CHANGING TAB SETTINGS

WP5.1

Let's make our first tab stop 1" instead of the WordPerfect default of .5".

1. Go to the beginning of the first line of the document and press [Shift][F8], [1] for Line, and [8] for Tab Set.

They have no lawyers among them, for they consider them as a sort of people whose profession it is to disguise matters.
Thomas More
Utopia [1516].
Of Law and Magistrates

2. With the cursor on the L (for Left Tab) at position .5", press [Del] to remove the tab. Notice that both the tabbed and indented text shifts automatically to the new 1" tab stop. See Figure 1-7.

3. Press [F7] twice to return to the document.

■ *If you turn on Reveal Codes you'll notice a rather long and apparently confused jumble of numbers. A closer look reveals that the code simply indicates the position of every tab in your present Tab Set. If you look closely you won't see one indicated at .5" because we deleted it. You should also notice that the first triangle is missing from the Reveal Codes ruler.*

WP5.0

1. Go to the beginning of the first line of the document and press [Shift][F8], [1] for Line, and [8] for Tab Set.

FIGURE 1-8

The Tab Set ruler near the page bottom indicates there is no tab at position +.5". It has been deleted. The text in the first paragraph is aligned with the tab at +1". (The + indicates that the tab is to the right of the 0 on the ruler; –, to the left.)

MACRO

Use the [Alt][F11] macro to quickly change tab settings.

2. Place your cursor on the L (for Left Tab) that corresponds to the position of the beginning of the paragraph (at 1.5") and press [Del] to remove that tab.

3. Press [F7] twice to return to the document. You will notice that the paragraph begins at the new tab position.

■ *If you turn on Reveal Codes you'll notice a rather long and apparently confused jumble of numbers. A closer look reveals that the code simply indicates the position of every tab in your present Tab Set. If you look closely you won't see one indicated at 1.5" because we deleted it. You should also notice that the first triangle is missing from the Reveal Codes ruler.*

1.4.9 UNDERLINING, BOLDING, AND ITALICIZING TEXT AND VIEWING THE DOCUMENT

In legal writing, cases are generally underlined or italicized, while text that has been emphasized by the author is often italicized or bold. The two most commonly used attributes, underlining and bolding, are added with the [F8] and [F6] keys, respectively. All other attributes are added via the [Ctrl][F8] (Font) menu.

■ *What you see on your screen will depend on what type of monitor and graphics card you have and what your settings are in Display—Colors/Fonts/Attributes under Initial Settings. (See Appendix A for more information on using Setup.)*

Let's add these text attributes to our sample text. We'll begin by underlining the case names.

1.4.10 UNDERLINING EXISTING TEXT

1. Place your cursor at the beginning of "Lemon" and turn on block. (Press [Alt][F4] or [F12].)
2. Press [Ctrl][→] three times, then [←] twice so that the entire case name of Lemon v. Kurtzman is blocked out.
3. Press [F8] (Underline).

> ■ *If you are using a color monitor, WordPerfect makes the text or background a different color instead of actually underlining. To see how it will look when printed, you must use the View Document feature discussed below. However, if you Reveal Codes, you will note the word surrounded by two codes: [UND] and [und]. The first code indicates that bolding begins at that point, and the second one indicates where it ends. Other attributes in WordPerfect work much the same way.*

TIP

You'll save yourself time by turning on underlining or bolding before entering text. For example, press [F8] [UND], type the text you want underlined, and then press [F8] again. You can also press [→] once to take your cursor beyond the code and outside of the underlining attribute.

1.4.11 BOLDING EXISTING TEXT

1. Place the cursor at the beginning of the emphasized quote "An excessive government entanglement..." in the second paragraph and turn on block. (Press [Alt][F4] or [F12].)
2. Press the period (.) to block out the rest of the sentence.
3. Press [F6] (Bold).

1.4.12 ITALICIZING EXISTING TEXT

1. Place the cursor at the beginning of the next occurrence of Lemon v. Kurtzman in your document and block it out using [Alt][F4] or [F12].
2. Press [Ctrl][F8] (font), [2] for Appearance, [4] for Italic.

> ■ *Make a mental note of the other formatting options available from the Appearance menu. Do the same for [Ctrl][F8] and [1] for Size. (We'll be discussing some of the options in the size menu in Chapter 6.)*

MACRO

Use the [Alt][I] macro to turn italics on and off.

1.4.13 USING VIEW DOCUMENT TO SEE HOW YOUR WORK WILL LOOK WHEN PRINTED

You've probably already noticed that WordPerfect does not always display an attribute on the editing screen as it will look when printed. In all probability, what you see merely symbolizes the attribute. In computerese, the editing screen is not WYSIWYG (What You See Is What You Get).

WordPerfect does let you achieve WYSIWYG, however, using the View Document function ([Shift][F7], [6] for View). The View Document function will also allow you to see headers, footers, footnotes, and endnotes that wouldn't normally be visible on the editing screen, as well as different typefaces and special print effects. The catch? You can't *edit* in this mode—you can only *view* your work.

> *WordPerfect is not WYSIWYG for technical reasons involving speed and memory, because WYSIWYG capabilities require substantial additional computing power. However, WordPerfect for Windows is WYSIWYG, as will be the forthcoming WordPerfect 6.0. To run these programs, you must have state of the art hardware. We recommend at least a 386-33 MHz class computer with 4MB of RAM and a VGA monitor.*

1. Press [Shift][F7] (Print), [6] for View Document.
2. Press [1] for 100% magnification, [2] for 200%, [3] for Full Page view, and [4] for facing pages. See Figure 1-9.

MACRO

Use the [Alt][V] macro to view quickly document.

TIP

Use the navigating keys when in View Document. For example, [Home], [↑] will take you to the top of the screen, [Home], [Home], [↑] to the beginning of the document, [PgUp] to the previous page, and so on.

FIGURE 1-9

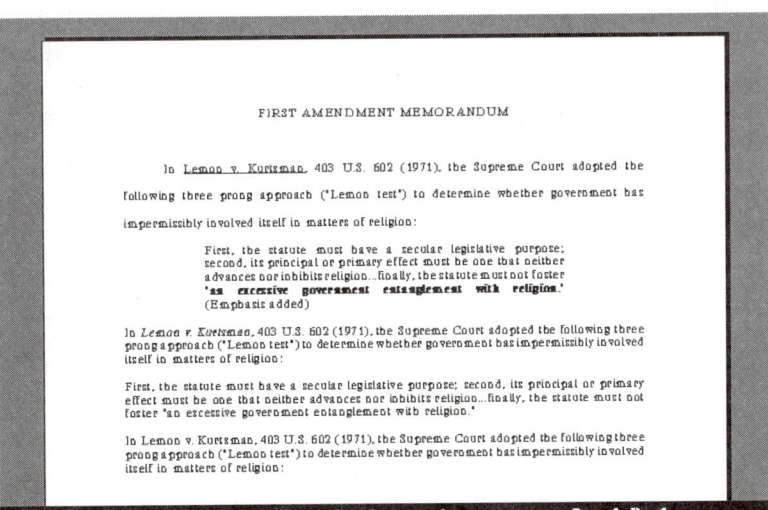

Our sample First Amendment document in view mode, at 100%. To see the entire page, choose [3] for Full Page. This will reduce the size, but show the complete text on the page.

> And do as adversaries do in law,
> Strive mightily, but eat and drink as friends.
> William Shakespeare
> The Taming of the Shrew [1593–1594]

3. Press [F7] (Exit) to return to the editing screen.

■ *Frequent use of the View Document mode, especially before printing, will save time and paper because errors that are often visible on this screen are not visible on the regular editing screen.*

1.4.14 DELETING CODES IN A DOCUMENT

As we have seen so far in this exercise, all of WordPerfect's formatting commands and attributes are created by inserting codes in the text. These codes can be seen using the Reveal Codes function. It follows logically, then, that you can edit a document or change its appearance by deleting these same codes. We're going to explore this important concept by deleting some of the codes in our sample document.

Deleting an attribute code

As mentioned previously, attribute codes such as [UND] and [BOLD] bracket the selected text. (Example: [UND]This text is underlined[und].) To get rid of underlining, you can delete either code. Here's how:

1. With the 1STAMEND.MEM document on the screen, press [Home], [Home], [↑] to move the cursor to the beginning of the document

2. Press [Alt][F3] or [F11] to Reveal Codes, then move the cursor to the beginning of Lemon v. Kurtzman in the first paragraph. Note that the cursor in the Reveal Codes bottom half of the screen is tracking the cursor on the normal editing screen above.

> **TIP**
>
> In **WP5.1**, you can adjust how many lines to use for the Reveal Codes screen under Setup, Display, Edit Screen Options by pressing [Shift][F1] (Setup), [2] for **D**isplay, and [6] for **E**dit-Screen options.

3. Place the cursor directly on top of the [UND] code and press [Del] to delete the code. The text will lose the underline attribute.

■ *If you decide you want to restore a code you just deleted, use the undelete function* [F1].

4. When finished, don't forget to save 1STAMEND.MEM by pressing [F10] (Save), [Enter], [Y].

You can use the same technique to delete any code inserted by WordPerfect. For example, if you wanted to get rid of the single spacing in the second paragraph, Reveal Codes and delete the [Ln Spacing:1] code. The trickiest thing is getting used to tracking the cursor in the Reveal Codes screen. Our advice is to look at the Reveal Codes (bottom) portion of the screen.

1.5 EXERCISE 4: PAGE NUMBERING; HEADERS, FOOTERS, AND FOOTNOTES; USING THE SPELL CHECKER AND THESAURUS

In this final exercise, we'll explore some of the refinements you might want to add to a document before printing the final copy. We'll also explore the much-loved spell checker and thesaurus feature.

To begin, let's give this document some page numbering.

1.5.1 ADDING PAGE NUMBERS IN WP 5.1

1. With our 1STAMEND.MEM document on the screen, press [Home], [Home], [Home], [↑] to bring your cursor to the very beginning of the document in front of any codes that might be there as well as text.

2. Press [Shift][F8].

3. Press [2] for **P**age, [6] for Page **N**umbering, and [4] for Page Number **P**osition.

4. This screen is graphically intuitive. Pick option 6 and our page numbering will appear on every page at the bottom center. You'll see that information in the Format: Page Number Position screen shown in Figure 1-10.

5. Press [Enter] three times and turn on your Reveal Codes. You should see the [Pg Numbering: Bottom Center] code. Go into View Document mode ([Shift][F7], [6]) and select [3] for Full Page view. You will see that little 1 centered at the bottom of the page.

MACRO

Use the [Alt][N] macro to quickly place page numbers bottom center.

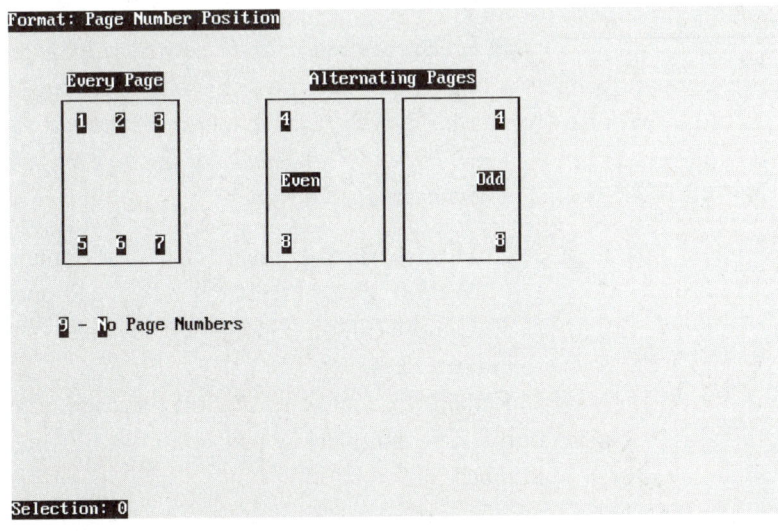

FIGURE 1-10

The Format: Page Number Position screen has a graphical look that makes it easy to choose numbering options.

Wherever Law ends, Tyranny begins.
*John Locke
Second Treatise of Government [1690]*

■ *You can see page numbers only when in the View Document mode. They will print correctly even if you do not invoke this mode.*

1.5.2 ADDING PAGE NUMBERS IN WP 5.0

1. With 1STAMEND.MEM on the screen, press [Home], [Home], [Home], [↑] to bring your cursor to the very beginning of the document in front of any codes, as well as before text.

2. Press [Shift][F8], [2] for **P**age.

3. Press [7] for **P**age Numbering.

4. The screen you will see is graphically intuitive. Pick option 6 and your page numbering will appear on every page at the bottom center. You'll see that information in the Format: Page screen at option 7, "Page Numbering." It will indicate that the page number is at Bottom Center.

5. Press [Enter] three times and turn on your Reveal Codes. You should see the [Pg Numbering: Bottom Center] code. If you go into View Document mode ([Shift][F7], [6]) you will see the little 1 at the bottom center of the page.

1.5.3 SUPPRESSING PAGE NUMBERS

Many legal documents don't have a page number on the first page—the numbering generally starts on the following page. Here's how we suppress the page number on page 1.

MACRO

Use the [Alt][A] macro to suppress all headers, footers, and page numbers.

1. With the cursor at the very top of the first page [Home], [Home], [↑], press [Shift][F8] (Format).

■ *Unless the cursor is at the very top of the page when you are performing this procedure, you will suppress the page number on the following page. Similarly when you are inserting page numbering in your document, be sure you're at the very top of the page you want your numbering to begin on.*

2. **WP5.1** Press [2] for Page, [8] for Suppress (this page only).
   WP5.0 Press [2] for Page, [9] for Suppress (this page only).

3. Choose option [4] for Suppress Page Numbering and press [Y] to indicate "yes."

Remember, you've turned off the page numbering for "this page only." The numbering will continue on the next page with page number 2.

One last word about page numbering. If you want to turn off page numbering at any point in the document for more than one page, you don't have to keep putting in suppress page number codes. Option 9 on the Format: Page Number Position screen: No Page Numbering will do the trick. Make sure it's placed on the first character of the page you want to stop numbering on or it won't work for that page. When you want to resume numbering, repeat steps 2–4 in Section 1.5.1.

■ *For information on using special page numbering features such as a small roman page number for table of contents and table of authorities, see Chapter 5.*

1.5.4 HEADERS, FOOTERS, AND FOOTNOTES

Creating headers and footers

We're going to place a header in the document that will begin on the second page. Here we go. Press [Home], [Home], [Home], [↑] to bring your cursor all the way to the beginning of the document. (Actually, to place a header it doesn't matter whether your cursor is in front of the codes or not, as long as it's before all the text.)

MACRO

Use the [Alt][H] and [Alt][F] macros to quickly create headers and footers.

1. Press [Shift][F8] (Format).
2. Press [2] for **Page**, [3] for **Header**, and [1] for Header **A**.

■ *You have two Header options: Header A and Header B. This is because WordPerfect allows you to place two headers (or footers) on a page.*

MACRO

WP5.1 The [Alt][B] macro will insert a footer B with the document's path and file name.

3. Now select option 2 for every page.

■ *You are now in the Header editing screen, which looks almost identical to the regular editing screen except for the prompt in the bottom left-hand corner of the screen indicating Header A:. You can use in this screen all the standard formatting commands that you've learned so far in this chapter, including underlining, bolding, etc.*

4. Type `Draft 1 of First Amendment Brief` (see Figure 1-11), then press [F7] (Exit) to exit the screen.

■ *Notice that Your Format Page screen indicates HA every page.*

■ *For a more complete discussion of using headers and footers, see Chapter 2.*

5. Press [F7] (Exit) to return to your document.

FIGURE 1-11

The Header editing screen shows a prompt at the bottom left-hand corner: you are reminded to press Exit when done to return to the document editing screen.

6. Press [Shift][F7], [6] (View Document) to see your handiwork.

■ *As with the page number code, you can only view headers and footers in the View Document mode.*

Suppressing headers and footers

Now let's suppress the header on the first page. It takes the same procedure as suppressing the page number, with one small exception. (Remember, press [Home], [Home], [↑] to place the cursor at the very beginning of the page or else you'll be suppressing the header on the next page.)

1. Press [Shift][F8] (Format).
2. **WP5.1**   Press [8] for Suppress (this page only).
   WP5.0   Press [9] for Suppress (this page only).
3. Press [5] for suppress Header A. (Be sure to type the [Y].)

You can check out the results by going into view mode.

■ *Footers work in exactly the same manner.*

Inserting footnotes

We'll be talking about footnotes later in the book, in Chapter 5, but we can certainly get you started by placing a footnote in our sample quote from the famous First Amendment case of *Lemon v. Kurtzman*:

TIP

When you Reveal Codes and place your cursor on the newly created header code, it indicates not only the nature of the header, but also the contents. (With longer headers or footers, only the initial part is shown.)

MACRO

Use the [Alt][A] macro to quickly suppress headers and footers on the first page.

If the law supposes that, said Mr. Bumble . . . "the law is a ass, a idiot."

Charles Dickens
Oliver Twist
[1837–1838]

1. With the 1STAMEND.MEM document on the screen, move the cursor to the end of the second paragraph that quotes *Lemon* (after Emphasis Added).
2. Press [Ctrl][F7] (**Footnote**).
3. Choose [1] for **Footnote** and [1] for **Create**.

Just as in the case of our header (the same thing applies to footers), we know we're not in the document edit screen from the prompt "Footnote: Press [Exit] when done" (**WP5.0** "Press [Exit] when done").

You can now, depending on the manner in which you format your footnotes, either place a few spaces after the 1, insert a tab, or press indent before inputting the footnote text. The same formatting rules apply as in the regular document edit screen; i.e., you can bold or italicize any of the text, change the spacing between lines (although you'd be unlikely to do that in a footnote), or make the footnote text smaller by changing the size of the typeface (or change the typeface itself). There is, however, a better way of doing that document-wide, without having to go into each footnote and putting a font code in at the beginning. We'll get to that in Chapter 5.

4. Type the following text:

```
Lemon v. Kurtzman, 403 U.S. 602, 612-13 (1970)
(quoting Walz v. Tax Commission, 397 U.S. 664, 674
(1970)).
```

5. When you're finished, press [F7] (**Exit**) as the prompt indicates to exit the footnote editing screen and return to the main body of the document. (See Figure 1-12.) You will note that the number 1 is automatically placed directly at the end of the text paragraph.

FIGURE 1-12

The Footnote editing screen shows our sample text indented to the first tab stop.

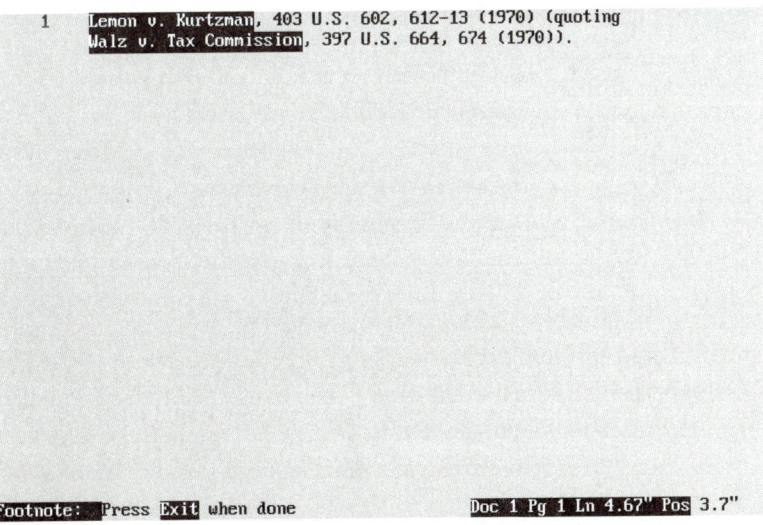

Chapter 1 Getting Started with WordPerfect—A Tutorial
§1.5

FIGURE 1-13

The cursor in the Reveal Codes screen is highlighting the footnote code. This shows the footnote number and the first few words of text, together with formatting codes; allowing you to easily identify footnotes in text.

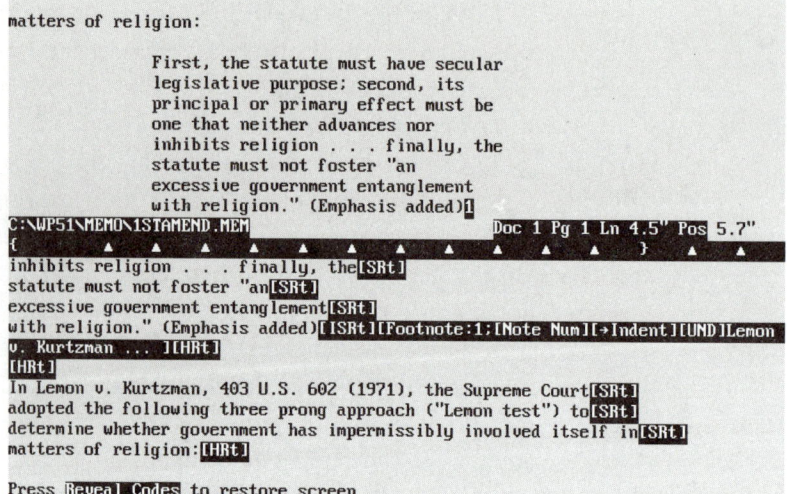

6. Place your cursor directly on the number and press Reveal Codes. Hmmm, as shown in Figure 1-13, there's some rather valuable information here.

■ *Not only are you reminded of which footnote you're looking at, but you can see what text it contains. Obviously, it's not all visible, but there's probably enough to make it identifiable.*

As we mentioned, there will be a lot more material on footnotes in Chapter 5, but we didn't think it would hurt if you got your feet wet at this point.

1.5.5 USING THE SPELL CHECK AND THESAURUS

SOFTWARE

West Publishing has now made Black's Law Dictionary available on disk for WordPerfect users. Both Black's Law Dictionary and Black's Legal Speller can be ordered from West at (800) 328-9352.

WordPerfect has a 125,000-word dictionary, including approximately 25,000 legal and medical terms. The Thesaurus contains approximately 150,000 words. Together, these are two of the most powerful tools in WordPerfect. They are especially valuable to touch typists, because it allows them to quickly type out the document and use Spell Check to catch the obvious errors later.

Get into the habit of running the spell checker before printing your documents, but remember that it is not fail-safe. Spell checkers do not check grammar—so if you use "their" instead of "there," WordPerfect will not catch the error because both are spelled correctly.

FIGURE 1-14

Spell Check here gives two possible spellings for the highlighted word. Typing the letter next to the desired spelling will automatically replace the word.

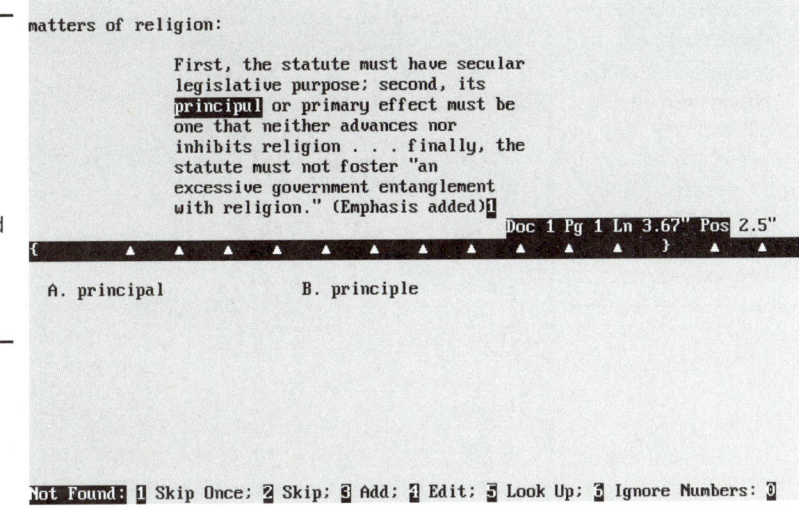

Spell Check

1. Press [Ctrl][F2] (Spell).

2. Choose [1] to check the current **W**ord, [2] to check the current **P**age, [3] to check the entire **D**ocument, [4] to use a **N**ew supplementary dictionary, [5] to **L**ook up the spelling of a word without first typing it on the screen, and [6] to get a word **C**ount of the document.

3. If a word is misspelled in or absent from WordPerfect's spelling dictionary (which is often the case for proper names), the word is highlighted and possible correct spellings are displayed.

4. If a correct spelling is displayed, type the letter assigned to the word. This will automatically replace the highlighted word. For example, in Figure 1-14, the proper choice would be **A** for "Principal." However, if the word is incorrectly spelled and WordPerfect's dictionary can't make a good guess, press [4] for **E**dit. You'll be allowed back into the document to make the correction yourself. Press [F7] to resume the spell checking.

5. When completely finished, press [F7] (Exit) to return to the document.

6. If Spell Check has made any changes to your document, press [F10] to save the document again, or your changes will be lost when you exit WordPerfect.

TIP

If a word is not listed and is correctly spelled (a case name, for example), you can tell WordPerfect to skip the word by choosing [1] to skip the word once or [2] to skip all further occurrences of the word. However, if it is a name or word that you will use frequently, press [3] to **A**dd the word to the supplementary dictionary, which you create and have control over.

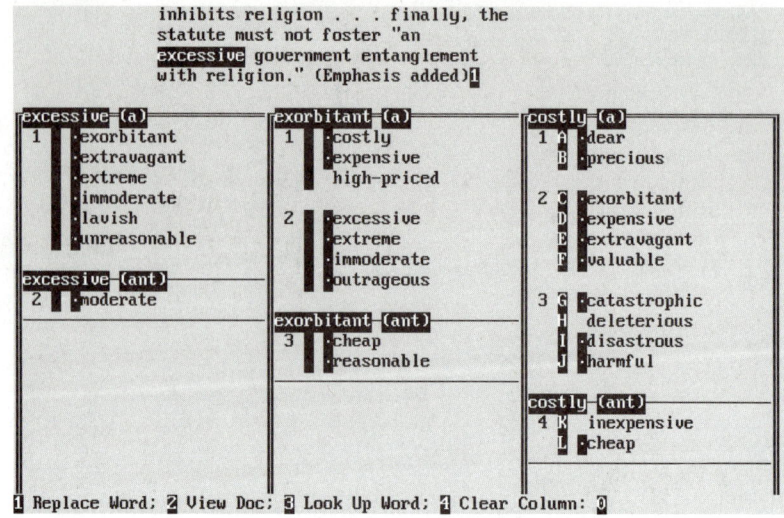

FIGURE 1-15

A Thesaurus menu providing a myriad of synonyms and antonyms for "excessive," while showing the word in the context of the document.

Thesaurus

Great cases, like hard cases, make bad law.
Justice Oliver Wendell Holmes, Jr., dissenting, Northern Securities Co. v. United States 193 U.S. 197, 400 [1904]

1. Press [Alt][F1] (Thesaurus) on the word "excessive."
2. The list of alternatives is displayed on the screen in three columns, as shown in Figure 1-15. You can use the [←] and [→] keys to move from column to column. (The boldface letters that label the words in the Thesaurus list indicate which column is current.) After moving to the column with the correct alternative, choose [1] to Replace the word in the text and then type the letter for the word.
3. To return to the document, press [F7] (Exit).
4. If the Thesaurus has made any changes to your document, press [F10] to save the document or your changes will be lost when you exit WordPerfect.

■ *If the cursor is not on a word, you are prompted to enter a word. If the cursor is on a word, but that word is not found in the Thesaurus, the message "Word not Found" is displayed and you are prompted to enter a word.*

■ *A word having its own group of alternatives is sometimes referred to as a headword. Each word listed in the Thesaurus with a bullet is a headword. There are approximately 10,000 headwords in the Thesaurus with an overall word count of 150,000.*

1.6 SOME "POWER USER" TECHNIQUES

Although this introductory chapter only represents the tip of the iceberg in revealing all the features and capabilities that WordPerfect offers you, we feel that since you stuck with us we'd show you a couple of "power user" techniques to whet your appetite for the forthcoming chapters.

1.6.1 USING THE [Esc] KEY'S REPEAT VALUE

TIP

You can change the repeat key's default value by pressing [Shift][F1], [4] ([5] for **WP 5.0**) for initial settings, and [6] for Repeat Value ([5] for **WP 5.0**). Enter a new number and when you press [Esc] the repeat value will reflect your new value.

Besides allowing you to back out or "escape" from a procedure, [Esc] has a repeat value function. Strike it right now. You should see it say "Repeat Value = 8." Press it again and it disappears. "Not much of a trick," you say. Press [Esc] again and now type a hyphen. Beginning to catch on? Go to the beginning of a new line. Now press [Esc] again and type 67. The Repeat Value = 67. Press the hyphen key. Voilà, a dashed line across the document. This feature can sometimes be very handy, especially when writing macros (something you'll learn all about in later chapters).

1.6.2 MOVING TEXT BETWEEN DOCUMENT SCREENS

We're finally going to show you that trick about how to move text from one document to the other on the same screen.

1. With 1STAMEND.MEM on the screen, press [Ctrl][F3] (Screen) and type [1] for **Window**.

2. Now type 12 in response to "Number of lines in this window:" then press [Enter]. You've got two document windows that should appear exactly the same except for one notable difference: the status line in the bottom window indicates that it is Document 2.

3. Press [Shift][F3] (Switch) and your cursor moves to the second document in the lower portion of your screen. Did you notice how the little triangles flipped over to indicate that you were in the bottom screen? Your screen should look something like Figure 1-16.

Now that you're in Document 2, you can start creating a new document and give it a name, or you can retrieve a document you've already created. If you want to exchange text or data between the two

FIGURE 1-16

The screen has been split into two parts, each a separate document. Although you can't see it, the cursor is in the second screen here, because the arrows in the graphic ruler are pointing down.

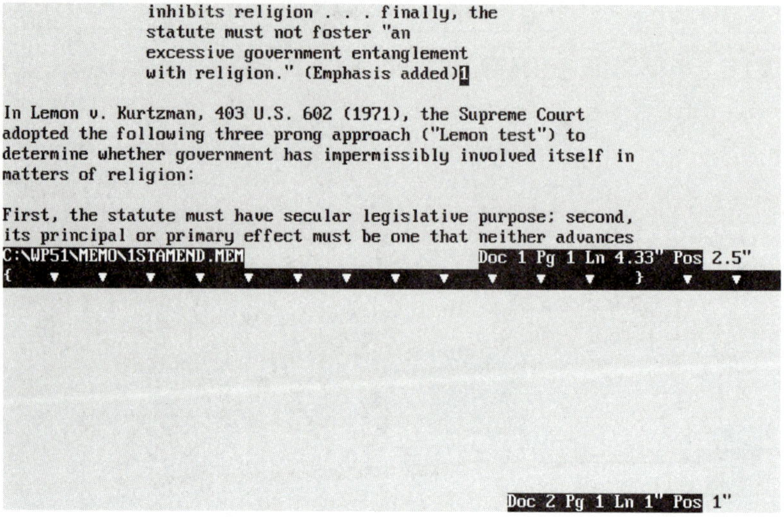

```
               inhibits religion . . . finally, the
               statute must not foster "an
               excessive government entanglement
               with religion." (Emphasis added)
In Lemon v. Kurtzman, 403 U.S. 602 (1971), the Supreme Court
adopted the following three prong approach ("Lemon test") to
determine whether government has impermissibly involved itself in
matters of religion:

First, the statute must have secular legislative purpose; second,
its principal or primary effect must be one that neither advances
C:\WP51\MEMO\1STAMEND.MEM                    Doc 1 Pg 1 Ln 4.33" Pos 2.5"




                                             Doc 2 Pg 1 Ln 1"    Pos 1"
```

documents, either by copying or moving text or data, the process is simple. Use the same commands you learned earlier in the chapter and simply use the [Shift][F3] (Switch) key combination to move the cursor from one document to the other to paste whatever you intend to move or copy. Let's try it.

If you're in the Document 2 window, move back to Document 1. Copy page 1 of 1STAMEND.MEM ([Ctrl][F4], [3], [2]), then press [Shift][F3] to move the cursor back to Document 2. Press the [Enter] key to retrieve the text. You can practice moving and copying text between the two documents if you're so inclined. We think you get the picture.

1.6.3 RESTORING A SPLIT SCREEN

1. When you're finished exploring the marvels of the split screen feature, press [Ctrl][F3] and [1] for **W**indow again.

2. This time, instead of inputting a number, use the [↓] cursor to move the bar all the way down to the bottom of the screen till it disappears. Notice that the prompt "Number of lines in this window:" changes to reflect the position of the bar. You could also move the bar upwards to achieve the same effect if you wanted to work exclusively in Document 2. (Press [Enter] to confirm your decision.)

TIP

You can also use the up or down arrows when you initially create the split screen to interactively change the size of the two windows.

■ *Although the second document has disappeared from the screen, it is still in memory. That means that after you are finished with Document 1 and you exit it, WordPerfect will still want to know about your intentions concerning the future of Document 2—"Do you want to save it, replace the existing version, etc.?"*

Well, there you have it—a quick introduction to WordPerfect. Armed with what you have learned, you are certainly capable of performing many of the tasks needed to produce legal documents quickly and professionally. However, WordPerfect offers much more in the way of features that will make those tasks a great deal easier to perform. It will also enable you to produce documents, if need be, that are much more sophisticated and attractive than the run-of-the-mill letter or memo.

We'll see you again in one or more of the following chapters.

> *No freeman shall be taken, or imprisoned, or outlawed, or exiled, or in any way harmed, nor will we go upon him nor will we send upon him, except by the legal judgment of his peers or by the law of the land.*
> —Magna Carta Clause 39

1.7 COMMAND REVIEW

Document navigation keystrokes

[Ctrl][←], [Ctrl][→], word to word

WP5.1 [Ctrl][↑], [Ctrl][↓], paragraph to paragraph

[End], end of line

[Home], [←] beginning of line

[Home], [Home], [↑], beginning of document

[Home], [Home], [↓], end of document

[PgUp] first line of previous page

[PgDn] first line of next page

[Ctrl][Home], [↑] first line of page you're on

[Ctrl][Home], [↓] last line of page you're on

[Home], [↑] top of visible screen

[Home], [↓] bottom of visible screen

[Ctrl][Home] + page number, beginning of that page

Printing a document

[Shift][F7], [1] for Full Document

Saving a document

1. [F10], type document name, [Y] to replace document
2. [F7], [Y], type document name, [Y] to replace document, [N] to remain in WordPerfect and clear the screen, [Y] to exit WordPerfect

Using the Undelete function

[F1], [1] for **R**estore (use [↑] to view last three deletions)

Deleting procedures

[Ctrl][Backspace] or [Ctrl][Del]—from cursor forward
[Ctrl][End] to end of line
[Ctrl][PgDn], [Y] to end of page
[F12] or [Alt][F4], [Del], [Y] to delete a block of text

Cutting, pasting, and copying

[Ctrl][F4], [1] for **S**entence, [1], [Enter] to move a sentence
[Ctrl][F4], [2] for **P**aragraph, [2] for **C**opy, [Enter] to copy a paragraph
[Ctrl][F4], [3] for **P**age, [2] for **C**opy, [Enter] to copy a page

Storing and retrieving text in memory

[Ctrl][F4], [2] for **P**aragraph, [1] for **M**ove, [F1], move to new position, [Ctrl][F4], [4] for **R**etrieve, [1] for **B**lock

Using List Files to find and retrieve a file

[F5], [Enter], [N] for **N**ame Search, type first two or three letters of document, [Enter], [1] for **R**etrieve

Changing the margins

[Shift][F8], [1] for **L**ine, [7] for **M**argins, enter desired left and right margins

Centering text

[Shift][F6], type text, [Enter] for one line of text

[F12] or [Alt][F4], block desired text, [Shift][F8], [Y] for more than one line of text

Changing text justification

[Shift][F8], [1] for Line, [3] for Justification, [1] for Left, [4] for Full

WP5.0 [Shift][F8], [1] for Line, [3] for Justification, [N] for no justification

Changing line spacing

[Shift][F8], [1] for Line, [6] for Line Spacing, type desired spacing, e.g., [2] for double spacing

Changing tab settings

[Shift][F8], [1] for Line, [8] for Tab Set, delete tab or tabs by placing cursor on tab, [Del], or add tab (type desired position [Enter])

Underlining text

1. [F8], type text, [→], or block text, [F8]
2. [Ctrl][F8], [2] for Appearance, [2] for Undln

Bolding text

1. [F6], type text, [→], or block text, [F6]
2. [Ctrl][F8], [2] for Appearance, [1] for Bold

Italicizing text

[Ctrl][F8], [2] for Appearance, [4] for Italc

Using View Document

[Shift][F7], [6] for View Document

Deleting an attribute code

[Alt][F3] or [F11], place cursor on code, [Del]

Adding page numbers

[Shift][F8], [2] for **P**age, [6] for Page **N**umbering, [4] for Page Number Position, enter Page Number Position, e.g., [6] for center bottom, every page

WP5.0 [Shift][F8], [7] for Page **N**umbering, enter Page Number Position

Suppressing page numbers

Place cursor at the top of the appropriate page [Home], [Home], [↑], [Shift][F8], [2] for **P**age, [8] for **S**uppress, [4] for Suppress **P**age Numbering, [Y]

WP5.0 [2] for **P**age, [9] for **S**uppress, [4] for Suppress **P**age Numbering, [Y]

Creating headers/footers

[Shift][F8], [2] for **P**age, [3] for **H**eader ([4] for Footer), [1] for Header/Footer **A**, [2] for Every **P**age, enter text, [F7]

Suppressing headers/footers

Place cursor at the top of the appropriate page, [Shift][F8], [2] for **P**age, [8] for **S**uppress, [5] for Suppress Header **A**, or [7] for Suppress Footer **A**, [Y]

Inserting footnotes

[Ctrl][F7], [1] for **F**ootnote, [1] for **C**reate, type footnote, [F7]

Using Spell Check

[Ctrl][F2], [3] to check **D**ocument, select letter next to correct spelling, e.g., [A], [B], or [C] to replace word, or [4] for **E**dit and [F7]; when finished, [F7] to return to document

Using the Thesaurus

`Alt`+`F1`, `1` to replace word, type letter next to desired word, `F7`

Moving text from one document to another using split screen

1. `Ctrl`+`F3`, `1` for **W**indow, indicate size of window by typing desired number of lines

2. `Shift`+`F3` and retrieve document `Shift`+`F10`

3. Cut and paste in usual manner and use `Shift`+`F3` to move from window to window

4. `Shift`+`F3`, `1` for **W**indow, type 24 or use `↑` or `↓` to restore window, depending on which window you're in

Using WordPerfect for Legal Correspondence

FUNCTIONS USED

- Basic formatting options: changing margins and tab sets, centering the page, adding text attributes, using headers and the date function §2.1.2–2.1.7
- Using the Styles feature to automate letter formatting §2.2.1–2.2.2
- Using the Macro feature to create simple named macros for frequently used addresses and text §2.2.3–2.2.4
- Using simple keyboard merges to automate routine letters §2.3.1
- Printing the address block onto envelopes §2.3.4
- Performing a mass mailing using the Merge feature §2.3.5–2.3.16
- Using the Sort feature for mass mailings §2.3.12–2.3.14
- Merges using the WordPerfect Office Notebook program §2.3.17
- Printing addresses onto labels §2.3.18–2.3.19

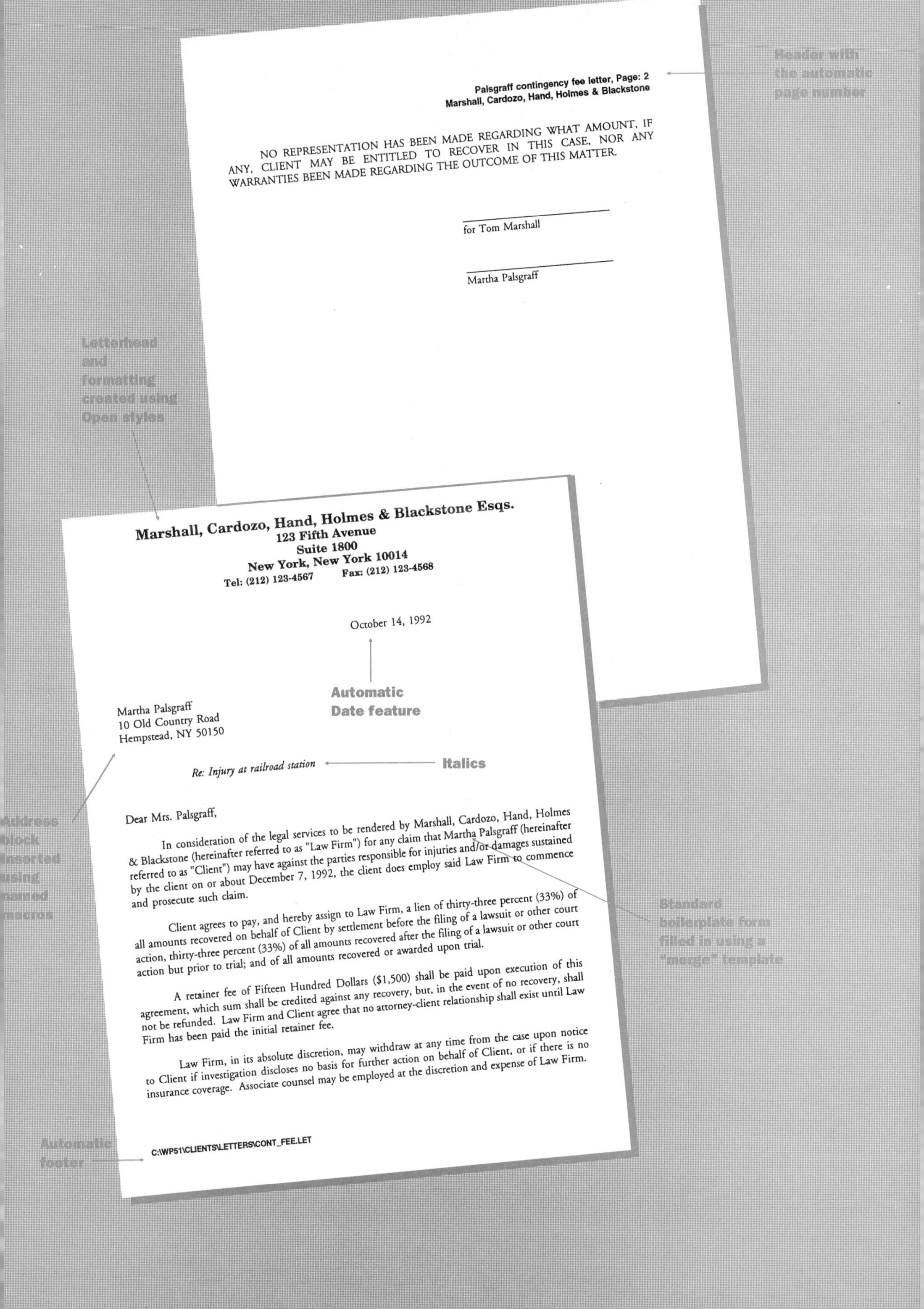

Annotations (margin labels):
- Header with the automatic page number
- Letterhead and formatting created using Open styles
- Automatic Date feature
- Italics
- Address block inserted using named macros
- Standard boilerplate form filled in using a "merge" template
- Automatic footer

Page 2:

Palsgraff contingency fee letter, Page: 2
Marshall, Cardozo, Hand, Holmes & Blackstone

NO REPRESENTATION HAS BEEN MADE REGARDING WHAT AMOUNT, IF ANY, CLIENT MAY BE ENTITLED TO RECOVER IN THIS CASE, NOR ANY WARRANTIES BEEN MADE REGARDING THE OUTCOME OF THIS MATTER.

_____
for Tom Marshall

_____
Martha Palsgraff

Page 1:

Marshall, Cardozo, Hand, Holmes & Blackstone Esqs.
123 Fifth Avenue
Suite 1800
New York, New York 10014
Tel: (212) 123-4567   Fax: (212) 123-4568

October 14, 1992

Martha Palsgraff
10 Old Country Road
Hempstead, NY 50150

Re: Injury at railroad station

Dear Mrs. Palsgraff,

In consideration of the legal services to be rendered by Marshall, Cardozo, Hand, Holmes & Blackstone (hereinafter referred to as "Law Firm") for any claim that Martha Palsgraff (hereinafter referred to as "Client") may have against the parties responsible for injuries and/or damages sustained by the client on or about December 7, 1992, the client does employ said Law Firm to commence and prosecute such claim.

Client agrees to pay, and hereby assign to Law Firm, a lien of thirty-three percent (33%) of all amounts recovered on behalf of Client by settlement before the filing of a lawsuit or other court action, thirty-three percent (33%) of all amounts recovered after the filing of a lawsuit or other court action but prior to trial; and of all amounts recovered or awarded upon trial.

A retainer fee of Fifteen Hundred Dollars ($1,500) shall be paid upon execution of this agreement, which sum shall be credited against any recovery, but, in the event of no recovery, shall not be refunded. Law Firm and Client agree that no attorney-client relationship shall exist until Law Firm has been paid the initial retainer fee.

Law Firm, in its absolute discretion, may withdraw at any time from the case upon notice to Client if investigation discloses no basis for further action on behalf of Client, or if there is no insurance coverage. Associate counsel may be employed at the discretion and expense of Law Firm.

C:\WP51\CLIENTS\LETTERS\CONT_FEE.LET

"My dear Sir, it is absolutely impossible for me to plead your case. You lack the most important piece of evidence . . . (aside) Evidence that you can pay my fee!"

OVERVIEW

Let's face it, lawyers spend a good deal of their time talking on the telephone. But they also depend on correspondence to stay in touch with their clients and opposing counsel. Consequently, writing (or dictating) letters is one of the most mundane tasks of the profession. The variety of letters drafted by lawyers is enormous, but almost all correspondence has standard repeating elements that lend themselves to automation by WordPerfect. Examples include the position of the date and address block on letterhead paper, the use of a RE: line, headers on page 2 and beyond, signature blocks, and printing addresses on envelopes.

Besides automating certain text elements of correspondence, WordPerfect can also be used to automate routine boilerplate letters that remain essentially unchanged except for perhaps the name and address of the recipient. WordPerfect's keyboard merge feature is ideal for turning ordinary letters into reusable boilerplate documents. The merge feature not only speeds routine correspondence but guarantees that the correspondence will look just like the original.

Finally, WordPerfect's powerful mail merge and sorting capabilities can make short work of mass mailings, enabling a law firm to send out hundreds, even thousands, of letters, newsletters, and so forth, to clients and prospective clients.

This chapter will describe how to use many of WordPerfect's most powerful features to automate the process of writing letters, including the macro and merge features. The skills discussed in each section are as follows:

Basic skills

> *The law . . . will not bend to the uncertain wishes, imaginations and wanton tempers of men. . . . On the one hand it is inexorable to the cries and lamentations of the prisoners; on the other it is deaf, deaf as an adder, to the clamors of the populace.*
> — John Adams
> Argument in Defense of the [British] Soldiers in the Boston Massacre Trials [December 1770]

- Changing margins
- Changing tab settings
- Adding text attributes such as italics and boldface
- Centering a letter on a page vertically
- Using headers and footers
- Using the automatic date feature

Intermediate skills

- Using styles to insert formatting commands
- Using the Advance feature to position text
- Using named macros to insert client names and addresses into the letter
- Revising macros using the macro editor

Advanced skills

- Using merge templates to create boilerplate documents
- Printing the address block on envelopes
- Using the Merge feature for mass mailings
- Using the Sort and Select features to alphabetize and sort mailings by zip code
- Printing labels

2.1 LEGAL CORRESPONDENCE—BASIC SKILLS

2.1.1 INTRODUCTION

With this chapter we begin the somewhat contrived, often frivolous, but undeniably entertaining tale of Tom, Linda, Steve, Sarah, and Larry. We've already introduced them to you in the Preface and mentioned that they've just started their own firm. The reason for this grand, somewhat frightening step is that they've seen more than a little of the world of mega-partner, big-city corporate law firms and have decided—over numerous, often contentious late-night dinners at Joe's Bar and Grill—to get together and form their own perhaps kinder, gentler firm.

Naturally, the startup costs for such a venture will be more than minimal. One of the ways firms can operate more efficiently is for lawyers to draft many documents themselves. In our fictitious firm of Marshall, Cardozo, Hand, Holmes & Blackstone, each member has limited experience with WordPerfect, having left that kind of thing to others more adept than them at their respective firms. Although they regret that hands-off approach now, they are determined to rectify matters. Before this book is finished, they will go where few attorneys have dared to go—and you will be the beneficiary. Follow them, then, on this journey.

Bear with us a bit longer. Each of the five (a number chosen more for the purposes of our narrative structure than for any other reason) has a particular area of expertise and will be guiding you through the chapter devoted to the document type associated with that area, as he or she grapples with the intricacies of WordPerfect. The five partners do the grunt work; you reap the benefits. We think you get the idea. This is going to work, trust us.

> *It is emphatically the province and duty of the judicial department to say what the law is. . . . If two laws conflict with each other, the courts must decide on the operation of each. . . . This is of the very essence of judicial duty.*
>
> Chief Justice John Marshall, Marbury v. Madison, 5 U.S. 137, 177-78 [1803]

ET'S get started in this chapter by introducing you to the first of the five partners, Tom Marshall, an extremely intense, focused, driven young lawyer. Tom has amazing, almost zen-like powers of concentration. His approach to any kind of challenge is to meet it head on and wrestle it to the ground. To meet the challenge of going beyond the basics of WordPerfect in order to maximize his efficiency, Tom has gone out of his way to pore through the WordPerfect manual and

as many aftersale books on the subject as he can get his hands on. His countless hours of research, gleaning ideas and tips from these tomes—many of them extremely dry and obscure—have been enervating but rewarding. Fortunately, he has committed his findings to paper for his own personal use and for that of his colleagues.

Like most attorneys, Tom has to write more correspondence than just about anything else, so he has decided to explore all of WordPerfect's many features that can be used to automate the task.

2.1.2 MARGINS AND TABS

Changing left and right margins

> *I will not say with Lord Hale, that The Law will admit of no rival . . . but I will say that it is a jealous mistress, and requires a long and constant courtship. It is not to be won by trifling favors, but by lavish homage.*
>
> *Joseph Story*
> *The Value and Importance of Legal Studies*
> *[August 5, 1829]*

The default margins for WordPerfect are 1" left and right margins and 1" top and bottom. However, it is not uncommon for letterhead to require slightly larger margins. In fact, the letterhead of Marshall, Cardozo, Hand, Holmes & Blackstone requires 1.5" margins both left and right. Here's how to change to those margin settings.

1. Making sure that the cursor is at the beginning of the page, press [Shift][F8] (**Format**).
2. Press [1] for **L**ine.
3. At the Format Line menu, press [7] for **M**argins.
4. Type 1.5" for left, press [Enter], type 1.5" for right, and press [Enter].
5. Press [F7] (**Exit**) to return to the editing screen.

■ *The "Pos" (position) indicator on the status line in the lower right-hand corner of the screen now reads 1.5".*

If you press [Alt][F3] or [F11] (Reveal Codes), you will see that a [L/R Mar:1.5",1.5"] has been inserted.

■ *If you are one of the many users of WordPerfect who began using the program before version 5.0, you may be used to the version 4.2 measurements of lines and columns. (For example, instead of a 1" left margin, the WordPerfect 4.2 measurement would read "10.") To change the default, press [Shift][F1] (Setup), [3] for **E**nvironment (WP5.1), [8] for **U**nits of Measure, [2] for **S**tatus line display. Then type* u *to use the WordPerfect 4.2 columns/line measurement system.*

Version 5.X will, however, automatically convert from one unit of measurement to another. If you've selected inches as your default unit, but type 10u as your left and right margin settings, WordPerfect will automatically convert these specifications to 1 inch for each. However, it is our opinion that the newer inches measurement system is easier to use for several reasons, the simplest being that WordPerfect settings can be handily measured with a ruler. The following example of changing the tab settings is a good illustration of this.

Changing tab settings

Like some electronic typewriters, WordPerfect 5.X defaults to tab stops every .5". However, for correspondence it may often be advantageous to change the tab settings. For example, let's assume that at Tom's firm the proper format for letterhead is to have the date and signature block aligned 3.3" from the left margin, which is set to 1.5" (in other words, 4.8" from the left edge of the paper).

> ■ *Tabs settings are measured from the left margin. A tab set at 1.5" in a document with a 1" left margin will be 1.5" inches from that margin and 2.5" from the edge of the page.*

Using WordPerfect's Tab Set feature, we can eliminate extraneous tabs so that the third tab stop is positioned where the date and signature block are to reside. (The first tab stop is positioned at 0", the second at .5", etc.) Here's how:

1. Make sure that the cursor is at the beginning of the page by pressing [Home], [Home], [↑], then press [Shift][F8] (Format).
2. Press [1] for **L**ine.
3. At the Format Line menu, press [8] for **T**ab Set. The Tab set line should appear. (Note that the cursor is at the left margin of the page, which is 0" on the Tab set line.) Each tab stop is represented by an L (for left tab).
4. Delete every tab stop from 1" onward by moving the cursor to the 1" tab stop and pressing [Ctrl][End] (Delete to End of Line). This leaves one tab stop at the beginning of the letter so that the first line of each paragraph can be indented.
5. Enter the number of the new tab setting desired (3.3") and press [Enter], or move the cursor to 3.3" on the Tab set ruler and type [L]. The tab set ruler should look something like Figure 2-1.
6. Press [F7] (Exit) to return to the editing screen. Now, the second tab stop should take the cursor to position 4.3".

MACRO

To quickly reset tabs to the default of every .5", use the [Shift][F11] macro.

MACRO

Use the [Alt][F11] macro for getting to the Tab Set line.

A [Tab Set:Rel: –1", –0.5", 0", +0.5", +1", +3.3"] code has been inserted. Also note that the Reveal Codes ruler (the bar separating the Reveal Codes screen from the normal editing screen) has only two triangles (each represents a tab stop) after the { curly brace (representing the left margin).

- **WP5.1** *WordPerfect 5.1 allows two types of tab settings: Relative and Absolute. The default for tab settings is Relative Tabs, which are measured relative to the left margin and which change when the left margin setting is changed. When relative tab stops are used, a + or – sign appears next to the ruler setting, indicating the distance from the left margin.*

- *WordPerfect 5.1 also allows the option of setting Absolute tab stops, which are positioned in relation to the absolute left edge of the page and do not change when the margins are changed. When absolute tab stops are chosen, the Tab Set ruler numbers do not display a + or – sign.*

To choose Absolute or Relative Tab Sets, bring up the Tab Set screen, press **T** for **Type**, then choose either **1** for **Absolute** or **2** for **R**elative to Margin.

> *If there were no bad people there would be no good lawyers.*
> Charles Dickens
> [1812–1870]

2.1.3 ADDING TEXT ATTRIBUTES TO THE RE: LINE

What follows is examples of the addition of common text attributes that are often used on the RE: line in correspondence.

Italics

1. Move the cursor to the position at which you wish to begin the RE: line.

FIGURE 2-1

Sample tab settings are shown for correspondence, with tab settings at .5" and 3.3".

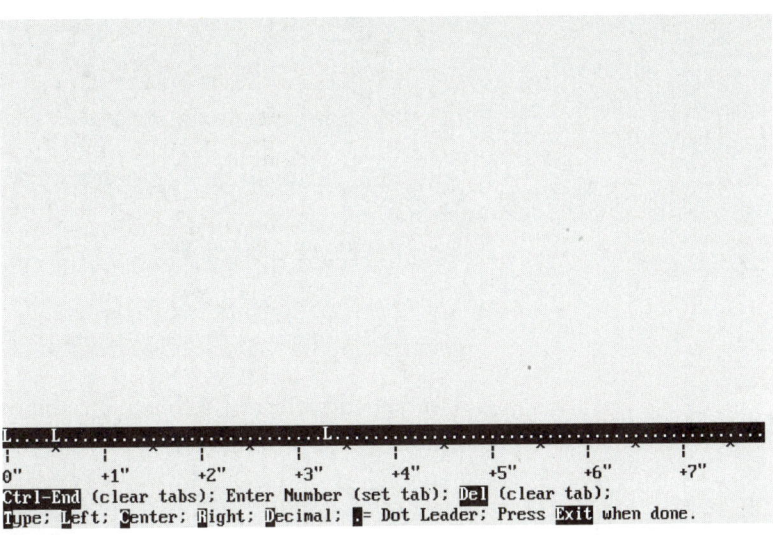

Chapter 2 Using WordPerfect for Legal Correspondence

§2.1

2. Enter the following keystrokes: [Ctrl][F8] (Font), [2] for **Appearance**, [4] for **Italics**. (On a color monitor, the position number on the status line will normally be yellow.)

> ■ *The text attributes menu ([Ctrl][F8] (Font), [2] for **A**ppearance) also allows you to enter Bold and Underline as text attributes. However, it is much easier to use the [F6] (Bold) and the [F8] (Underline) keys for these functions.*

3. Type the text you wish to appear in italics.
4. When finished, turn off italics by entering the following keystrokes: [Ctrl][F8] (Font), [3] for **Normal**.

> ■ *WordPerfect's ability to print italics depends on your printer and the fonts you have available. For example, the standard Hewlett-Packard II printer fonts do not include an italic font. To see if you can print in italics, use View Document [Shift][F7], [6] or the [Alt][V] macro to see how your italicized text will look when printed. You may need to magnify the text by pressing [1] for 100% or [2] for 200% to see it clearly. If your printer does not support italics, use an attribute such as underlining or bold, which are supported by virtually all printers.*

TIP

An easy way to turn off an attribute such as bold or underline is to press the [→] cursor arrow when you are finished. (This moves the cursor past the attribute code.) Watch the position number on the status line to see that the attribute is off.

Bolding and underlining new text

We did not create macros for these functions because they only require one keystroke.

1. Move the cursor to the position at which you wish to begin the RE: line.
2. Press [F6] (Bold) or [F8] (Underline) to turn on the attribute.
3. Enter the text.
4. Press [F6] (Bold) or [F8] (Underline) to turn off the attribute.

Bolding and underlining existing text

1. Move the cursor to the beginning of the text you wish to bold or underline.
2. Press [Alt][F4] or [F12] (Block).

> ■ *The "Block on" prompt will flash, and the position number on the status line will be highlighted in red if you have a color monitor.*

3. Use the cursor arrow to block out the text you wish to bold or underline.

4. Press [F6] (Bold) or [F8] (Underline) to apply the attribute to the selected text.

2.1.4 CENTERING A LETTER VERTICALLY

Another WordPerfect 5.X formatting option that law firms might find handy for short, one-page letters is the Center Page command. (This command is also convenient for the Title Pages of Briefs and Memoranda.) When inserted at the absolute beginning of a letter, this command will vertically center all the text between the top and bottom margins for that page only. However, be aware that the position of the text will move depending upon how long the letter is, so that the text of a longer letter might print over your firm's letterhead.

1. If the cursor is not already at the top of the page, press [Home], [Home], [↑] or [Ctrl][Home][↑].
2. Press [Shift][F8] (Format).
3. Choose [2] for **P**age.
4. Choose [1] for **C**enter Page.
5. Press [Y] to insert the [Center Page] code
6. Press [F7] (Exit) to return to the editing screen.

TIP

If you decide you don't like the page centered, press [Alt][F3] or [F11] to Reveal Codes, place the cursor on the [Center Page] code and press [Del].

MACRO

Use the [Alt][V] macro to view the letter before printing to see what the page-centering effect will look like.

2.1.5 USING HEADERS AND FOOTERS

Yes, we know you probably are already familiar with the header and footer features—after all, they're pretty simple. But bear with us while we bring up to speed those of you who were too busy to explore them.

Most letters of more than one page require some kind of header on the pages following the first page, with information such as the name of the addressee, the date, the draft number, or the page number. We recommend placing your header at the beginning of the first page and then suppressing that header on the first page. It will then appear on every subsequent page, but not on the first one. Let's try it.

Creating Headers/Footers

1. Move the cursor to the very top of the first page by pressing [Home], [Home], [↑].
2. Press [Shift][F8] (Format), [2] for **P**age.
3. Select [3] for **H**eaders or [4] for **F**ooters.

FIGURE 2-2

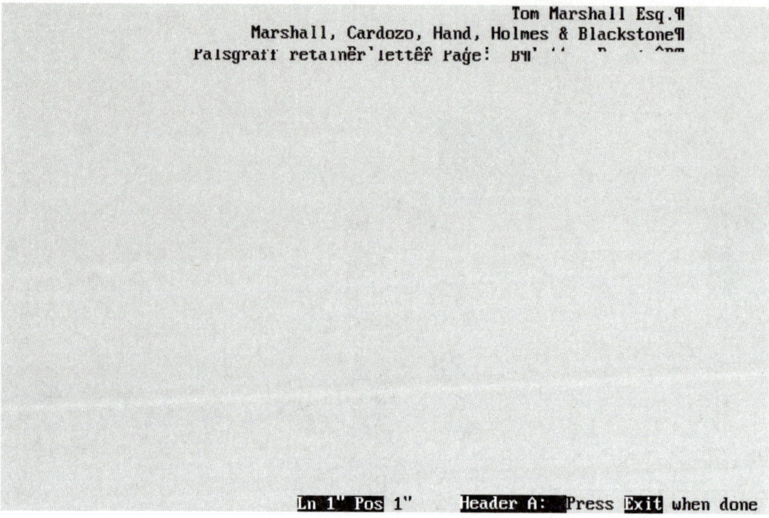

```
                                         Tom Marshall Esq.¶
                    Marshall, Cardozo, Hand, Holmes & Blackstone¶
              Palsgraff retainer letter Page: B¶
```
Ln 1" Pos 1"   Header A: Press Exit when done

4. Select [1] for Header/Footer **A**, or [2] for Header/Footer **B**.

▪ *You can place two headers (or footers) on the same page with the Header (or Footer) B option. For instance, say you want the firm name on the upper left-hand side of the page and the date on the upper right, you could place the firm name in header A, then create another header (B) and put the date in it. Both the firm name and the date will appear on the same line in the header. If you want them to appear on separate lines, you'll have to move one side down using hard returns in the appropriate header.*

5. Select [2] for Every **P**age, [3] for **O**dd Pages, or [4] for E**v**en Pages.

6. Type the text of your header or footer. You can use most of WordPerfect's formatting commands in headers and footers. For example, you might want the text flush right [Alt][F6], bolded [F6], or underlined [F8]. To place an automatic page number in your header or footer, press [Ctrl][B] (it will appear onscreen as ^B). For an example, see Figure 2-2.

▪ *Your header or footer will take on the base font of your document at the point it was inserted. If you wish to use a different font for the header/footer, press [Ctrl][F8], [4] for **B**ase Font and select a different font. Choosing a different font for the header/footer will not affect the document's base font.*

7. Press [F7] (Exit) twice to return to your document.

▲▲▲▲▲▲▲▲▲▲▲▲▲▲▲▲▲▲▲▲▲▲▲▲▲▲▲▲▲▲▲▲▲▲▲▲▲

A [Header A: Every Page;*text of header or footer*] or equivalent code has been placed in your document.

■ *Because headers/footers are inserted as codes, they do not appear on the editing screen. To see your handiwork, you must press* [Shift][F7] *(Print Preview).*

Editing a header/footer

> **MACRO**
>
> Use the [Alt][H] and [Alt][F] macros to create headers and footers.

1. Press [Shift][F8] (Format), [2] for **P**age.
2. Select [3] for **H**eaders or [4] for **F**ooters.
3. Select [1] for Header/Footer **A**, or [2] for Header/Footer **B**.
4. Select [5] for **E**dit.
5. When finished editing, press [F7] (Exit) twice to return to your document.

Deleting headers/footers

1. Reveal Codes [Alt][F3] or [F11] and find the header or footer code you wish to delete.
2. Place the cursor on the code and press [Del].

Suppressing (hiding) headers/footers

WordPerfect's Suppress feature (see Figure 2-3) allows you to hide headers/footers on a specific page. This is handy if, for example, you've placed all your codes on the first page of the letter, but don't want the header or footer to appear on the first page.

1. Press [Shift][F8] (Format), [2] for **P**age, [8] (**WP5.1**) or [9] (**WP5.0**) for **Su**ppress.

> **FIGURE 2-3**
>
> The Suppress Format screen allows you to suppress headers, footers, and page numbering or each individually. If you want to suppress any of these on the current page, make sure your cursor is at the beginning of the page.

```
Format: Suppress (this page only)

    1 - Suppress All Page Numbering, Headers and Footers

    2 - Suppress Headers and Footers

    3 - Print Page Number at Bottom Center      No

    4 - Suppress Page Numbering                 No

    5 - Suppress Header A                       No

    6 - Suppress Header B                       No

    7 - Suppress Footer A                       No

    8 - Suppress Footer B                       No


Selection: 0
```

> **MACRO**
>
> Use the [Alt][A] macro to suppress all headers, footers, and page numbers on the first page. (You should be at the very top of the page when you execute the macro.)

2. Select the appropriate option and type [Y] for **Yes**.
3. Press [F7] (Exit) to return to your document.

A [Suppress:*options*] code has been inserted.

■ *You must be at the top of the page when suppressing the page number or you will suppress the page numbering on the following page. The same thing applies to starting page numbering.*

2.1.6 POSITIONING AND AUTOMATICALLY INSERTING THE DATE

There are several ways to position text such as the date: using the Tab Set feature described above; using the Center feature; and using the Flush Right feature.

■ *Never use the [Spacebar] to position the date or any other text. Not only does this give you less control than other methods, it can also lead to major reformatting headaches. A space is a hard character. In other words, spaces do not automatically adjust to changes in formatting. Formatting commands, on the other hand, are inserted as codes that can be easily searched for, edited, and deleted. To make life as simple for yourself as possible, remember this rule:* Only use the [Spacebar] to insert spaces between words. *Let WordPerfect's commands handle the positioning of text.*

Centering the date

> **TIP**
>
> With WordPerfect, you can type some text at the left margin and then center more text on the same line.

[Shift][F6] (Center) is used to center one line of text between the left and right margins. However, do not use the Center function if you wish to align the left edge of the date with the left edge of the signature block, for example. Remember that the Center function only centers one line of text at a time and that the position of the left edge of the text will vary depending upon the length of the text block being centered.

1. Press [Shift][F6] (Center). The cursor will jump to the middle of the page.
2. Enter the date, then press [Enter] to return the cursor to the left margin.

A [Center] code will be inserted.

■ *The Center feature is automatically turned off when a hard return* [Enter] *is pressed.*

■ *To delete text centering, use Reveal Codes to find the [Center] code, highlight the code with your cursor, and press* [Del].

Positioning the date flush right

The Flush Right feature of WordPerfect is very handy for aligning the right edge of the date text with the right margin of the letter.

1. Press [Alt][F6] (Flush Right). The cursor will jump to the right margin of the document.

2. Enter the date.

A [Flsh Rgt] code is inserted.

■ *The Flush Right function is automatically turned off when a hard return (*[Enter]*) is pressed.*

■ *To delete the Flush Right function, use Reveal Codes to find the [Flsh Rgt] code, highlight the code with your cursor, and press* [Del].

2.1.7 USING THE AUTOMATIC DATE FEATURE

> If by the mere force of numbers a majority should deprive a minority of any clearly written constitutional right, it might, in a moral point of view, justify revolution—certainly would if such a right were a vital one.
>
> Abraham Lincoln
> First Inaugural Address
> [March 4, 1861]

The Date feature of WordPerfect is one of the many timesaving devices that a savvy attorney can use to automate the creation of letters. WordPerfect offers two date options: Date Text and Date Code. The Date Text option puts the date into your document (based on your computer's clock) as text. In other words, once the date is inserted, it will not be updated automatically by the computer. This is the option that should be used for most legal correspondence, since it provides the attorney with a record of when the letter was created (assuming the letter was saved to disk). The Date Code feature, on the other hand, automatically updates the date based on the computer's clock. This feature is ideal for reusable boilerplate documents.

FIGURE 2-4

The Date Format screen shows the default as 3 1, 4—e.g., January 1, 1993.

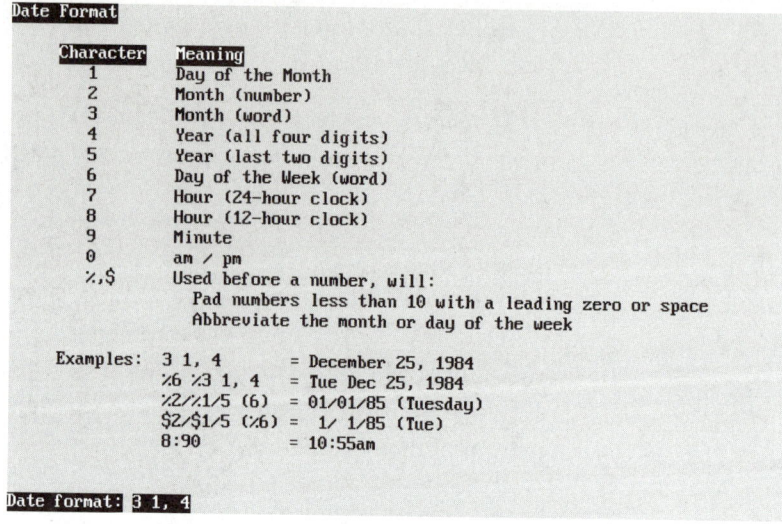

Using the Date Text and Date Code features

1. Position the cursor at the point at which you wish to insert the date using either the tab key, the Center function, or the Flush Right function. (Remember, don't use that [Spacebar]!)
2. Press [Shift][F5] (Date/Outline) to bring up the Date menu.
3. Choose [1] for Date Text, or [2] for Date Code.

■ *If you Reveal Codes [Alt][F3] or [F11], you will notice that with Date Text, the date is inserted as ordinary text, whereas with Date Code, Word-Perfect inserts a [Date:3 1, 4] code. The significance of this code will become immediately apparent if you press [Shift][F5], [3] for Date Format. What you see (in Figure 2-4) is, we think, self-explanatory, so we won't belabor the issue. Try [1][3], [4] as the format. Now insert the date using Date Text. You'll see the day in front of the month, with the year following.*

2.2 INTERMEDIATE WORDPERFECT LETTER WRITING SKILLS

2.2.1 USING WORDPERFECT STYLES TO INSERT FORMATTING COMMANDS

Styles are one of WordPerfect's most powerful features for automating the proper formatting of a document. (The other is *macros*, which are discussed in this chapter and other chapters in the book.) Styles can contain multiple formatting codes and text. If you can learn how to use styles to quickly format the various legal documents your firm works on, you are well on your way to becoming a power user of the program. Let's see how styles can be used to automate the formatting of correspondence.

So far, you and Tom have learned how to set up the margins and tab sets for a letter, and how to position and insert the date using the Date Text and Date Code features. As you can see, a number of different steps are needed to perform each of these formatting commands so that the proper codes are inserted at the head of the letter. Tom, already staggering under a heavy workload, does not want to have to go through these steps each time he writes a letter. Furthermore, his fledgling law firm has not yet decided on any standardized letterhead style and already is using two that he's aware of: the formal firm letterhead requires 2" margins and a centered date, while the plain letterhead uses 1.5" margins and a flush-right date.

> **MACRO**
>
> Use the [Alt][R] macro to call up a style. (See also the sample paired-style letterhead illustrated in Appendix C under the [Alt][R] macro.)

Tom, taking to heart our motto that no repetitive task should ever be done manually more than once, has set up different styles for each of the letterhead formats that his firm uses. Now, instead of having to manually put in all the various formatting codes illustrated above, he merely chooses the appropriate style, and the codes are put in automatically by WordPerfect.

Creating a style for the firm's letterhead

The plain letterhead format at Tom's firm is 1.5" left and right margins with a tab stop at 3.3" from the left margin at which both the date and signature block are aligned. Finally, the date's position is 1" from the top margin (which is also 1"; in other words, the date is 2" from the top edge of the letter).

> **SHAREWARE**
>
> The LTRHD.ZIP file, available as shareware on the supplementary disks, is a sophisticated letterhead kit that can be used to create letterhead; it includes over 50 graphical business messages, such as "Confidential" and "Next Day Air."

■ *Be careful to insert a Date Code into a style if you want to know when the letter was written.*

Tom has created a style called Plain Letterhead that contains all of these codes. Here's how he's done it:

Configuring WordPerfect to use styles

Before he created his styles, Tom went into [Shift][F1] (Setup) to see what directory his styles were being kept in and the name of the style

TIP

Use a macro to call up a style and then insert Date Text. See the [Alt][R] macro in Appendix C for an example.

library file he was using. (When the WordPerfect default installation procedure is used, it automatically installs all style files in the C:\WP5X directory, and the default style library is a file called LIBRARY.STY. In WordPerfect, each style is *not* kept as a separate file. Rather, each style you create is kept in one file, known as a style library. The default style library is called LIBRARY.STY, but this can be changed or renamed to suit your needs.) The settings (in Setup) allow the styles to be used globally; that is, they can be used in any document you create on any directory in the computer.

Because the process of creating styles does not beget many separate files that need to be kept track of, the default does not generally need to be changed. Should you wish to change the default style library or the location of that style library, follow these steps:

1. Press [Shift][F1] (Setup) to access the setup menu.
2. Choose [6] (**WP5.1**) or [7] (**WP5.0**) for Location of Files.
3. Press [5] (**WP5.1**) or [6] (**WP5.0**) for **S**tyle Files and enter the new directory for your styles or the new Library file name. Be sure to use the extension .STY. Press [Enter] when done.
4. Press [F7] (Exit) to return to your document.

2.2.2 TYPES OF STYLES

There are three types of styles you can create: Paired, Open, and Outline.

I think that we should be men first, and subjects afterward. It is not desirable to cultivate a respect for the law, so much as for the right.
  Henry David Thoreau
  Civil Disobedience
  [1849]

Open Styles: An Open style takes effect from the point at which the style code was inserted until the end of the document. Because any text inserted after an Open style code conforms to that style, Open styles are generally used to insert global formatting commands that apply throughout the document. A perfect example is an Open Letterhead Style that sets up global formatting for letterhead such as margins, tab stops, etc. Note that the only way to turn off this kind of style is to delete the code. The [Style Off] function only works with Paired Styles, discussed below.

Paired Styles: A Paired Style has both a beginning and an end, denoted by Style On and Style Off codes. Any text between the On and Off codes conform to the style. For this reason, they are often used in desktop publishing documents, where special font and attribute codes are used to format specific blocks of text. In a legal environment, Paired Styles have fewer uses than Open Styles. A possible application, if you have a laser printer with the appropriate fonts, might be reproducing the firm letterhead using various font sizes and attributes such as Small Caps (see the example next to the [Alt][R] macro entry in Appendix C). Other uses include creating special headings in briefs and corporate documents (such as a prospectus) that require unusual fonts or font sizes. For a detailed discussion of creating and using Paired Styles, see Chapter 6.

WP5.1 Outline Styles: An outline style is used with the Outline and Paragraph numbering features of WordPerfect 5.1. These features can be very useful in a legal environment, especially in contracts that contain numbered clauses. The use of these styles is discussed in depth in Chapter 3.

Creating an Open Style for letterhead

1. Press [Alt][F8] (Style). The Style screen and menu appear, listing all the styles currently available in your Style Library file name, along with their type and description.

2. Choose [3] for Create.

3. At the Styles: Edit screen, choose [1] for Name, type in a name, and press [Enter]. (Tom called his `plain lh`.) The name for a style can be up to 12 characters and can include spaces.

4. Choose [2] for **T**ype, then choose [2] for **O**pen. (Open styles are used for global formatting.)

5. Choose [3] for **D**escription, then enter a descriptive name for your style. The description can be up to 54 characters and can include spaces. (Tom called his: `Plain letterhead`.)

6. Choose [4] for **C**odes. You will be taken to a blank screen with Reveal Codes displayed. At this point, you go through the keystrokes necessary to insert the codes you wish to use in the style. The codes will be displayed in the Reveal Codes portion of the screen. Tom did the following for his letterhead style: see Figure 2-5.

7. Press [F7] (Exit) twice to return to the Style main menu.

8. Choose [6] for Save. At the "Filename:" prompt, enter the name of the Style Library Filename you are using. (The default is LIBRARY.STY.)

9. Answer [Y] at the "Replace Library.sty"? prompt.

■ *Every time you create a new style, you must update the Style Library file by replacing the old one with the updated one when you save it,*

> **TIP**
>
> An excellent use for Paired Styles is duplicating your firm's letterhead. To do this, you'll probably need a variety of fonts that duplicate your current letterhead. (For a discussion of fonts and typefaces, see Chapter 6.)

FIGURE 2-5

Tom's letterhead style is shown with left and right margins set at 1.5" and tab stops at .5" and 3.3".

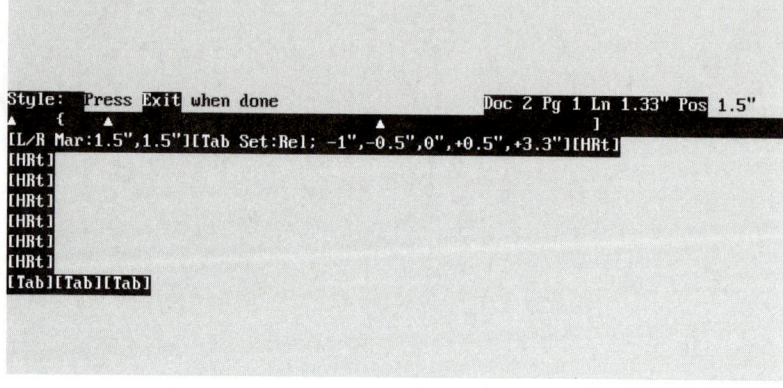

otherwise your new style will only be available in the current document.

10. To use your new style, highlight it in the Style main menu, and press [1] for On.

An [Open Style: *Name of Style*] is placed in the document. If you place the cursor on the [Open Style:] code, all the codes in that style will be displayed.

EXERCISE: SAMPLE LETTERHEAD STYLE

1. **Margins 1.5"**: [Shift][F8] (Format), press [1] for Line, [7] for **M**argins, type 1.5" for left, press [Enter], type 1.5" for right, and press [Enter]. Press [F7] (Exit) to return to the Styles editing screen.

2. **Tab Stops at 2" and 4.8"**: [Shift][F8] (Format), press [1] for Line. At the format Line menu, press [8] for Tab Set. At the Tab set line, delete every tab stop from 2" onward by moving the cursor to the 2" Tab stop and pressing [Ctrl][End] (delete to end of line). Enter the number of the new tab set desired (3.3") and press [Enter] or move the cursor to 3.3" on the Tab set ruler and type **L**. Press [F7] (Exit) to return to the Style editing screen.

3. **Positioning the date 1" from the top margin and at 4.8" (the second tab stop)**: Press [Enter] six times to put in six hard return codes. (This places the cursor at 2".) Press [Tab] twice to place the cursor at 4.8". Press [Shift][F5] (Date/Outline), [2] for Date **C**ode.

   ■ See also "Using the Advance feature to position text," below.

4. **Moving the cursor to the beginning of the address block**: Press [Enter] four times to move the cursor three lines down from the date.

Using the Advance feature to position text

WordPerfect's Advance feature is an esoteric but elegant method for positioning text precisely on the page. It is often used for filling out forms and setting up letterhead.

For example, let's pretend that our date and address block have to start further down the page on certain kinds of firm letterhead that have all the partners' names at the top. (Tom and his cohorts have agreed that everyone fits into this category at their firm.) If the names take up 3" of space, and we need another .5" between the names and the date, we might want to start our letter at line 5" (taking into account the 1" margin at the top of the page). That would begin the actual letter .5" below the date. We would insert that advance code in our style.

We might also want to place an advance code in our header, instead of inserting several returns, to move the header information down below the firm name on the upper left-hand side of the page. (You can be more precise this way.) In this instance, we would put a code that advances 1" or 1.5" inch in our header before the addressee name.

1. Press [Shift][F8].
2. Choose [4], then [1].
3. Choose [2] for **D**own and type the appropriate number of inches.

> ■ *You can indicate how far you want to move up, down, left, or right on the page. You can also indicate a particular line or position on a line. When you do this, your cursor will not move but you will know that you're at that new position by looking at the status line.*

Using existing codes in a document to create a style

If you already have a document with different formatting codes inserted, you can create a new style directly from the document by following these steps:

1. Reveal Codes by pressing [Alt][F3] or [F11].
2. Place the cursor at the beginning of the block of text containing the codes you wish to use in the style, and use the block function, [Alt][F4] or [F12], to select it. Be sure to select only the text containing the codes you want in the style, not any extraneous text.
3. With the codes selected, press [Alt][F8] (Style), then [3] for **C**reate.

In my youth, said his father, I took to the law,
And argued each case with my wife;
And the muscular strength, which it gave to my jaw,
Has lasted the rest of my life.

Lewis Carroll
Alice's Adventures in Wonderland
[1865], Ch. 5. You are old, Father William

4. At the "Styles: Edit" screen, enter a name, type, and description for the style. Notice that when you press [4] for **C**odes, the codes you blocked out in your document appear. Edit them if necessary.

5. Press [F7] to return to the Style main menu, then press [6] for **S**ave to add the new style to your Style Library file.

Using Retrieve to copy styles from documents into a Style Library file

If you are using several different Style Library files, you can retrieve styles from either a document or another Style Library into your current Style Library (as indicated in Setup).

1. Press [Alt][F8] (Style), then [7] for **R**etrieve.
2. At the "Filename:" prompt, type in the full file name including the path (e.g., `c:\wp51\legal.sty`) or press [F5] (List Files).
3. At the "Style(s) already exist. Replace?" prompt, choose [Y].
4. Choose [6] for **S**ave to permanently add the retrieved style to the Style Library file.

Not to confuse matters, but you can also retrieve styles attached to another document that are not actually part of any style library and include them in your default style library by using the same procedure. Simply include the name of the document in your path instead of the style file name.

By the way, you don't have to save styles to a style library or file—that is, if you are not interested in using that set of styles with other documents. When you create styles while in a document, those styles are automatically made part of the document because they are saved when the document is saved. Each time the document is retrieved, those styles automatically accompany it.

> *The law embodies the story of a nation's development through many centuries, and it cannot be dealt with as if it contained only the axioms and corollaries of a book of mathematics.*
>
> Oliver Wendell Holmes, Jr.
> The Common Law
> [1881]

2.2.3 USING NAMED MACROS TO INSERT CLIENT NAMES AND ADDRESSES

So far, you and Tom have learned how to set up margins and tab sets for a letter, and how to position and automatically insert the date. Then, you both learned how to automate the process of inserting formatting codes into a document by saving them as a style. Now, after all that, you've finally gotten to the point at which you are ready to insert the address block at the top of the letter. Of course, you can always just type in the name and address you need, but that probably means stopping, looking through your Rolodex or files, finding the name and address, and then carefully typing it in and proofreading it. In essence, this is using your PC armed with WordPerfect as a glorified typewriter, when it is capable of so much more. To put it in a different way, using WordPerfect as a typewriter would be the computer equivalent of making Oliver Wendell Holmes the judge of a small claims court—a true waste of great talent.

As you've probably guessed by now, you can use the WordPerfect macro feature to automate the task of inserting frequently used names and addresses.

What is a named macro?

A simple named macro is a recorded series of keystrokes that can be played back at a later time by entering the name of the macro. (This is in contrast to [Alt] and [Ctrl] key macros, discussed in Chapter 5, which are invoked by pressing either the [Alt] or [Ctrl] key in conjunction with a letter. In fact, this book comes with many such macros, and you will see references to them throughout.) Knowing how to create and use simple macros is within even the first-time user's grasp and is essential to a complete understanding of the program. It is not an exaggeration to state that one of the secrets to unlocking the true power of WordPerfect is to use macros (and styles) to automate all of your most repetitive word processing tasks.

Congress shall make no law respecting an establishment of religion, or prohibiting the free exercise thereof; or abridging the freedom of speech, or of the press; or the right of the people peaceably to assemble, and to petition the government for a redress of grievances.
Constitution of the
United States
First Amendment
[1791]

■ *Macros can be complex and extremely sophisticated, depending upon how far you are willing to explore the WordPerfect macro language (a simple computer programming language) that is built into the program. For those willing to take the plunge, this book describes several examples of advanced macros in Appendix C that can be used in a legal office. (They are also available on disk from the authors for a small fee, along with hundreds of the best shareware macros available. Please see the order form at the back of the book.) A detailed discussion of advanced WordPerfect macro programming is beyond the scope of this book. However, if you are interested in learning more about the subject, we highly recommend Gordon McComb's excellent* WordPerfect 5.1 Macros and Templates. *The book comes with two disks that include over 300 macros.*

While named macros can be used to automate virtually any repetitive word processing function in a law office, they are best suited to recalling specific blocks of text. There are two especially useful examples of this feature in the writing of correspondence—inserting name and address blocks, and inserting a signature block.

EXERCISE: CREATING NAMED MACROS

Tom is constantly corresponding with the Clerk of the Court for the District Court of the Southern District of New York, so he created a simple macro he called SDCLERK to quickly recall the address.

■ Named macros can have up to 8 letters (no spaces) and are automatically given the extension .WPM. In our example, the full path name of Tom's macro is C:\WP5X\MACROS\SDCLERK.WPM)

1. Press [Ctrl][F10] (Define Macro) to turn on the macro definition process (i.e., turn on the keystroke recorder).

2. At the "Define Macro:" prompt, enter a name of up to 8 letters (e.g., SDCLERK) and then press [Enter].

3. At the "Description:" prompt, type a description and press [Enter]. (Tom called his: Address for clerk of the southern district). You will be returned to the editing screen and "macro def" will be flashing, alerting you that WordPerfect will record every keystroke you make.

■ A description may contain up to 39 characters. The description can be viewed via the Look option in the List Files menu.

4. Type in the address block you wish to use, exactly as you want it to appear on your correspondence.

```
Clerk of the Court
U.S. District Court
Southern District of
 New York
1 St. Andrew's Plaza
New York, New York 10001
```

5. When finished, press [Ctrl][F10] again to turn off the keystroke recorder. The "macro def" flashing prompt will disappear. That's all there is to it!

■ The above macro will be saved to disk as SDCLERK.WPM. (WordPerfect automatically assigns the extension .WPM to all macros.) If you have properly configured WordPerfect using the Location of Files option in Setup [Shift][F1], the macro will be stored in the \WP5X\MACROS subdirectory.

■ *If you haven't done so already, please refer to Appendix A to make sure that WordPerfect is properly configured to use macros.*

Using Named Macros in your documents

SHAREWARE

The ADDBK.ZIP file, available as shareware on the supplementary disks, is a sophisticated address book macro.

Now that the macro has been created, it is a simple process to play it back.

1. Position the cursor on your document at the point at which you wish to insert the macro text. (In our example, this is at the beginning of the address block.)

2. Press [Alt][F10] (Start macro).

3. At the "macro:" prompt, type the name of the macro and press [Enter].

Renaming your macros

When you create a macro, you are actually creating a discrete file that is stored in the directory specified in [Shift][F1] (Setup). (If you have scrupulously followed our instructions, all of your macros are in a separate subdirectory called MACROS, and not in your \WP5X directory.) Because each macro is a separate file, you can use the List Files feature to rename it by following these steps:

1. Press [F5] (List Files) once, and at the "Dir" prompt, change the path to where your macros are stored (e.g., C:\WP51\MACROS). Then press [Enter] to bring up the List Files screen.

■ **WP5.1** *If the Long Document Names feature is on, you will not be able to see the macro files. Turn it off by choosing* [5] *for Short/Long Display, then choosing* [1] *for Short Display.*

2. Use the cursor to highlight the name of the macro you wish to rename, or press [N] for **N**ame Search and type the first few letters of the macro.

3. With the macro highlighted, choose [3] for **M**ove/Rename.

4. At the "New name" prompt, move the cursor to highlight the name of the macro, then enter the new name, and press [Enter].

CAUTION: Be sure to leave the .WPM extension. Otherwise, the macro will not be recognized by WordPerfect as a macro.

5. Press [F7] (Exit) to return to your document.

Creating a Named macro (signature block) using Pause

The Pause feature of WordPerfect 5.X macros allows the user to insert a pause into the macro while it is being created. When the macro is run, it will stop at the point where the pause was inserted and allow you to enter text from the keyboard. When the user presses [Enter], the pause ends and the macro resumes until finished or until the next pause. This feature is especially useful for macros that contain text that changes on a regular basis. An example might be a generic signature block macro that is used firmwide.

The love of justice in most men is simply the fear of suffering injustice.
Francois, Duc de La Rochefoucauld
Reflections; or, Sentences and Moral Maxims

EXERCISE: CREATING A NAMED MACRO USING THE PAUSE FEATURE

Tom has been staying late for the last several days to create named macros for all of his most frequently used names and addresses, as well as to create separate named macros for his plaintiff and defendant signature blocks. However, he has recently discovered a much easier and less time-consuming way to create this kind of macro—using the Pause feature. Eager to test this recent discovery of his, he goes through the following steps to create his signature block:

1. Press [Ctrl][F10] (Define Macro) to turn on the macro definition process (i.e., turn on the keystroke recorder).

2. At the "Define Macro:" prompt, type Sigblock (or whatever he wishes to name it) and press [Enter].

3. At the "Description:" prompt, type signature block with pauses and press [Enter]. The "Macro Def" prompt should now be flashing, indicating that any keystroke you enter will now be recorded by WordPerfect.

4. Type the text as illustrated below, up to the first "PAUSE":

Law Offices of Marshall, Cardozo, Hand, Holmes, & Blackstone

BY_____
Tom Marshall
123 Fifth Avenue
New York, New York 10014
(212) 555-1212
Attorneys for {PAUSE}

Copies of the foregoing have been {PAUSE} this {PAUSE}

5. At the first instance of "PAUSE," press [Ctrl][PgUp] to display the Macro Commands menu.

6. Choose [1] for **Pause**.

■ There is no indication on the screen that a pause has just been inserted.

7. Press [Enter] to turn off the Pause and continue with the macro creation.

8. Continue to enter the text of the signature block as illustrated, inserting Pauses where necessary.

9. When finished, press [Ctrl][F10] to end the macro definition (i.e., turn off the keystroke recorder).

To play back the above macro, do the following:

1. Press [Alt][F10] (Start macro).

2. At the "Macro:" prompt, type sigblock and press [Enter].

3. When the macro pauses, type in the required text, then press [Enter].

2.2.4 EDITING A WORDPERFECT MACRO

WordPerfect comes with a built-in macro editor that allows you to edit a macro that has already been created. Using the macro editor, you can correct mistakes or add new features to existing macros without being forced to create a new one. (It seems to be a WordPerfect variation of Murphy's Law that once the macro recorder is turned on, one inevitably makes an error while creating the macro!) Furthermore, WordPerfect has a highly developed macro programming language that can only be accessed via the Macro Editor. The macro language allows you to embellish macros you have already created, as well as to create very sophisticated macros from scratch. For example, you can use the macro language to sound a beep every time a macro reaches a pause, thereby alerting a user to enter text.

HIS initial foray into the world of macros a resounding success, Tom creates all kinds of sophisticated macros that include pauses. Unable to contain his enthusiasm, he rushes to recount his triumphs to his colleagues. Actually, they're a little too mired in work to do anything but nod and smile vaguely. Tom is not particularly disheartened by this tepid reaction; he knows that this is an important breakthrough, the significance of which they'll soon appreciate.

Undeterred, he returns to his office and decides to work on making the macros even more user-friendly. To do this, he decides to add the beep feature to his macros before he distributes them. The following example demonstrates editing the SIGBLOCK macro created above, but the procedures are the same for all macros.

1. Press [Ctrl][F10] (Define Macro) to define a macro (i.e., turn on the keystroke recorder).

2. At the "Define Macro:" prompt, type `sigblock` and press [Enter].

3. At the "Macro already exists:" prompt, choose [2] for Edit. (**WP5.0** Press [2] for **A**ction to access the editor.) The cursor should now be inside the macro editing screen.

4. Move the cursor to the first {PAUSE} code in the macro, then press [PgUp]. This will display the Macro Commands menu.

5. Press [B] or cursor down until the {BELL} code is highlighted, then press [Enter]. The bell code is now inserted in the macro.

■ *Make sure that the {BELL} code is before, not after, the {PAUSE} code, or it will not work properly. See Figure 2-6 for the completed macro.*

6. When finished editing the macro, press [F7] (Exit) to return to your document. Then, run the macro to make sure it beeps at every prompt.

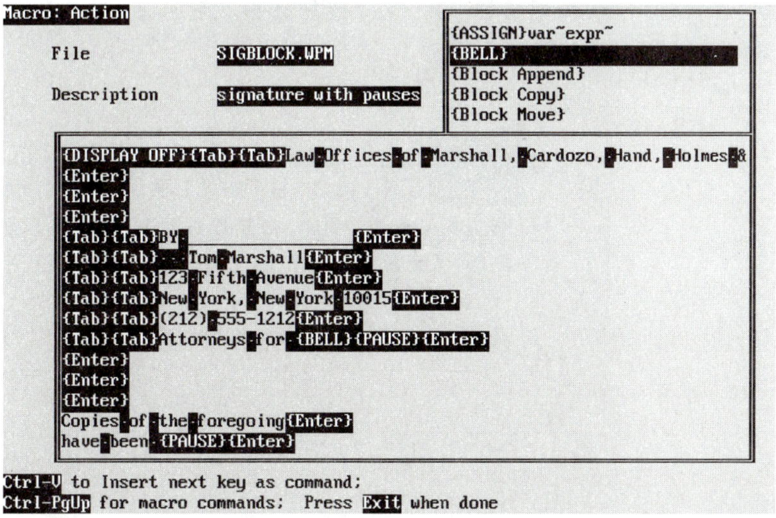

FIGURE 2-6

The SIGBLOCK.WPM macro is seen in its entirety, as seen in the macro editor. Pressing [Ctrl][PgUp] accesses the macro code menu.

Entering codes in the macro editor

When you create a simple macro, WordPerfect codes are inserted in a variety of ways, depending upon the code required. For example, codes for standard WordPerfect functions, such as underline, are inserted by pressing the appropriate function key(s), in this case [F8] (Underline). This holds true for most of the WordPerfect functions except those keys that are normally used to format and edit a document. These include the [Enter] and [Del] keys, the cursor keys, and [F7] (Exit). There are two ways to insert these commands:

- Press [Ctrl][V] (Compose) before pressing the desired key. This is best used when you only need to enter one code at a time; *or*

- Press [Ctrl][F10] (Macro Define) to toggle back and forth between the default editing mode and the WordPerfect commands mode. Use this mode when you have to enter many codes into your macro.

Macro commands, on the other hand, are inserted by pressing [Ctrl][PgUp], highlighting the code you wish to use, and pressing [Enter].

Congratulations, you and Tom have survived your initiation into the exciting world of macros unscathed. You may now be tempted to quit law and take up programming full time. After all, you tell yourself, computers will always be with us, but eventually society is going to have to put its foot down and say: "No more lawyers." Although you're probably not yet ready for object-oriented programming in C++ (whatever that is), you *are* ready to learn about merge templates.

SOFTWARE

To write and edit long, complex macros, we recommend purchasing WordPerfect Office, which, among other applications, includes a very powerful macro editor. The macro editor lets you easily copy and move blocks of text and codes, edit two macros at a time, and use search and replace.

2.3 ADVANCED WORDPERFECT LETTER WRITING SKILLS

2.3.1 USING SIMPLE KEYBOARD MERGES TO CREATE REUSABLE BOILERPLATE LETTERS (TEMPLATES)

One of WordPerfect's great strengths in the legal office is its ability to quickly and easily create reusable *templates*. A template is a boilerplate document that can be frequently reused without changing the original text. Instead, a copy is made automatically with your additions that can then be saved with a different file name. Thus, the

> *People of the same trade seldom meet together, even for merriment and diversion, but the conversation ends in a conspiracy against the public, or in some contrivance to raise prices. It is impossible indeed to prevent such meetings by any law which either could be executed, or would be consistent with liberty and justice.*
>
> Adam Smith
> Wealth of Nations
> [1776]

original form can be reused countless times without being edited. And if you need to edit the template itself, it is as easy as editing a regular WordPerfect document.

The advantages of using merge templates for boilerplate legal letters and forms are many. First of all, merge templates can give the user detailed instructions on how to fill in the blanks. This makes it much easier and faster for secretaries, paralegals, and attorneys to fill out forms and contracts. And, with a little bit of extra work, you can make your templates "smart" so that repeating text in a form only needs to be entered once; the other occurrences will automatically be filled in by WordPerfect. An example of this might be a contract where the names of the parties are mentioned numerous times in the course of the document. (For more information on creating and using advanced merge templates, refer to Chapter 3.)

A second important advantage of merge templates is that they guarantee greater accuracy. Ironically, the ease of use of word processors has contributed to inaccuracy. Secretaries and lawyers sometimes get sloppy when editing an old version of a form or contract and overlook information from a previous client. With a template merge system, you never have to fear having missed a part of the form that contained old and erroneous information because blanks on the original are never filled in.

If you plan on fully exploiting WordPerfect's template features and you're currently using WordPerfect 5.0, *you should upgrade to WordPerfect 5.1*. If you are already using WordPerfect 5.1, you'll be glad to know that the capabilities of its merge language have been greatly enhanced over those of 5.0. In essence, WordPerfect 5.1's expanded merge language now brings all of the power of the WordPerfect macro language to regular WordPerfect documents. Combined with the use of macro menu systems, WordPerfect 5.1 has the power to become a full-fledged document assembly program.

This chapter will talk you through the steps of turning a sample Attorney Fee Letter into a merge template and then using the template. Because boilerplate letters are usually relatively short (unlike contracts), only simple keyboard merges will be discussed. For information on more advanced uses of the merge template feature, including how to combine macros with templates, please refer to Chapter 3.

BY dint of sheer will and hard work, Tom has automated much of the process of writing letters. He's created styles for the different kinds of letterhead that he uses, and his most frequently used names and addresses are now stored as named macros, as are the different signature blocks that he regularly uses. He's made it much easier for his partners, even if they're not yet aware of it, to turn out flawless-looking correspondence.

Tom is not one to rest on his laurels, however. During the course of his work, he has realized that there are several letters, such as the firm Attorney Fee Letter, that he constantly reuses. Like his partners, he has been retrieving the old version of the letter, deleting the old names and other information, and then typing in the new information. Because information from a prior client is in the old version of the Fee Letter, Tom also has to be sure to carefully review it several times before giving it to a new client. To Tom, this whole process seems, well, very "inelegant." Confident that WordPerfect has a better way to do things, he plunges back into the reference book. After some digging, he finds the answer—the simple keyboard merge.

Creating a template by retrieving, rather than loading, text

The easiest way to create a template is to retrieve your boilerplate form into a blank file, rather than loading the file itself. This creates a new document and ensures that the original is not changed. (However, this system will not prompt the user to fill in the blanks.) Follow these steps:

SOFTWARE

West's Express Forms contain dozens of high-quality forms on disk. Currently available are consumer bankruptcy and California litigation forms, including pleadings and jury instructions. For more information on Express Forms, call 1-800-328-9352.

1. On a blank editing screen, press the [Spacebar] once. By putting in one space, you have effectively created a new document.

2. Press [Shift][F10] (Retrieve) or [F5] (List Files) and retrieve the document you wish to use. If you get the message "Retrieve into current document?," answer [Y].

3. If you wish to save the new document you have created, press [F10] to save and give it a new name. Remember to use a proper extension!

> ■ *Because you have inserted a document into another document (albeit one that contains a single space), note that it does not have a name until you save it. This is the tip-off that you have created a new document and that the original remains unchanged.*

You can enhance this system by creating a named macro that performs the above steps for each of your mostly commonly used boilerplate forms. Figure 3-10 (in the next chapter) shows what the macro would look like from the macro editor for a template called RETAINER.TEM kept in the directory C:\WP51\FORMS. You could also use the {Pause} macro code discussed previously to make it more generic.

> *The republican is the only form of government which is not eternally at open or secret war with the rights of mankind.*
>
> Thomas Jefferson
> Letter to William Hunter [March 11, 1790]

Creating a user-prompting merge template using merge codes

The following illustrates how to turn a sample Attorney Fee Letter into a simple keyboard merge template using the **{INPUT}** merge code (**WP5.1**) or the **^O** and **^C** codes (**WP5.0**). Theses codes prompt the user to enter information at each variable. We will use as our example the first paragraph of a sample Attorney Contingency Fee Letter found at the beginning of this chapter. Alternatively, if your firm has a standard Fee Letter, feel free to use that instead.

1. Type the first sentence of the Attorney Fee Letter as illustrated on the following page up to the word "by."

2. Press [Shift][F9] (Merge Codes) to display the merge codes menu.

3. **WP5.1** Choose [3] for Input. At the "Enter Message:" prompt, type the prompt to be used for the keyboard merge, then press [Enter]. For example, for the [ATTY NAME] variable, you might want to type: Enter attorney name, then press [F9] to continue:

WP5.0 Choose [O] to insert a ^O code (Output message to screen), type the prompt to be used during the keyboard merge, press [Shift][F9] again and choose [O] to insert a closing ^O code. Next, press [Shift][F9] [C] to insert the ^C code (Request input from Console) after the output message. For example, at the [ATTY NAME] variable, your message might look something like this: "**^O**Enter attorney name, press F9 to continue:**^O^C**"

> ■ *The {INPUT} merge code is just one of many different merge codes that are available in WordPerfect 5.1. If you would like to learn how to use advanced merge codes to create sophisticated keyboard templates, see Chapter 3 and Appendix C.*

TIP

Because templates are merge documents, the merge is continued by pressing the [F9] (End Field) key, not the [Enter] key. Because users will often instinctively press [Enter], it is wise to remind users in the prompt that the [F9] key continues the merge. For an example, see step 3.

4. Repeat the above steps for each variable in the fee letter. When completed, the letter should look like one of the figures below, depending on which version of the software you're using.

> ■ **WP5.1** *If you do not see any merge codes on the regular editing screen, you must make sure that Merge Codes Display is set to Yes on the Edit Screen Options under Setup. Press [Shift][F1] (Setup), [F2] for Display, [F6] for Edit-Screen Options, [F5] for Merge Codes Display and [Y].*

TIP

If you plan to use many different templates, it is advisable that you store all templates in a separate subdirectory, such as C:\WP51\FORMS.

5. When finished, save the template by pressing (Save) or by using the [Alt][S] macro. We highly recommend that merge templates be clearly identified by using a distinct three-letter extension such as TEM. Example: `fee_let.tem`.

WP5.1 sample:

ATTORNEY FEE LETTER - CONTINGENCY

In consideration of the legal services to be rendered by {INPUT}Enter Attorney Name, then press [F9] to continue~ (hereinafter "Law Firm") for any claim that {INPUT}Enter Client name, then press [F9] to continue~ (hereinafter "Client"), may have against the parties responsible for injuries and/or damages sustained by the client on or about {INPUT}Enter Date of Injury, then press [F9] to continue~, the client does employ said Law Firm to commence and prosecute such claim.

WP5.0 sample:

ATTORNEY FEE LETTER - CONTINGENCY

In consideration of the legal services to be rendered by ^OEnter Attorney Name, then press [F9] to continue^O^C (hereinafter "Law Firm") for any claim that ^OEnter Client name, then press [F9] to continue^O^C (hereinafter "Client"), may have against the parties responsible for injuries and damages sustained by the client on or about ^OEnter Date of Injury, then press [F9] to continue^O^C, the client does employ said Law Firm to commence and prosecute such claim.

2.3.2 USING MERGE TEMPLATES

Templates are in reality sophisticated keyboard merges. Therefore, to use templates you must follow the steps needed to merge documents. When you are performing a keyboard merge, the template is the primary merge file; there is no secondary merge file.

1. Press [Ctrl][F9] (Merge/Sort) to access the merge menu.
2. Choose [1] for **Merge**.
3. At the "Primary File:" prompt, enter the entire file name of the merge template you wish to use, including the path name (if it is

located in a different subdirectory than the one you are presently in, and press [Enter]. (For example, if you were currently in the C:\WP51\LETTERS directory and you wished to use the Fee Letter template created above, called FEE_LET.TEM, which is stored in the C:\WP51\FORMS directory, you would have to type out C:\WP51\FORMS\FEE_LET.TEM to use it. You may also use List Files [F5] to retrieve it).

■ *WordPerfect will give the error message "File not Found" if you enter the wrong document name or fail to give the proper path for the file.*

4. At the "Secondary File:" prompt, simply press [Enter]. (There is no secondary file when performing a keyboard merge.)

5. The cursor will stop at the location of the first merge code in the document, and the relevant merge prompt will appear at the bottom left-hand side of the screen. Type in the proper text and press [F9] (End Field) to continue the merge.

6. When all the merging is completed, you may also edit the document as you would any normal WordPerfect document. When finished editing, name and save the document by pressing [F10] (Save), or print it by pressing [Shift][F7] (Print). Note that the completed merge document does not have a name, because it is a new document that has just been created as a result of the merge process.

2.3.3 EDITING A TEMPLATE

One of the beauties of the WordPerfect 5.X merge template feature is the ease with which templates can be changed and edited. Because templates are simply normal WordPerfect documents with the addition of merge codes, they may be retrieved and edited in the same way. Just use [F5] (List Files), or [Shift][F10] (Retrieve). Even the merge prompts that are part of the merge codes can be edited like normal text.

■ **WP5.1** *When editing a template, make sure that you do not delete the all important tilde (~)! The tilde acts as a delimiter for the merge code. If it is accidentally deleted, the merge will not function properly.*

> WE THE PEOPLE of the United States, in Order to form a more perfect Union, establish Justice, insure domestic Tranquility, provide for the common defence, promote the general Welfare, and secure the Blessings of Liberty to ourselves and our Posterity, do ordain and establish this CONSTITUTION for the United States of America.
> — Constitution of the United States, Preamble

2.3.4 PRINTING A LETTER ADDRESS BLOCK ON ENVELOPES

Although computers and word processing programs have replaced typewriters in all but the most stubborn legal offices, many offices still use typewriters to type names and addresses onto envelopes. However, if you have a printer within reach of your computer, it is faster and easier to let WordPerfect do the work of properly spacing, aligning, and printing the address block on the envelope—to say nothing of accurately reproducing the correct information.

There are several different ways to print an envelope. The easiest is to use the [Alt][E] macro supplied with this book. (This macro works only for standard 9.5" X 4" envelopes.) Alternatively, you can insert the necessary codes to define an envelope yourself. These codes can then be saved as a style, macro, or template.

Printing on an envelope

MACRO

Use the [Alt][E] macro to print an address block on an envelope.

To print on an envelope, you must tell WordPerfect what paper size and type you are using. The kind of paper you can use depends on the type of printer you are using. Therefore, the printer definition file contains the relevant paper definitions. (Printer definition files in WordPerfect end with the extension .PRS and are normally stored in the WordPerfect directory [e.g., HPLASEII.PRS].)

Step 1: Define a document as an envelope

TIP

Save the envelope definition as either an open Style or a Macro. You could further embellish the style or macro by including a return address on the top left of the envelope, or by inserting a base font code ([Ctrl][F8], [4]) so that the address block gets printed in a certain font.

Before typing an address block on the screen, you must first define your document as an envelope and change the margins by following these steps:

1. Press [Shift][F8] (Format).
2. Press [2] for **P**age.
3. Press [7] (**WP5.1**) or [8] (**WP5.0**) for Paper **S**ize/Type.
4. **WP5.1**   At the Format: Paper Size/Type menu, highlight the **Envelope - Wide** paper size, then press [1] for **S**elect.

    WP5.0   At the Format: Paper Size/Type menu, select [5] for Envelope, then select [5] for Envelope again at the Format: Paper Size/Type menu.
5. Press [F7] (Exit) to return to the document. If you press [Shift][F7], [6] or [C] (View Document), you should see a blank envelope.

TIP

A smart way of using WordPerfect is to write the letter in Document 1 and make Document 2 your envelope. Then, using Copy Block or the [Alt][C] macro, copy the address block from your letter in Doc 1 and insert it onto the envelope in Doc 2, using [Shift][F3] (Switch) to alternate between the two documents. Alternatively, use the [Alt][E] macro.

A [Paper Sz/Typ: 9.5" X 4", Envelope] code has been inserted.

▪ **WP5.1** *This example assumes that you are using a printer such as a Hewlett Packard Series II laser printer or compatible that comes with an envelope page definition for 9.5" x 4" standard envelopes. If your printer does not have an envelope paper size predefined, you can add it by pressing [2] for Add, then [5] for Envelope from the Format: Paper Size/Type menu.*

Step 2: Change the margins on the envelope

1. Change the left and right margins to 3.5" and 1", respectively, by pressing [Shift][F8] (Format), [1] for **Line**, [7] for **Margins**.

2. Change the top and bottom margins to 2" and .5", respectively, by pressing [Shift][F8] (Format), [2] for **Page**, [5] for **Margins**. Press [Enter], then [F7] (Exit) to return to the document edit screen.

If you Reveal Codes, you should see the following codes: [Paper Sz/Typ: 9.5" X 4", Envelope] [L/R Mar:3.5", 1"][T/B Mar:2",1"].

3. Type the address block, then print.

2.3.5 USING MERGE TO AUTOMATE MASS MAILINGS

OM, in his infinite ambition, has taken it upon himself to take charge of a fairly large mailing of over 200 letters to potential clients in order to drum up more business. Characteristically, he sees this as another opportunity to try out a feature of WordPerfect under game conditions.

Using Merge to do mass mailings

Every nation has the government it deserves.
    Joseph de Maistre
    Letter to X [1811]

Every so often, a law firm has to send out numerous letters, brochures, etc., at the same time. Examples might be employment rejection letters sent to recent applicants, a notice to inform clients that an associate has made partner, brochures advertising the services of the firm, and so on. For large mailings, the WordPerfect merge feature can be a godsend, producing hundreds of letters in minutes. The

Merge feature can also be used to print on envelopes and mailing labels.

A merge is made up of two elements: the primary document and the secondary document. The primary document is the document that you wish to mail out to all your clients. The secondary document is the list of names of the people who will receive the letter. During the merge process, merge codes inserted in the primary document pluck the names from the secondary document (the list) and insert it in the proper place in the primary document (letter). At the very minimum, when you have learned how to do a merge, you will have discovered the secret of how junk mail comes to your door with your name inserted throughout the document!

It should not surprise you by now that WordPerfect 5.1 has greatly improved upon the merge capabilities of 5.0. As we've mentioned previously, the full glory and power of WordPerfect's macro language has now been incorporated into WordPerfect's merge language. Because of these improvements, we have separate sections for WordPerfect 5.1 and 5.0 merges.

Because the secret to using the merge feature resides in properly creating a secondary merge file, we'll start there first.

2.3.6 CREATING A WORDPERFECT SECONDARY FILE—OVERVIEW

Before creating your secondary file (think of it as a Name List from now on), you've got to take a minute to carefully plan out what information from the Name List you want merged into your primary document or letter. A Name List consists of a record for each individual, with each record composed of different fields for each different data element, e.g., First Name, Last Name, Zip Code, etc. For example, to personalize your letters, you may want to address them to either the first or last name of the person you are sending them to, not the full name (e.g., Dear John, or Dear Mr. Smith, instead of Dear John Smith). To do so, you must have separate fields for first name and last name. You may also want separate fields for Salutation, Title, Company, etc. Finally, if you want to be able to use WordPerfect's Sort feature (the best in the business), the data to be sorted should be kept in a separate field. A perfect example of this might be sorting your mailing by zip code so that you can take advantage of less expensive bulk mail rates.

SHAREWARE

The DBM.ZIP file, available as shareware on the supplementary disks, is a macro system to manage secondary merge files as databases.

With these considerations in mind, we'll create a secondary file called CLIENTS.SF with different fields for each element of our list. The first step is to define the field names to be used in the secondary file.

2.3.7 CREATING A SECONDARY MERGE FILE IN WORDPERFECT 5.1

Step 1: Define field names for a secondary file

Prior to WordPerfect 5.1, fields could only be identified by number. With the {FIELD NAMES} merge code in 5.1, fields can now be given names, which are easier and more intuitive to use and remember. Follow these steps to define the field names:

1. Press [Shift][F9] (Merge Codes), [6] for **M**ore to bring up the Merge Codes box. Or press [Shift][F9] twice.

2. Press [F] to move to the codes that begin with f, press [↓] once to highlight the {FIELD NAMES} code, then press [Enter].

3. At the "Enter Field 1:" prompt, type the name of the first field you plan to use (e.g., First Name), the press [Enter]. Continue to enter the field names you plan to use, making sure to press [Enter] after each field name. When you have finished defining all of the field names you plan on using, press [Enter] at a blank "Enter Field N:" prompt. A {FIELD NAMES} code with the field names you have chosen will be inserted, followed by a hard page break.

▪ *WordPerfect inserts a tilde (~) to separate each field in the {DEFINE NAMES} statement. The entire statement is ended with two tildes (~~).*

4. Save your document by pressing [F10] and name the document CLIENTS.SF.

> **TIP**
>
> It is not necessary to use the {FIELD NAMES} code to assign names to fields, because WordPerfect will also perform merges based on the field number. However, we strongly recommend using {FIELD NAMES} to define field names. Using field names instead of numbers makes it easier and more intuitive to create primary merge files and enter information into secondary merge files.

Step 2: Enter information into your secondary file (list)

1. Now that you've defined the Field Names, you're ready to create your first record, field by field. Type the contents of the first field, then press [F9] (End Field) to end the first field and begin the second. Notice that the "Field: field name" prompt at the bottom left of the screen changes each time you press [F9]. This prompt will always tell you what the proper contents of each field are.

FIGURE 2-7

The WordPerfect 5.1 Advanced Merge Codes menu is accessed by pressing [Shift][F9] twice.

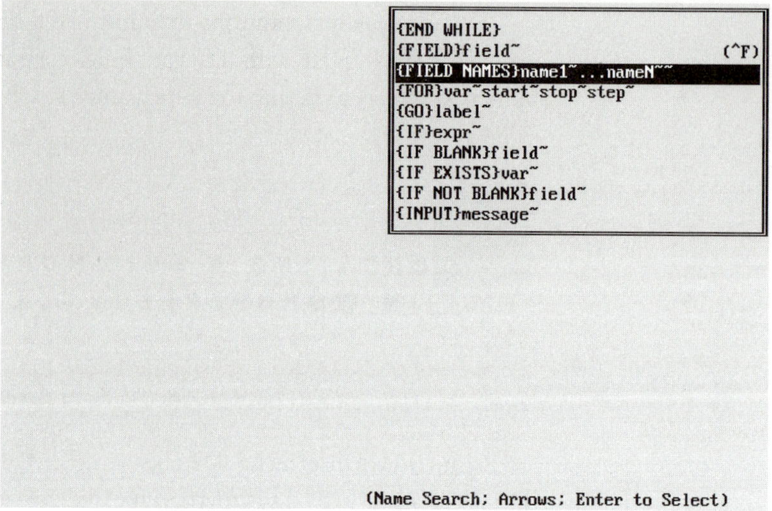

```
{END WHILE}
{FIELD}field~                                        (^F)
{FIELD NAMES}name1~...nameN~~
{FOR}var~start~stop~step~
{GO}label~
{IF}expr~
{IF BLANK}field~
{IF EXISTS}var~
{IF NOT BLANK}field~
{INPUT}message~
```

(Name Search; Arrows; Enter to Select)

■ *The contents of a field can be as long as you wish and include a number of hard returns. For example, if an address block is two lines, simply press* [Enter] *at the end of the first line, then type out the second line of the address. Press 9 (End Field) when you're ready to move on to the next field. Both lines of the address block will appear in the final merge.*

■ *If your list contains a field such as Title that does not apply to that particular record (i.e., that particular person does not have a title), simply leave that field blank and end it by pressing* [F9] *(End Record) to move on to the next field. The key point is: you must keep the order and number of the fields consistent from record to record.*

TIP

As always, you should name your documents properly, making consistent use of extensions. We recommend that secondary merge files be given the extension .SF and primary merge files the extension .PF (example: CLIENTS.PF).

2. When finished with the first record, press [Shift][F9], [2] for End Record to insert the {END RECORD} code. Notice that this code inserts a page break and begins the next record.

3. Repeat steps 1 and 2 until your list is done, remembering to save the file frequently as you go along. Be sure that the order and number of fields is consistent from record to record.

Figure 2-8 shows our sample secondary merge file, called CLIENTS.SF. Notice that it includes separate fields for Greeting, Title, and Company.

FIGURE 2-8

A sample WordPerfect 5.1 secondary merge file is shown. Note that the field names have been defined with the use of the {FIELD NAMES} code.

```
{FIELD NAMES}First Name~Last Name~Greeting~Title~Company~Address~City~State~Zip~
==============================================================================
Guy{END FIELD}¶
Wiggins{END FIELD}¶
Mr. Wiggins{END FIELD}¶
President{END FIELD}¶
Legaltek Research{END FIELD}¶
518 Park Avenue{END FIELD}¶
Hoboken{END FIELD}¶
NJ{END FIELD}¶
07030{END FIELD}¶
{END RECORD}¶
==============================================================================
Lawrence{END FIELD}¶
Nussbaum{END FIELD}¶
Larry{END FIELD}¶
CEO{END FIELD}¶
CIDEX Computer Systems{END FIELD}¶
2 Willow Terrace{END FIELD}¶
Hoboken{END FIELD}¶
NJ{END FIELD}¶
07030{END FIELD}¶
{END RECORD}¶
==============================================================================
Field: First Name                                    Doc 2 Pg 2 Ln 1" Pos 1"
```

2.3.8 CREATING A WORDPERFECT 5.1 PRIMARY MERGE FILE

Now that the hard work of creating a secondary merge file has been done, the primary merge file (letter) must be created and the two merged together. Like the merge template discussed previously, a primary file is a regular WordPerfect document except that it includes certain merge codes. The success of a useful primary merge file is actually based on how carefully you created your secondary merge file. In general, if each data element (such as First Name) is given its own field in the secondary merge file, you can be more flexible in creating a primary merge document. The following letter illustrates this concept.

To properly insert the merge codes, you must know the field names you will use for the merge (see above). The following example uses the First Name, Last Name, Greeting, Title, Company, Address, City, State, and Zip fields from the secondary merge file discussed above.

1. Insert the formatting codes you wish to use in your letter (i.e., any styles you wish to use, fonts, etc.). Also, put in today's date. If this is a form letter you plan to reuse, you can use the Date Code feature ([Shift][F5], [2]) to automatically insert the date. Alternatively, you can also use the merge code {DATE} feature ([Shift][F9] twice, [D] for {DATE}, then press [Enter]).

2. At the point where you wish to insert the first merge code (generally the address block of the letter), press [Shift][F9] (Merge Codes), [1] for Field, then enter the field name you wish to use (e.g.,

TIP

To help you remember field names/numbers when creating your primary file, retrieve your secondary file into Document 2 and use the Switch feature ([Shift][F3]) to switch back and forth between them.

First Name) and press [Enter]. WordPerfect will insert the following code: {FIELD}First Name~. Repeat this step for all the other fields you wish to insert as part of the merge, being careful to put in the proper spaces and punctuation.

CAUTION: When you insert a field into a primary merge document, the field name is delimited by the tilde (~). Make sure that all punctuation and spacing occurs *after* the use of the tilde, or the merge won't work properly. (For example, when placing a colon after a salutation as in "Dear {FIELD}Greeting~:" the placement of the colon is correct, while in "Dear{FIELD}Greeting:~" the colon placement is incorrect. With the incorrect version, there will be no space between the Dear and the Salutation, and WordPerfect will be looking to merge with a field called Greeting:, not Greeting.

3. When all the merge codes have been entered and the text of the letter typed, press [F10] to save the primary merge file. We recommend that you give primary merge documents the .PF extension. (e.g., FORMLET.PF).

■ *It is not necessary for a primary merge file to have this extension, but using it makes the file name easier to find and remember.*

4. After saving the document, clear the file from the computer's memory by pressing [F7], [N], [N] to exit the document without quitting WordPerfect.

The letter in Figure 2-9 is an example of a primary merge document.

FIGURE 2-9

In this sample WordPerfect 5.1 primary merge file, note that the fields are named, not numbered as in WordPerfect 5.0. Using names makes merges more intuitive

```
{DATE}

{FIELD}first name~ {FIELD}last name~
{FIELD}address~
{FIELD}city~, {FIELD}state~ {FIELD}zip~

Dear {FIELD}greeting~,

     The law firm of Marshall, Cardozo, Hand, Holmes & Blackstone
is proud to announce that it is open for business. We are a general
practice firm in areas of expertise in Corporate, Criminal and
First Amendment issues. For more information on our firm, please
see our enclosed brochure or call us at (212) 123-4567.

                         Sincerely,


                         Tom Marshall, Esq.
                         Marshall, Cardozo, Hand, Holmes & Blackstone

                                         Doc 2 Pg 1 Ln 3.5" Pos 1"
```

2.3.9 CREATING A SECONDARY MERGE FILE IN WORDPERFECT 5.0

In WordPerfect 5.0, fields are given numbers (Field 1, Field 2, etc.), not descriptive field names as in WordPerfect 5.1. Therefore, you have to decide on the number of separate fields you need. Our example will have 9 fields: First Name (field 1), Last Name (field 2), Greeting (field 3), Title (field 4), Company (field 5), Address (field 6), City (field 7), State (field 8), and Zip (field 9). The key to properly creating and using a secondary merge file is to *rigorously adhere to the structure you've decided on!* For example, if a particular client does not have a title, you would leave that field blank (in our example, field 4)—you would put her company name (field 5) there instead.

With these few rules in mind, create a secondary merge file by following these few steps:

1. On a blank screen, type the first name of a client, then press [F9] (End Field) to insert an End Field code.

2. Type the last name of a client, then press [F9] to insert an End Field code (^R). Type the rest of the information for that particular record (Greeting, Title, Company, etc.), making sure that each field appears on a different line and ends with the ^R code.

3. When finished with the first record, press [Shift][F9] (Merge Codes), [E] for ^E (the End Record code).

4. Repeat the above steps for each subsequent record (i.e., client) that you wish to include in your secondary merge file (list).

5. Press [F10] (Save) to save your work. A sample secondary merge file appears in Figure 2-10.

■ *We strongly recommend that you use the extension .SF when naming your secondary merge file. Using descriptive file name extensions helps you remember and identify the file later on (e.g., CLIENT.SF).*

> **TIP**
>
> Using a greeting field in a secondary merge file permits greater flexibility during merges. For example, if the client is a close friend, you could put a nickname or first name in the field instead of the more formal salutation and last name.

> **TIP**
>
> Don't worry about alphabetizing the names in your secondary merge file (list). WordPerfect's powerful Sort feature can do this for you automatically after you create the list.

2.3.10 CREATING A WORDPERFECT 5.0 PRIMARY MERGE FILE

Now that the hard work of creating a secondary merge file has been done, the primary merge file (letter) must be created and the two merged together. Like the merge template discussed previously, a primary file is a regular WordPerfect document except that it includes certain merge codes. The trick to creating a useful primary merge file is actually based on how carefully you created your secon-

FIGURE 2-10

A sample WordPerfect 5.0 secondary merge file shows two records. Each record is separated by an End Record (^E) code.

```
Daniel^R¶
Webster^R¶
Danny^R¶
Managing Partner^R¶
Webster, Cardozo & Hand^R¶
123 Fifth Avenue^R¶
New York^R¶
New York^R¶
10128^R¶
^E¶
================================================================================
John^R¶
Marshall^R¶
Mr. Marshall^R¶
President^R¶
Marbury and Madison Associates^R¶
258 West 3rd Street^R¶
New York^R¶
New York^R¶
10014^R¶
^E¶
================================================================================
                                                          Doc 2 Pg 1 Ln 1.67" Pos 1.7"
```

dary merge file. In general, if each data element (such as First Name) is given its own field in the secondary merge file, you can be more flexible in creating a primary merge document. Our sample letter of congratulations illustrates this concept.

To properly insert the merge codes, you must know the field numbers and what information they correspond to in your secondary merge file. The following example uses Field 1 (First Name), Field 2 (Last Name), Field 3 (Greeting), Field 4 (Title), Field 5 (Company), Field 6 (Address), Field 7 (City), Field 8 (State), and Field 9 (Zip) from the secondary merge file discussed above.

1. Insert the formatting codes you wish to use in your letter (i.e., any styles you wish to use, fonts, etc.). Also, put in today's date. If this is a form letter you plan to reuse, you can use the Date Code feature ([Shift][F5], [2]) to automatically insert the date. Alternatively, you can also use the Date merge code ^D feature ([Shift][F9], [D] for ^D, then press [Enter]).

TIP

If you have a primary merge file that you can constantly reuse for many different mailings, you may want to include it as one of your firm's basic boilerplate forms and store it in a separate FORMS directory.

2. At the point where you wish to insert the first merge code (generally the address block of the letter), press [Shift][F9] (Merge Codes), [F] for ^F (Field), then enter the field number you wish to use (i.e., [1] for First Name etc). WordPerfect will insert the following code: ^F1^. Repeat this step for all the other fields you wish to insert as part of the merge, being careful to put in the proper spaces and punctuation.

3. When all the merge codes have been entered and the text of the letter typed, press [F10] to save the primary merge file. We recommend that you give primary merge documents the .PF extension (e.g., FORMLET.PF). Our sample primary file appears in Figure 2-11.

FIGURE 2-11

A sample WordPerfect 5.0 primary merge file is shown. The fields correspond to the fields as defined in the secondary merge file illustrated in Figure 2-7.

```
^D
^F1^  ^F2^
^F4^
^F5^
^F6^
^F7^,  ^F8^  ^F9^

Dear ^F3^,

     The law firm of Marshall, Cardozo, Hand, Holmes & Blackstone
is proud to announce that it is open for business. We are a general
practice firm in areas of expertise in Corporate, Criminal and
First Amendment issues. For more information on our firm, please
see our enclosed brochure or call us at (212) 123-4567.

          Sincerely,


          Tom Marshall, Esq.
          Marshall, Cardozo, Hand, Holmes & Blackstone



                                      Doc 2 Pg 1 Ln 3.67" Pos 2"
```

■ *It is not necessary for a primary merge file to have the .PF extension, but using it makes the file name easier to find and remember.*

4. After saving the document, clear the file from the computer's memory by pressing [F7], [N], [N] to exit the document without quitting WordPerfect.

EXERCISE: CREATING AN ENVELOPE PRIMARY MERGE DOCUMENT

Now that you've learned how to use WordPerfect to create a primary merge document for letters, you may perform the same procedure to create a primary merge envelope. The only difference is that you have to define an envelope first before entering the merge codes. In other words, instead of typing or addressing the envelopes by hand, let WordPerfect do the work for you. We'll use the envelope form or style that we discussed earlier in this chapter along with the same field names from the secondary merge file CLIENTS.SF that we created above.

1. Define a document as an envelope as described in Section 2.3.4. If you have created an envelope style, you can use that as well. See above.

WP5.1

{FIELD}First Name~ {FIELD}LastName~
{FIELD}Title~
{FIELD}Company~
{FIELD}Address~
{FIELD}City~, {FIELD}State~ {FIELD}Zip~

WP5.0

^F1^ ^F2
^F4^
^F5^
^F6^
^F7^, ^F8^ ^F9^

3. Save this primary merge document by pressing [F10] and call it ENVELOPE.PF.

2. Enter the following field names by pressing [Shift][F9] (Merge Codes), [1] for **Field:**

4. Merge ENVELOPE.PM with CLIENTS.SM by pressing: [Ctrl][F10] (Merge), [1] for **M**erge and entering the names of the two files at the prompts.

2.3.11 ELIMINATING BLANK LINES DURING A MERGE

If you have defined a secondary merge file similar to our example above, it may frequently be the case that some of the records in the list will have blank fields. For example, it may often be true that certain individuals do not have formal titles. In that case, you'll want to make sure that you eliminate blank lines caused by empty fields when you perform a merge. There are two techniques for performing this bit of magic, depending on which version of WordPerfect you are using.

Using the ?

The first method to eliminate blank lines in either WP5.1 or WP5.0 is to place a question mark (?) after the field name or number, but not outside of the caret (^). Note, however, that WordPerfect will delete *everything* after the question mark that appears on that line, including subsequent text and fields. See Figure 2-12.

Using the {IF NOT BLANK} merge code (WP5.1)

The {IF NOT BLANK} merge code in WordPerfect 5.1 gives you much greater control over the printing of blank lines. Most importantly, it will not delete text after the {IF NOT BLANK} code. Simply put, the {IF NOT BLANK} merge code tells WordPerfect to print

FIGURE 2-12

WordPerfect uses the question mark (?) to prevent blank lines from printing during a merge.

```
¶
^D¶
¶
^F1^ ^F2^¶
^F4?^¶
^F5^¶
^F6^¶
^F7^, ^F8^ ^F9^¶
¶
¶
Dear ^F3^,¶
¶
    The ^F4^ field above corresponds to the Title field in the
secondary merge file. Because I have placed a question mark within
this field, if the field is empty, the blank line will not print
during a merge.




C:\WP50\LETTER.PF                             Doc 2 Pg 1 Ln 3.5" Pos 2.5"
```

FIGURE 2-13

WordPerfect 5.1 uses the {IF NOT BLANK} merge code to prevent blank fields from inserting blank lines during a merge. The hard return forcing a new line was placed before the {END IF} code. This ensures that it will not print if the field is blank.

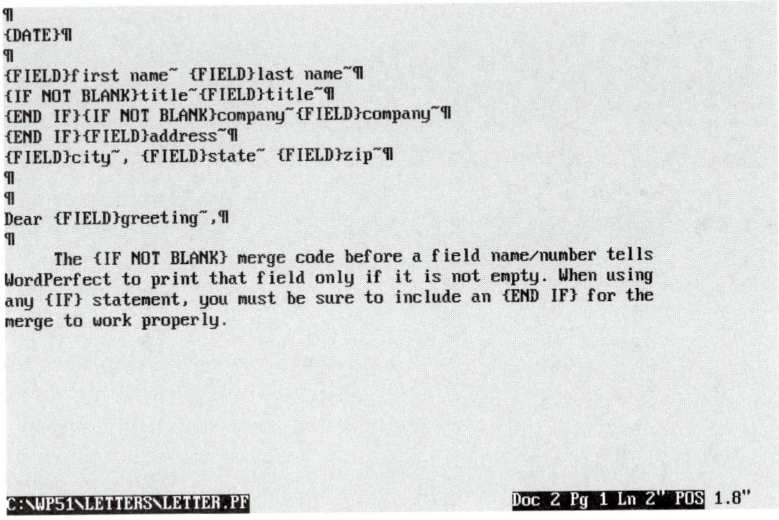

```
¶
{DATE}¶
¶
{FIELD}first name~ {FIELD}last name~¶
{IF NOT BLANK}title~{FIELD}title~¶
{END IF}{IF NOT BLANK}company~{FIELD}company~¶
{END IF}{FIELD}address~¶
{FIELD}city~, {FIELD}state~ {FIELD}zip~¶
¶
¶
Dear {FIELD}greeting~,¶
¶
    The {IF NOT BLANK} merge code before a field name/number tells
WordPerfect to print that field only if it is not empty. When using
any {IF} statement, you must be sure to include an {END IF} for the
merge to work properly.




C:\WP51\LETTERS\LETTER.PF                              Doc 2 Pg 1 Ln 2" POS 1.8"
```

the contents of that field only if it is not blank. (The {IF BLANK} code does the opposite.) When using any {IF} merge code, you must include an {END IF} statement for the merge to work properly.

1. At the point at which you need to insert the code (before the {FIELD}~ code), press [Shift][F9] twice to access the Advance Merge codes.

2. Press [↓] to quickly scroll down, then highlight the {IF NOT BLANK} merge code and press [Enter].

3. Enter the name of the field you wish to check, then press [Enter].

4. When finished, be sure to insert an {END IF} code by pressing [Shift][F9] twice, highlighting the proper code, and pressing [Enter]. For an example, see Figure 2-13.

WP5.1 Proofreading secondary files before performing the merge

You may very well wish to proofread your secondary file before the final merge. Think how inefficient and environmentally wasteful it would be if every record had its own page. You can avoid this inefficiency and waste by setting up a temporary primary file that includes a {Page Off} code. This tells WordPerfect to eliminate the hard page breaks when you do the merge.

1. At the beginning of your primary file, press [Shift][F9], [4] to insert the {PAGE OFF} code.

2. Enter the remaining fields you wish to proof.

3. Save this primary file and perform the merge.

The following illustrates a WP5.1 temporary primary file from the CLIENTS.SF file:

```
{PAGE OFF}
{FIELD}First Name~ {FIELD}Last Name~
{FIELD}Title~
{FIELD}Company~
{FIELD}Address~
{FIELD}City~, {FIELD}State~ {FIELD}Zip~
{FIELD}Greeting~
```

After reviewing and editing the resultant document, you can make whatever changes are necessary to the secondary merge file before the final merge.

If you like, you can simply delete the temporary primary merge file when it's served its purpose to avoid confusion.

2.3.12 SORTING A SECONDARY MERGE FILE BEFORE MERGING

Now that you have created both your primary and secondary merge files, you are ready to execute and print the merge. Or are you? Remember, the final merge will reflect the order of the records in the secondary merge file, and this might force you to do a lot of sorting manually after you print the letters. For example, the post office requires that all bulk mailings be sorted by zip code before being mailed. But, once again, WordPerfect comes to the rescue with its easy-to-use Sort feature. Sort is one of WordPerfect's most powerful features and, when used together with secondary merge files, it can automatically sort records by last name, zip code, or any other field. The WordPerfect Sort feature also allows you to include operators such as > (greater than) and <> (not equal to) to filter out records that are not needed. This is very handy when you have a secondary merge file that is made up of hundreds or even thousands of names. For example, you can tell WordPerfect to display only those records that have NY as the state, or that have a zip code between 10014 and 20014. In brief, the sort feature gives WordPerfect users many of the most powerful features of a full-blown database program when sorting secondary merge files.

The following exercises will show you how to sort by last name and by zip code (essential for large bulk mailings), and how to limit your sorts to specific records by using "operators." We will be using the

---

Within these limits the power vested in the American courts of justice of pronouncing a statute to be unconstitutional forms one of the most powerful barriers that have ever been devised against the tyranny of political assemblies.
Alexis Charles Henri Maurice Clerel de Tocqueville
Democracy in America [1835]

Table 2.1 This secondary merge file contains five records plus a number of fields for data.

{FIELD NAMES}First Name~Last Name~Greeting~Title~ Company~Address~ City~State~Zip~
===
Tom{END FIELD}
Jones{END FIELD}
Mr. Jones{END FIELD}
President{END FIELD}
Legaltek Research{END FIELD}
518 Park Avenue{END FIELD}
New York{END FIELD}
NY{END FIELD}
10020{END FIELD}
{END RECORD}
===
Edith{END FIELD}
Smith{END FIELD}
Ms. Smith{END FIELD}
President{END FIELD}
Cidex Publishing{END FIELD}
2 Willow Terrace{END FIELD}
Hoboken{END FIELD}
NJ{END FIELD}
07030{END FIELD}
{END RECORD}
===
Harold{END FIELD}
Jones{END FIELD}
Harry{END FIELD}
Vice President{END FIELD}
Jones Widgets{END FIELD}
5 Main Street{END FIELD}
Westfield{END FIELD}
MD{END FIELD}
21230{END FIELD}
{END RECORD}
===
Marilyn{END FIELD}
Robbins{END FIELD}
Ms. Robbins{END FIELD}
CEO{END FIELD}
Robbins & Robbins{END FIELD}
205 Broadway{END FIELD}
New York{END FIELD}
NY{END FIELD}
11353{END FIELD}
{END RECORD}
===
Rachel{END FIELD}
Gruhin{END FIELD}
Ms. Gruhin{END FIELD}
Treasurer{END FIELD}
Valmore Communications{END FIELD}
1414 Madison Avenue{END FIELD}
New York{END FIELD}
NY{END FIELD}
10305{END FIELD}
{END RECORD}

CLIENTS.SF secondary merge file created in Table 2-1. We do not claim that these lessons are all-inclusive, because the sort feature has other capabilities not discussed here that are considerably more esoteric and of doubtful use to most law firms. What follows are the most practical uses of the Sort feature when used with large secondary merge files.

2.3.13 USING SORT TO ALPHABETIZE RECORDS BY LAST NAME

SHAREWARE

The BLKBOOK.ZIP file is an easy-to-use client database/rolodex program. Keystroke-compatible with WordPerfect, it includes an autodialer and the ability to export names as secondary merge files.

AFTER many long hours, Tom has created a secondary merge file that is over 1,000 records long and contains just about anybody who might want to retain his firm's services. Naturally, the names in the records were not compiled in alphabetical order. Furthermore, because it is such a large mailing, the envelopes must all be bundled in zip code order before they are sent to the post office. Tom knows that once the merge is done he can't possibly further endanger his relationship with his partners by taking even more time to organize all those letters and envelopes alphabetically. Tom, after slogging through the WordPerfect manual, masters the Sort feature. Here's what he learned:

1. Press [Ctrl][F9], [2] for **S**ort.

2. At the "Input File to sort:" prompt, enter the name of the file you wish to sort. (We will be using the CLIENTS.SF file below.) If the file you wish to sort is already on the screen, just press [Enter].

3. At the "Output file for sort:" prompt, press [Enter] to display the results of the sort on the screen. Alternatively, you can save the results to a file name, but to view its contents you will have to retrieve the file first.

WordPerfect will split the screen, with the sort menu displayed below the ruler and the secondary merge file above the ruler.

4. Press [7] for **T**ype, then [1] for **M**erge. This ensures that the sort is performed on a merge file. Note that the title "Sort secondary merge File" appears and that Merge Sort appears under the Title/Type heading (Type in **WP5.0**).

5. Press [6] for **O**rder, then [1] for **A**scending. This ensures that when you sort by last name, the sort will proceed from A to Z.

6. Now comes the tricky part. Press [3] for **K**eys. The cursor jumps to **Key 1** and the menu options below change.

■ *The Keys option is the most crucial part of the Sort feature—and the most difficult to understand.*

FIGURE 2-14

The Keys submenu in the Sort screen shows that the user has chosen an alphanumeric sort on the second field (last name) in ascending order.

```
{FIELD NAMES}First Name~Last Name~Greeting~Title~Company~Address~City~State~Zip
===============================================================================
Tom{END FIELD}
Jones{END FIELD}
Mr. Jones{END FIELD}
President{END FIELD}
Legaltek Research{END FIELD}
518 Park Avenue{END FIELD}
New York{END FIELD}
NY{END FIELD}
                                                      Doc 3 Pg 1 Ln 1" Pos 1"
{      ▲     ▲     ▲     ▲     ▲     ▲     ▲    ▲   }    ▲     ▲
─────────────────────────── Sort Secondary Merge File ───────────────────────
Key Typ Field Line Word    Key Typ Field Line Word    Key Typ Field Line Word
 1   a    2    1    1       2                          3
                            5                          6
 4                          8                          9
 7
Select

Action                     Order                      Type
Sort                       Ascending                  Merge sort

Type: a = Alphanumeric; n = Numeric; Use arrows; Press Exit when done
```

7. With the cursor under the **Typ** heading, press [A] for **Alphanumeric** to make sure that WordPerfect will sort by character, not by number.

8. Next, with the cursor under the Field heading, enter the number of the field you wish WordPerfect to sort on. In our CLIENTS.SF example, Last Name is the second field in each record (First Name is first), so you would enter 2.

9. Make sure that the number 1 (the default) occurs under the Line and Word headings respectively. This tells the Sort feature to sort on the first line of the field you chose (a field can have more than one line), and to sort from the first word or number from the left. Your screen should look like Figure 2-14.

TIP

If you need to view the secondary merge file without leaving the sort feature, press [F2] for **V**iew. This option does not appear in the Keys menu, so you have to press [F7] to return to the original Sort menu. When finished viewing, press [F7] to return to the Sort menu.

▪ *WordPerfect allows you to use negative numbers to make WordPerfect count words from the right. For example, if a field contained both first and last names, such as "Sherlock Holmes," and you wished to sort by last name, you would enter -1 to sort by the first word from the right. In this case, entering [2] would have the same effect, but you'll quickly run into trouble if some names have two words and some are three or four. Starting from the right and entering -1 ensures that you would always be sorting on the last name in a field containing both first and last, and possibly middle, names.*

10. Press [F7] to exit the Keys menu and return to the main sort menu. The screen should now look like Figure 2-15.

▪ *Sorting on the Last Name field requires using only one key, but WordPerfect allows you to sort on up to nine different keys at one time, allowing for very sophisticated and powerful sorts.*

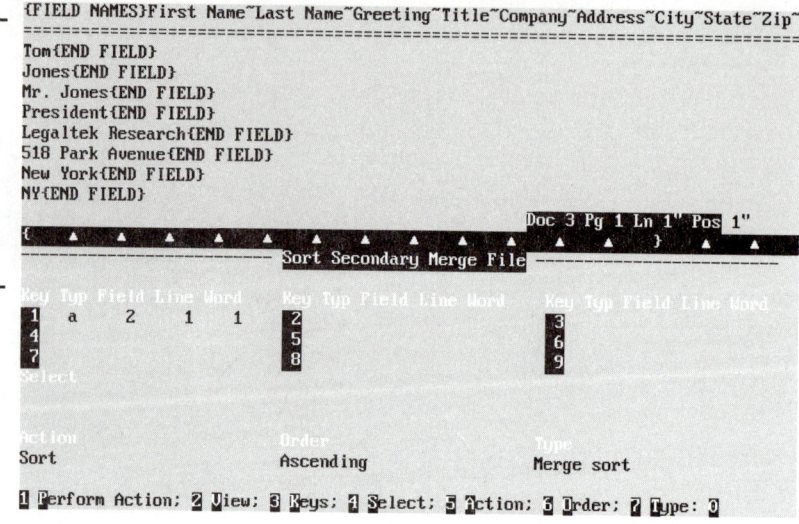

FIGURE 2-15

The Sort screen is shown after the user has exited the Keys submenu. Pressing 1 at this point will perform the sort.

11. Press 1 for **P**erform Action. WordPerfect performs the sort and will give you a count of how many records it is selecting. When finished, the results of the sort will appear on the screen.

12. Press F10 to save the results of the sort. You may wish to give it the same name as the original secondary merge file (this will replace the old, unsorted list with the sorted version). Otherwise, give it a new name.

2.3.14 SORTING A SECONDARY MERGE FILE BY ZIP CODE

1. Press Ctrl F9, 2 for **S**ort.

2. At the "Input File to sort:" prompt, enter the name of the file you wish to sort. (We will be using the same CLIENTS.SF file.) If the file you wish to sort is already on the screen, just press Enter.

3. At the "Output file for sort:" prompt, press Enter to display the results of the sort on the screen. Alternatively, you can save the results to a file name, but to view its contents you will have to retrieve the file first. WordPerfect will split the screen, with the sort menu displayed below and the secondary merge file above the ruler.

4. Press 7 for **T**ype, then 1 for **M**erge. This ensures that the sort is performed on a merge file. Note that the title "Sort secondary merge File" appears and that Merge Sort appears under the Title/Type heading (Type in **WP5.0**).

5. Press [6] for **O**rder, then [1] for **A**scending. This ensures that when you sort by zip code, the sort will proceed from the lowest to the highest number.

6. Now comes the tricky part. Press [3] for **K**eys. The cursor jumps to **Key 1** and the menu options below change.

7. With the cursor under the **Typ** heading, press [N] for Numeric to make sure that WordPerfect will sort by number, not character. (When sorting numbers by character, WordPerfect will sort 100 before 2 because 1 comes before 2. However, a numeric sort will recognize the value of the number.)

> **TIP**
>
> Sort on both Last Name and Zip if you have several records with the same last name that you want to sort by zip code. To sort on Last Name first, make that key 1, then make Zip key 2. Sort will first alphabetize by last name, then sort on the zip codes.

8. Next, with the cursor under the Field heading, enter the number of the field you wish WordPerfect to sort on. In our CLIENTS.SF example, Zip is the ninth field in each record, so you would enter 9.

9. Make sure that the number 1 (the default) occurs under the Line and Word headings respectively. This tells WordPerfect to sort on the first line of the field you chose, and to sort from the first word or number from the left.

10. Press [F7] to exit the Keys menu and return to the main sort menu. The screen should look like Figure 2-16.

■ *Sorting on the Zip field requires using only one key. If you need to sort on both state and zip, use two keys.*

11. Press [1] for **P**erform Action. WordPerfect performs the sort and will give you a count of how many records it is selecting. When finished, the results of the sort will appear on the screen.

12. Press [F10] to save the results of the sort.

FIGURE 2-16

The Sort screen is shown once again. This time the user intends to perform a numeric sort on the 9th field (zip code).

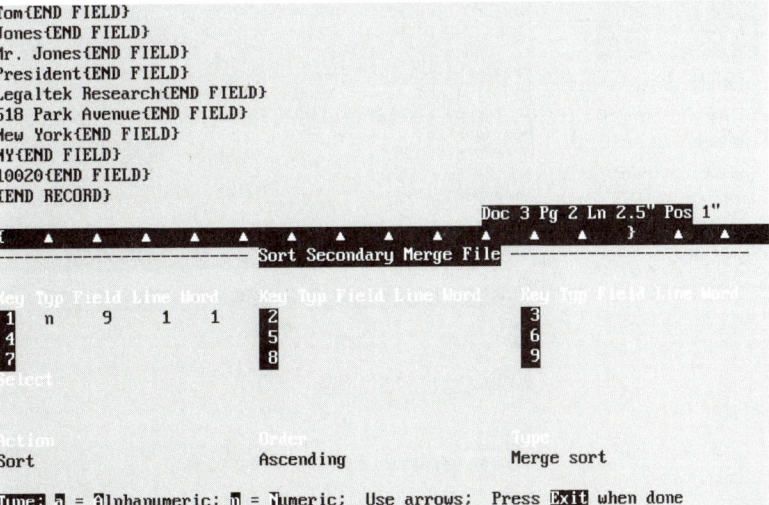

Chapter 2 Using WordPerfect for Legal Correspondence
§2.3

2.3.15 USING SELECT TO SORT SPECIFIC RECORDS ONLY

Let's say you have a large secondary merge file of over 1,000 records with names and addresses from all over the United States. However, you only wish to send mail to those people on the list who lived in areas with zip code numbers from 10007 to 15000. You would use the Select feature to find only the records that matched your criteria, and to filter out all the other unwanted records.

We'll use the same secondary merge file CLIENTS.SF, and we'll use the above criteria for our sort in our next example. For other examples of Select statements, see Table 2-3.

1. Repeat steps 1 through 10 in the previous example on how to sort a secondary merge file by zip code. *Key point*: Be sure to define your keys before using the Select feature.

2. Press [4] for **S**elect. Enter the following statement to have WordPerfect sort only those records with zip codes greater or equal to 10007 and less than or equal to 15000: `Key1>=10007*Key1<=15000`. When finished, press [F7] to return to the main sort menu. Note that **Action** is now changed to Select and Sort. The Select options will appear at the bottom of the menu as illustrated in Figure 2-17. See Table 2-2 for a full explanation of each symbol and its function.

3. Press [1] for **P**erform Action. WordPerfect performs the sort and will give you a count of how many records it is selecting. When finished, the results of the sort will appear on the screen.

4. **WARNING**: Press [F10] and save the results of your Select and Sort *with a different file name!*

FIGURE 2-17

On the Sort Select screen, the user intends to sort zip codes between and including 10007 and 15000 in ascending order.

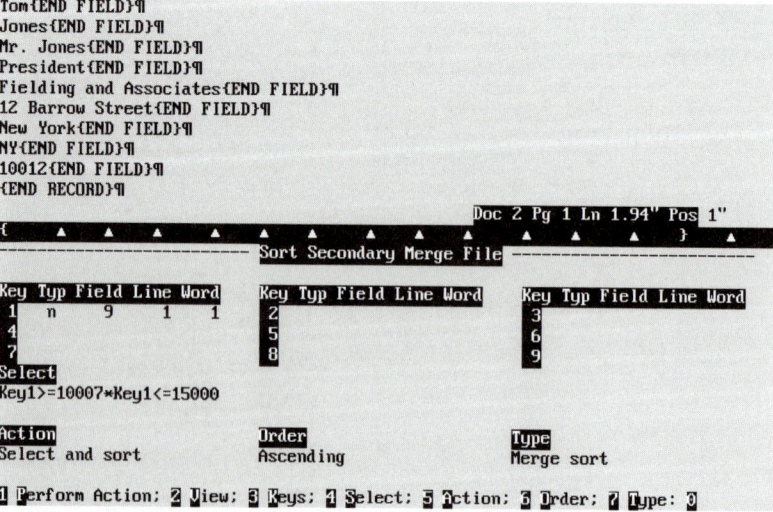

TABLE 2.2 Various symbols used to Sort and Select data in preparing a merge file.

SYMBOL	FUNCTION
+(or)	Place between keys to select records that meet one condition or the other.
*(and)	Place between keys to select records that meet one condition and the other.
=	Equal to
<>	Not equal to
>	Greater than
<	Less than
>=	Greater than or equal to
<=	Less than or equal to
()	Place around keys that should be considered one group. Sort will consider whatever is in the parentheses first, then sort from left to right.

> **TIP**
>
> Press [F10] and save the results of your Select and Sort *with a different file name* than your secondary merge file or else you will lose valuable data.

Do not save the results of this type of sort with the same name as your original secondary merge file. This would cause your original secondary merge file to be overwritten with the results of the Select and Sort, leaving you with a potentially small fraction of the names in the original list. For example, if the original CLIENTS.SF had 1,000 names and there were only 100 clients who matched the above Select and Sort (i.e., who lived in zip codes from 10007 to 10014), and you saved the results as CLIENTS.SF, your secondary merge file would now only have the 100 names with those zip codes. The others would have been overwritten!

The examples in Table 2-3, which use the secondary merge structure we defined earlier, demonstrate the use of Select operators for sophisticated sorts.

TABLE 2.3 Examples of Sorts Performed Using Select Statements

SELECT STATEMENT	EXPLANATION
key1>=10001*key1<=10028	Select all records having a zip code greater than or equal to 10001 and less than or equal to 10028.
key 1=NY+ key 1=NJ	Select all records that have either NY or NJ as the state.
key 1>a*key 1<j	Select all records where the last name starts with the letter "B" through "I."
key 1<>NY	Select all records except those from New York.
key 1=President + key1+CEO	Select all records with the title of either President or CEO.
(key 1>=10001) * key2=Smith	Select all records having a zip code greater than or equal to 10001 and Smith as the last name. Note that two different keys would have to be defined because two different fields are being sorted.

For complicated sorts, various Select statements are used to find and merge the data.

2.3.16 MERGING PRIMARY AND SECONDARY MERGE FILES

Once the primary file has been created and saved, and the names entered into the secondary merge file and sorted according to your needs, only a few short steps remain to perform the merge:

1. From a blank screen, press [Ctrl][F9] (Merge/Sort), [1] for Merge.
2. At the "Primary file:" prompt, type the full name of the primary merge file you wish to use, including its extension. (See how using consistent extensions can make life easier for you?)

> ■ *WordPerfect will search for the name of the file you indicated. If it does not find it, WordPerfect will display the message: "ERROR: FILE NOT FOUND—FILE NAME." If WordPerfect can't find the file, you misspelled it or you didn't specify what directory the file is stored in. For example, if you are currently in the C:\WP51\LETTERS directory, and the primary merge document you wish to use is MERGELET.PF and is in a directory called C:\WP51\FORMS, you must type* `C:\WP51\FORMS\ MERGELET.PF`.

3. At the "Secondary file:" prompt, type the name of the secondary merge file you are using and press [Enter]. Be sure to include the full path name, if necessary. WordPerfect will display the message "*Merging*." The time needed to complete the merge will vary depending on the speed of your equipment and the size of your secondary merge file (i.e., how many names are in your list).

4. When the merge is completed, the result of the merge will appear on the screen. Review the merged letters to make sure that no errors occurred during the merge and to do any cleaning up, if necessary, before printing. Note that the merge result is a completely new document and that it has not yet been saved to disk.

5. Save the results of the merge if you want to review or edit it later by pressing [F10] (Save). We recommend using the extension .MRG for merge results.

TIP

If you forgot the name of the primary or secondary files you are using, or you don't want to type out the full path name, you can use [F5] (List Files) to retrieve the file.

TIP

If you caught a simple error in the merge results, try using [Alt][F2] (Replace) to quickly correct it. However, if the error was in your primary merge document and you have a long list of names in your secondary merge file, it may be faster to correct the error in the primary merge file and run the merge again.

2.3.17 USING WORDPERFECT NOTEBOOK AS A SECONDARY MERGE FILE (FOR WORDPERFECT OFFICE USERS ONLY)

If I were asked . . . to what the singular prosperity and growing strength of that people [the Americans] ought mainly to be attributed, I should reply: To the superiority of their women.
  Alexis Charles Henri Maurice Clerel de Tocqueville Democracy in America [1840]

As we mentioned before, WordPerfect Office 3.1 is a set of programs that work adroitly with WordPerfect. (There is a stand-alone version and also a network version that includes electronic mail and scheduling.) If you are using WordPerfect Office, then you probably already know that one of its handiest programs is called Notebook. Notebook is a simple, easy-to-use flatfile database program that stores data automatically as a secondary merge file. (A flatfile database is self-contained—the fields in this type of database do not reference those in another database.) Notebook also includes powerful sorting capabilities; if you have a modem, you can even dial automatically from it. The beauty of using Notebook over a standard secondary merge file is that you can create all kinds of databases containing useful information that your firm can then use on a daily basis (such as a Notebook for clients, a Notebook for closed cases, etc.). And anytime you need to, this information can be easily merged with WordPerfect.

WordPerfect Notebook comes with a sample Notebook file called ADDRESS.NB. In the following example, we'll use ADDRESS.NB to talk you through performing a merge with a Notebook file instead of a regular secondary merge file.

Viewing Notebook field names in order to create a primary merge file

Because Notebook records are automatically created as WordPerfect secondary merge files, merging them with WordPerfect is relatively easy. Before you do the merge, however, you must make sure that you know the names of the fields in the Notebook file you wish to merge. The easiest way to do this is to view the Notebook file using WordPerfect's Look feature available from the List Files menu. Then, you must make sure that you have properly inserted the field names used in your Notebook file into your WordPerfect primary merge file (i.e., your form letter) using [Shift][F9] (Merge Codes). These steps will be demonstrated using the ADDRESS.NB file that comes with WordPerfect Office, stored in the C:\OFFICE31 directory. (See Figure 2-18.) However, the procedure is the same for all Notebook files.

FIGURE 2-18

A record is shown from the ADDRESS.NB notebook file that comes with WordPerfect Office. Notebook files function as secondary merge files.

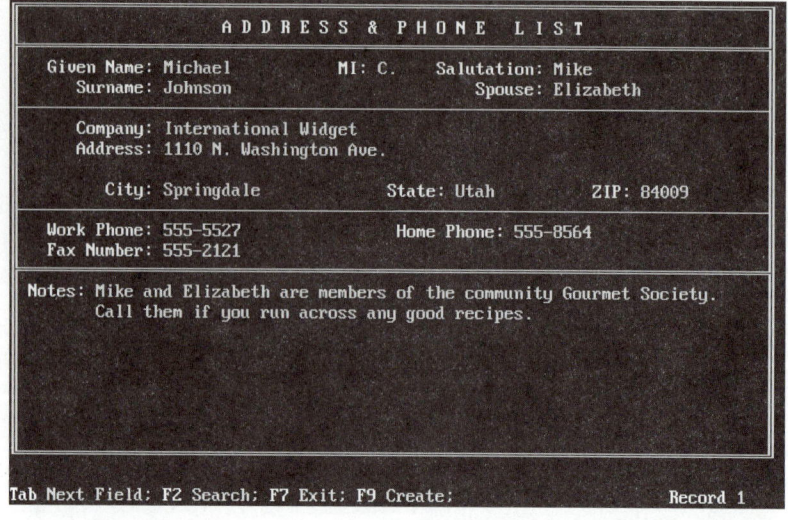

1. In WordPerfect, press [F5] for List Files, type the path name of the directory where the Notebook files are stored (usually C:\OFFICE31), then press [Enter].

WP5.1 IMPORTANT: If the Long Document Feature is on, turn it off by pressing [5], [1] in List Files ([F5]). This way, you'll be able to see all the files in the directory.

2. Highlight the ADDRESS.NB file, and press [Enter] or [6] to view it. See Figure 2-19. For WordPerfect 5.1 users, the Field names for the Notebook file are in **bold**, with a corresponding Field number for WordPerfect 5.0 users to the left (i.e., 01 **First Name**, 02 **MI**). Write down the field names/numbers you wish to use in your primary merge file.

FIGURE 2-19

The ADDRESS.NB notebook file is shown as viewed in List Files in WordPerfect. The field names (in bold) are for WordPerfect 5.1 merges, the numbers to their left are for WordPerfect 5.0.

3. Create a primary merge document using [Shift][F9], [1] for **Field**, then enter the field names or numbers that you wish to use from the Notebook file. For example, ADDRESS.NB has 14 different fields but you may only wish to merge from fields: **First Name**, **Last Name**, **Address**, **City**, **State**, and **Zip**. For more information on creating primary merge files, please see sections 2.3.8 and 2.3.11. Don't forget to save the primary merge file using [F10] (Save). We recommend using the .PF extension for all primary merge files.

Merging the primary and Notebook files

Once the primary file has been created and saved, follow these steps to merge it with the contents of the Notebook file:

1. Press [Ctrl][F9] (Merge/Sort), [1] for **M**erge.
2. At the "Primary file:" prompt, type the full name of the primary file you wish to use (you may have to give the full path name if it is in another directory, e.g., C:\WORDPERFECT\LETTERS\MERGELET.PF).
3. At the "Secondary file:" prompt, type the name of the Notebook file you are using, including the full path (e.g., C:\OFFICE31\ADDRESS.NB), and press [Enter] to execute the merge.
4. When the merge is completed, go through the merged letters and do any necessary cleanup.
5. Save the results of the merge, if you want to review or edit it later, by pressing [F10].

> **TIP**
> By pressing [4] for **O**ptions, [5] for **T**ext while in Notebook, you can specify whether the secondary merge text should be in WordPerfect 5.0 or 5.1 format.

2.3.18 PRINTING ADDRESSES ON LABELS

For most correspondence, you will generally want to print the address directly on the envelope. However, if you are sending out hundreds of letters at a time, and you don't have an envelope sheet feeder, you will find it much more convenient to print your addresses onto labels and then affix them to your envelopes.

One of the major improvements made to WordPerfect 5.1 is its flexibility and ease of use when printing labels. Because of these substantial differences, we have a separate section for each version of the program. We will discuss two ways of using labels: manually and by using the Labels macro that comes with WordPerfect 5.1. For our example, we will print on 2.63" x 1" standard Avery-brand labels, but it's the same procedure for other label sizes.

> **TIP**
> If you will be printing long lists of names to labels, create the list as a secondary merge file and merge them to the labels. See sections 2.3.6 to 2.3.16. Another good use for labels is for creating file folders with client information, case number, and so forth.

2.3.19 USING LABELS (WP5.1)

Step 1: Define paper size/type as a label

Just as we did for envelopes, you must first define the paper size/type as a label before you use it. There are a number of steps involved here, because you will have to edit the paper definition before you can use the labels.

1. Press [Shift][F8] (Format).
2. Press [2] for **P**age.
3. Press [7] for Paper **S**ize/Type.
4. At the "Format: Paper Size/Type" menu, press [2] for **A**dd, [4] for **L**abels. This step creates Labels as a new paper type for your printer to use.
5. At the "Format: Edit paper definition" menu screen, press [8] for Labels, [Y]. This step is critical because it takes you to the "Format: Labels" menu and ensures that WordPerfect treats the paper size as labels.
6. At the "Format: Labels" menu (see Figure 2-20), you will be presented with a number of options, including Label Size, Number of Labels, Distance Between Labels, etc. Because the labels we are using (2.63" x 1" with 30 to a page) are the default size, press [F7] (Exit) to accept. If you are using a different size label, you must enter its measurements manually. (This can be done with decimals or fractions—WordPerfect will convert the fractions to decimals automatically.) To help explain the options on the Labels menu, we will use as our example the Avery 5260 labels, which are standard 2.63 x 1" labels and come 30 to a page.

Label Size: Enter the height and width of the label you wish to use. You may type the measurements in fractions—WordPerfect will automatically convert them to decimals.

Avery 5260: 2.63" x 1"

Number of Labels: Tells WordPerfect the number of labels on a sheet, divided by columns and rows.

Avery 5260: 3 x 10

Top-Left Corner: This option tells WordPerfect where the top-left corner of the first label on the sheet of labels is located. Using this measurement, WordPerfect properly aligns the labels before printing. To find this measurement, you will need to measure from the top

---

TIP

If you normally use WordPerfect 4.2 columns and rows as Units of Measure, be sure to change to inches (the default) by pressing [Shift][F1], [3], [8] before defining Labels. This will make it much easier to find the proper measurements.

TIP

At the Format: Labels menu, you can press [F3] for context-sensitive Help at any of the specific menu options.

FIGURE 2-20

The Format: Labels screen in WordPerfect 5.1 allows for standard 2.63" X 1" labels, 30 to a sheet.

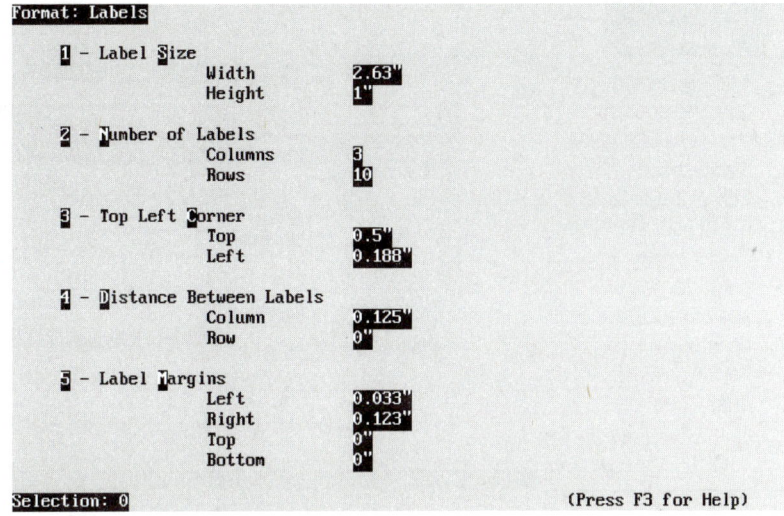

edge of the label sheet to the top edge of the first label and from the left edge of the sheet to the left edge of the first label.

Avery 5260: The top edge of the first label is .5" from the edge of the sheet, while the left edge is 3/16" (or .188").

If you are using tractor fed labels, the measurements should be 0", 0" and you should position the labels in the printer so that it prints on the first line of the top-left label.

Distance Between Labels: This consists of two measurements: distance between rows and distance between columns. Make sure the distance is measured between the edges of two labels.

Avery 5260: Distance between columns: $\frac{1}{8}$ or .125". Distance between rows: 0".

Label Margins: This option allows you to set the margins for each label individually. The default of .113" left and .113" right, 0" top and 0" bottom, is generally fine.

> ■ *WordPerfect treats each label as a separate or Virtual page. Therefore, you can apply codes to one label that will not affect other labels.*

7. Press [F7] to return to the Format: Paper Size/Type menu. Notice that a Labels paper definition now exists. Highlight the Labels paper size, then press [1] for **S**elect. Note that on the Format: Page menu, the paper type is now **Labels** and the Labels heading says "3 x 10." Press [F7] again to return to the editing screen.

TIP

WP5.1 Use the WordPerfect LABELS macro to automatically define the most commonly used Avery and 3M labels. See below for detailed instructions.

The [Paper Sz/Type: 8.5" X 11", 1 1/2" X 2 5/6", 2.63" X 1"] has been inserted. Also note that the position number on the status line reads: .0333". You are now ready to enter text onto these labels.

FIGURE 2-21

A screen is shown from the sophisticated LABELS.WPM macro that comes with WordPerfect 5.1. If your LABELS macro screen looks any different, you should request the updated version from WordPerfect Corp. The most recent 5.1 release is 3/9/92.

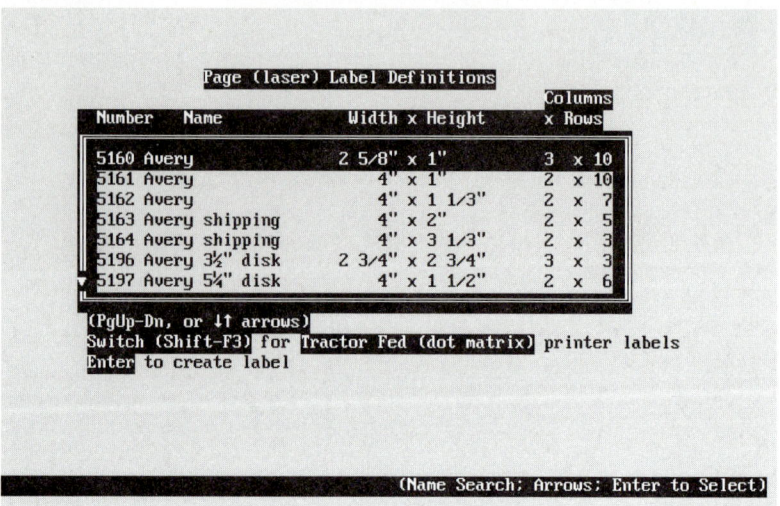

Step 2: Use the WordPerfect 5.1 Labels macro

WordPerfect 5.1 comes with a very sophisticated macro called LABELS.WPM that allows you to automatically define and use the most popular Avery and 3M labels on the market. To use the macro, make sure that it is located in the directory you specified in Location of Files in Setup ([Shift][F1], [6]) as the directory for all your macros and keyboard layouts. Then, follow these steps *(only in 9/25/91 and later releases)*:

1. Press [Alt][F10] (Macro), then type Labels at the "Macro:" prompt. Alternatively, if you are using our keyboard macros, press [Ctrl][M] for Macro Main Menu, [3] for Labels.

2. If you are using labels with a laser printer, highlight the label you wish to use and press [Enter] to create it. If you are using labels on a dot-matrix printer, press [Shift][F3] (Switch) to display the dot-matrix label choices.

3. At the "Location:" prompt, choose [1] for **C**ontinuous if you do not wish to be prompted to manually feed the printer the label paper before printing. Otherwise, choose [3] for **M**anual. Choose [2] for **B**in only if you are keeping labels in a separate bin on your laser printer.

■ *WordPerfect will notify you that it is creating the label. Then, if you are using a laser printer such as an HP Laserjet II or compatible, you will see the following error message: "Label Margins Increased due to Printer's Minimum Margin." Don't worry, this message simply means that WordPerfect had to make an adjustment to the label margins so that they would print properly. All laser printers have a small unprintable region, which is generally .25" from the edge of the paper. To compensate, WordPerfect increases one of the other label margins, and this change takes effect for all labels on a page.*

4. At the "Insert Label Definition in Document Initial Codes?" prompt, choose [Y] if you wish to define that document as the sheet of labels you've just chosen. If you choose [N], the document will not be defined as labels, but the definition will be added to your Format: Paper Size/Type menu so that you can select it later on as a paper size option.

▪ *If you decided to add the definition to the Document Initial Codes, notice that the line and position numbers on the status line have changed. If you Reveal Codes [F11] or [Alt][F3], the new margins are displayed on the ruler bar. You can access the initial codes screen of a document by pressing [Shift][F8], [3] for **D**ocument, [2] for Initial Codes.*

Entering addresses on the labels

TIP

If your text will not fit on one label, try using a smaller font if it is available on your printer. Alternatively, you can try changing the label margins. See above for details.

Now that the hard work of defining the labels is done, you are ready to type in the addresses you wish to print. Remember that WordPerfect treats each label as a *logical (separate) page* (as opposed to a physical page) and that WordPerfect numbers logical pages from left to right, starting from the top left of the page (like the flow of text in a book), as illustrated below.

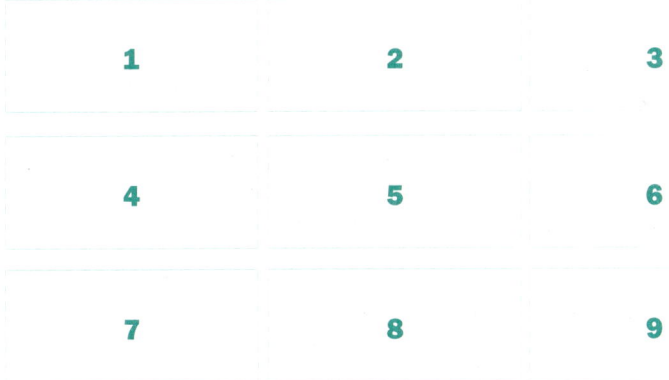

What follows are some useful tips when entering text:

Using [Ctrl][Enter] (Hard Page) to start a new label

WordPerfect will put in a soft page break after a certain number of lines, depending on the size of the label you are using. For example, if you are using the 2.63" X 1" label that we defined above, WordPerfect will put in a page break after every six lines to separate one label from another. If you wish to force the start of a new label, press [Ctrl][Enter] to enter a hard page break. You can also use [Ctrl][Enter] to leave a label blank (perhaps it has already been peeled off) or to start the text at a certain label. Remember that WordPerfect works from left to right, starting at the top left of the page.

Use secondary merge files when creating long lists of names

If you will be doing long lists of names, it is much better to create them as secondary merge files and then merge them onto a primary merge file defined as a label. That way, the list of names can be sorted and used for other types of merges, such as letters. The trick to creating a label as a primary merge file is to be sure *not* to have WordPerfect enter a soft page break. In other words, insert the proper merge codes but don't press [Enter] enough times to start a new label. The example in Figure 2-22 uses some of the fields that we created in the secondary merge file CLIENTS.SF created above. See sections 2.3.7 and 2.3.10 for more details.

Printing labels

The trick to printing labels properly is to pay close attention to the measurements that you entered when you defined the label. Because it takes some finessing to properly align labels, and because labels are generally more expensive than regular paper, test print on scrap paper

TIP

Use View Document ([Shift][F7], [6]) to view your work. In the edit mode, WordPerfect does not display the labels across the page, even though they may print three across. Be sure to save your work regularly. We recommend using the .LBL extension when naming documents defined as labels.

FIGURE 2-22

A sample primary merge file for labels shows that there is no soft page break.

```
{FIELD}First Name~ {FIELD}Last Name~¶
{FIELD}address~¶
{FIELD}city~, {FIELD}state~ {FIELD}zip~¶
```

Doc 2 Pg 1 Ln 0.415" Pos 0.033"

before printing to labels. What follows are some helpful tips when printing labels.

Use Print Preview to view labels before printing: The labels should look exactly as needed when printed. If you only see one label on an entire sheet of paper, you have not entered the Paper Size/Type code for the labels you are using. See "Step 1: Define paper size/type as a label," above, or rerun the LABELS.WPM macro. Use [1] for 100% magnification and [2] for 200% magnification if you need to check finer details.

Use the Print Multiple Pages option to print selected labels: Because each label is on its own logical page, you can specify which labels you want printed by pressing [Shift][F7], [5] for **Multiple Page**, and then entering the page numbers you want printed, separated by a comma. For example: 4, 8, 12, 25. If you wish to print a range of pages, use the hyphen. For example, to print from label 4 to 25, enter: 4-25.

> ■ *When printing different labels (logical pages), WordPerfect will print on a single physical page until that page is full. For example, if you have 1,000 labels and you wish to print both label 1 and label 1,000, they will both appear on the same sheet.*

TIP

Do yourself a favor—print some labels experimentally on scrap paper before printing on the more expensive labels themselves.

2.4 COMMAND REVIEW

Changing left/right margins

[Shift][F8], [1] for Line, [7] for Margins, type desired measurements. Press [F7].

Changing tab sets

[Shift][F8], [1] for Line, [8] for Tab Set. Enter the position of the new tab (or tabs) to be set and press [Enter], e.g., 3.3" [Enter]. To delete a tab, place your cursor on the tab and press [Del]. Press [F7].

Adding text attributes such as italics, bold, and underline

[Ctrl][F8], [2] for Appearance, [1] for bold, [2] for underline, [4] for italics, type text, [→] once.

If the text has already been entered, move to the beginning of the text, [F12] or [Alt][F4], block the text using the cursor keys, and [Ctrl][F8] and the appropriate attribute

Centering text vertically on a page

Go to the very top of the page; [Shift][F8], [2] for Page, [1] for Center Page, [Y]

Creating headers/footers

1. Move to the top of the first page on which you want to place the header or footer, [Shift][F8], [2] for Page, [3] for Headers, [4] for Footers
2. [1] for Header/Footer A, [2] for H/F B
3. [2] for Every Page, [3] for Odd Pages, [4] for Even
4. Type the text of the H/F, press [F7] twice to return to document

Editing headers/footers

1. [Shift][F8], [2] for Page, [3] or [4] for Header/Footer
2. [1] for H/F A, [2] for H/F B
3. [5] for Edit, [F7] twice to return to document

Deleting headers/footers

Find the Header/Footer code using Reveal Codes, [Alt][F3] or [F11]; delete it by backspacing over it or using the [Del] key

Suppressing headers/footers

Place your cursor at the top of the page on which you want the H/F suppressed. [Shift][F8], [2] for Page, [8] for Suppress ([9] in **WP5.0**). After selecting the desired option from the menu, press [F7]

Using Flush Right to position the date

[Alt][F6], enter the date

Using the Automatic Date feature

[Shift][F5], [1] for Date Text, [2] for Date Code

Using Open styles to automatically format your letterhead

1. Configure WordPerfect to use styles. [Shift][F1], [6] for Location of Files [7] (in **WP5.0**), [5] Style Files [6] (in **WP5.0**), enter appropriate directory and Library Filename, and press [Enter]

2. [Alt][F8], [3] for Create, [1] for Name, and type a name (e.g., C:\WP51\LIBRARY.STY) for the style; press [Enter]

3. [2] for Type, [2] for Open, [3] for Description. Enter an appropriate description

4. [4] for Codes and insert desired codes. Press [F7] several times to return to document

5. Use the new style by highlighting it in the Style menu and pressing [1] for On

Using the Advance feature to position text

[Shift][F8], [4], [1]. Choose appropriate menu option and input desired distance, i.e., [2] for Down, 2.5".

Using a document's formatting codes to create a style

1. Block the text containing the desired codes and include all the desired codes. [Alt][F8], [3] for Create

2. At the Styles: Edit screen, enter the appropriate information (i.e., name of style and description) and press [4] for Codes to see the formatting codes to be included in the style; edit them if necessary

3. Press [F7], [6] for Save

Creating a named macro using the Pause feature

1. [Ctrl][F10], give the macro a name, [Enter], type a description

2. Type the desired text. At the point the user is supposed to provide text, [Ctrl][PgUp], [1] for Pause

3. Press [Enter] to turn off the pause and continue inputting text

4. When finished, [Ctrl][F10] to end the macro definition

5. To play it back, [Alt][F10], type the macro name. When the macro pauses, type the desired text and press [Enter]

Editing a macro

[Ctrl][F10] and type macro name, [Enter], [2] for Edit [2] for Action in **WP5.0**). [F7] when finished editing macro

Creating a simple merge template using merge codes to prompt the user

[Shift][F9], [3] for Input. At "Enter Message:" type appropriate prompt, [Enter]; when finished, save template [F10]

WP5.0 [Shift][F9], [O] to insert ^O code (type prompt), [Shift][F9], [O] to insert closing ^O code. [Shift][F9], [C] to insert ^C

Using a simple merge template

[Ctrl][F9], [1] for Merge. At "Primary File:" type name of the template (including the entire path), at "Secondary File:" press [Enter]. Input text when prompted and [F9] to continue

Printing an address block on envelopes

1. [Shift][F8], [2] for Page
2. [7] for Paper Size [8] (in **WP5.0**)
3. Highlight Envelope—Wide, [1], [F7] ([5] for Envelope, [5] again in **WP5.0**)
4. Change left and right margins to 3.5" and 1"
5. Change top and bottom margins to 2" and .5"
6. Type address, then print

Performing a mass mailing using merge in WP5.1

1. Create secondary file. [Shift][F9], [6] for More, highlight {FIELD NAMES}, [Enter]
2. At "Enter Field 1:" type first field, [Enter]. Enter the other fields and press [Enter] each time. When finished with all the fields, [Enter] at a blank "Enter Field N:" prompt. Save
3. Type contents of each field followed by [F9]

4. When finished with first record, [Shift][F9], [2] for End Record

5. Do entire list this way and save file

6. Create primary merge file. Insert all appropriate formatting codes

7. Insert merge codes in appropriate places, [Shift][F9], [1] for Field and enter the field name. Do the same for all other fields. Save

8. Merge the two files. [Ctrl][F9], [1] for Merge. Type primary file name and secondary file names, [Enter]

Performing a mass mailing using merge in WP5.0

1. Create a secondary file. Type first name, last name, title, company, address, etc., each on a separate line, followed by [F9] each time

2. When finished with the record, [Shift][F9], [E]. Save file after all records are done this way

3. Create primary merge file. Insert all appropriate formatting codes

4. Insert merge codes in appropriate places, [Shift][F9], [F], followed by field number, e.g., [1] for First Name. Save

5. Merge the two files. [Ctrl][F9], [1] for Merge. Type primary and secondary file names, [Enter]

Sorting a secondary merge file before merging by last name

1. [Ctrl][F9], [2] for Sort

2. At "Input File to sort:" enter file name

3. At "Output File for sort:" [Enter] to print results to screen, or type name of a new file

4. [7] for Type, [1] for Merge

5. [6] for Order, [1] for Ascending

6. [3] for Keys

7. [A] for Alphanumeric

8. -1 to ensure that the sort occurs on last name

9. [1] for Perform action

Defining paper size/type as a label

1. [Shift][F8], [2] for Page
2. [7] for Paper Size/Type
3. [2] for Add, [4] for Labels
4. [8] for Labels, Yes
5. At Format: Labels menu, type appropriate label size

Assembling Contracts and Standard Legal Forms

FUNCTIONS USED

- Automatic paragraph numbering §3.1.2–3.1.5
- Keeping text together §3.1.6
- Using the Master Document feature for long documents §3.2.1–3.2.2
- Redlining and strikeout (blacklining) §3.2.3
- Document assembly using merge templates §3.2.4–3.2.6
- Generating a table of contents §3.2.7

HATFIELD, MCCOY & EARP
PARTNERSHIP AGREEMENT

THIS AGREEMENT OF GENERAL PARTNERSHIP entered into on November 11, 1992, by and among, Joseph Hatfield, Thomas McCoy and Wyatt Earp (hereinafter collectively referred to as "Partners" and individually as "Partner").

1. <u>Name and Purpose</u>. The Partnership shall be carried on under the name of Hatfield, McCoy & Earp (hereinafter referred to as "Partnership"). The Partnership has been formed for the purpose of operating a saloon. The Partnership may engage in any and all other activities as may be necessary, incidental or convenient to carry out the business of the Partnership as contemplated by this Agreement.

2. <u>Place of Business</u>. The principal office of the Partnership shall be located at 5 Dead Gulch Road, Dodge City, Kansas 34567, or at such other place as shall be agreed upon by a majority in interest of the Partners from time to time.

3. <u>Partners</u>. The name and address of each of the Partners are as follows:

Name	Address
Joseph Hatfield	258 West 4th Street Dodge City, Kansas 34567
Thomas McCoy	718 Adams Street Dodge City, Kansas 34567
Wyatt Earp	2 Willow Terrace Dodge City, Kansas 34567

4. <u>Consent to Operation</u>. The procedure for the operation of the Partnership shall be as follows:

(A) The day-to-day affairs of the Partnership shall be handled by the Managing Partner.

(B) The following actions shall require the vote and unanimous approval of all the Partners:

   (1) The purchasing and developing of new properties; and

   (2) The admission of new partners to the Partnership.

(C) All other actions taken by the Partnership, excluding those mentioned in subparagraphs (A) and (B) above, shall require the vote and approval of Partners owning a majority ~~in interest of the capital of~~ the Partnership.

"Listen, witness, it is extremely important that you tell us every single detail of the events that you observed last April 12th."

"But, your honor, that was 9 months ago!"

"That doesn't matter ... please proceed."

OVERVIEW

> [The Constitution] was framed upon the theory that the peoples of the several states must sink or swim together, and that in the long run prosperity and salvation are in union and not division.
> — Justice Benjamin Nathan Cardozo, Baldwin v. G.A.F. Seelig, Inc., 294 U.S. 511, 523 [1935]

Writing and assembling contracts and standard legal documents is the bread and butter of many law firms, small and large. Whether you are writing a standard will, assembling documents for real estate closings, or drafting detailed business contracts, WordPerfect has a battery of features that can be used to generate the paper work faster, more easily, and with less error. For law offices that specialize in an area of the law such as real estate that lends itself to the constant reuse of standard boilerplate text, the greatly enhanced merge features of WordPerfect 5.1 will be greatly appreciated. This chapter will discuss the functions that are most commonly used when writing contracts and legal forms, including those that enable you to create and use a simple document assembly system with templates. But before we go into the specifics of using different functions, let's briefly discuss some basic rules to keep in mind when preparing clauses. Sticking to these rules will make it easier for your firm to get the most out of Word-Perfect's features.

Basic skills

- Auto paragraph numbering

- Block protect
- Conditional end of page
- Widow/orphan protection
- Hard hyphens/spaces

Intermediate skills

- Using the Master Document feature
- Using the Document Compare feature

Advanced skills

- Document assembly using merge templates
- Generation of a table of contents

3.1 BASIC WORDPERFECT CONTRACT ASSEMBLY SKILLS

3.1.1 BASIC CLAUSE PREPARATION TIPS

SOFTWARE

West's Express Forms contain dozens of high quality forms on disk that currently cover consumer bankruptcy law and California litigation, and are drafted by nationally recognized authors. For more information on Express Forms, please call 1-800-328-9352.

- Give each clause a number, using the automatic numbering feature of WordPerfect. You should have several macros to quickly insert automatic numbers. (Or use the macros that come with this book and are reproduced in Appendix C.)
- Give each clause a short title that is part of the clause. This short title can then be used in a table of contents or as part of a synopsis clause.
- Try to limit each numbered clause to one function or idea. This makes it easier to create interchangeable clauses.
- Try to be gender neutral and try to eliminate singular/plural problems. Again, this makes your clauses more interchangeable.
- Use Schedules to list the major variables (i.e., text that changes from document to document, such as the names of parties).

3.1.2 AUTOMATIC PARAGRAPH NUMBERING

Like many of the features that we cover in this book, automatic paragraph numbering is one of those options that can save a lot of time and reduce tedium if used properly. Many, if not most, legal forms and contracts use some kind of numbering system to label clauses and articles. Before WordPerfect's automatic paragraph numbering feature was incorporated, every time a number was deleted or changed, all the numbers had to be adjusted manually. But with automatic numbering, if you delete one number, all others will renumber accordingly. If you add another automatic number, all the others will renumber correctly. Think what a time-saver that can be with long contracts!

SHAREWARE

The AUTONUM.EXE file, available as shareware on the supplementary disks, is a stand-alone program that converts paragraph, section, and article numbers to WordPerfect automatic paragraph numbering codes.

WE promised you an opportunity to meet Sarah Holmes. Sarah is a very capable corporate attorney, although she believes in a life outside of the office. If truth be told, she doesn't really have the time or inclination to learn any more than the basics of WordPerfect on her own—in fact, she likes to get out of the office no later than 6:00 p.m. if she can.

Greta, a computer-literate friend of Sarah's, arrives just in the nick of time, because Sarah is in the process of putting together the first draft of a major contract for one of the firm's biggest clients. The contract will consist of many different clauses drafted by various associates at the firm that must all be numbered. It goes without saying that many of the clauses will either be deleted or moved during the drafting process. Fortunately, the paragraph numbering feature will automatically insert and adjust paragraph numbers up to eight levels deep. And, as with the outline feature, you can choose from different paragraph number styles, including a legal style (such as the one used in this book).

Greta wastes no time in informing Sarah of the pertinence of this feature for the task at hand and shows her how to go about using it.

Paragraph numbering versus outlining

Because WordPerfect's Outline feature and automatic Paragraph numbering feature are defined on the same screen and use the same codes ([Par Num] and [Par Num Def]), it can be easy to confuse the two. When you use the Outline function, the numbers (actually, a [Par Num:Auto] code) are inserted automatically every time you press [Enter] and will automatically change each time the [Tab] key is pressed. In other words, the Outline feature inserts the number and decides on the level according to tab levels (first, second, and so on). By contrast, Paragraph numbering lets you place a number anywhere you want, at any level you want.

For example, in the following illustration, Paragraph numbering allows you to make the 3 after ARTICLE a level 1 number and the 3.1 that numbers the first clause a level 2 number, even though 3 is centered on the page and is therefore several tab stops in from the left relative to 3.1.

> ARTICLE 3
>
> Allocation of Profit or Loss; Distributions
>
> 3.1 <u>Profit or loss.</u> Profit, loss and investment tax credits for each fiscal period of the partnership shall be allocated among the partners as follows:

SHAREWARE

The CLX.ZIP file, available as shareware on the supplementary disks, is a clause cross referencer for WordPerfect 5.1. It analyzes a document, identifies clause numbers, and produces a report listing references in the text to the clause numbers.

What this means to the practicing attorney/legal secretary is that you should only use the Paragraph numbering feature, not the Outline feature, when writing contracts and forms. As its name implies, the Paragraph numbering feature is much more suited to numbering paragraphs because of its flexibility. Stick with using the Outline feature for outlining ideas. (For an example of how to use the Outline feature, see Chapter 5.)

Defining an automatic numbering style

WordPerfect comes with a number of predefined numbering styles, including an Outline style (the default), a Paragraph style, and a Legal style. Each style can be up to eight levels deep. If these styles don't conform to your practice, WordPerfect allows you to create your own numbering style. See Figure 3-1.

1. Press [Shift][F5] (Date/Outline).
2. Choose [6] to Define outline numbering.
3. Choose [2] for Paragraph, [3] for Outline, [4] for Legal, etc. (Note that Current Definition changes to reflect the style you've chosen.
4. Press [7] (Exit) to return to the (Date/Outline) menu options.

FIGURE 3-1

The Paragraph Number Definition screen is shown. By looking at Current Definition you can see that the Outline style has been chosen.

```
Paragraph Number Definition

1 - Starting Paragraph Number              1
    (in legal style)
                                      Levels
                           1    2    3    4    5    6    7    8
2 - Paragraph              1.   a.   i.   (1)  (a)  (i)  1)   a)
3 - Outline                I.   A.   1.   a.   (1)  (a)  i)   a)
4 - Legal (1.1.1)          1    .1   .1   .1   .1   .1   .1   .1
5 - Bullets                •    o    -    ■    *    +    ·    x
6 - User-defined

Current Definition         I.   A.   1.   a.   (1)  (a)  i)   a)
Attach Previous Level      No   No   No   No   No   No   No   No

7 - Enter Inserts Paragraph Number         Yes

8 - Automatically Adjust to Current Level  Yes

9 - Outline Style Name

Selection: 0
```

When you use a paragraph numbering style other than the default style (e.g., legal), WordPerfect inserts a [Par Num Def:] code first. This allows you to use as many paragraph numbering styles as you wish in a document. If you want to change the numbering style back to the default style, simply delete the [Par Num Def:] code.

3.1.3 PARAGRAPH AND OUTLINE NUMBERING OPTIONS

Starting paragraph number (in legal style)

This option lets you manually override the next paragraph or outline number in the document. In other words, if the next automatic paragraph number would normally be 5, but you want it to return to 1, type 1 here. Always enter your new starting paragraph number in legal style (e.g., 1, 1.2, etc.), even if you are using another style. This option can be particularly useful if you are drafting a contract and you want the numbers in each clause to start from the beginning.

WP5.1

Attach Previous Level: This is the default only for the legal style. For example:

1   Level 1

    1.1   Level 2 (attached to previous level)

        1.1.1   Level 3 (attached to level 2)

> **TIP**
>
> If you need to change the position of the levels for the paragraph numbers, you must change the tab settings. Press [Shift][F8] (Format), [1] for Line, [8] for Tab Set to get to the Tab Set screen, or use the Tab Set macro that comes with this book.

However, you can change this for any style you choose (or one you custom create by selecting the User-defined option) by doing the following:

1. After choosing one of the Paragraph numbering styles, press [6] for User-Defined. (The cursor will jump down to the Current Definition line and a list of options will appear at the bottom of the screen.)
2. Press [Tab] to move to the second number of the definition, press [↓], then [Y] or [N]. Repeat these steps for the remainder of the levels.

■ *In **WP5.0** you don't have nearly this kind of flexibility. You may only select the default legal style and you may not alter it in the manner described in the previous steps.*

Enter Inserts Paragraph Number: Pertains only to the Outline feature.

Automatically Adjust to Current Level: Pertains only to the Outline feature.

> **TIP**
>
> To quickly insert automatic paragraph numbers, define either an [Alt] or a [Ctrl] key macro (available only as a keyboard layout macro) to quickly repeat the above steps. (If you need to learn how to define a macro, refer to chapters 1 and 2.).

3.1.4 USING PARAGRAPH NUMBERING

WordPerfect has two types of numbering options: fixed and automatic. Automatic numbers are based on the tab stop your cursor is on (each tab stop is considered a level), and change automatically each time you press [Tab] or [F4] (Indent). Fixed numbers keep the same appearance regardless of the tab stop. Fixed numbers are the most flexible because different numbering styles can be used regardless of the position of the cursor in the document. (See the exercise below for an example of this.)

1. Move the cursor to where you wish the paragraph number to appear. (Use the [Tab] key, if you wish to place the number one or more levels in.)
2. Press [Shift][F5] (Date/Outline).
3. Choose [5] for **P**ara Num.
4. At the "Paragraph Level (Press Enter for Automatic):" prompt, press [Enter] if you want WordPerfect to insert an automatic paragraph number, or type the level (1 through 8) if you wish to use a fixed number style.

EXERCISE: CREATING A USER-DEFINED LEGAL PARAGRAPH NUMBERING STYLE

Sarah's firm does not use the default WordPerfect legal style for numbering its contracts. Rather, it has a four-level style broken down as follows:

Level 1: Articles use a digit with no trailing period.

Level 2: Paragraphs use a digit with a trailing period that is attached to the previous level (i.e., the number of the article).

Level 3: Subparagraphs use an uppercase letter enclosed in parentheses that is not attached to the previous level.

Level 4: Sub-sub paragraphs use a lowercase Roman number enclosed in parentheses that is not attached to the previous level.

The style looks like this:

ARTICLE 1
1.1
   (A)
      (i)

For this lesson, you will create the above user-defined style and then apply it to the sample Agreement of Limited Partnership.

Step 1: Create a user-defined style

1. Input the text in the Agreement below. Press [Home], [Home], [↑] to move the cursor to the beginning of the document.

2. Press [Shift][F5] (Date/Outline).

3. Choose [6] to **D**efine outline numbering.

4. Press [6] for **U**ser-defined, then enter the definitions for the first four levels of the numbering style as shown in Figure 3-2. Make sure that Level 2 is attached to the previous level but that the other levels are not.

If you Reveal Codes, you should see the [Par Num Def] code at the beginning of your document.

5. When finished, press [F7] three times to return to the edit mode.

Step 2: Enter paragraph numbers

1. Move the cursor one space past the word ARTICLE and press [Shift][F5]. At the "Paragraph Level:" prompt, type [1] and press [Enter].

2. Move the cursor to the beginning of the title for the first clause of article 1 (Restrictions...) (making sure, with Reveal Codes on, that your cursor is on the [UND] code) and press [Shift][F5], [5]. At the "Paragraph Level:" prompt, type [2] and press [Enter]. (You may put a space or two in after.)

3. Use the above steps to place automatic paragraph numbering for levels 3 and 4.

In the paragraph beginning "Without the Consent . . ." press [Tab] after inserting the automatic number.

In the last two paragraphs, after placing the automatic paragraph number, press [Tab] then [Home][←], then [F4] to achieve the same format.

The completed exercise should look like the numbered document that follows.

"**T**HAT wasn't so bad, Sarah, now was it?" asks Greta. "You've been a real trooper so far, and I'm going to reward you for your attentiveness by showing you a great little feature that few users of WordPerfect 5.1 are aware of. It's the Outline Style feature, which is related to the automatic Paragraph numbering feature you've just learned. You may

Sample Clause for Exercise Without Paragraph Numbers

AGREEMENT OF LIMITED PARTNERSHIP
OF
NAME, L.P.

THIS AGREEMENT OF LIMITED PARTNERSHIP dated as of this evidences the mutual agreement of the General Partners....

ARTICLE
Rights, Powers and Duties of General Partners and Designation of Tax Matters Partner

<u>Restrictions on Authority of the General Partners</u>.

Without the Consent of the Limited Partner, the General Partners shall not have the authority to:

sell, exchange, lease, mortgage, pledge, or transfer all or substantially all of the assets of the Partnership other than in the ordinary course of business;

incur indebtedness by the Partnership other than in the ordinary course of business; or

---

find it a useful alternative for numbering contract clauses, and it's very handy for creating outlines of your ideas when you're in the initial drafting stage.

Sample Clause with Automatic Paragraph Numbers Inserted

AGREEMENT OF LIMITED PARTNERSHIP
OF
NAME, L.P.

THIS AGREEMENT OF LIMITED PARTNERSHIP dated as of this evidences the mutual agreement of the General Partners ...

ARTICLE 1
Rights, Powers and Duties of General Partners and Designation of Tax Matters Partner

1.1 <u>Restrictions on Authority of the General Partners</u>.

(A) Without the Consent of the Limited Partner, the General Partners shall not have the authority to:

(i) sell, exchange, lease, mortgage, pledge, or transfer all or substantially all of the assets of the Partnership other than in the ordinary course of business;

(ii) incur indebtedness by the Partnership other than in the ordinary course of business; or

3.1.5 THE OUTLINE STYLE FEATURE

This feature, new to WordPerfect 5.1, allows you to format each outline level individually in a style, so you don't have to manually enter the same formatting codes each time. Once you create your Outline Style, all you have to do is select it and the rest is automatic.

For instance, let's say that you wanted the number in the first level of a particular automatic numbering style you use frequently to be bolded and the text following that number to be indented, like this:

> I. **This is the first level of a frequently used automatic numbering style. The first level is bolded and at the left margin, and the text is indented at the first tab stop.**

And you want the second level of the outline to look like this:

> A. This is the second level of the outline. The text on the first line begins at the second tab stop, and the rest of the text is indented at the second tab stop.

Now imagine a few more levels in this particular outline requiring a variety of other formatting codes: you get the picture. Using the Outline Style feature requires you to input these codes but once. You can then apply this style to the beginning of any document and the outline you produce will comprise this format. You can also easily edit any of the styles you produce in this fashion. Let's see how this works.

Government implies the power of making laws. It is essential to the idea of a law, that it be attended with a sanction; or, in other words, a penalty or punishment for disobedience.

*Alexander Hamilton
The Federalist
[1787–1788]*

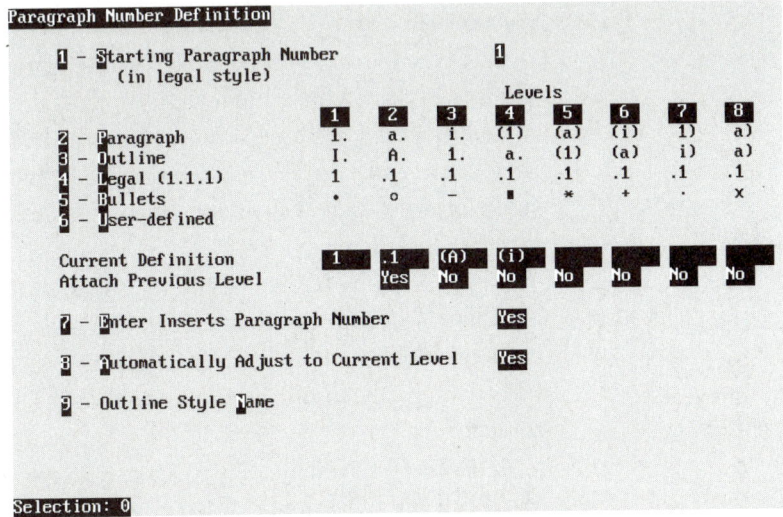

FIGURE 3-2

A user-defined style of four levels, with the second level attached to the first.

FIGURE 3-3

The Outline Styles menu is shown before any styles have been created. You will probably see WordPerfect's default Outline Style.

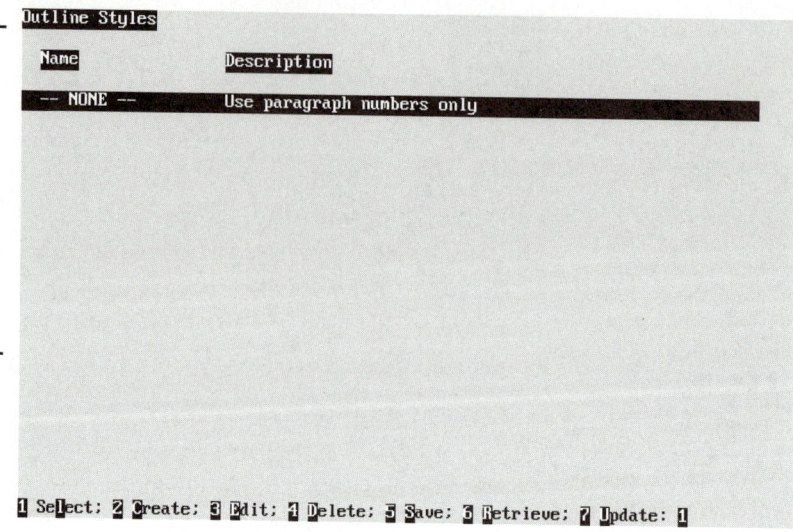

By the way, you might well want to look at Chapter 2 for a complete discussion of how to use WordPerfect styles to automatically insert formatting codes. Although there's more than a little to learn about this feature, it is, for the most part (as you'll see), pretty straightforward. Once you learn how to implement this tool, you'll find that it can really cut down on the amount of work you'll have to do to format a variety of documents, including long contracts.

OK, enough verbal meandering; let's give you a practical example. We're going to produce a three-level Outline Style, we'll save it to your default Style Library, and then we'll show you how to apply it to a newly created document.

1. Press [Shift][F5] to access the Date/Outline menu and choose [6] for **D**efine. We're going to use the default Outline style here, i.e., I., A., 1., a., etc., but remember—you can choose any of them or create your own.

2. Press [9] for Outline Style **N**ame. You'll find yourself in the Outline Styles menu, which will look something like Figure 3-3.

You may very well see some styles already there: in all likelihood, they came with WordPerfect and exist in the Style Library, which (unbeknownst to you) you are probably using. We'll talk about that library a little later.

3. Press [2] for **C**reate. You'll see the menu shown in Figure 3-4.

This is where you actually create the style. You'll see eight levels, each of which can be formatted separately, although you needn't format them all. In our example, we'll only be dealing with the first three levels.

4. Press [1] for **N**ame. Try to make it easily identifiable if possible. We'll call ours "Example" for this example. Press [Enter]. You may, if

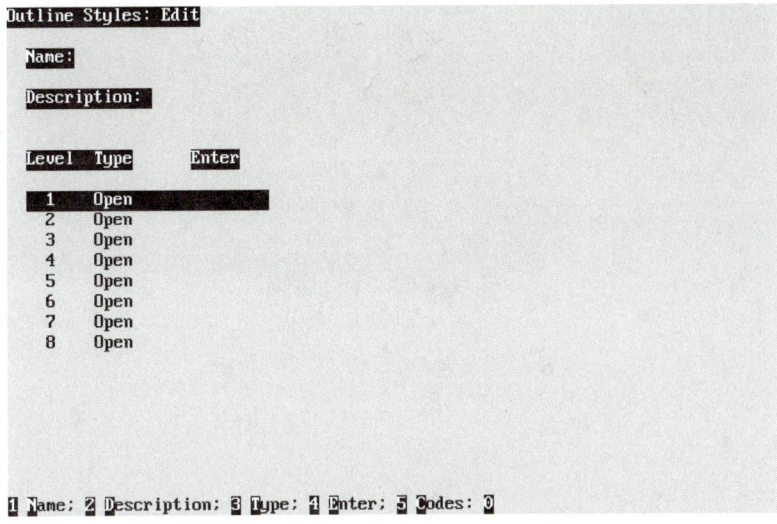

FIGURE 3-4

The Outline Styles: Edit menu is shown before the Outline Style has been named. The next step is to enter the format codes for each desired level.

you like, also opt to give your style a description to make it even easier to identify. Press [2] for **D**escription if you so choose. Press [Enter] again.

5. You'll notice (if you look under the Type heading) that all the Outline levels are "Open." They can also be Paired, but we're not going to explore that option here, because it can make matters somewhat more complicated. Again, if you want to learn about Paired Styles vs. Open Styles, consult Chapter 2. We can assure you that you'll be able to create Outline Styles that are more than adequate for your needs, using only Open Styles.

6. Now we're ready to do some formatting. Instead of bolding the number, as in the example above, we're going to put a Decimal Tab in front of the number so the Roman numerals will all right-align on the decimal. Press [5] for **C**odes. Press [Ctrl][F6] to insert the [DEC TAB] code. Move your cursor past the [ParNum:1] code and press [F4] to indent the text. Your screen should look like Figure 3-5.

Press [F7] and move your cursor down to the second level. Press [5] for **C**odes again. You'll see an A. and a [ParNum:2] code in the bottom half of the screen. Remember, A. is the second level of the default Outline style that we chose in step 1.

▪ *You can place any number level code in any of the levels in this screen. Delete the number code already there, press [Shift][F5], choose [5] for Para Num, and type the level you desire. The corresponding number for that level will appear at the top of the screen.*

7. Let's enter the codes for level 2. Press [F4] to indent this level. Now move your cursor to the right once and place a [Tab] after the number. Press [F7] to exit. One more level to go.

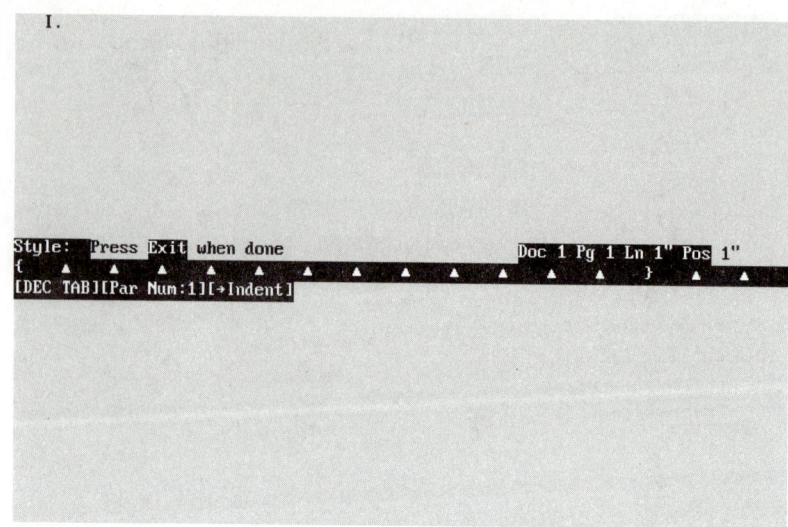

FIGURE 3-5

The format codes are shown for the first level of our Outline Style.

8. In this last level (level 3), we're first going to insert two indent codes in front of the number. (You can do that now.) Next we're going to bold the number. Press [F6] to turn on bold and then press [→] once to move the cursor past the number and press [F6] again to turn off bold. (We don't want the text to be bolded.) Finally, press [F4] to indent the text. Press [F7] twice. You should now be in the Outline Styles menu again. See Figure 3-6.

9. At this point we're going to save this style so that it can be used in the future. Press [5] to **S**ave and type the name of your Library file name at the "Filename:" prompt. It will probably be LIBRARY.STY. (You can check this by pressing [Shift][F1], [6] for **L**ocation of files, and checking **S**tyle Files: Library Filename).

Now let's see how our Example Style looks.

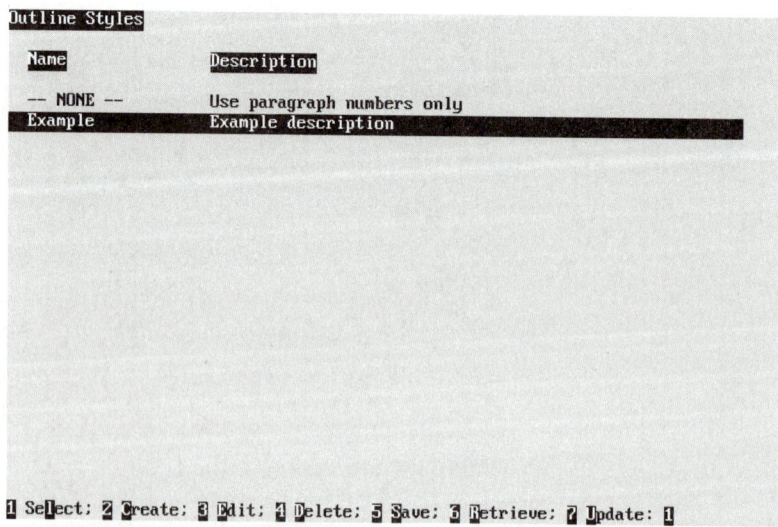

FIGURE 3-6

The Outline Style menu is again shown with our newly created "Example" Outline Style.

1. Press [1] to Select the Style. You should now be in the Paragraph Number Definition screen. Note that the Outline Style **N**ame is "Example." Press [Enter].

2. Press [4] for **O**utline and [1] for On. "Outline" should appear in the bottom left-hand area of your screen, indicating that Outline is on.

3. Press [Enter]. The Roman numeral I. appears at the first tab stop, because we placed a Decimal Tab in front of it in the first-level style. Type a couple of lines of text and press [Enter] twice. See how the Roman numeral II. aligns itself with the Roman numeral I. at the decimal. Type a few more lines and press [Enter] twice again. The same thing happens.

4. Press [Enter] twice again and press [Tab]. The second level goes into effect. Type a line or two of text. Notice how it indents on the second (and subsequent lines) at the first tab stop.

5. Press [Enter] twice again and press [Tab] once more. There's the third level with our bolded number at the second tab stop.

Turn on Reveal Codes.

Cautious, careful people, always casting about to preserve their reputation and social standing, never can bring about a reform. Those who are really in earnest must be willing to be anything or nothing in the world's estimation.
— Susan Brownell Anthony
On the campaign for divorce law reform
[1860]

▼▲▼▲▼▲▼▲▼▲▼▲▼▲▼▲▼▲▼▲▼▲▼▲

Place your cursor on the first style code. You will see [Outline Lvl 1 Open Style;[DEC TAB][Par Num:1][Indent]. This code is chock full of information. It's telling you that you're looking at an Outline Level 1, which is an Open Style with the following codes: a Decimal Tab, a first-level number, and an indent. Place your cursor on a second-level number and take a look. There are the format codes for Level 2.

3.1.6 HOW TO KEEP TEXT TOGETHER: BLOCK PROTECT, WIDOW/ORPHAN PROTECTION, AND CONDITIONAL END OF PAGE

"**S**ARAH, when writing contracts, you're often going to want to keep certain text together," says Greta. "For example, you want to keep the title of a clause and the first two lines of text together, as in the following example:"

ARTICLE 1

Restrictions on Authority of the General Partners.
Without the Consent of the Limited Partner, the
General Partners shall not have the authority to...

Greta continues: "WordPerfect has two different options you can use to ensure that the title and several lines of text following it stay together through thick and thin."

Block Protect: Block Protect is used to ensure that a block of text does not get separated by a page break. (Widow/Orphan does not solve this problem because Article 1 is separated from the text by a blank line.) To invoke Block Protect, block out the entire text you wish to remain together using [Alt][F4] or [F12], press [Shift][F8], then [Y] at the "Protect Block?" prompt.

The [Block Pro: On] and [Block Pro: Off] have been inserted.

Conditional End of Page: The difference between Conditional End of Page and Block Protect is that the Conditional End of Page function protects a specific number of lines while Block Protect protects a block of text. Block Protect is easier to use, because you can see the text you wish to protect and it does not require as many keystrokes. (Conditional End of Page must be done from a menu.) To determine which function is better to use, decide whether it is important to keep certain lines together (as with our sample heading and text above) or whether the block must be kept together regardless of the amount of text added or deleted.

1. Count the number of lines to be protected before entering the menu (you won't be able to see the text once you are in the menu), then position the cursor on the line just above the section of lines you wish to keep together.

2. Press [Shift][F8] (Format), [4] for **O**ther, [2] for **C**onditional End of Page.

3. At the "Number of Lines to Keep Together:" prompt, enter the number of lines, including any blank spacing caused by double spacing.

■ *If the protected lines fall near the end of a page, the page break will occur just after the [Cndl EOP:n] code and right before the protected lines.*

4. Press [F7] to return to the document.

Widow/Orphan Protection: This colorful term comes from typography. An *Orphan* is the first line of a paragraph that is alone at the bottom of the page, a *Widow* the last line of a paragraph when alone at the top of the page. If you place a Widow/Orphan code [W/O On] code at the beginning of a document, WordPerfect can put a page break one line earlier or later than the default, which is normally 54 lines per page.

In the new code of laws which I suppose it will be necessary for you to make, I desire you would remember the ladies and be more generous and favorable to them than your ancestors. Do not put such unlimited power into the hands of the husbands. Remember, all men would be tyrants if they could. If particular care and attention is not paid to the ladies, we are determined to foment a rebellion, and will not hold ourselves bound by any laws in which we have no voice or representation.

Abigail Adams
Letter to John Adams [March 31, 1776]

■ *This does not work to ensure that headings and text remain together, unlike the Block Protect and Conditional End of Page features.*

1. Press [Shift][F8] (Format), [1] for Line, [9] for Widow/Orphan, then [Y].
2. Press [F7] to return to your document.

Hard hyphens/spaces

Hard hyphens and hard spaces are used to keep words together. For example, if you've turned on WordPerfect's auto hyphenation feature, a word such as Co-stipulator might get broken at the hyphen if only "Co-" would fit at the end of a line. To make sure hyphenated words always stay together, press [Home], [-] instead of just the [-].

The hard hyphen will appear as a regular hyphen: -. The regular hyphen will look like this [-] in Reveal Codes.

For words such as New Jersey that you wish to keep together, press [Home], [Spacebar] instead of just [Spacebar] to insert a hard space. The hard space will look like this in Reveal Codes: [ ].

3.2 INTERMEDIATE WORDPERFECT CONTRACT ASSEMBLY SKILLS

3.2.1 USING THE MASTER DOCUMENT FEATURE

SOFTWARE

West's Express Forms contain dozens of high-quality forms on disk. Currently available are consumer bankruptcy and California litigation forms, including pleadings and jury instructions. For more information on Express Forms, call 1-800-328-9352.

Large, complex contracts consist of many different clauses, a number of which might be drafted by various lawyers in a firm. In other words, the final draft of the contract can be conceptualized as the skeleton document composed of many smaller files. This is the idea behind the Master Document feature. When you are working on a large project consisting of many smaller files, the Master Document ties all the files and subdocuments together. You can then create tables of contents, tables of authorities, and indexes for all the separate files as if they were one.

The Master Document feature is also a good way to assemble boilerplate forms from different standard clauses. With this technique, you could convert your favorite clauses into subdocuments that could then be dropped into different master documents at will. This method works well as long as you have on hand a good record of the file names of your different clauses. However, it is our opinion that the Master Document feature is only worthwhile when used on long, complex contracts with many clauses. If your contracts are generally just several pages, a better way to automate them is to create a simple document assembly system using merge templates. (See Section 3.2.4.)

What is a master document? A master document contains two types of files: a master document and subdocuments. A master document might contain a title page, a page numbering code, and a formatting code. The subdocument(s) contain the text, such as commonly used boilerplate clauses. When not expanded, the subdocument appears as a code in the master document, saving memory and disk space. By using this function, a 50-page contract composed of 100 different clauses that are each stored as a separate file will only take up a few pages when not expanded. When the master document is expanded, the text is formatted according to whatever codes are present in both the master document and subdocuments.

The codes that enter and number graphics, footnotes, pages, and paragraphs can be entered in either the master document or the subdocument. However, it is often best to put formatting codes such as margins, fonts, paragraph number definitions, etc., in the master document, not in the subdocuments. This ensures that the subdocuments will be consistently formatted when expanded.

> *Res iudicata pro veritate habetur [A matter which has been legally decided is considered true].*
> — Anonymous, Latin legal maxim

SARAH listens patiently to Greta's discussion of the advantages of the Master Document feature and reluctantly realizes that it could become a good way of automating the creation of the firm's contracts. Nonetheless, she feels obligated to put up a bit of a struggle.

"This seems so difficult," she laments.

"Nonsense, this isn't rocket science," says Greta. "You're more than capable of learning this stuff in an hour or two, and when you start using it regularly it will become second nature to you."

After a little more half-hearted kvetching, Sarah recovers her professional demeanor and decides to get down to business.

> **SHAREWARE**
>
> The DOC.EXE file, available as freeware on the supplementary disks, is a document assembly macro for creating master documents and subdocuments.

3.2.2 CREATING A CONTRACT AS A MASTER DOCUMENT

For this exercise, we'll have Sarah and you input a small part of a contract, AGREEMENT.FRM, create subdocuments from its different clauses, then create a new master document using the subdocuments you have created. Finally, we'll show you how to expand and contract a master document.

Creating subdocuments

Any amount of text can be used as a subdocument. The text can come from previously existing WordPerfect files or from new files. Furthermore, there is no limit to the number of subdocuments you can include in a master document (short of disk space, that is!).

1. Input the following:

```
            AGREEMENT OF LIMITED PARTNERSHIP
                           OF
                       LTD PARTNER
```

```
THIS AGREEMENT OF LIMITED PARTNERSHIP dated as of
this DATE evidences the mutual agreement of the Gen-
eral Partners, FIRST PARTY and SECOND PARTY, and LIM-
ITED PARTNER as the limited partner ("Limited Part-
ner"), to join together in a limited partnership,
under and governed by the provisions of the laws of
PRTNSP STATE as contained in the Revised Code, for
the purposes and upon the terms and conditions set
forth below.
```

```
                          ARTICLE 1
                         Organization
```

```
1.1 Formation of Limited Partnership. The Partner-
ship shall commence on ORDINAL DATE and shall con-
tinue without interruption as a limited partnership
pursuant to the governing regulations for partner-
ships under the laws of the state of PRTNSP STATE.
```

```
1.2 Name. The name of the Partnership shall be LTD
PARTNER ("Partnership"). However, the business of
the Partnership may be conducted, upon compliance
with all applicable laws, under any other name desig-
```

> nated in writing by the General Partners to the Limited Partner.
>
> 1.3 <u>Principal Place of Business</u>. The Partnership's principal place of business shall be PRTNRSHP ADD, PRTNRSP CITY, PRTNSP STATE PRTNRSHP ZIP, or such other place as the General Partners may from time to time designate in writing to Limited Partner. The Partnership may maintain other offices at such other places as the General Partners deem advisable.

This form consists of an introductory section and three separate clauses. The introduction and the three clauses will be turned into subdocuments.

2. Turn on the Block feature by pressing [Alt][F4] or [F12], then block out the introductory section up to clause 1.

3. Press [F10] to save, and at the "block name:" prompt, type: `introduc.sub`.

> ■ *The "block name:" is actually a DOS file name. Therefore, it is limited to eight characters and a three-character extension.*

4. Repeat the above steps for each numbered clause in the contract. You may wish to identify each subdocument by its title (e.g., *Formation of Limited Partnership* might be named FORMLIMP.SUB). When finished, you should have a total of four subdocuments.

5. Clear the screen without saving.

> ■ *The above steps show how to save discrete clauses as subdocuments. However, any WordPerfect file can be a subdocument.*

Creating the master document

A master document is made up of subdocuments plus any formatting and other codes you have inserted. Some examples of codes you could put in your master document include page numbering, margins, automatic Paragraph numbering styles, etc. You would also put the title in the master document.

1. Press [Alt][F5] (Mark Text).
2. Choose [2] for **Subdoc**.
3. At the "Subdoc Filename:" prompt at the bottom of the page, enter the *exact* DOS file name (not the Long Document Name!) of the subdocument to be inserted into the master document. For example, type `introduc.sub` to retrieve the introductory clause subdocu-

---

TIP

Use the automatic Paragraph numbering feature to number the paragraphs or clauses in subdocuments. That way, when you delete or move the position of the suddocument, the paragraphs will renumber themselves automatically when the master document is expanded.

TIP

If you use the Master Document feature while assembling a contract that will contain automatic paragraph numbers, insert the appropriate [Par Num Def:] code at the beginning of the master document. All of the automatic paragraph numbers in the separate subdocuments will then conform to this numbering style, as long as another [Par Num Def:] code has not been inserted in one of the subdocuments.

FIGURE 3-7

The subdocument INTRODUC.SUB is inserted into the master document.

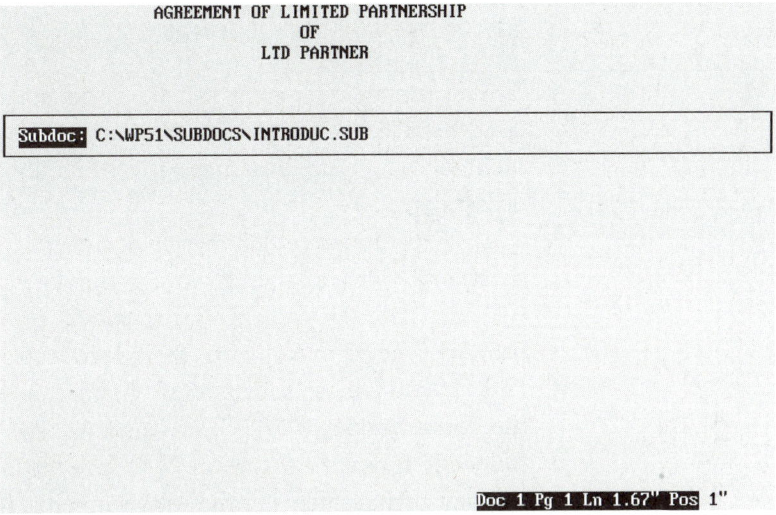

```
              AGREEMENT OF LIMITED PARTNERSHIP
                            OF
                        LTD PARTNER

  Subdoc:  C:\WP51\SUBDOCS\INTRODUC.SUB




                                          Doc 1 Pg 1 Ln 1.67" Pos 1"
```

ment you created above. You should see a screen like Figure 3-7 to indicate that a subdocument has been inserted.

■ *Be sure to give the entire path name if the document is in another directory. For example, if you keep all your clauses in a directory called C:\WP51\SUBDOCS and you are currently in another directory, you would type* `c:\wp51\subdocs\introduc.sub`.

4. Repeat the above steps until all subdocuments have been inserted in the master document. Your master document should look something like Figure 3-8.

FIGURE 3-8

The master document is shown with four subdocuments inserted. Note that the entire path for each has been included.

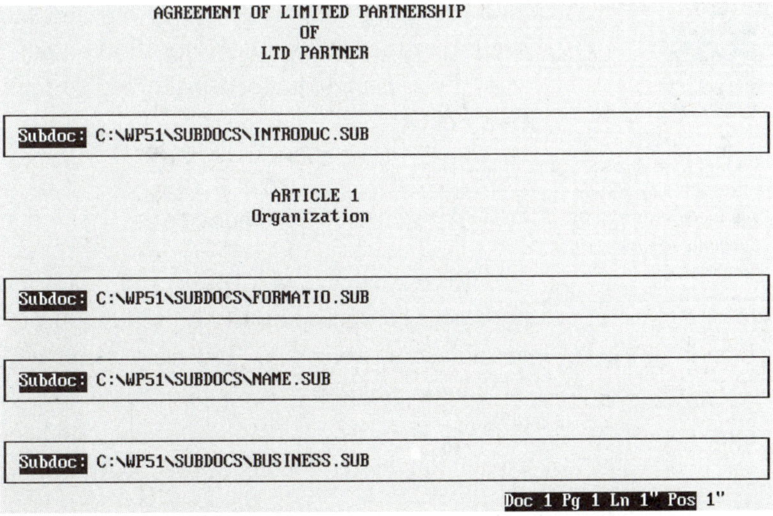

```
              AGREEMENT OF LIMITED PARTNERSHIP
                            OF
                        LTD PARTNER

  Subdoc:  C:\WP51\SUBDOCS\INTRODUC.SUB

                         ARTICLE 1
                        Organization

  Subdoc:  C:\WP51\SUBDOCS\FORMATIO.SUB

  Subdoc:  C:\WP51\SUBDOCS\NAME.SUB

  Subdoc:  C:\WP51\SUBDOCS\BUSINESS.SUB
                                          Doc 1 Pg 1 Ln 1" Pos 1"
```

Saving the master document

The master document can be saved in either the expanded or condensed version. However, because the expanded master document takes up more disk space, it is generally preferable to condense it first.

1. With the expanded master document on the screen, press [F7] (Exit) or [F10] (Save), then [Y] to save the document.

2. At the "Document is expanded, condense it? (Y/N) Yes" prompt, type [Y] to condense, [N] to leave expanded.

3. If you choose to condense the master document, you will see the "Save Subdocs? (Y/N) Yes" prompt. A "Yes" will give you the following options: Press [1] or [Y] to save the individual subdocument and any changes made to the subdocuments, [2] or [N] not to save the changes to the subdocuments, and [3] or **R**eplace to automatically save all the subdocuments before condensing.

4. When the Master Document is condensed, you will get the familiar "Document to be saved: *file name*" prompt. As always, use a unique three-letter extension to identify this particular type of document (Example: IMPART.MST). Press [Enter].

Moving, copying, and deleting subdocuments

One of the key advantages of using the Master Document feature is the ease with which you can move, copy, or delete subdocuments. In other words, instead of moving, copying, or deleting long blocks of text, you can manipulate the subdocument codes instead.

1. Press [F11] or [Alt][F3] (Reveal Codes) and move the cursor in front of the subdocuments you wish to move or copy.

2. Press [F12] or [Alt][F4] (Block on) and block out the code. You should see the subdocument box blocked out.

3. Press [Ctrl][F4], [1] for **B**lock, then [1] for **C**opy, [2] for **M**ove, or [3] for delete.

Expanding a master document

The convenience of a condensed master document is that a long document composed of different files appears merely as a collection of subdocument codes. However, if you wish to print the master document, edit any of the subdocuments, or mark the subdocuments in order to create a table of contents or table of authorities, you must expand the master document first. When you have finished with your

---

TIP

Like all WordPerfect codes, a subdocument can be deleted by using Reveal Codes, placing the cursor on the [Subdoc:*filename*] code, and pressing [Del].

MACRO

Using the [Alt][M], [Alt][C], and [Alt][D] macros provided in Appendix C will facilitate moving, copying, and deleting documents.

TIP

Another advantage of the Master Document feature is that it allows you to quickly make changes in several different files at once. Let's say you needed to search and replace a name that appeared on many different clauses saved as separate files. Instead of retrieving each file individually and making the change, you could include all the files as subdocuments in a master document, expand the master document, and make the change in all the files at once.

changes or corrections, they can be automatically saved in the separate files (subdocuments) when you condense the master document.

1. With the master document on the screen, press [Home], [Home], [↑] to move the cursor to the top of the document.
2. Press [Alt][F5] (Mark Text).
3. Choose [6] for **G**enerate.
4. Choose [3] for **E**xpand Master Document.

■ *If WordPerfect cannot find a specified file, the following message will appear: "Subdoc not found (Press **Enter** to Skip):* file name.*" Either enter the correct file name or press* [Enter] *to have WordPerfect skip to the next subdocument. If you do not know the file name, cancel the operation by pressing* [F1]*, then use the List Files feature* [F5] *to get the proper file name. See Appendix B on how to use List Files for more information.*

■ *Each expanded subdocument now has a marker at the beginning and at the end of the text, as illustrated in Figure 3-9.*

Condensing a master document

There are two ways to condense the master document. A master document can be condensed using the Condense Master Document option from the Mark Text: Generate menu. It can also be condensed during the exit procedure by selecting the Condense Master Document option. The steps that follow are for condensing the Master Document from the Mark Text: Generate menu, but are substantially similar to the Exit procedure.

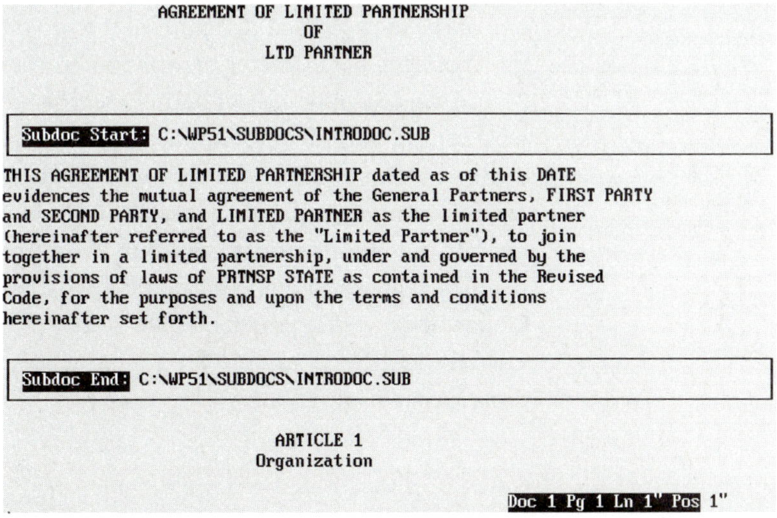

FIGURE 3-9

An expanded subdocument shows the Subdoc Start and Subdoc End markers surrounding it.

```
                    AGREEMENT OF LIMITED PARTNERSHIP
                                 OF
                             LTD PARTNER

┌─────────────────────────────────────────────────────────────────────┐
│ Subdoc Start:  C:\WP51\SUBDOCS\INTRODOC.SUB                         │
└─────────────────────────────────────────────────────────────────────┘
THIS AGREEMENT OF LIMITED PARTNERSHIP dated as of this DATE
evidences the mutual agreement of the General Partners, FIRST PARTY
and SECOND PARTY, and LIMITED PARTNER as the limited partner
(hereinafter referred to as the "Limited Partner"), to join
together in a limited partnership, under and governed by the
provisions of laws of PRTNSP STATE as contained in the Revised
Code, for the purposes and upon the terms and conditions
hereinafter set forth.

┌─────────────────────────────────────────────────────────────────────┐
│ Subdoc End:  C:\WP51\SUBDOCS\INTRODOC.SUB                           │
└─────────────────────────────────────────────────────────────────────┘

                              ARTICLE 1
                             Organization

                                              Doc 1 Pg 1 Ln 1" Pos 1"
```

> **TIP**
>
> If all the subdocuments have been previously marked to create a table of contents or table of authorities, you do not have to expand the master document first before generating the table. Press [Alt][F5], [6] for Generate, [5] for Generate Tables..., and WordPerfect will automatically expand the master document before generating the table.

1. With the expanded Master Document on the screen, press [Alt][F5] (Mark Text).
2. Choose [6] for **G**enerate.
3. Choose [4] for **C**ondense Master Document.
4. At the "Save Subdocs (Y/N) Yes" prompt, type [Y] to save the subdocument with any of the changes made or [N] to condense the master document without saving the changes to the subdocuments.
5. If you typed [Y], the name of each subdocument is displayed one at a time and you are asked if you want to replace the original file. This prompt is the same as the "Replace *file name* (No) Yes?" prompt that you get when you normally save a file. In other words, you are being asked if you wish to replace the old version of the subdocument with a new version that contains changes. If you want WordPerfect to automatically save all the subdocuments with the new changes, press [3] for **R**eplace All Remaining.

3.2.3 USING REDLINING AND STRIKEOUT (BLACKLINING)

As lawyers go through numerous drafts of a contract, they frequently have to add or delete text. These insertions and deletions must often be highlighted to check for accuracy, a process commonly referred to as *redlining* and *blacklining* (or *strikeout*). WordPerfect has a feature called Document Compare that allows the user to compare a document on the screen with one on disk and automatically inserts the proper redline and blackline marks. Redline and strikeout marks may also be added manually.

> **SHAREWARE**
>
> The COMPARE.ZIP file, available as shareware on the supplementary disks, is a stand-alone program that performs word-for-word comparison of WordPerfect documents.

CAUTION: WordPerfect's document compare feature is not one of the most refined functions of the program. Instead of comparing character by character or word by word, it compares phrase by phrase where a phrase is defined as a section of text from one comma, hard return, period, question mark, or colon to the next. Therefore, while it will highlight changes in a document, it is not accurate enough for serious legal redlining and strikeout. If your firm frequently uses redlining and strikeouts in contracts, it is highly recommended that you use a dedicated computer package such as Docu-Comp from Advanced Software (call (800) 346-5392) or the COMPARE.ZIP shareware program available on the supplementary disks for your important work.

Using Document Compare

Document Compare works in the following manner. If text was added on screen, it will be redlined. If text was found on disk that was not on the screen, that text will be copied onto the screen document with strikeout marks through it.

1. Retrieve the contract or form, make the necessary changes, but do not save it to disk yet.
2. Press [Alt][F5] (Mark Text), then [6] for **G**enerate.
3. Choose [2] for **C**ompare Screen and Disk Documents.
4. At the prompt, type the path and name of the file on disk to be used for comparison, e.g., B:\CONTRACT.DOC, and press [Enter].

■ *While WordPerfect is comparing documents, a counter will appear indicating how much progress is being made.*

Manually inserting redline and strikeout marks

TIP

To see how the redlining and strikeout will actually print, press [Shift][F7], [6] to preview the document, or use the [Alt][V] macro.

Because of the limitations of the Document Compare function, you may wish to insert strikeout and redline marks manually. Both options are found under the Appearance menu under Font.

1. Block out the text you wish to redline or strikeout by pressing [F12].
2. Press [Ctrl][F8] (Font).
3. Choose [2] for **A**ppearance.
4. Choose either [8] for **R**edln (Redline) or [9] for **S**tkout (Strikeout).

TIP

Use the Search function [F2] to quickly find the [STKOUT] and [REDLN] codes.

See the samples of strikeout and redlined text below.

```
1.4 Agent. The agent for the service of process on
the Partnership shall be AGENT NAME, or such other
agent as the General Partners may from time to time
designate in writing in the Certificate of Limited
Partnership.
```

Removing redline and strikeout marks

Automatically: With the marked document on the screen, press [Alt][F5] (Mark Text), [6] for **G**enerate, then [1] for **R**emove Markings and Strikeout text from Document, [Y] for **Y**es.

Manually: Press [F11] or [Alt][F3] (Reveal Codes). Place the cursor on the [STKOUT] or the [REDLN] codes that you wish to delete, and press [Del].

3.2.4 CREATING A SIMPLE DOCUMENT ASSEMBLY SYSTEM USING THE MERGE TEMPLATE FEATURE

> *The fundamental article of my political creed is that despotism, or unlimited sovereignty, or absolute power, is the same in a majority of a popular assembly, an aristocratical council, an oligarchical junto, and a single emperor.*
>
> *John Adams*
> *Letter to Thomas Jefferson [November 13, 1815]*

As we discuss in both Chapter 2 and Chapter 4, the greatly expanded merge language of WordPerfect 5.1 is one of the most exciting new features of the program and one that can be of great benefit to any law firm that regularly uses standard boilerplate forms and contracts. With the 5.1 merge language, WordPerfect can turn any of your standard contracts into a "Merge Template," so called because the original template is not changed by the merge process. In other words, a merge template can be reused hundreds of times for different clients without ever being changed.

In Chapters 2 and 4, we discuss how to create simple merge templates using WordPerfect 5.1's {INPUT} code and WordPerfect 5.0's ^O^C codes. We will cover this again in the present chapter. However, because contracts are generally longer, more complex documents with many more variables, this chapter will primarily focus on how to create advanced merge templates using a variety of different WordPerfect 5.1 advanced merge codes. Since advanced templates are "smart," a repeating variable need only be entered once for all other occurrences to be automatically filled in by WordPerfect. This is only possible with version 5.1—if you want this capability for your office, you know the answer. Upgrade!

The following examples of merge templates are easy to use and will suffice for the needs of most legal offices.

 N no time at all Sarah, under Greta's tutelage, is becoming a WordPerfect power user, and loving it. In her enthusiasm, she has even shared her latest discovery with Steve.

Is this the same Sarah we met only 20 or so pages ago, the one for whom computers represented an imposition on her social life? Apparently not, because Sarah is now actually looking forward to the vital task of computerizing and automating the numerous boilerplate forms and contracts the firm uses. (In essence, she wants to produce a sort of computerized form book for the firm.) In very little time, and with Steve's active encouragement and Greta's guidance, Sarah distills the necessary steps down to the following six sections.

Creating a simple template by retrieving text

The easiest way to create a template is to retrieve your boilerplate form into a (blank) file, rather than loading the file itself. This creates a new document and ensures that the original is not changed. However, this system will not prompt the user to fill in the blanks. Follow these steps:

1. On a blank editing screen, press the [Spacebar] once. By putting in one space, you have effectively created a new document.

2. Press [Shift][F10] (Retrieve) or [F5] (List Files) and retrieve the document you wish to use. If you get the message "Retrieve into current document?," answer [Y].

3. If you wish to save the new document you have created, press [F10] to save and give it a new name. Remember to use a proper extension!

> ■ *Because you have inserted a document into another document (albeit one that contains a single space), note that it does not have a name until you save it. This is the tip-off that you have created a new document and that the original remains unchanged.*

You can enhance this system by creating a named macro that performs the above steps for each of your most commonly used boilerplate forms. Figure 3-10 shows what the macro would look like

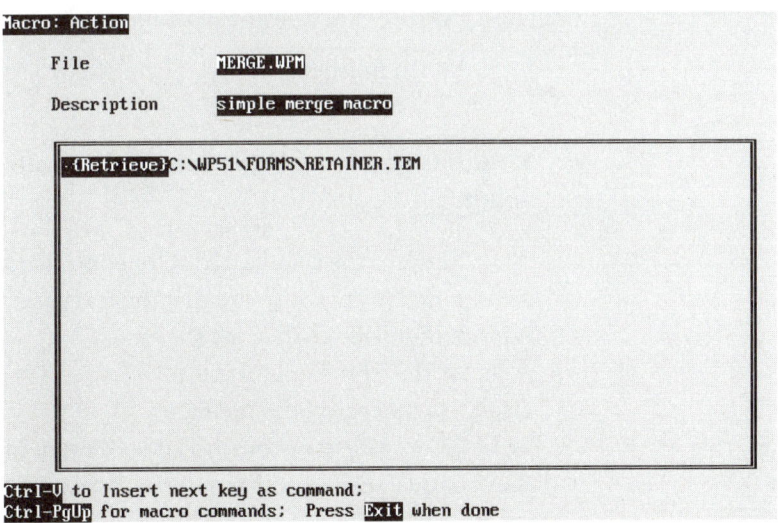

FIGURE 3-10

The MERGE.WPM macro here simply retrieves a template called RETAINER.TEM. Note the space in front of the {Retrieve} code to ensure that the original template does not change.

from the macro editor for a template called RETAINER.TEM kept in the directory C:\WP51\FORMS.

WP5.1 Creating a simple merge template using the {INPUT} code

The following illustrates how to create a simple keyboard merge template using the {INPUT} merge code. The {INPUT} code prompts the user to enter information at each variable. It does not automatically fill in repetitive text variables in a document.

1. Retrieve the standard form or contract that you wish to convert into a template, making sure that the text variables (blanks where new information will be filled in) are empty.

2. At the first blank in the form, press [Shift][F9] (Merge Codes) to display the merge codes menu.

3. Choose [3] for Input. At the "Enter Message:" prompt, type the prompt to be used for the keyboard merge. For example, if the variable is the name of the first party in a contract, you might want to type:
Enter name of the first party, press [F9] to continue:.

> **TIP**
>
> If you plan to use many different templates, it is highly recommended that you store all templates in a separate subdirectory such as C:\WP51\TEMPLATE. Also, templates will be easier to identify if they are given the same three-letter extension. Example: CONTRACT.TEM.

■ *Because templates are merge documents, the merge is continued by pressing the [F9] (End Field) key, **not** the [Enter] key. Because users will often instinctively press the [Enter] key, it is wise to remind users in the prompt that the [F9] key continues the merge.*

4. Repeat the above steps for each variable in the contract or form.

■ *If you do not see any merge codes on the regular editing screen, you must make sure that Merge Codes Display is set to Yes on the Edit Screen Options under Setup. Press [Shift][F1] (Setup), [2] for Display, [6] for Edit screen options, [5] for Merge Codes Display, and [Y].*

5. When finished, save the template by pressing [F10] (Save).

WP5.0 Creating a simple merge template using the ^O^C codes

1. Retrieve the standard form or contract that you wish to convert into a template, making sure that the text variables (blanks where new information will be filled in) are empty.

2. At the first blank in the form, press [Shift][F9] (Merge Codes) to display the merge codes menu.

3. Choose [O] to insert a ^O code (Output message to screen), type the prompt to be used during the keyboard merge, press [Shift][F9] again

and choose [O] to insert a closing ^O code. Next, press [Shift][F9][C] to insert the ^C code (Request input from Console) after the output message. For example, at the [ATTY NAME] variable, your message

EXERCISE: CREATING AN ADVANCED TEMPLATE USING {VARIABLE} AND {TEXT} CODES

The following exercise uses the INDEMNI.FRM document at the top of the next page. It is a sample indemnification agreement with the text variables FIRST PARTY and SECOND PARTY repeating throughout. Each of the text variables to be replaced with merge codes is in capital letters.

Step 1: Inserting the codes at the first occurrence of repeating text

1. Input the Indemnification Agreement above and name it INDEMNI.FRM. Note that FIRST PARTY and SECOND PARTY are the repeating text variables.

2. Delete the first instance of FIRST PARTY, then press [Shift][F9] (Merge Codes) twice to access the pop-up merge codes.

3. Type [T] to scroll down to the {TEXT}var~message~ code and press [Enter].

4. At the "Enter variable:" prompt, type the variable name 1stpart and press [Enter]. (Variable names should be easy to remember and should reflect the subject matter of the text to be entered as much as possible.)

5. At the "Enter message:" prompt, type: Enter the full name of the first party, [F9] to continue, then press [Enter]. The following merge code should be inserted in your document:

{TEXT}1stpart~Enter the full name of the first party, [F9] to continue~

6. Press [Shift][F9] (Merge Codes) twice to access the merge codes, type [V] to scroll down to the {VARIABLE}var~ code and press [Enter].

7. At the "Enter variable:" prompt, type: 1stpart and press [Enter]. Your document should now have these codes inserted:

{TEXT}1stpart~Enter the full name of the first party, [F9] to continue~{VARIABLE}1stpart~

8. Repeat the above steps for the text variable SECOND PARTY.

Step 2: inserting the codes for the repeating occurrences of text

1. Press [Alt][F2] (Search and Replace), [N].

2. At the "-> Srch" prompt, type: FIRST PARTY, then press [F2].

3. At the "Replace With:" prompt, press [Shift][F9] (Merge Codes) twice to access the merge codes, [V] to scroll down to the {VARIABLE}var~ code, and press [Enter]. The [Mrg: VARIABLE] code is inserted.

4. Type: 1stpart~ after the merge code. Be sure to include the tilde (~). The complete "Replace With:" prompt should look as follows:

Replace With:[Mrg: VARIABLE]1stpart~

Press [F2] again to execute the Search and Replace.

5. Repeat the following steps for the SECOND PARTY text variable. Your completed template should look like the agreement at the bottom of the next page, which we have named INDEMNI.TEM, because it is now a merge template.

6. Press [F10] to save the template, call it INDEMNI.TEM, then clear the screen.

INDEMNIFICATION AGREEMENT

This indemnification agreement is made and entered on by and between FIRST PARTY, and SECOND PARTY.

WHEREAS FIRST PARTY and SECOND PARTY have agreed to resolve certain disputes which have arisen between them; and

****

FIRST PARTY and affiliates hereby jointly and severally agree to indemnify and hold harmless SECOND PARTY and any affiliate of SECOND PARTY from every liability, claim, action, cause of action resulting from:

****

IN WITNESS WHEREOF the undersigned set their hands.

_____

FIRST PARTY

_____

SECOND PARTY

INDEMNIFICATION AGREEMENT

This indemnification agreement is made and entered on by and between {TEXT}1stpart~ENTER NAME OF FIRST PARTY, [F9] TO CONTINUE~ {VARIABLE}1stpart~ and {TEXT}2ndpart~ ENTER NAME OF SECOND PARTY, [F9] TO CONTINUE~{VARIABLE}2ndpart~.

WHEREAS {VARIABLE}1stpart~ and {VARIABLE}2ndpart~ have agreed to resolve certain disputes which have arisen between them; and

****

{VARIABLE}1stpart~ and affiliates hereby jointly and severally agree to indemnify and hold harmless {VARIABLE}2ndpart~ and any affiliate of {VARIABLE}2ndpart~ from every liability, claim, action, cause of action resulting from:

****

IN WITNESS WHEREOF the undersigned have hereunto set their hands.

_____

{VARIABLE}1stpart~

_____

{VARIABLE}2ndpart~

might look something like this: "^OEnter attorney name, press [F9] to continue:^O^C"

4. Repeat the above steps for each variable in the contract or form.
5. When finished, save the template by pressing [F10] (Save).

WP5.1 Creating an advanced merge template using the {TEXT} and {VARIABLE} codes

Using the {INPUT} code as described above is an ideal solution when the document variable occurs only once in the document. However, in many legal forms and contracts, a document variable such as a name or address might be repeated many times in the same document. Using the steps described below, you will only have to enter the document variable once and it will automatically be filled in anywhere else in the document you need it. Together, simple and advanced merge codes can dramatically speed up the production of standard legal documents.

Before getting to the exercise on how to create an advanced merge template, it is necessary to briefly explain the concept of memory variables and to illustrate the two WordPerfect merge codes {TEXT} and {VARIABLE} that perform this neat trick.

An explanation of memory variables

Earlier in the chapter, we discussed how the {INPUT} code is employed to allow the user to fill in text variables from the keyboard. (The term *text variable* has been used to describe text such as names or addresses that change from document to document.) A key point: The {INPUT} code does not store the text variable in memory for future use.

By contrast, a different kind of variable, called a *memory variable*, is also used in WordPerfect macro and merge programming. For our purposes here, by this we mean text temporarily stored in memory that can be retrieved by the use of the {VARIABLE}variable~ code. ("Temporarily" because when you exit WordPerfect, the variable disappears from memory.) When using memory variables, you must follow these rules:

➢ Variable names can be a number from 1 to 9 or any name up to 7 characters.

Examples: {VARIABLE}1stname~, {VARIABLE}address~, {VARIABLE}newname~. (Note the use of the tilde.)

> Variables can store a maximum of 129 characters: WordPerfect will ignore anything past the size limit.

{VARIABLE} and {TEXT} merge codes explained

{TEXT}variable~message~: Prompts the user with a message and then stores the keystrokes (the user's response) in a variable. This code is used to assign a value to a particular variable. The variable assigned by {TEXT} can be no longer than 128 characters.

The **{VARIABLE}variable~** code then retrieves that value.

Example: "{TEXT}1stname~Enter the first name, press [F9] to continue:~" If the user types "David," the variable "1stname" will have the value "David."

The contents of that variable ("David") can then be retrieved at any point in the document with the {VARIABLE}variable~ merge code. (In this case "variable~" is "1stname.")

Here's how it might look in a document:

```
{TEXT}1stname~Enter the first name, press [F9] to
continue:~
Dear {VARIABLE}1stname~:
```

> *The judicial power ought to be distinct from both the legislative and executive, and independent upon both, that so it may be a check upon both, as both should be checks upon that.*
>
> John Adams
> Thoughts on Government [1776]

3.2.5 USING MERGE TEMPLATES (EXECUTING THE MERGE)

Templates are, in reality, sophisticated keyboard merges. Therefore, to use templates, you must follow the steps needed to merge documents. The template is the primary merge file, and there is no secondary merge file.

1. Press [Ctrl][F9] (Merge/Sort) to access the merge menu.
2. Choose [1] for **M**erge.
3. At the "Primary File:" prompt, enter the file name `INDEMNI.TEM` if you did our exercise on creating an advanced template. If you prefer, you may also use List Files [F5] to retrieve it.

> ■ Remember that if you are in another subdirectory from the one in which your template is stored, you must type the entire path name of the file. WordPerfect will give the error message "File not Found" if you enter the wrong document name or fail to give the proper path for the file.

4. At the "Secondary File:" prompt, simply press [Enter].

5. The cursor will stop at the location of the first {TEXT} merge code in the template, and you will see at the bottom left of the screen the prompt that you created. Type the name of the First Party and press `F9` (End Field) to continue the merge.

6. When all the merging is completed, you may save the document by pressing `F10` (Save) or print it by pressing `Shift`+`F7` (Print).

The result of the merge is a new document (it has not yet been saved so it does not have a name). In our example, you will see that every occurrence of FIRST and SECOND PARTY has been automatically replaced by the actual names you entered.

3.2.6 EDITING A TEMPLATE

A government of laws, and not of men.
— John Adams
"Novanglus" papers, Boston Gazette [1774]. Incorporated [1780] into the Massachusetts Constitution

One of the beauties of the WordPerfect 5.0 and 5.1 merge template feature is the ease with which templates can be changed and edited. Because templates are normal WordPerfect documents with the addition of merge codes, they may be retrieved and edited in the same way as normal text files. Even the merge prompts and variable names that are part of the merge codes can be edited like normal text. **IMPORTANT**: *Just make sure that, when you edit the variable name or prompt in a merge code, you do not delete the all-important tilde (~). The tilde acts as a delimiter for the merge code. If it is accidentally deleted, the merge will not function properly.*

For an explanation of how macros can be incorporated into merge templates, please see Chapter 4.

"**I**'M eternally in your debt, Greta," exclaims Sarah. "Not only have you taught me all these neat, time-saving techniques, but you've turned me into a true believer in the power of the computer. Never again will I look with disdain upon those who toil in front of a VDT, or show contempt for some hacker I meet at a party who has just sold his program for a million bucks."

"You're welcome, Sarah. Listen, I gotta go. Do you have any more questions?" asks Greta.

"Sorry, I got carried away," Sarah replies. "Oh yeah, one more thing. How about a table of contents? I'm sure WordPerfect makes it much easier to create one—how does it work?"

Here's what Greta shows Sarah.

3.2.7 CREATING A TABLE OF CONTENTS

Like other long legal documents, such as briefs, a lengthy contract benefits greatly from a table of contents. At the very least, a table of contents will make it easier for your client to read the contract! Because contracts almost always go through numerous changes and revisions before they are finally signed, creating a table of contents manually was a tedious and time-consuming chore. No longer. WordPerfect's Table of Contents feature can generate a table automatically. Best of all, it can be regenerated at will to reflect changes in the contract.

The steps involved in creating a table of contents are:

➤ Define the table.

➤ Renumber the pages.

➤ Mark the text to be included as entries in the table.

➤ Generate the table.

➤ Touch up the generated table.

A table of contents in WordPerfect can consist of up to five levels. Once the necessary text is marked in the document as entries, new tables can be generated as needed.

In the following exercise, you will create a two-level table of contents for the first two articles and Schedule A of a limited partnership agreement called LIMITED.CON, illustrated below.

```
                AGREEMENT OF LIMITED PARTNERSHIP

THIS AGREEMENT OF LIMITED PARTNERSHIP dated as of
this DATE evidences the mutual agreement of the
General Partners, FIRST PARTY and SECOND PARTY, and
LIMITED PARTNER as the limited partner ("Limited
Partner"), to join together in a limited
partnership....

                         ARTICLE 1
                        Organization

1.1 Formation of Limited Partnership.  The
Partnership shall commence on ORDINAL DATE and shall
thereafter continue without interruption as a
limited partnership pursuant ...

1.2 Name.  The name of the Partnership shall be ABC
PARTNER (hereinafter referred to as the
```

```
"Partnership"). However, the business of the
Partnership may be conducted, upon compliance with
all applicable laws, under any other name designated
in writing by the General Partners to the Limited
Partner....

               ***************

                  ARTICLE 2
Partners' Names, Addresses, and Capital Contributions

2.1 General Partners.

The name and address of each General Partner is set
forth in Schedule "A" hereto attached, as amended
from time to time....

               ***************

                  SCHEDULE A

FIRST PARTY

ADDRESS 1

CITY 1, STATE 1, ZIP 1
```

Step 1: Define a table of contents

The Limited Partnership Agreement is composed of Articles, each of which is composed of a number of clauses. There is also a Schedule A. Therefore, this table of contents will consist of two levels.

To define a table of contents with this structure, follow these steps:

1. Press [Home], [Home], [↑] to move the cursor to the very beginning of the contract.

2. Press [Ctrl][Enter] (Hard Return) to create a new page.

3. Move the cursor up to the line at which the title for the table of contents will appear and type `Table of Contents`.

4. Press [Enter] several times to move the cursor to the line at which the first line of the table of contents will appear.

5. Press [Alt][F5] (Mark Text).

6. Choose [5] for **D**efine.

7. Choose [1] for Define **T**able of **C**ontents.

8. Choose [1] for **N**umber of Levels that will be included in the table of contents, then press [2]. The other options will be left at their default settings (No for Display Last Level in Wrapped Format and Flush right with leader for both levels, as shown in Figure 3-11.)

> *Facts are stubborn things; and whatever may be our wishes, our inclinations, or the dictates of our passions, they cannot alter the state of facts and evidence.*
>
> John Adams
> Argument in Defense of the [British] Soldiers in the Boston Massacre Trials [December 1770]

FIGURE 3-11

The Table of Contents Definition screen shows two levels defined with the traditional "Flush right with leader" format.

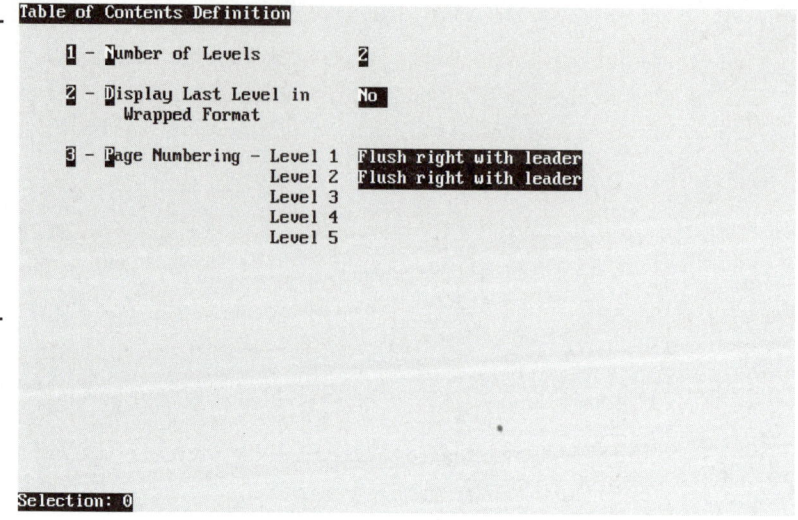

9. Press [F7] (Exit) to return to the document screen.

▲▲▲▲▲▲▲▲▲▲▲▲▲▲▲▲▲▲▲▲▲▲▲▲▲▲

The following code has been inserted: [Def Mark: ToC, 2:5, 5]. This means you have defined a table of contents with two out of five possible levels.

WordPerfect allows a number of different listing styles for tables of contents. Although Sarah's firm uses the Flush Right Page Numbers with Leaders style, the following example shows the other listing styles available:

No Page Numbers:
Page Numbers Follow Entries: 1; 5; 7
(Page Numbers) Follow Entries: (1); (5); (7)
Flush Right Page Numbers: 1, 5, 7
Flush Right Page Numbers with Leaders: 1, 5, 7

Step 2: Renumber the pages

MACRO

Use the TOCTITLE.WPM macro to quickly set up a table of contents title page, including new page numbering

There are two important steps that must now be taken to ensure the page accuracy of the table of contents. Because new pages have been added for the table of contents, we must ensure that the table is given a Roman numeral page number and that page 1 of the contract begins at the start of the text, not at the table of contents.

1. Press [Home], [Home], [↑] to move the cursor to the beginning of the table of contents.
2. Press [Shift][F8] (Format).
3. Choose [2] for Page.
4. Choose [6] for Page Numbering.

5. Choose [4] for Page Number **P**osition, then [6] for bottom center.
6. Choose [1] for New Page **N**umber.
7. Type i, then press [Enter].
8. Press [F7] (Exit) to return to the document.

▲▲▲▲▲▲▲▲▲▲▲▲▲▲▲▲▲▲▲▲▲▲▲▲▲▲▲▲▲▲▲▲▲▲▲▲

A [Pg Numbering:Bottom Conter] [Pg num:i] code should now be inserted.

Now, start the text of the contract at page 1.

1. Move the cursor to the beginning of the page where the actual text of the brief begins.
2. Press [Shift][F8] (Format).
3. Choose [2] for **P**age.
4. Choose [6] for Page **N**umbering.
5. Choose [1] for **N**ew page number.
6. Type [1] and press [Enter].
7. Press [F7] (Exit) to return to the document.

▲▲▲▲▲▲▲▲▲▲▲▲▲▲▲▲▲▲▲▲▲▲▲▲▲▲▲▲▲▲▲▲▲▲▲▲

A [Pg Num:1] code should now be inserted. Also note that the page indicator on the status line on the bottom right of the screen should now properly indicate 1.

Step 3: Mark text for the table of contents

I always consider the settlement of America with reverence and wonder, as the opening of a grand scene and design in providence, for the illumination of the ignorant and the emancipation of the slavish part of mankind all over the earth.

*John Adams
Notes for "A Dissertation on the Canon and Feudal Law" [1765]*

Now that the table has been defined, each heading to appear on the table must be marked.

1. Move the cursor to ARTICLE 1, the first heading to be included in the table of contents, press [F12] or [Alt][F4] (Block), and block out the text.

   ■ *Any codes that are included in the block, such as bold, underline, etc.,* will *appear on the generated table. To ensure that no extraneous codes are included, turn on Reveal Codes* [F11] *or* [Alt][F3] *before blocking text to make sure you don't include these formatting codes.*

2. Press [Alt][F5] (Mark Text).
3. Choose [1] for ToC.
4. Enter the number of the ToC level to which this heading will be assigned and press [Enter]. For example, ARTICLE 1 would be on level 1 of our ToC. (See Figure 3-12.)

▲▲▲▲▲▲▲▲▲▲▲▲▲▲▲▲▲▲▲▲▲▲▲▲▲▲▲▲▲▲▲▲▲▲▲▲

Reveal Codes should display [Mark:ToC, 1]ARTICLE 1[End Mark:ToC,1].

FIGURE 3-12

Reveal Codes shows that ARTICLE 1 of this document has been marked as level 1.

```
                              OF
                         LTD PARTNER
THIS AGREEMENT OF LIMITED PARTNERSHIP dated as of this DATE evidences the
mutual agreement of the General Partners, FIRST PARTY and SECOND PARTY, and
LIMITED PARTNER as the limited partner (hereinafter referred to as the "Limited
Partner"), to join together in a limited partnership, under and governed by the
of laws of PRTNSP STATE as contained in the Revised Code, for the purposes and u
the terms and conditions hereinafter set forth.
                           ARTICLE 1
ToC Level: 1
{  ▲   ▲   ▲   ▲   ▲   ▲   ▲   ▲   ▲   ▲   ▲   }   ▲   ▲
of laws of PRTNSP STATE as contained in the Revised Code, for the purposes and u
pon[SRt]
the terms and conditions hereinafter set forth.[HRt]
[HRt]
[Center][Block][Mark:ToC,1]ARTICLE 1[End Mark:ToC,1][HRt]
[Center]Organization[HRt]
[HRt]
1.1  [UND]Formation of Limited Partnership[und].  The Partnership shall commence
 on ORDINAL[SRt]
DATE and shall thereafter continue without interruption as a limited partnership

Press Reveal Codes to restore screen
```

5. Move the cursor to the paragraph number and title of the first clause of Article 1 and mark it for the table of contents by repeating the above steps. However, be sure to assign it to level 2 of the table of contents.

6. Repeat this procedure for the other articles and clauses in the contract.

7. When finished, save the contract.

Step 4: Generate a table of contents

Now that the necessary text has been marked, the pages properly numbered, and the table defined, it only remains to generate and touch up the table. (It doesn't matter where you are in the document when you generate.)

1. Press [Alt][F5] (Mark Text).
2. Choose [6] for **G**enerate.
3. Choose [5] for Generate Tables, Indexes, Cross references, etc.
4. At the "Existing tables, lists, and indexes will be replaced. Continue?" prompt, type [Y] to tell WordPerfect to generate the Table. This will delete any prior versions of the table of contents that you may have created.

■ *During generation, the following message appears in the status line: "Generation in progress. Pass #, Page #." WordPerfect will make a number of passes through the entire document. Depending on the size of the contract, this step may take a while.*

4. Press [Home], [Home], [↑] to move the cursor to the top of the document to view the table.

Error messages

Because creating and generating a table of contents is a complex process, you may see the following error messages:

Not Enough Memory: WordPerfect uses Document 2 to generate tables, lists, and the like. Document 1 is allotted twice as much memory as Document 2. Therefore, if you are running out of memory, retrieve the contract or form into Document 2. The Generate option can then use the additional memory available in Document 1.

No [DefMark] found: The [DefMark] code is created when you first define the tables of authorities. If you forgot to define the location and format of the table, WordPerfect will be unable to generate the table. Follow the steps above to define a table of contents and regenerate.

Can't find end of Table of Contents, Lists or Index Text: This message generally means that the [EndDef] code was deleted accidentally. The [EndDef] code is created when you first generate a table and is found at the end of each section in the table. (Each [DefMark] code has a corresponding [EndDef] code.)

If WordPerfect can't find an [EndDef] code, that section will be generated again, without deleting the first table. Therefore, you have two options: delete the prior duplicate table you have regenerated or, if possible, copy an existing [DefMark] code from another section of the table to the section that's missing it.

Touching up the finished table of contents

> **TIP**
>
> To manually create flush-right dot leaders press [Alt][F6] twice. To manually create center dot leaders, press [Shift][F6] twice.

When generation is complete, you will have to touch up the table of contents. Use Reveal Codes to delete any extraneous codes and align the flush-right dot leaders.

The complete table for the Limited Partnership agreement should look something like the table below.

```
                    TABLE OF CONTENTS
                LIMITED PARTNERSHIP AGREEMENT

    ARTICLE 1  . . . . . . . . . . . . . . . . . . . . . 1

    1.1   Formation of Limited Partnership  . . . . . . 1

    1.2   Name  . . . . . . . . . . . . . . . . . . . . 1

                         ********

    ARTICLE 2  . . . . . . . . . . . . . . . . . . . . . 2

    2.1   General Partners. . . . . . . . . . . . . . . 2

                         ********

    SCHEDULE A . . . . . . . . . . . . . . . . . . . . . 3
```

Printing documents on disk with several sections, each beginning with a new number

If your document is divided into more than one section, each beginning with a new number, you must take that fact into account when printing selected pages.

Let's use the purely hypothetical example of a document that consists of the following sections:

Table of Contents i–iv
1st part of the body of the document 1–25
2nd part of the body of the document 1–30
Exhibit i–iv

To select individual pages, at the Print Document on Disk menu, after entering the file name of the document you want to print, type the appropriate section number first, followed by a colon, then the desired pages in that particular section. Let's see how this might be done:

You must enter `1:ii` to print the second page of the Table of Contents (or simply `ii`, because it is the first instance of the Roman numeral ii).

Enter `2:18` to print page 18 of the first part of the body of the document (or simply `18`, because it is the first instance of the Arabic numeral 18).

Enter `2:iii` to print the third page of the Exhibit, because it is the second instance of the Roman numeral iii.

> **TIP**
>
> You may also print pages from various sections in a multisection document in this manner, from within the document. Simply enter the desired pages at the Page(s): prompt when you select [5] for **M**ultiple pages in the Print menu.

Enter 2:16 to print page 16 of the second part of the body of the document, because it is the second instance of the Arabic numeral 16. If you wanted to print page 29 of the second part of the body of the document, all you'd have to do would be to enter the number 29, because it is the *first* instance of the Arabic number 29 in the document. Got it?

3.3 COMMAND REVIEW

Using automatic paragraph numbering

[Shift][F5] (Date/Outline), [6] to define style, [Enter], [5] for **P**ara Num, press [Enter] for automatic numbering or enter the level you wish to assign to the paragraph

Keeping text together

Widow/Orphan: [Shift][F8], [1], [9], [Y]
Block protection: - [Shift][F8], [Y]
Conditional End of Page: [Shift][F8], [4], [2]

Hard hyphen/spaces

[Home], [-], [Home], [Spacebar]

Creating a master document

[Alt][F5] (Mark Text), [2] for **S**ubdoc, enter the name of the file to be placed at that location, including the path (drive and directory)

Expanding a master document

[Alt][F5] (Mark Text), [6] for **G**enerate, [3] for **E**xpand Master Document

Condensing a master document

[Alt][F5], [6] for **G**enerate, [4] for **C**ondense Master Document, [Y] to save any changes made to the subdocuments or [N] to ignore any changes before removing the contents of the subdocuments from the screen

---

Creating a simple keyboard merge template (text must be entered manually for each variable)

WP5.1

1. Write or retrieve the text you wish to use as a template
2. Press [Shift][F9] (Merge Codes), [3] for Input
3. At the "Enter Message:" prompt, type the prompt to be used for the keyboard merge

WP5.0

1. Write or retrieve the text you wish to use as a template
2. Press [Shift][F9] (Merge Codes), [O] (type prompt), [Shift][F9], [O], [Shift][F9], [C]

Creating an advanced keyboard merge template (repeating variables are automatically filled in)

1. Write or retrieve the text you wish to use as a template
2. At the first instance of a repeating variable, insert the following merge codes by pressing [Shift][F9] twice or by pressing [Shift][F9], [6]: {TEXT}*var~message~* {VARIABLE}var~
3. At the next instance of the repeating variable, insert the {VARIABLE}var~ code, making sure that you are using the correct variable name

---

Retrieving and using a keyboard merge template

[Ctrl][F9] (Merge Sort), [1] for **Merge**, type in name of primary file at the prompt, press [Enter] at the "Secondary File:" prompt. Press [F9] to continue the keyboard merge until finished

---

Using Document Compare to insert redline and strikeout marks

1. Retrieve a document from disk and make the necessary revisions
2. With the revised document on screen, press [Alt][F5] (Mark Text), [6] for **Generate**, [2] for **Compare Screen and Disk Documents and**

Add Redline and Strikeout. Press [Enter] to accept the file name or enter a different one

Removing redline markings and deleting strikeout text

[Alt][F5] (Mark Text), [6] for **G**enerate, [1] for **R**emove Redline Markings and strikeout text from document

Defining a table of contents

[Alt][F5] (Mark text), [5] for **D**efine, [1] for **D**efine Table of **C**ontents, select **N**umber of levels and **P**age numbering style

Creating a table of contents (must be defined first—see above)

[Alt][F4] or [Alt][F12] (Block options), block appropriate text, [Alt][F5] (Mark Text), choose [1] for **T**o**C**, enter number of the ToC level

Generating a table of contents (must be created first—see above)

[Alt][F5] (Mark Text), [6] for **G**enerate, [5] for **G**enerate Tables, [Y]

Assembling Pleadings and Court-Related Documents

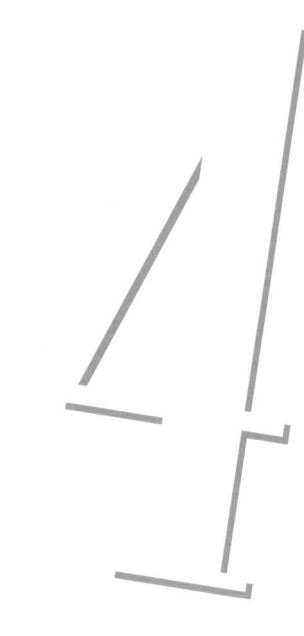

FUNCTIONS USED

➤ Creating a case caption using the WP 5.1 Tables feature §4.1.2

➤ Creating a case caption using Newspaper Columns and Line Draw §4.1.3

➤ Using merge templates to automate pleadings §4.2.1–4.2.3

➤ Creating pleading paper §4.2.4

Creating Pleading Paper using Graphic Lines and Styles

Creating Case Captions using the Tables and Newspaper Columns features

Using Line Draw for captions and pleading covers

Using Merge templates for basic document assembly of boilerplate

1 MARSHALL, CARDOZO, HAND,
   HOLMES & BLACKSTONE
2 Attorneys at Law
   123 Fifth Avenue, Suite 1800
3 New York, New York 10014
   (212) 123-4567
4 Attorneys for Plaintiff John Hatfield
5
6 CIVIL COURT OF THE CITY OF NEW YORK
   COUNTY OF NEW YORK
7 ─────────────────────────────
8 John Hatfield   Plaintiff(s),   Index no: 1234
9   -against-   STIPULATION OF
                                                      SETTLEMENT
10 Tom McCoy   Defendant(s),
11
12 ─────────────────────────────
13
14   It is stipulated and agreed among the parties as follows: Plaintiff shall dismiss with
15 prejudice its action against the defendant and the defendant shall dismiss with prejudice
16 its counterclaims against the plaintiff. Defendant shall release and discharge the plaintiff
17 from any and all obligation pursuant to a note and mortgage dated September 20, 1992
18 in which defendant is the mortgagee and plaintiff is the mortgagor. The parties shall
19 execute and forward to counsel for the Plaintiff, a Discharge of Mortgage for recording
20 with the clerk of the clerk of the court.
21   We hereby understand and agree to the terms of the within stipulation.
22
23   _____
                John Hatfield
24
25   _____
                Tom McCoy
26   BY: _____
27   Sarah Holmes, Esquire
                Attorneys for the Plaintiff
28

He defends the widow and the orphan, that is, when he is not attacking the widow and the orphan.

OVERVIEW

A pleading, as defined by Black's Law Dictionary, is a statement in logical and legal form of the facts that constitute the plaintiff's cause of action and the defendant's ground of defense. The stock in trade of trial lawyers, pleadings include complaints, answers, replies, motions, and myriad other documents that must be filed in court and with the opposing side. Because certain elements of pleadings, such as caption headings, pleading covers, pleading paper, etc., are constantly being used in any litigation practice, they lend themselves to automation with WordPerfect.

This chapter will describe how to use WordPerfect's table, macro, merge, and other features to speed up the production of pleadings. It will also demonstrate how some of the desktop publishing features of WordPerfect can be used to great effect in producing pleadings, from the creation of pleading paper to professional-looking typeset documents. The skills discussed in each section are as follows:

Beginning skills

➤ Creating a case caption using the WP 5.1 Tables feature

- Creating a case caption using the WP 5.0 Newspaper Column feature
- Using the Line Draw feature to create a case caption box and pleading cover

Intermediate skills

- Using WP 5.1 advanced merge codes to create a pleading template
- Using WP 5.0 advanced merge codes to create a pleading template
- Creating pleading paper using the graphic vertical line feature
- Creating pleading paper using the WP 5.1 pleading macro

4.1 BEGINNING WORDPERFECT PLEADING CREATION SKILLS

4.1.1 CASE CAPTIONS

> *Many forms of conduct permissible in a workaday world for those acting at arm's length, are forbidden to those bound by fiduciary ties. A trustee is held to something stricter than the morals of the market place. Not honesty alone, but the punctilio of an honor the most sensitive, is then the standard of behavior.*
>
> C. J. Benjamin Nathan Cardozo, Meinhard v. Salmon, 249 N.Y. 458, 464 [1928]

A fundamental element of every pleading is the case caption, where information concerning the names of the litigants, the court of venue, and the type of the pleading must be displayed. See page 159 for a sample case caption. The styles of case captions can vary from state to state and court to court, depending on local court rules and firm policy. Regardless of the style used, producing a good-looking case caption is not an easy task. In fact, for most legal offices, producing a case caption is probably one of the most sophisticated formatting tasks performed. However, knowledge of some of WordPerfect's more advanced features can make this task a great deal easier.

There are a number of features available in WordPerfect 5.X that can greatly aid in the creation of case captions. In the following pages, we describe two possible methods: one using newspaper columns for 5.0 and 5.1 users, the other using the Tables feature for 5.1 users. Both methods have their advantages and disadvantages. Your decision of which method works best for you will depend in part on the look and style of case captions used in your office and state. Either method will prevent much unnecessary aggravation and ensure that your case captions are perfect every time.

YES, it's that time. We're going to reintroduce one of the members of our fledgling law firm to you. You're going to like Steve Hand, trust us; you'll be in good "hands."

The aforementioned Steve already has some computer saavy from college: he was a history major and several of his courses required him to use the PC, much to his initial surprise and chagrin. He also had the opportunity to use an earlier version of WordPerfect (4.2) to write papers. Although WordPerfect has come a long way since those days, Steve doesn't anticipate too much trouble learning some of the more advanced features of 5.0 and 5.1 that he's going to need for his work.

Steve has a game plan that is simple yet elegant and just might work: he's going to take advantage of WordPerfect's world-famous technical support. The support staff's resourcefulness and patience are legendary; that's one of the major reasons WordPerfect users are so fanatically loyal to the product. (WordPerfect's technical support number is [800] 321-5906.) Steve figures he's got enough computer smarts to ask the right questions and to apply the answers to his document production.

Steve knows that the first (and perhaps most important) technical problem he has to solve is how to create case captions in the most efficient manner. He is already familiar with the newspaper column feature from version 4.2 and knows that this might be an answer; but he's also heard about the new and powerful Tables feature, which he suspects may ultimately be even more useful. After taking a quick look at the WordPerfect reference manual to give himself an idea of how tables work, he decides to make his first call to the good folks at WordPerfect. What follows is the result of Steve's research. Don't worry, he doesn't mind sharing all this with you.

In life, as in a football game, the principle to follow is: Hit the line hard.

*Theodore Roosevelt
The Strenuous Life:
Essays and
Addresses [1900].
The American Boy*

4.1.2 CREATING CASE CAPTIONS USING WORDPERFECT 5.1'S TABLES FEATURE

As we have discussed elsewhere in this book, the Tables feature is probably the most powerful and versatile feature added to WordPerfect 5.1. Its convenience in creating case captions is a perfect illustration. The Tables feature makes case captions a breeze and offers lawyers and their staff unprecedented control and ease of use when formatting and positioning text in captions. It is also better than the newspaper column method (discussed below) when using a font such as Times Roman for your pleading papers, because the lines display properly.

There is, however, one disadvantage to the Tables feature: it does not, as we shall see, allow the use of brackets, X's, and other characters when drawing the case caption box. The Tables feature allows only the use of dashed, dotted, or solid lines as shown below. However, if this is not a major concern, you are much better off using the Tables feature to create a case caption.

Sample case option using the 5.1 Tables feature

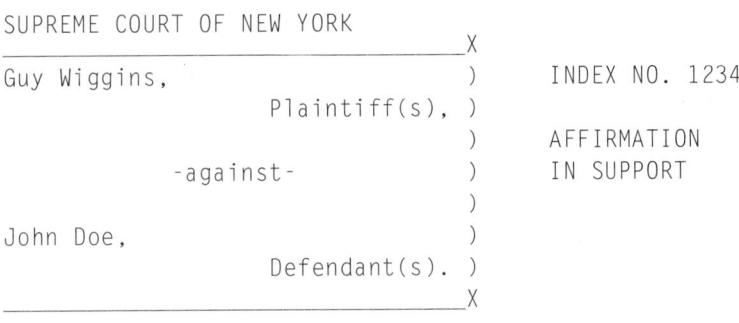

```
SUPREME COURT OF NEW YORK

Guy Wiggins,                                     INDEX NO. 1234
                  Plaintiff(s),
                                                 AFFIRMATION
         -against-                               IN SUPPORT

John Doe,
                  Defendant(s).
```

Sample case option using the 5.0 Newspaper Column feature

```
                _____
SUPREME COURT OF NEW YORK                        X
                _____
Guy Wiggins,                         )           INDEX NO. 1234
                  Plaintiff(s),      )
                                     )           AFFIRMATION
         -against-                   )           IN SUPPORT
                                     )
John Doe,                            )
                  Defendant(s).      )
                _____X
```

Creating the caption box

1. Type your firm name and address as it appears on your pleadings, then the name of the court where the case is to be pleaded.

2. Press [Alt][F7] (Columns/Tables), [2] for **Tables**, [1] for **Create**.

3. Enter [2] for number of columns, [1] for number of rows. A table will be created and you will be placed in the table edit mode. You will use the table edit mode to format the table lines.

MACRO

Use the [Alt][T] macro to set up a two-column, one-row table.

4. With the cursor in the left cell of the table, press [3] for **Lines**, [1] for **Left**, [1] for **None**. This should cause the left line of the first cell to disappear.

FIGURE 4-1

A two-column, one-row table is shown with all the lines eliminated from the right cell. The cell will automatically expand to accommodate text.

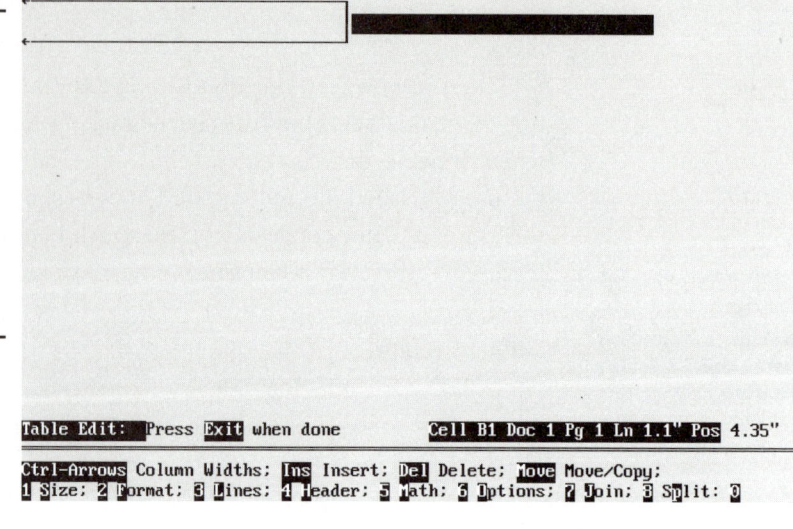

TIP

If you choose a line option such as thick or extra thick, use Print Preview ([Shift][F7], [6]) or the [Alt][V] macro to view the caption box before printing.

TIP

To quickly return to the table edit mode, place the cursor within a cell and press [Alt][F7] (Columns/Tables).

5. Press [3] for **L**ines, [3] for **T**op, then choose the style of line you wish to use, i.e. [2] for **S**ingle, [3] for **D**ouble, [4] for **D**ashed, etc. Repeat these steps for the bottom line of the first cell.

6. Once the lines of the first cell have been properly formatted, press [Tab] to move the cursor to the right cell.

7. With the cursor in the right cell of the table, press [3] for **L**ines, [3] for **T**op, [1] for **N**one. Then press [3] for **L**ines, [4] for **B**ottom, and [1] for **N**one and [3] for **L**ines, [2] for **R**ight, and [1] for **N**one to eliminate the bottom and right lines respectively. The completed table should look like Figure 4-1.

8. Now that the lines have been drawn properly, you may wish to adjust the size of the cells. For example, you may want the case caption box to be wider. To adjust the width of each cell, hold the [Ctrl] key down and press or [←] until the cell reaches the desired width.

9. Once the widths of the cells are properly adjusted, press [F7] to exit the table edit mode and return to the regular edit mode. You are now ready to enter text into the case caption.

■ *Don't worry about the narrowness of the case caption cell. The cell will expand automatically to accommodate any written text.*

Entering text in a case caption

Each cell in a table is a "virtual page." In other words, WordPerfect treats each cell as if it were an individual page.

1. With the cursor in the left cell, type the name of the plaintiff(s). If there are multiple plaintiffs in this litigation and the names extend further than one line, WordPerfect will wrap the text automatically

> **TIP**
>
> Use [Ctrl][→] and [Ctrl][←] (column width) in the table edit mode to quickly make adjustments to the amount of text that will fit on each line within a cell by adjusting the size of the cell.

within the cell. When finished, press [Enter] twice to insert several hard returns. Note that the table automatically expands as new lines are added.

- *When in the left cell, the status line should indicate A1; in the right cell, B1.*

- *Sometimes WordPerfect will make it appear as if the text is extending further than the width of the cell. Just continue typing, as WordPerfect will eventually wrap the text.*

2. While still in the regular edit mode, press [Alt][F8] (Flush Right) to jump the cursor to the right margin of the cell, then type `Plaintiff(s)`. Press [Enter] twice when finished.

- *You might be tempted to use [Tab] to align text, but remember that, in a WP 5.1 table, [Tab] moves you from cell to cell.*

3. Press [Shift][F6] (Center) to position the cursor in the center of the cell, then type `v.` or `-against-` or the equivalent used in your office and press [Enter] again twice.

4. Continue by typing the names of the defendant(s), etc., in the case caption.

> **5.1 MACRO**
>
> Use the TABLECAP.WPM macro to have WordPerfect create this case caption for you automatically.

5. Press [Tab] to jump the cursor to the next cell (notice how it moves automatically to the first line), then type the name of the pleading, the index number, and any other relevant information. When finished, press [↓] until the cursor is out of the caption. A completed case caption should look similar to the sample caption below.

```
SUPREME COURT OF NEW YORK
```

Guy Wiggins,
                         Plaintiff(s),
 	
           -against-
 	
John Doe,
                         Defendant(s).
	INDEX NO. 1234
	
	AFFIRMATION
	IN SUPPORT

4.1.3 CREATING A CASE CAPTION USING NEWSPAPER COLUMNS AND LINE DRAW

Using newspaper columns and Line Draw is an alternative method for creating case captions. However, this method is not as highly recommended as the Tables feature because it is more complicated and awkward. Nonetheless, it does have the advantage of allowing you to use any character you wish when drawing a case caption.

Creating a case caption using this method involves the following steps—and, yes, they are a bit tedious at first. If you decide that you have better things to do with your time, be aware that all of the following steps have been automated by the 50COLCAP.WPM and 51COLCAP.WPM macros described in Appendix C and included on the supplementary disks. For details on these macros, see below.

MACRO

Use the 50COLCAP.WPM macro to have WordPerfect 5.0 create the caption for you automatically, or 51COLCAP.WPM for WordPerfect 5.1.

Step 1: Create two newspaper columns and enter the name of the court

Case captions are divided into two discrete elements, the caption itself with the names of the plaintiff and defendant, and the case number with the name of the pleading. This construction lends itself to use of the newspaper columns feature. Newspaper columns provide boundaries for the Line Draw feature and ensure that editing and formatting changes in one element of the caption will not affect the other element. The following keystrokes create three columns, one approximately 4.4" long, one .1" long, and the third 2.2" long. However, the size of these columns may have to be altered depending on the particular style of your firm or jurisdiction.

WP 5.1

1. Press [Alt][F7] (Columns/Tables).
2. Select [1] Columns.
3. Choose [3] for **D**efine.
4. Choose [2] for **N**umber of Columns, type 3, and press [Enter].
5. Choose [4] for **M**argins, then enter the following lengths for each column: Column 1: 1", 5.4"; Column 2: 5.4", 5.5"; and Column 3: 5.7", 7.9". (You must press [Enter] to go from one margin to the next.) When finished defining the column margins, press [F7] (Exit).

■ *WordPerfect defaults to newspaper columns.*

6. Choose [1] for **O**n to turn on the columns mode (notice now that the bottom right of the screen now says "Col 1").

7. Type the name and district of the court that will appear at the top of the case caption, then press [Enter] (e.g., United States District Court, Southern District of New York).

WP 5.0

1. Press [Alt][F7] (Columns/Math).
2. Press [4] for Column **D**ef.
3. Select [2] for **N**umber of Columns, type 3, and press [Enter].
4. Choose [4] for **M**argins, then enter the following lengths for each column: Column 1: 1", 5.4"; Column 2: 5.4", 5.5"; and Column 3: 5.7", 7.9". (You must press [Enter] to go from one margin to the next.) When finished defining the column margins, press [F7] (Exit).
5. Choose [3] for **C**olumn On/Off.
6. Type the name and district of the court that will appear at the top of the case caption, then press [Enter] (e.g., United States District Court, Southern District of New York).

Step 2: Use Line Draw to draw the caption box

[Lawyers are a] society of men . . . bred up from their youth in the art of proving by words multiplied for the purpose, that white is black and black is white, according as they are paid.

Jonathan Swift,
Gulliver's Travels
[1667–1745]

WordPerfect's Line Draw feature allows you to draw lines and boxes using virtually any character you wish. As such, it is very handy for drawing caption boxes using single or double lines (as well as a host of other Line Draw characters). A disadvantage of Line Draw, however, is that there is often a major discrepancy between what you see on the editing screen and what actually gets printed. This is especially noticeable when you use proportionately spaced fonts such as Times or Helvetica. Fortunately, by using the three-column method, we can get around this limitation. (See Chapter 6 for a more complete discussion of fonts.)

In the following example, we will use Line Draw to create a caption using single lines. We'll then use column 2 to insert the close parenthesis mark [)], per the New York Rules of Court. And, because we have already defined our column widths, we can use the column boundaries as guides for the Line Draw feature. The horizontal length of the caption box will be 4.4" (if the above column margins are used), while the vertical length should generally be about 2".

Please follow our instructions scrupulously or else you may find yourself floundering and frustrated.

1. Press [Ctrl][F3] (Screen).
2. Choose [2] for **L**ine draw.

3. Choose [1] for a single line ([2] can be used for double lines and [4] presents you with another menu of Line Draw options, if you prefer). Hold down the [→] to draw the line to the margin of the first column. Note that the cursor will stop when it reaches the margin of the column.

4. With Line draw on and the cursor at the right margin of the first column, choose [6] for **M**ove and press [↓] for about 2".

5. Press [1] again to turn Line Draw back on, and press [←] until you reach the left margin of the page.

6. Press [F7] to exit Line draw. Voilà, you've drawn the first part of the caption.

Now, we have to move to column 2 before we complete the caption box. Follow these next steps carefully or you'll have a mess on your hands.

7. **THIS STEP IS EXTREMELY IMPORTANT!** Press the [End] key to move the cursor to the end of the line you've just drawn, then press [Enter] to place a hard return after the line. This puts you in position to create column 2.

> ■ *WARNING: If you press [Ctrl][Enter] before placing a hard return after the bottom line of the case caption, lines from the first column will move to the second column. Press Reveal Codes ([Alt][F3] or [F11]), place the cursor on top of the [HPg] (Hard Page) code, and press [Del] to restore the appearance of the first column.*

8. Now, press [Ctrl][Enter] (Hard Page) to move to column 2. Press [Enter] until the cursor is at the same level as the first case caption line, and press [Shift][O] to insert the close parenthesis mark [ )] for the case caption.

> ■ *Because the column is only .1" wide, the brackets flow down the column without having to press the [Enter] key.*

9. When finished, press [Ctrl][Enter] (Hard Page) to move to the third column. Your completed case caption should look something like this:

```
SUPREME COURT OF NEW YORK
_____ )
                                     )
                                     )
                                     )
                                     )
                                     )
                                     )
                                     )
                                     )
_____ )
```

> **TIP**
>
> If you should make a mistake while in the Line Draw function, choose for **E**rase and retrace your steps to delete the mistake. You can also move the cursor to another position on the screen without drawing by pressing [6] for **M**ove.

> **TIP**
>
> After you've finished drawing a line, eliminate those little arrowheads at the ends by placing your cursor on each of them and pressing the [End] key while still in Line Draw. Not only will this make your captions and whatever other graphics you create attractive on the screen, but it will keep the ends of your lines straight on your printouts.

5.1 TIP

To quickly move the cursor from column to column, press Alt→ or Alt← to move to the right or left column, respectively.

5.0 TIP

To quickly move the cursor from column to column, press 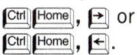 Ctrl-Home, → or Ctrl-Home, ←.

Step 3: Insert text in the caption box

1. Press Ctrl← to move the cursor back to the first column.
2. Use Tab, Center (Shift-F6), Flush Right (Alt-F6), and cursor keys to place text.

   ▮ *The Tab key and the Flush Right function are especially useful for aligning words such as Plaintiff and Defendant. By contrast, we recommend never using the Spacebar to position text since this is often very inexact and spacing can vary from printer to printer, depending on the kind of font used, etc. If you need to delete an entire line, use the Delete to End function (Ctrl-End).*

3. After you input the caption text, press Ctrl→ twice to move to the third column. Then, enter the case or index number and pleading title, if any.

Step 4: Turn the newspaper columns off

Once the case number and pleading title have been entered in column 3 of the case caption, use the following keystrokes to turn off the columns mode and return WordPerfect to the regular editing mode.

1. Press Alt-F7 (Columns/Tables).
2. **WP5.1** Choose 1 for **C**olumns.
   WP5.0 Choose 3 for **C**olumn On/Off.
3. Choose 2 for **O**ff.

▼▲▼▲▼▲▼▲▼▲▼▲▼▲▼▲▼▲▼▲▼▲▼▲▼▲▼▲▼▲▼▲

A [Col Off] code has been inserted.

The cursor should jump to the bottom-left margin of the document, and the status line at the bottom-right hand corner of the screen should no longer include a column number indicator.

4. Press Shift-F7 (Print Preview) or Alt-V to view the caption, which we have no doubt will look exactly like the one below.

```
SUPREME COURT OF NEW YORK
────────────────────────────────X
Guy Wiggins,                    )    INDEX NO. 1234
                 Plaintiff(s),  )
                                )    AFFIRMATION
        -against-               )    IN SUPPORT
                                )
John Doe,                       )
                 Defendant(s).  )
────────────────────────────────X
```

4.1.4 USING THE CAPTION MACROS

The 50COLCAP.WPM or 51COLCAP.WPM macros, described in Appendix C and included on the supplementary disks, automatically perform the steps described above. In addition, the macros will prompt the user for the court name, the name of the litigants, the case number, and the pleading title. To use it, follow these steps:

1. Press [Alt][F10] (Macro) and type `50colcap` or `51colcap` at the "Macro:" prompt.

2. Type the name of the court and press [F7] to continue the macro. The macro will prompt you at each part of the case caption.

> ■ *We have designed the WordPerfect 5.1 macro so that the user must press the [F7] (Exit) key to go from one prompt to another. The WordPerfect 5.0 macro uses the [Enter] key. The advantage of being able to use [F7] is that you can use [Enter] to insert a hard return for text and names that require more than one line. Please note, however, that the case caption created by the macro conforms to the New York Rules of Court and may have to be modified for other jurisdictions.*

4.2 INTERMEDIATE WORDPERFECT PLEADING CREATION SKILLS

If you followed our directions fastidiously, you have completed the previous exercise with little or no trauma. Your reward is the opportunity to learn about what is one of WordPerfect's most powerful features, merge templates.

4.2.1 USING MERGE TEMPLATES TO AUTOMATE PLEADINGS

In this chapter, as in just about every other one, you will find us extolling the virtues of merge codes in turning ordinary legal documents into reusable merge templates. We believe that the greatly enhanced merge language of WordPerfect 5.1 is one of WordPerfect's strongest features for the legal profession and something that every law firm should use to automate their document production. In fact, many pleadings are perfect candidates for merge templates. For example, this chapter will show you how to create a Notice of Motion template that incorporates a case caption and a pleading cover template. (*Note*: The template example used in this chapter is based on the form for a notice of motion as described in 212.10 of the Uniform Civil Rules for the District Courts of New York State.)

If you've read Chapter 2, you've already been introduced to the use of the {INPUT} code (WP5.1) and the ^O and ^C codes (WP5.0) to create simple keyboard merges. (If you haven't, don't worry. We'll go over their use again.) This chapter will introduce several new merge codes that can be used in creating templates as well. The merge codes discussed in this chapter are as follows, depending on the version you are using. Both use similar concepts, although WP5.1's codes are much more powerful and intuitive to use.

WP5.1

- **The {INPUT} command**: allows the user to enter text from the keyboard into a document during a merge.
- **The {NEST PRIMARY} command**: turns control of the merge over to the named primary file. When the commands in the nested file have been executed, control is returned to the original primary file.
- **The {NEST MACRO} command**: turns control of the merge over to the named macro. When the macro has been executed, control is returned to the original primary file.
- **The {CHAIN PRIMARY} command**: turns control of the merge over to the named primary file, and does not return to the original primary file.
- **The {CHAIN MACRO} command**: turns control of the merge over to the named macro, and does not return to the original primary file.

SOFTWARE

West's Express Forms contain dozens of high quality forms on disk that currently cover consumer bankruptcy law and California litigation, including pleadings and jury instructions. For more information on Express Forms, please call 800-328-9352.

WP 5.0

> - The ^O*message*^O code: displays the message on the status line. Used in conjunction with the ^C code.
> - The ^C code: temporarily pauses the merge so that text can be entered from the keyboard. [F9] is pressed to continue the merge.
> - The ^G*macro name*^G code: turns control of the merge (known as *Chaining*) to the named macro.
> - ^P*file name*^P code: inserts the named file in the merge (also known as *nesting*).

Basically, what you will be learning here are some simple but potent programming concepts. Do not be alarmed by the use of the term *programming*. Not only will our explanation be lucid and unintimidating, but what's more you will be rewarded when you understand these concepts and are able to use them effectively. Take our word for it, you will enjoy this!

I once heard you say that it took you twenty years to recover from your legal training—from the habit of mind that is bent on making out a case rather than on seeing the large facts of a situation in their proportion.

W. H. Page [1855–1918], American diplomat and publisher; to Woodrow Wilson

4.2.2 NESTING AND CHAINING

Nesting and chaining are powerful functions that are available in both macro and merge operations. They perform two distinct operations, but together can greatly increase the power of both your macros and merges. In merge operations, these codes are accessed by pressing [Shift][F9] twice (**WP5.1**) or once (**WP5.0**). In macro operations, they are available while in the macro editor by pressing [Ctrl][PgUp].

Nesting

When you nest a macro or a document, you are telling WordPerfect to temporarily branch off to the specified macro or document and, when finished, return to the original document or macro. In our example, the 5.1 merge command {NEST PRIMARY}caption.tem~ or the 5.0 code ^Pcaption.tem^P in the MOTION.TEM template will instruct WordPerfect to execute the CAPTION.TEM template and when finished return to the MOTION.TEM template. Alternatively, if you used the 5.1 {NEST MACRO}tablecap.wpm~ merge code, the MOTION.TEM template would execute the macro, then return to the template.

- There is no equivalent in WordPerfect 5.0 for the {NEST MACRO} merge code.

MACRO

For the adventurous, the COVERMEN.WPM macro described in Appendix C and available on the supplementary disks presents the user with menu options for a pleading cover, including a Notice of Entry and an Affidavit of Service.

Chaining

The opposite of nesting, chaining instructs WordPerfect to leave the current document and execute the specified macro or document. For example, in our sample MOTION.TEM template, the WP 5.1 {CHAIN PRIMARY}cover.tem~ code instructs WordPerfect to switch to and execute the COVER.TEM template without returning to the MOTION.TEM document. (*Note*: There is no equivalent in WP 5.0 for the {CHAIN PRIMARY} code.) Alternatively, if you used the WP 5.1 {CHAIN MACRO}cover.wpm~ command or the WP 5.0 ^Gcover.wpm^G code, control of the merge would switch to the Cover macro and would not return to the original merge document.

STEVE'S not about to pat himself on the back yet for solving the pleading problem; he's aware that this is only the first step, albeit an important one, in the process of automating the creation of pleadings he will routinely be using for his cases.

Once again, you will be the beneficiary of Steve's labors.

4.2.3 CREATING A PLEADING MERGE TEMPLATE THAT INCLUDES A CASE CAPTION AND A PLEADING COVER

The purpose of creating templates is to automate as much as possible all routine, repetitious, and tedious tasks. Besides the filling in of text, examples of this might include the creation of the case caption and the pleading cover necessary to file the pleading in court. For our example, Steve will create three different templates: (1) a case caption, (2) a notice of motion, and (3) a pleading cover, and tie them together using the WP 5.1 {NEST PRIMARY} and {CHAIN PRIMARY} merge codes. (Steve will also demonstrate how the ^P code is used in WP 5.0.) The complete merge operation will work like this:

1. The merge will retrieve the Notice of Motion template.

2. The {NEST PRIMARY} or ^P code will make the merge branch off temporarily to the case caption template. Once that is filled in, the user will be returned to the Notice of Motion template.

3. When the Notice of Motion template is completed, the {CHAIN PRIMARY} or ^P code will retrieve the pleading cover template.

Steve's first order of business is to turn the case caption, notice of motion, and pleading cover into simple merge templates by using the 5.1 {INPUT} code and the 5.0 ^O and ^C codes. Then he'll tie them together by using the {CHAIN PRIMARY}, {NEST PRIMARY} and ^P codes.

> **TIP**
>
> The {INPUT}~ or the ^O merge code prompts may be easily edited in the same fashion as regular text. Just keep in mind that the length should be limited to about 40 characters or the prompt will become obscured by the status line at the bottom right-hand side of the screen. Also, *never* delete the all-important tilde sign (~) or the merge will not work.

Step 1: Create a case caption and pleading cover template

To create a template from a case caption and pleading cover, simply replace the Court of Venue, names of plaintiffs and defendants, etc., with the {INPUT} or ^O^C codes by using the following steps:

1. Retrieve the case caption or cover you wish to use as a template.

■ *The double lines in our sample pleading cover template were drawn using the Line Draw feature:* [Ctrl][F3] *(Screen),* [2] *for Line draw,* [2] *for a double line. For details on the Line Draw feature, please see the instructions above on how to create a case caption.*

2. **WP5.1** Delete the Name of the Court and insert an {INPUT} code by pressing [Shift][F9] (Merge Codes), [3] for **I**nput. At the "Enter Message:" prompt, type the prompt to be used for the keyboard merge (example: ENTER COURT OF VENUE, [F9] TO CONT.).

WP5.0 Delete the Name of the Court, insert a ^O message code by pressing [Shift][F9] (Merge Codes), [O], type the message, then follow the message with another ^O code and the ^C code to pause the merge (for example: ^OENTER COURT OF VENUE, [F9] TO CONT.^O^C).

> **TIP**
>
> Most legal documents do not require special fonts in order to be filed in court so you can get away with using the Courier 10- or 12-point typeface that comes standard on most laser printers. However, you generally cannot file a pleading cover in court using the Courier typeface. Pleading Covers are an example of a legal document that requires the use of special fonts, such as Times Roman or Helvetica. For an in-depth discussion of using and choosing fonts in WordPerfect, turn to Chapter 6.

3. Repeat the above steps for the names of the parties, pleading number and name, etc. The finished caption heading and pleading cover should look something like Figures 4.2 and 4.3.

4. Save the caption or cover by pressing [F10] (Save). We recommend using the .TEM extension when naming template files.

WP5.1 Step 2: Create a Notice of Motion template

Our sample Notice of Motion pleading template MOTION.TEM (see Figure 4-5) begins with the {NEST PRIMARY} code to retrieve

FIGURE 4-2a

A sample WordPerfect 5.1 Case Caption template is shown (CAPTION.TEM).

```
{INPUT} ENTER NAME OF COURT, F9 TO CONT.~
{INPUT}ENTER PLAINTIFF NAME,
[F9] TO CONT.~                    INDEX NO: {INPUT} ENTER
                                  INDEX #, [F9] TO CONT.~
              Plaintiff(s)
       v.                         {INPUT}ENTER NAME OF
                                  PLEADING, [F9] TO CONT.~
{INPUT}ENTER DEFENDANT NAME,
[F9] TO CONT.~
              Defendant(s)
_____
```

FIGURE 4-2b

A sample WordPerfect 5.1 Notice of Motion Pleading (NOTICE.TEM) is shown.

{NEST PRIMARY}caption.tem~

Upon the affidavit of {INPUT}ENTER FULL NAME~, sworn to on {INPUT}ENTER DATE~, and upon {INPUT}LIST SUPPORTING PAPERS~, the {INPUT}ENTER PLAINTIFF OR DEFENDANT~ will move this court at {INPUT}SPECIFY THE PART~, at the {INPUT}ENTER NAME OF COURTHOUSE~, {INPUT}ENTER LOCATION OF COURTHOUSE~, New York, on the {INPUT}SPELL OUT THE DAY~ of {INPUT}ENTER MONTH~, 1992, at 9:30 a.m. for an order {INPUT}ENTER THE RELIEF REQUESTED~.

The above entitled action is for {INPUT}STATE NATURE OF ACTION~. This action {INPUT}ENTER IS/IS NOT~ on a trial calender. Pursuant to CPLR 2214(B), answering affidavits, if any, are required to be served upon the undersigned at least 7 days before the return date of this motion.

Dated:

_____
{INPUT}ENTER ATTORNEY NAME~
{INPUT}ENTER ATTORNEY ADDRESS~
{INPUT}ENTER TELEPHONE NUMBER~

TO:_____
{INPUT}ENTER ATTORNEY NAME FOR OTHER PARTY~
{INPUT}ENTER ATTORNEY ADDRESS FOR OTHER PARTY~
{INPUT}ENTER TELEPHONE NUMBER FOR OTHER PARTY~

TO:_____
{INPUT}ENTER ATTORNEY NAME FOR OTHER PARTY~
{INPUT}ENTER ATTORNEY ADDRESS FOR OTHER PARTY~
{INPUT}ENTER TELEPHONE NUMBER FOR OTHER PARTY~
==
{CHAIN PRIMARY}cover.tem~

FIGURE 4-3a

A sample WordPerfect 5.0 Case Caption template (CAPTION.TEM) is shown.

```
^OENTER NAME OF COURT, F9 TO CONT.^O^C
^OENTER PLAINTIFF NAME,
[F9] TO CONT.^O^C                    INDEX NO: ^O ENTER
                                     INDEX #, [F9] TO CONT.^O^C
              Plaintiff(s)
        v.                           ^OENTER NAME OF
                                     PLEADING, [F9] TO CONT.^O^C
^OENTER DEFENDANT NAME,
[F9] TO CONT.^O^C
              Defendant(s)
```

FIGURE 4-3b

A sample WP5.0 Notice of Motion Pleading (NOTICE.TEM) is shown.

^Pcaption.tem^P

Upon the affidavit of ^OENTER FULL NAME^O^C, sworn to on ^OENTER DATE^O^C, and upon ^OLIST SUPPORTING PAPERS^O^C, the ^OENTER PLAINTIFF OR DEFENDANT^O^C will move this court at ^OSPECIFY THE PART^O^C, at the ^OENTER NAME OF COURTHOUSE^O^C, ^OENTER LOCATION OF COURTHOUSE^O^C, New York, on the ^OSPELL OUT THE DAY^O^C of ^OENTER MONTH^O^C, 1992, at 9:30 a.m. for an order ^OENTER THE RELIEF REQUESTED^O^C.

The above entitled action is for ^OSTATE NATURE OF ACTION^O^C. This action ^OENTER IS/IS NOT^O^C on a trial calender. Pursuant to CPLR 2214(B), answering affidavits, if any, are required to be served upon the undersigned at least 7 days before the return date of this motion.

Dated:

_____
^OENTER ATTORNEY NAME^O^C
^OENTER ATTORNEY ADDRESS^O^C
^OENTER TELEPHONE NUMBER^O^C

TO:_____
^OENTER ATTORNEY NAME FOR OTHER PARTY^O^C
^OENTER ATTORNEY ADDRESS FOR OTHER PARTY^O^C
^OENTER TELEPHONE NUMBER FOR OTHER PARTY^O^C

TO:_____
^OENTER ATTORNEY NAME FOR OTHER PARTY^O^C
^OENTER ATTORNEY ADDRESS FOR OTHER PARTY^O^C
^OENTER TELEPHONE NUMBER FOR OTHER PARTY^O^C
==
^Pcover.tem^P

the CAPTION.TEM template. (Alternatively, you could use the {NEST MACRO} code to retrieve the CAPTION.WPM macro.) After the caption is completed, the merge returns to the body of the

FIGURE 4-4

The WordPerfect 5.1 Advanced Merge Codes menu is shown, accessed by pressing [Shift][F9] twice.

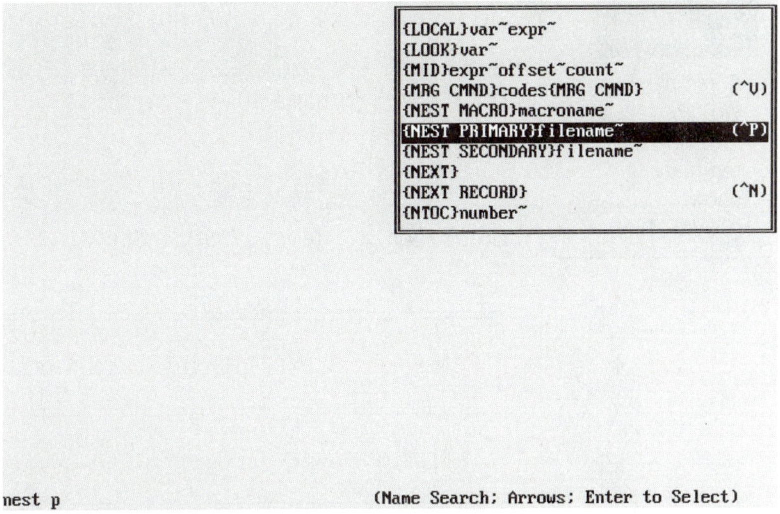

```
{LOCAL}var~expr~
{LOOK}var~
{MID}expr~offset~count~
{MRG CMND}codes{MRG CMND}           (^U)
{NEST MACRO}macroname~
{NEST PRIMARY}filename~             (^P)
{NEST SECONDARY}filename~
{NEXT}
{NEXT RECORD}                       (^N)
{NTOC}number~
```

nest p   (Name Search; Arrows; Enter to Select)

TIP

The simplest (but least powerful) way to create a template is to retrieve it into a blank document, rather than loading the file itself. For more information on this technique, look at in Chapter 2.

pleading, which uses the {INPUT} code to prompt the user to fill in the blanks. Finally, the pleading ends with the {CHAIN PRIMARY} code, which retrieves the pleading cover template COVER.TEM. Note that a hard page ([Ctrl][Enter]) has been inserted before the {CHAIN PRIMARY} code to ensure that the pleading cover is created on a new page. Use the following steps to insert the nest and chain merge codes:

Inserting advanced merge codes

1. At the first location you wish to insert the merge code in your document, press [Shift][F9] twice or press [Shift][F9], [6] for **More**.

2. When the pop-up box of merge codes appears, either scroll down the list until you find the one you need or press the first letter(s) of the code (e.g., N for {NEST MACRO}, CH for {CHAIN MACRO}). See Figure 4-4.

3. Press [Enter] to insert the code into the document, and answer the prompt, if any. For instance, when you select {Nest Primary} from the list of merge codes, you are asked to supply the name of the template. (The tilde is automatically supplied after you type the name of the template and press [Enter].)

4. Save the caption or cover by pressing [F10] (Save). We recommend using a name such as NOTICE.TEM.

The result should look like Figure 4-7.

FIGURE 4-5

A sample WordPerfect 5.1 Pleading Cover template is shown (COVER.TEM).

```
{INPUT}Enter name of court, [F9]~

{INPUT} Enter name of Plaintiff(s), [F9] to cont.~,
                                        Plaintiff(s),

            -against-
{INPUT} Enter name of Defendant(s), [F9] to cont.~,
                                        Defendant(s).


      Case No. {INPUT}Enter case number, [F9] to cont.~


       {INPUT}Enter name of pleading, [F9] to cont.~


    MARSHALL, CARDOZO, HAND, HOLMES, & BLACKSTONE, ESQS.
       Attorneys for {INPUT} Enter Plaintiff or Defendant,
                         [F9] to cont.~
                      123 Fifth Avenue
                        Suite 1800
                     New York, NY  10014
                      (212) 123-4567
```

WP5.0 Step 2: Create a Notice of Motion template

Our sample Notice of Motion pleading template MOTION.TEM (see Figure 4-7) begins with the ^P code to retrieve the CAPTION.TEM template. After the caption is completed, the merge returns to the body of the pleading, which uses the ^O^C code combination to prompt the user to fill in the blanks. Finally, the pleading ends with the ^P code, which retrieves the pleading cover template COVER.TEM. Note that a hard-page ([Ctrl][Enter]) has been inserted before the ^Pcover.tem^P code to ensure that the pleading cover is created on a new page. Use the following steps to insert these merge codes:

Inserting advanced merge codes

1. At the first location you wish to insert the merge codes in your document, press [Shift][F9] (Merge Codes).
2. Press [P] to insert the ^P code and [O] and [C] to insert the ^O^C combination. See Figure 4-6.

FIGURE 4-6

The WordPerfect 5.0 Merge Code menu is shown.

^C; ^D; ^E; ^F; ^G; ^N; ^O; ^P; ^Q; ^S; ^T; ^U; ^V;

3. Save the caption or cover by pressing [F10] (Save). We recommend using a name such as NOTICE.TEM.

The result should look like Figure 4-7.

FIGURE 4-7

A sample WordPerfect 5.0 Pleading Cover template is shown (COVER.TEM).

```
^OEnter name of court, [F9]^O^C

^OEnter name of Plaintiff(s), [F9] to cont.^O^C,
                              Plaintiff(s),

           -against-
^OEnter name of Defendant(s), [F9] to cont.^O^C,
                              Defendant(s).


     Case No.^OEnter case number, [F9] to cont.^O^C


     ^OEnter name of pleading, [F9] to cont.^O^C


  MARSHALL, CARDOZO, HAND, HOLMES, & BLACKSTONE, ESQS.
     Attorneys for ^OEnter Plaintiff or Defendant,
                [F9] to cont.^O^C
                 123 Fifth Avenue
                   Suite 1800
                New York, NY  10014
                  (212) 123-4567
```

Executing the merge

"That wasn't really that difficult," thinks Steve. "Now it's time to see if this thing really works. Here goes."

1. Press `Ctrl`+`F9` (Merge Sort), `1` for Merge, type in the name of primary file at the prompt, including the full path if not in the current directory (e.g., `c:\wp51\template\notice.tem`).

2. Simply press `Enter` at the "Secondary File:" prompt because keyboard merges do not use secondary files.

3. Enter the necessary information at each prompt and press `F9` to continue the keyboard merge until finished. If the merge did not work properly, make sure your templates are in the same directory, and that the merge codes reference the correct documents.

> **5.1 TIP**
> To stop a keyboard merge at any time, press `Shift`+`F9`, `3` for **S**top.

DON'T think we fail to appreciate how great you guys have been, conscientiously plodding step by step through these procedures and dutifully completing your exercises. Well, we're going to reward you with a brief discussion of how to use some of the desktop capabilities of WordPerfect in pleadings.

4.2.4 HOW TO CREATE PLEADING PAPER

WordPerfect comes with many desktop publishing features that can help add pizzazz and aesthetic appeal to any document. They give you the ability to insert text and graphics boxes, horizontal and vertical lines of varying widths, and even mathematical equations. While most law firms will not regularly need to use these features, there is at least one instance where a specific feature can come in very handy—the creation of pleading paper, as shown in Figure 4-8. The following steps detail how to make pleading paper using the vertical Graphic Lines feature of WordPerfect. Once you have created the pleading paper, you can copy it and refeed it through your laser printer for an inexpensive alternative to commercial paper.

If you use WP5.1, you may prefer to use the Pleading style that comes with the program. It has the advantage of being very easy to set up and it allows you to type text directly on screen. However, it does not include a line on the right side of the page. (After reading the following steps, you'll understand how to add another line.) Either way, by following the steps below, you will understand how to use Graphic Lines so that you can create or modify your own pleading paper styles.

> **SHAREWARE**
> The DEPNOT.ZIP file, available as shareware on the supplementary disks, contains merge files for depostions and subpoenas.

> **SHAREWARE**
> The FEDS51.ZIP file, available as shareware on the supplementary disks, contains WP5.1 merge forms for Federal Service of Process.

FIGURE 4-8

Creation of pleading paper using WordPerfect's vertical Graphic Lines feature.

If we mean to have heroes, statesmen and philosophers, we should have learned women. . . . If much depends as is allowed upon the early education if youth and the first principles which are instilled take the deepest root, great benefit must arise from literary accomplishments in women.

*Abigail Adams
Letter to John Adams
[August 14, 1776]*

```
 1.
 2.
 3.
 4.
 5.
 6.
 7.
 8.
 9.
10.
11.
12.
13.
14.
15.
16.
17.
18.
19.
20.
21.
22.
23.
24.
25.
26.
27.
28.
29.
```

Creating pleading paper

MACRO

Use the [Alt][V] macro to quickly view the lines in graphics mode.

The most difficult part of creating pleading paper in WordPerfect is properly aligning the vertical lines. Please note that because these lines are treated as graphic objects by WordPerfect, they cannot be seen on the normal editing screen. To view the lines, you must press [Shift][F7], [6] for **V**iew document.

Step 1: Create vertical lines

1. Change the left and right margins to 1" and .4", respectively, and the top and bottom margins to .5" and .25", respectively. (The margin settings menu is found under [Shift][F8] [Format].)

   ■ *Don't worry if, when you enter .25" as the bottom margin, WordPerfect insists on changing the setting to a slightly larger measurement. You're simply being told that that's the smallest margin it will accept.*

   ■ *The margins must be changed so that the vertical lines can extend the full length of the page and be properly placed.*

2. Press [Alt][F9] (Graphics), [5] for Line, [2] for Vertical. The "graphics: vertical line" menu should appear.

3. Press [1] for Horizontal Position, [4] for Set Position, then enter 1.25" as the position for the first line. Although it might make perfect sense to you, we find this definition a bit confusing. In WordPerfect the horizontal position of a vertical line refers to how far in from the left margin it is.

4. With the "graphics: vertical line" menu still on the screen, press [4] for Width of line, then enter .01" for the line width of the first line. When finished, press [F7] to exit. The first line of the pleading paper has now been created, to view it press [Shift][F7], [6] or [Alt][V].

A second, slightly thinner line must now be created very close to the first line on the left. To do so, the above steps must be repeated but with slightly different settings.

5. Press [Alt][F9] (Graphics), [5] for Line, [2] for Vertical. The "graphics: vertical line" menu should appear.

6. Press [1] for Horizontal Position, [4] for Set Position, then enter 1.28" as the position for the second line.

7. With the "graphics: vertical line" menu still on the screen, press [4] for Width of line (under the vertical line menu), then enter .007" as the width for the second line. When finished, press [F7] to exit. The second line of the pleading paper has now been created. You might have to view it in 100% mode in View Document, because in a full page view you won't be able to distinguish between the two lines. Now there remains the task of creating one more line on the right-hand side of the page.

8. Press [Alt][F9], [5] for Line, [2] for Vertical.

9. At the "graphics: vertical line" menu, press [1] for Horizontal Position, [4] for Set Position, then enter 8.1" as the position for the third line.

MACRO

Use the [Alt][G] macro to create graphic lines, both horizontal and vertical.

SHAREWARE

The RULENO.ZIP and RULENO2.ZIP files, available as shareware on the supplementary disks, uses sophisticated style sheets to allow users to input text directly onto the pleading paper created by the styles.

10. With the "graphics: vertical line" menu still on the screen, press [4] for **W**idth of line, then enter .007" as the width of the third line. When finished, press [F7] to exit. The third line of the pleading paper has now been created.

Step 2: Insert the line numbers

The next and last step is to type in the line numbers for the pleading paper.

1. Press [Enter] several times until the cursor is at the Line 1", Position 1" position. (Look at the status line on the bottom right side of the screen for guidance.)

2. Press the [Spacebar] once, then type 1. Press [Enter] twice and continue to type consecutive numbers, being sure to place a space before each of the numerals from 1 to 9 and to leave a line between numbers. You should be able to enter numbers up to approximately 28 or 29 for letter-sized paper. To view the complete pleading paper, press [Shift][F7], [6] or use the [Alt][V] macro.

3. Print the completed pleading paper and make copies of it to feed through your laser printer.

TIP
If the line numbers are too close to the vertical lines, you can easily change their horizontal positions a bit until it looks right.

Using the Pleading style that comes with WordPerfect 5.1

The LIBRARY.STY style library that comes with WordPerfect 5.1 and is installed by default contains a style called Pleading that will automatically insert the vertical lines and line numbers. Obviously, the advantage of using this style is you don't have to perform all the tedious steps we just had you perform. The Pleading style performs this trick by inserting the vertical lines and line numbers in a header. (For more information on using styles, refer to Chapter 2).

1. Press [Alt][F8] (Style) to access the Styles menu.
2. Highlight Pleading and press [1] for **O**n.

■ *If you do not see a Pleading style, make sure that WordPerfect is using the LIBRARY.STY style library by pressing* [Shift][F1] *(Setup),* [6] *for Location of Files. The Library File name under* [5] *for Style Files should be LIBRARY.STY.*

4.3 COMMAND REVIEW

Creating a case caption using the 5.1 Table feature

1. Type firm name, address and name of court, press [Alt][F7], [2] for **Tables**, [1] for **Create**
2. Enter [2] for # columns, [1] for # rows
3. Alter the lines surrounding the left and right cells of the table using the line draw feature, e.g., [3] for **Lines**, [1] for **Left**, [1] for **None**, to obtain the appropriate format
4. Adjust the size of the cells—[Ctrl][→] or [←]
5. Press [F7] to exit Table Edit mode and enter text into the case caption

Creating a case caption using Newspaper Columns and Line Draw

1. **WP5.1** Press [Alt][F7] and select [1] for **Columns**, [3] for **Define**. Choose [2] for Number of Columns, type 3, and press [Enter]
2. Press [4] for **Margins** and and enter the following numbers: 1, 5.4; 5.4, 5.5; 5.7, 7.9. Press [F7] when done
3. Press [1] for **On** and type the name and district of the court. Press [Enter]

WP5.0 1. Press [Alt][F7] and select [4] for **Define**. Choose [2] for Number of Columns, type 3 and press [Enter]
2. Press [4] for **Margins** and and enter the following numbers: 1, 5.4; 5.4, 5.5; 5.7, 7.9. Press [F7] when done
3. Press [3] for Column On/Off and type the name and district of the court. Press [Enter]
4. Press [Ctrl][F3] (Screen), [2] for Line Draw, [1] for a single line. Use [→] to draw the line to the margin of the first column
5. Press [6] for **Move**, and press [↓] for about 2 inches; press [1] again to turn Line Draw on again; press [←] until you reach the margin, then press [F7] to exit Line Draw
6. Press [End] to move cursor to end of line, and press [Enter]
7. Press [Ctrl][Enter] (hard page) to move to second column; press [Shift][O] to insert end parenthesis

8. Press [Ctrl][Enter] to move to third column; then press [Ctrl][←] to move cursor to first column

9. Insert text and use [Ctrl][→] or [←] to move from column to column

10. Turn off columns [Alt][F7], [1] for Columns, [2] for Off ([3] in **WP5.0**)

Creating a simple keyboard merge template for pleading headings and bluebacks (text must be entered manually for each document variable)

1. Write or retrieve the text you wish to use as a template

2. Press [Shift][F9] (Merge Codes), [3] for Input

3. At the "Enter Message:" prompt, type the prompt to be used for the keyboard merge

WP5.0 [Shift][F9], [O] to insert ^O code (type prompt), [Shift][F9], [O] to insert closing ^O code. [Shift][F9], [C] to insert ^C code

---

Retrieving and using a keyboard merge template

1. [Ctrl][F9] (Merge Sort), [1] for **Merge**, type in name of primary file at the prompt, press [Enter] at the "Secondary File:" prompt. Press [F9] to continue the keyboard merge until finished

---

Line numbering

1. [Shift][F8], [1] for Line, [5] for Line Numbering, [Y]

Using Line Draw

1. [Ctrl][F3] (Screen), [2] for Line Draw, [1] for a single or [2] for a double line

2. Use cursor arrows to draw line

Creating pleading paper

1. Change the L/R margins to 1", .4" and the T/B margins to .5", .25"

2. Press [Alt][F9] (Graphics), [5] for Line, [2] for Vertical

3. Press [1] for **H**orizontal Position, [4] for **S**et Position, then 1.25". Also, press [4] for **W**idth of line (under the vertical line menu), then .01"

4. Press [1] for **H**orizontal Position, [4] for **S**et Position, then 1.28". Also, press [4] for **W**idth of line (under the "graphics: vertical line" menu), then .007"

5. Press [Alt][F9], [5] for **L**ine, [2] for **V**ertical

6. Press [1] for **H**orizontal Position, [4] for **S**et Position, then 8.1". Also, press [4] for **W**idth of line (under the "graphics: vertical line" menu), then .007"

7. Type the number for each line (from 1 to 28), with a space before each one-digit number, separating each number by a hard return

Writing and Assembling the Brief

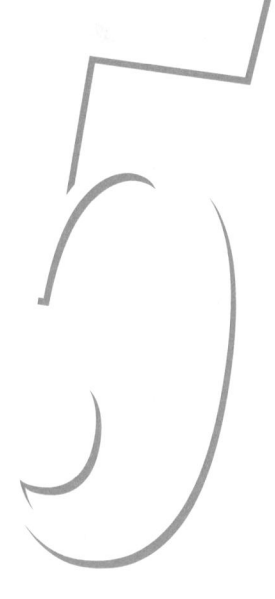

FUNCTIONS USED

- Creating an outline to structure ideas §5.2.1
- Placing footnotes §5.2.2–5.2.3
- Using endnotes to create exhibit lists §5.2.4
- Using text comments to annotate documents §5.2.5
- Using the Search and Replace function §5.2.6
- Using the Compose feature to insert special characters §5.2.8
- Creating and using macros to automate routine tasks §5.3.1–5.3.2
- Using the Tables and Parallel Columns features to create exhibit lists §5.3.3–5.3.5
- Creating a table of contents and a table of authorities §5.3.6–5.3.9

93-0000

United States Court of Appeals
for the
Second Circuit

GUARDIANS OF GOD AND GOVERNMENT

Petitioner-Appellant,

--against--

THE CITY OF SMALLVILLE

Respondent-Appellees.

ON APPEAL FROM THE UNITED STATES DISTRICT COURT
FOR THE SOUTHERN DISTRICT OF NEW YORK

BRIEF OF THE PETITIONER-APPELLANT

Marshall, Cardozo, Hand, Holmes & Blackstone
123 5th Avenue
Suite 1800
New York, NY 10014
(212) 123-4567

Of Counsel:
Linda Cardozo

"Look, a potential client.... I'm going to make sure we cross paths!..."

OVERVIEW

Upon the sacredness of property civilization itself depends—the right of the laborer to his hundred dollars in the savings bank, and equally the legal right of the millionaire to his millions.

Andrew Carnegie
Wealth. From the
North American
Review [June 1889]

Writing and assembling a legal brief or memorandum of law is without a doubt one of the most demanding tasks for both lawyers and their support staff. For lawyers, it requires legal research, writing skills, and the efficient and logical organization of ideas. For the support staff it generally means putting together a table of contents and a table of authorities and assembling exhibits, as well as the inevitable typing, retyping, and meticulous double checking of all work. Fortunately, WordPerfect can make everyone's job easier by performing much of the tedious work efficiently and with more accuracy.

This chapter will describe several WordPerfect functions that can be used to ease the burden of writing a brief, from the initial outlining of ideas to the final assembly of exhibits. It is divided into three sections: basic, intermediate, and advanced skills. (You may find it helpful to refer to the brief BRIEF.DOC we have included on the supplementary disk, available from the authors, which illustrates many of these concepts.) The skills discussed in each section are as follows.

Basic skills

- Changing line spacing
- Centering text
- Left/Right indenting text
- Underlining options
- Intermediate skills
- Using the Outline feature

Intermediate skills

- Using the Compose feature to insert the § and ¶ symbols
- Using and editing Comments
- Widows and orphans, block protect, and conditional end of page
- Using footnotes and exploring Footnote Options
- Using Endnote to number exhibits, and exploring Endnote Options

Advanced skills

- Creating and using temporary and keyboard macros
- Using the WordPerfect Tables feature and Parallel Columns feature for exhibits
- Creating a table of contents and a table of authorities

EFORE we get started we'd like to introduce you to Linda Cardozo. Linda is very competent, well organized, and resourceful. She works hard enough as a trial lawyer during the business day to find the thought of emulating Tom, who spends his after hours attempting to master WordPerfect, less than compelling. However, she is computer-savvy enough to know it has many features that can make her job much easier.

While pondering her dilemma, she hits on the wonderful idea of asking her friend Cindy, a woman she met at her previous firm, for help. If you must know, Cindy is a struggling young performance artist masquerading as a "temp" WordPerfect specialist. It might be a good idea, thinks Linda, to offer Cindy her legal services at some time in the foreseeable future in exchange for WordPerfect training.

5.1 WORDPERFECT BRIEF WRITING SKILLS— THE BASICS

5.1.1 BASIC WORDPERFECT FEATURES

SHAREWARE

The BREEF.ZIP macro file, available as shareware on the supplementary disks, includes several brief writing tools as well as a brief template.

Perhaps more than any other kind of legal document except sophisticated corporate filings, writing a brief requires a full gamut of WordPerfect skills, from the mundane to the most sophisticated. The following are the most basic ones required to write a brief or legal memorandum.

Centering text (for section headings, etc.)

MACRO

Use the [Alt][L] macro to quickly change line spacing.

Press [Shift][F6].

Changing line spacing (for long quotes, etc.)

Press [Shift][F8] (Format), [1] for Line Numbering, [6] for Line Spacing, then [1] for single spacing, [2] for double spacing.

■ *If the body of the text is double-spaced and you wish to insert a long quote that must be single-spaced, you must place a single-space code before the start of the quote and a double-space code after the quote so that the body text returns to double spacing.*

Left/right indenting (for long quotes)

TIP

Instead of pressing [F8] again to turn off underlining, press [→] once to bypass the second underlining code. This works for all appearance attributes, including italics and bold.

Press [Shift][F4].

■ *Indenting in WordPerfect is based on the tab stops. The default for tab stops is every half inch (.5") from the left margin (not from the left edge of the paper). Therefore, if you wish to indent a quote 1" from both the left and right margins, press* [Shift][F4] *twice.*

Underlining text (for cases, headings, etc.)

If the text has not been typed yet, turn on underlining by pressing [F8], type the text, and then press [F8] again. If the text has already been typed and you wish to add underlining, press [F12] or [Alt][F4] (Block), block out the text, then press [F8].

> **MACRO**
>
> Use the [Alt][I] macro to Italicize and the [Alt][U] macro for underlining options.

Underlining words only (Roe v. Wade.)

WordPerfect lets you choose whether or not to underline spaces between words. To change this option:

1. Press [Shift][F8] (Format), [4] for Other, [7] for Underline.
2. Press [N] to not underline spaces and/or tab stops.

> **SHAREWARE**
>
> The CITER2.ZIP file, available as shareware on the supplementary disks, is a sophisticated macro system that produces correct citation formats from a database of bluebook forms.

Double underlining (Roe v. Wade)

1. Press [Ctrl][F8] (Font), [2] for **Appearance**, [3] for **D**bl Und. If the text has already been typed and you wish to add double underlining, press [F12] or [Alt][F4] (Block), block out the text, then press [Ctrl][F8], [2], [3]. Just as with single underlining, you can choose the option of double underlining the words only, not the spaces.

Italicizing

1. Press [Ctrl][F8] (Font), [2] for **Appearance**, [4] for Italic. If the text has already been typed and you wish to italicize it, press [F12] or [Alt][F4] (Block), block out the text, then press [Ctrl][F8], [2], [4]. See Figure 5-1.

> **FIGURE 5-1**
>
> WordPerfect's text attributes menu includes italics, bold, and so on.

```
and federal grants.  It is capable of displaying illuminated
words and images and operates 7 days a week, 365 days a year
during the hours between sunset and sunrise.  Due to its great
size and brilliant candlepower, it is visible at night to a large
section of the community as well as to thousands of motorists who
travel along a nearby interstate highway. The uniqueness of the
Sentinel as an advertising medium has given Smallville much
national publicity, including a widely acclaimed news documentary
on network television entitled, "The Little Town with the Big
Sign."¶
     On September 1, 1989 the Smallville City Council adopted a
proposal to display symbols representing the Christian cross and
1 Bold 2 Undln 3 Dbl Und 4 Italc 5 Outln 6 Shadw 7 Sm Cap 8 Redln 9 Stkout: 0
```

5.2 INTERMEDIATE WORDPERFECT BRIEF WRITING SKILLS

5.2.1 USING THE OUTLINE FEATURE TO STRUCTURE IDEAS

The Outline feature of WordPerfect is ideal for lawyers and law students who wish to construct a framework for their ideas before beginning the task of writing a brief (or class outline). It allows them to automatically create and number an outline with up to eight levels and sublevels. And when a level is changed or deleted, the other levels are renumbered *automatically*, saving time and reducing tedium. The Outline feature makes it easy for the user to move ideas around in order to play with the structure of the document. WP5.1 has improved upon the function by allowing a *family* (defined as the current level and sublevels for that level) to be copied, moved, or deleted. Other features allow you to:

> Change the outline numbering style

> Turn the outline function on or off

If you do any writing at all, get familiar with this feature. Once you have done so, you'll wonder how you ever did without it.

> **TIP**
>
> The first time [Enter] is pressed, the first level of the outline is inserted. If you press [Enter] again without indenting or spacing, that level moves down one line (i.e., one hard return). If you want to insert a hard return after indenting or spacing in, press [Ctrl] [V] (Compose), then press [Enter].

Creating an outline

1. Press [Shift] [F5] (Date/Outline).
2. Choose [4] for **O**utline.
3. **WP5.1**   Choose [1] for On.
4. Press [Enter] to insert the first number.

 "Outline" should appear in the lower-left corner of the screen.

4. Press [4] (Indent) or space in, then type the text for that entry. When finished, press [Enter] to create the next level of the outline.

> **TIP**
>
> If you want to insert an actual tab (instead of indenting or spacing over) after the outline number before you input text, press [Home], [Tab].

Adding or changing sublevels

1. With the cursor immediately after the outline number (actually, the [Par num: Auto] code), press [Tab] to move the number to the next tab setting, thereby changing the level number. Remember to then

TIP

If the numbers of the sublevels misbehave, Reveal Codes and delete the **[-Mar Rel]** (Margin Release) codes until the proper number of the sublevel appears. (Margin Release codes are inserted when pressing [Shift][Tab].)

use the [F4] (Indent) key or the [Spacebar] before typing the text at that entry.

2. With the cursor immediately after the outline number, press [Shift][Tab] (Left Margin Release) if you need to move back a level.

Turning the Outline function on/off

With WordPerfect, you can easily turn the outlining feature on or off. However, WordPerfect 5.1 allows you to have several different outlines in the same document. Each time you turn outlining on, the new outline will begin with the number 1 or the first level's equivalent.

1. Press [Shift][F5] (Date/Outline).
2. Choose [4] for **O**utline.
3. **WP5.1** Choose [1] for On or [2] for Off.

■ *Deleting the [outline on] code is the functional equivalent of turning the outline function off.*

Changing to the Legal outline style

TIP

When you use an outlining style other than the default style (e.g., Legal), Word-Perfect inserts a **[Par Num Def:]** code first. If you want to change the outline you've already created back to the default style, simply delete the code.

WordPerfect 5.1 comes with four outline styles and allows the user to create his or her own as well. The default style is Outline—i.e., I., A., 1., a. (1), (a), i), a). However, it is likely that a law office may want to use the Legal outline style, especially when numbering clauses in a contract. (Example: 1, 1.1, 1.1.1, etc.)

1. Press [Shift][F5] (Date/Outline).
2. Choose [6] to **D**efine outline numbering.
3. Choose [4] for **L**egal.
4. Press [F7] (Exit) to return to the (Date/Outline) menu options.
5. Choose [4] for **O**utline.
6. **WP5.1** Choose [1] for On.

Creating a User-defined outline

When the four outline styles do not meet your needs, WordPerfect 5.1 allows you to define your own. You can use numbers, upper- and lowercase letters, Roman numerals, even punctuation.

1. Press [Shift][F5] (Date/Outline).
2. Choose [6] to **D**efine outline numbering.
3. Press [6] for **U**ser-defined. A menu will appear at the bottom of the screen and the cursor will jump to the current definition line. Now change the numbering scheme to whatever style you desire. For

EXERCISE: USING THE OUTLINE FEATURE

After reviewing the basics with Linda, Cindy suggests an exercise on which Linda can practice her new-found skills. She tells Linda to take any good-sized brief she wrote during her tenure at her former law firm and use the Outline feature to . . . you guessed it, write an outline of the brief. "After you do it once this way, you'll never stop using this feature," declares Cindy.

This brief was an important pro bono assignment given to Linda by a rather formidable senior partner. As an exemplar of the old school, he strongly believed that every attorney in the firm should perform pro bono work on an ongoing basis. The case is a fascinating First Amendment issue pitting the Guardians of God and Government (GGG) against the city of Smallville. The GGG has sought a declaratory judgment and an injunction to prevent the city from displaying a cross and a menorah on a large electronic billboard owned by the city on the grounds that it violates the establishment clause of the First Amendment. Judge Drew of the District Court, in a written opinion, has dismissed the claims against the city. Besides the First Amendment issue, there is also a procedural issue concerning the timeliness of the appeal.

Linda's firm represented the GGG in its appeal against the city of Smallville, and she had to write the first draft of the brief in one week. Naturally, the distinguished senior partner was a stickler for organization and the logical flow of ideas.

As Cindy advised, the first thing to do is to outline one's ideas and arguments. In the following exercise, we'll create an outline for the brief Linda wrote, then we'll practice moving, copying, and deleting families.

Below is a partial view of the outline that Linda has created for her brief. Try to reproduce the outline using the Outline feature as faithfully as possible. (The outline file is also available on disk as BRIEF.OUT.) The keystrokes are as follows:

Creating an outline

1. Press [Shift][F5] (Date/Outline).

2. Choose [4] for **O**utline.

3. Choose [1] for **O**n. (Note that "Outline" appears in the lower-left corner of the screen.)

4. Press [Enter] to insert the first number, press [F4] (Indent) to indent, then type the text for that entry. (Order of 12/9/92... etc.)

PARTIAL OUTLINE FOR SMALLVILLE APPELLATE BRIEF

I. Order of 12/9/91 was not a final judgement in accordance with Rule 58 FRCP. Therefore, Appellants appeal to the USCA for the 2nd Circuit from the order dated January 18, 1992, was timely under Rule 4 of FRAP/

    A. **KGL** case: Order is not a seperate judgement.

    B. **National Railroad**: Recent 2nd Cir case that follows KGL.

    C. **Indrelunas:** Re: Rule 58. Simple judgements are to be prepared by the court.

        1. Quotes Moore: separate document must be mechanistically applied

            a. Rule should be interpreted to prevent loss of the right of appeal.

II. The District Court erred in refusing to find that the Smallvillle proposal to display the cross and the menorah on the Smallville sentinel violated the 1st Amendment of the Constitution.

    A. The proposal as it currently stands clearly violates the **Lemon** test, which the Supreme Court uses as the standard for determining whether governmental conduct violates the establishment clause.

When finished, press [Enter] to create the next level of the outline, Roman numeral II, and again to put a line of space between the levels.

▲▲▲▲▲▲▲

The [Par Num:Auto] code has been inserted.

5. With the cursor underneath the II, press [Tab] to move the outline down one level to A., press [F4] to indent, then type the text for that level. (The District Court erred...) Type the rest of the outline, using the above steps. (Press [Shift][Tab] to move back a level.)

6. When finished, turn the outline feature off by pressing [Shift][F5], [4] for **O**utline, [2] for **O**ff. See "Partial Outline for Smallville Apellate Brief" on previous page.

Moving, copying, and deleting families

One of the enhancements of WordPerfect 5.1 over 5.0 is the ability to move, copy, and delete outline families. A family is defined as a level and any sublevels under that level. For example, in our sample outline, I. and its sublevels A., B., and C. all constitute a family, but A. and B. are childless. C. has one lovely little one, 1.

Place the cursor anywhere on the very first line of our example and press [Shift][F5]

(Date/Outline), [4] for **O**utline, and choose [3] to **M**ove, [4] to **C**opy, or [5] to **D**elete. That line and every line below it until II is highlighted. Try it with the line below (A., that is) and you'll see only that line highlighted. This is because that line has no sublevels below it; it thus comprises an entire family itself. Now place the cursor anywhere in the line on the C. level and follow the same procedure. Levels C., 1., and a. are highlighted.

Now things get a little trickier. If you have chosen Move or Copy, the message "Press Arrows to Move Family; **Enter** when done" will appear. Press any arrow to move the highlighted block to the desired location and press [Enter] when finished.

Let's try a few examples. First, something simple. Let's move level a. up a level. Place the cursor on the line, go into Outline mode, and choose [3] for **M**ove. Move the level up one line and it becomes 1. Move it up another level and it becomes a sublevel of B, or 1. Note that each time you move it up, it leapfrogs the level immediately above it and becomes a sublevel of whatever new level it is beneath. When it reaches the top it becomes a first level number.

Let's try the same thing with a family comprising more than one level. Place the cursor

anywhere on level 1. and select **M**ove family. Notice that 1. and level a. are highlighted. Now press [←] once. 1. becomes D. and its level becomes 1. Once more to the left and D. becomes Roman numeral II and its little one becomes A under level II.

It's the same routine with copying, except that when you choose Copy, the highlighted family replicates almost instantly before you are asked to "Press Arrows to Move Family; **Enter** when done." Then you can move the new family wherever you desire with the same results as in our previous exercise.

Deleting a family is self-explanatory. Simply choose [Del] to highlight the family. At the "Delete Outline Family?" prompt, press [Y] for yes. In this manner WordPerfect prevents you from making any editing changes that might cause you to later suffer trauma or despair, unless you go out of your way to do such a thing. Of course, if you delete a family despite these warnings, you can always use the undelete feature, ([F1], [1], for **R**estore). But be careful when using the undelete feature. If you wait too long before invoking it, the deleted family (or any other text you may wish to retrieve) may be gone from memory. (See Chapter 1 for more about this feature.)

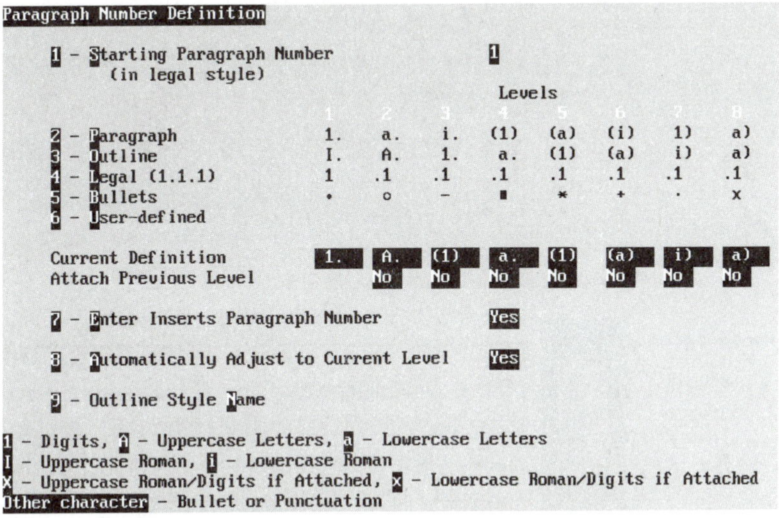

FIGURE 5-2

The Paragraph Number Definition screen is used to define Outline styles and automatic Paragraph numbers. This screen shows a User-Defined outline style.

```
Paragraph Number Definition
 1 - Starting Paragraph Number           1
     (in legal style)
                                         Levels
                            1    2    3    4    5    6    7    8
 2 - Paragraph              1.   a.   i.   (1)  (a)  (i)  1)   a)
 3 - Outline                I.   A.   1.   a.   (1)  (a)  i)   a)
 4 - Legal (1.1.1)          1    .1   .1   .1   .1   .1   .1   .1
 5 - Bullets                •    o    -    ■    *    +    .    x
 6 - User-defined

 Current Definition         1.   A.   (1)  a.   (1)  (a)  i)   a)
 Attach Previous Level      No   No   No   No   No   No   No   No

 7 - Enter Inserts Paragraph Number      Yes

 8 - Automatically Adjust to Current Level  Yes

 9 - Outline Style Name

 1 - Digits, A - Uppercase Letters, a - Lowercase Letters
 I - Uppercase Roman, i - Lowercase Roman
 X - Uppercase Roman/Digits if Attached, x - Lowercase Roman/Digits if Attached
Other character - Bullet or Punctuation
```

instance, suppose you want A. instead of I. at the first level. Type A. and it replaces I. Now let's say you want the next level to be .1. Tab over once and type .1, replacing A. Do the same for the other levels.

4. Press [F7] twice when finished to exit the outline menu.
5. Choose [4] for Outline (and [1] for **On** in **WP5.1**). See Figure 5-2.

SOFTWARE

West Publishing has now made Black's Law Dictionary available on disk for WordPerfect users. Both Black's Law Dictionary and Black's Legal Speller can be ordered from West Disk at 800-328-9352.

5.2.2 USING FOOTNOTES

Footnotes, of course, are an integral part of legal writing, especially in documents like briefs and memoranda. WordPerfect's ease of use in creating and editing footnotes is yet another reason why the program is so popular in the legal profession. For example, WordPerfect's powerful footnote feature allows you to number footnotes, place them on the same page as the note numbers, and renumber them automatically as the document is edited and as footnote codes are deleted or removed. The footnote function also does the following:

➢ Automatically reduces the text on a page to accommodate the size of the footnote. When a footnote is too long and needs to continue on the next page, WordPerfect offers the option of showing a (Continued...) message at the end of the footnote and again at the top of the footnote that continues on the next page.

➢ Allows you to specify numbering style and spacing within and between footnotes.

TIP

You can use WESTCheck to automate cite checking and verification.

- Gives you the ability to specify a minimum amount of the note that should be kept together if the footnote is split between pages.
- Allows footnotes to be spell checked along with the body of the document and legal cites in footnotes to be automatically added to a table of authorities.

CINDY is adamant that Linda learn the ins and outs of footnoting in WordPerfect. "It's a well-designed feature and easy to use," she declares. "But it sure helps to know some of the more esoteric options and a few of the little tricks I'm going to show you."

Creating a new footnote

1. Press [Ctrl][F7] (Footnote) to display the Footnote/Endnote menu.

2. Choose [1] for Footnote, then [1] for Create. The footnote/endnote screen appears, and the appropriate number is inserted.

3. Type the text for the footnote. The footnote editing screen allows all the formatting and text attributes of the regular document editing screen, so you can underline, bold, etc.

4. Press [F7] (Exit) to return to the document.

> **MACRO**
>
> Use the [Ctrl][F] macro to quickly create a footnote.

A [Footnote:*n*;[Note Num]*text*] code has been inserted.

■ *When you have created the footnote, the footnote number will appear on the screen in the color or font scheme that you have chosen to represent superscript. (Superscript means above the normal script.) As with most font and text attributes in WordPerfect, you will not see the number superscripted in the editing screen. You must go to Print Preview ([Shift][F7], [6]) to see how it will look when actually printed or use the [Alt][V] macro.*

> **MACRO**
>
> Use the [Alt][E] macro found in the SHORTCUT.WPK keyboard that comes with WP5.1 to quickly edit the footnote code. To do so, press [F11] to Reveal Codes, place the cursor on the [Footnote:*n*;[Note Num]*text*] code so that it is highlighted, and press [Ctrl][E].

Editing a footnote

1. Press [Ctrl][F7] (Footnote).
2. Choose [1] for Footnote.
3. Choose [2] for Edit. The prompt "Footnote Number?" is displayed with the number of the next available footnote.

> *These are times in which a genius would wish to live. It is not in the still calm of life, or in the repose of a pacific station, that great challenges are formed. . . . Great necessities call out great virtues.*
>
> Abigail Adams
> Letter to John
> Quincy Adams
> [January 19, 1780]

4. Press [Enter] to edit the displayed footnote, or enter the number of the note to be edited, then press [Enter].

5. When finished editing, press [F7] (Exit) to return to the document screen.

Deleting a footnote

1. Position the cursor on the footnote number to be deleted.
2. Press the [Del] key.
3. Type [Y] in response to the "Delete [Footnote:*n*]?" prompt.

■ *When you delete a footnote, WordPerfect will automatically renumber the other footnotes in the document.*

Creating a footnote from previously entered text

It is often the case in legal writing that text that was to appear originally in the body of a brief must subsequently be moved to a footnote. One of our cardinal rules is that the smart WordPerfect user never has to retype text to make an editing change, and this is true for footnotes. Instead, you can simply retrieve the text into your footnote. This can be accomplished in three ways. You can do any of the following:

> ➤ Simply delete the desired text, create a footnote (or edit an existing one), and use the Undelete feature ([F1], [1])
>
> ➤ Use the Block and Move feature by blocking the text you wish to move with [F12] or [Alt][F4], pressing [Ctrl][F4], [1], [1] (to move the block), creating or editing a footnote, and retrieving the blocked text by pressing [Enter].

TIP

To download WESTLAW documents in WordPerfect format, you need WESTMATE 4.8 or higher. For more information, call 800-937-8529.

■ *If you don't wish to retrieve the text into the footnote immediately, you may press cancel when asked to "Move cursor; press enter to retrieve" and later retrieve the text from memory by using the Move, Retrieve, Block feature keys. Remember, however, that only one block of text placed in the Retrieve memory buffer using the block and copy or move feature can be stored in that memory buffer at a time. The next operation of this sort will replace the text in the buffer with new text.*

> ➤ Block the desired text and then save it as you would a document by pressing [F10] and naming it. Then, after creating or editing a footnote, retrieve it as you would a document by pressing [Shift][F10], typing the name of the document (or in this case the block of text), and pressing [Enter]. Note that WordPerfect con-

EXERCISE: CREATING A FOOTNOTE FROM PREVIOUSLY ENTERED TEXT

With little difficulty, Linda has gotten over the first hurdle that Cindy has tossed in her way. "Too bad I didn't have this advantage when I wrote the brief two years ago; it might have saved me a lot of trouble," she thinks. Inspired by this modest triumph, she feels confident about confronting Cindy's second hurdle. "Pretend it's the second draft of the brief," announces Cindy. "Drop some of the body text on page 4 into a footnote." Here's how she does it:

1. Retrieve your brief and find some text you wish to drop into a footnote. If you are using our sample documents, retrieve the BRIEF.DOC file, and move the cursor to the last sentence of the first paragraph on page 4 ("The Supreme Court, quoting from . . .").

2. Press [Ctrl][F4] (Move), [1] for Sentence, [1] for Move. Alternatively, you can block out the sentence first, using [F12] or [Ctrl][F4], [1] for Block, [1] for Move.

3. Press [Ctrl][F7], [1] for Footnote, [1] for Create. Then, press [Enter] to retrieve the sentence.

4. Press [F7] to exit the footnote.

TIP

A quick way to jump to a specific page is to use [Ctrl][Home], enter the page number, and press [Enter].

---

siders this text to be a real document, so using this method frequently could soon lead to quite a bit of clutter on your hard disk. You might keep track of the documents you're creating each time you use this method and, after completing your revisions, go into List Files and delete each one. This method seems to us a bit awkward and would probably only work well for very long footnotes. But don't let us prejudice you in any way.

Adjusting footnote margins to conform with document margins

The default margin setting for all footnotes is 1". This remains the case *even* when you change the document margins. For example, if you changed the document margins to 2", the footnotes will stick out past the text. To ensure that both the document and the footnotes have the same margin settings, you must place the [Ftn Opt] code after the [L/R Mar:*n,n*] code. The steps are as follows.

1. Press [Home], [Home], [↑] to move to the beginning of the document, then press [F11] or [Alt][F3] (Reveal Codes) to reveal the codes.

2. Move the cursor beyond the Margin Set Code [L/R Mar: *n,n*].

3. Press [Ctrl][F7] (Footnote).

4. Choose [1] for **F**ootnote.

5. Choose [4] for **O**ptions. The Footnote Options menu is displayed.

> *How amazing it is that, in the midst of controversies on every conceivable subject, one should expect unanimity of opinion upon difficult legal questions! In the highest ranges of thought, in theology, philosophy and science, we find differences of view on the part of the most distinguished experts—theologians, philosophers and scientists. The history of scholarship is a record of disagreements. And when we deal with questions relating to principles of law and their application, we do not suddenly rise into a stratosphere of icy certainty.*
>
> Charles Evans Hughes
> Speech to the American Law Institute
> [May 7, 1936]

6. Press [F7] (Exit) to return to the document.

■ *The [Ftn Opt] code is created merely by entering and exiting the Footnote Options menu. You needn't make any changes.*

▲▲▲▲▲▲▲▲▲▲▲▲▲▲▲▲▲▲▲▲▲▲▲▲▲▲▲▲▲▲▲

The Footnote Option code [Ftn Opt] is now inserted. All footnotes will now take on the margins that were set when the [Ftn Opt] code follows the Left/Right Margin code.

Making the footnotes smaller than the body of the document

If you would like your footnotes to be a smaller point size than the text of the body of the document, and you want to avoid the bother of editing each individual footnote and inserting a code to effect this change, we've got a shortcut for you.

1. Press [Shift][F8], [3] for Document, and [2] for Initial Codes.
2. In the Initial Codes screen, press [Ctrl][F8] and [4] for base font.
3. From the list of fonts, select one by pressing [1] and type the desired footnote point size (usually 1 point smaller than the body text) at the "Point Size:" prompt. Press [F7] three times to return to the document editing screen.
4. With your cursor at the very beginning of the document, press [Ctrl][F8] and [4] for base font.
5. From the list of fonts select the one you desire by pressing [1], and enter the point size.

The font code in Document Initial Codes will affect only your footnotes. The font code you placed at the beginning of your document editing screen will override the code in Document Initial Codes and affect the appearance of the rest of the document. (For a more complete discussion of fonts, point size, and other desktop publishing mysteries, see Chapter 6. For more about Initial Codes, see Appendix A.)

5.2.3 EXPLORING FOOTNOTE OPTIONS

In keeping with its tradition of offering its users full power and flexibility in document production, WordPerfect allows users to customize virtually every aspect of creating a footnote. Most of the WordPerfect defaults do not generally have to be changed. However, the following examples might prove useful to many offices. *Key point*: If you want any option change to occur for all footnotes in the document, remember to go to the beginning of the document first by pressing [Home], [Home], [↑], then change the options. WordPerfect will

> **TIP**
>
> If you want the same footnote options in all your documents, make the changes in the Initial Codes section of Initial Settings under the Setup menu [Shift][F1]. The code will then be inserted for all documents.

insert the [Ftn Opt] code and any modifications will take place from that point on. The following options can be accessed by pressing [Ctrl][F7], [1] for Footnote, [4] for Options.

Changing the footnote line spacing

The first choice in the Footnote Options menu allows you to change both the line spacing within footnotes and the amount of space between footnotes on the same page. If you want to make the spacing within the text of the footnotes double space, simply go into this option and change 1 to 2. To change the default for space between footnotes, select [1], press [Enter] once, and type in a value. Simple.

Changing the amount of footnote text to be kept together

The second option, "Amount of note to keep together," refers to the minimum size of the footnote text if the footnote is split between pages. The default is .5", meaning that, if WordPerfect decides in whatever way it does these things (this is not your decision) that the footnote must be continued on the following page, the depth of the footnote text on the first page will be .5". You can change that to whatever amount you'd like (within reason).

Changing the appearance of footnote numbers

> **MACRO**
>
> To see how the footnote character will look when printed, go to the View Document mode by pressing [Shift][F7], [6], or use the [Alt][V] macro.

Options 3 and 4 control the style for footnote numbers in the text and note, respectively. The default for the footnote number style in the text is superscripted (i.e., higher and smaller than the normal text). You can alter this. In the following example, we'll change the footnote number in the text from plain superscript to superscript, bold italic.

1. Select [3] and press [←] once. Don't worry if you don't see the cursor move; it's not supposed to.

2. Now press [F6]. You'll see the Bold code appear.

3. To italicize, choose [Ctrl][F8] (Font), [2] for Appearance, [4] for **I**talic.

4. Move the cursor to the end by pressing [End] and insert the bold and italics codes by pressing [F6] and [Ctrl][F8] (Font), [2] for **A**ppearance, [4] for **I**talic again. The footnote options screen should look like Figure 5-3.

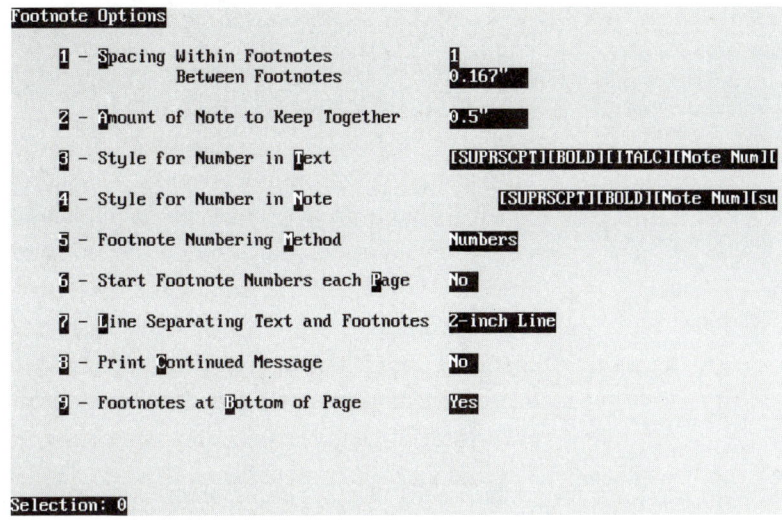

FIGURE 5-3

The Footnote Options screen shows the Style for Number in Text changed to superscript, bold, italics.

5. Press [F7] or [Enter] twice to exit. Voilà, an italicized, superscripted, bold footnote number. You can also simply eliminate the superscript option by deleting the codes.

Changing the indenting of footnote text

As you can see, the default style for footnote numbers in the actual footnote is superscript and the first line is indented five spaces. You may, if you would prefer the first line of the footnote text to be flush left, delete those spaces. Simply select [4] and press [Del] five times. You can also change the style in the same manner as you would in the prior example.

Changing the footnote numbering method

In the vast majority of cases, you will want to use numbers for footnotes. However, there may be that special occasion when you want to use a dagger, a double dagger, or an asterisk instead. Word-Perfect will use the character you choose, and then double it, triple it, etc., for each new footnote. The following steps take you through the use of either a single (or double) dagger as a footnote character (**WP5.1** only), or an asterisk.

1. Press [Ctrl][F7] (Footnote).
2. Choose [1] for **F**ootnote.
3. Choose [4] for **O**ptions. The Footnote Options menu is displayed.
4. Choose [5] for Footnote Numbering **M**ethod. The numbering method menu is displayed.

Chapter 5 Writing and Assembling the Brief
§5.2

> One who belongs to the most vilified and persecuted minority in history is not likely to be insensible to the freedoms guaranteed by our Constitution. . . . But as judges we are neither Jew nor Gentile, neither Catholic nor agnostic.
>
> Justice Felix Frankfurter, dissenting, *West Virginia State Board of Education v. Barnette* (Flag Salute Cases), 319 U.S. 624, 646-47 [1943]

5. Choose [3] for **C**haracters. (Pay attention; things get a little tricky here.)

6. Press [Ctrl][2] or [Ctrl][V] (Compose).

7. **WP5.1** Type 4,39, then press [Enter] for a single dagger (†) or 4,40 and [Enter] for a double dagger (‡). A small box will be inserted, which will appear as a single or double dagger in print view mode after you've created your footnote or footnotes. These numbers signify the 39th and 40th characters in the 4th WordPerfect character set (Typographic symbols). (For more information on WordPerfect character sets and the Compose feature, refer to or consult your WordPerfect manual.) To make your footnote an asterisk, simply press [Shift][8].

> ■ *WP5.0 does not print many special characters. To see if a special character is supported, use Compose, then Print Preview ([Shift][F7], [6]) and see if it appears on the screen. If it does, you should be able to print it.*

If you move the cursor to the square, you will see the numbers that represent that character (e.g., [4,40] for the double dagger).

8. Press [F7] (Exit) twice to return to the document.

Renumbering footnote numbers on each page

To begin footnote numbering anew on each page so that the first footnote (on each page) begins with the number 1, press [Ctrl][F7], [1] for **F**ootnote, [4] for **O**ptions, [6] for Start Footnote Numbers Each **P**age, and press [Y].

> ■ *If you want to change the number of a particular footnote (i.e., make footnote number 7 number 9), place your cursor on the footnote number in the text, press [Ctrl][F7], [1] for **F**ootnote and [3] for **N**ew Number. Type the desired number, then press [↑] or [↓]—you'll see the new number. A [New Ftn Num:#] code will be placed in front of the existing footnote code. However, the footnote number following 9 (if there is one) will be 10 and the next one will be 11, etc.*

Changing the line size separating text from footnotes

Option 7 really gives you only three options for the size of the line separating the text from the footnote: the standard 2", all the way across the page, and none.

Inserting a "Continued..." message for long footnotes

Legal footnotes are often long and detailed enough to get split between different pages of a brief. When this happens, you may want WordPerfect to add a (Continued...) message to the bottom of the page. The (Continued...) message will appear at the end of the footnote on the first page and the same message will appear at the beginning of the footnote on the next page. You aren't allowed to be any more creative in the wording of this message; it's automatically generated and can't be edited.

If, for some reason, your firm places its footnotes at the end of the document on a separate page or pages, use the endnote feature (`Ctrl`+`F7`, `2`). The procedures are very similar, and we'll trust your ability to apply the knowledge gained from reading about footnotes to endnotes. However, there is another less obvious use of the Endnote feature: numbering exhibits and creating an exhibit list.

Footnotes often appear in a smaller point size than the body of the text. To achieve this without inserting a code into each separate footnote, do the following: Press `Shift`+`F8`, `3` for Document, and `2` for Initial Codes. In the Initial Codes screen press `Ctrl`+`F8`, `4` for Base Font, and `1` for Select. At this time you can input the desired point size. This point size will affect the text in all the footnotes in your document. Press `F7` several times to return to the document screen.

Now go to the very beginning of your document and press `Shift`+`F8`, `3` for Document, and `3` for Initial Base Font. Once again press `1` for Select and indicate the desired point size, i.e., a point larger than the point size selected for the footnotes. This size will affect the text of the document, but not the footnotes.

5.2.4 USING THE ENDNOTE FEATURE TO NUMBER EXHIBITS AND CREATE AN EXHIBITS LIST

The importance of footnotes is clear to all legal professionals. Endnotes, however, are not as commonly used in the legal profession, and it may be easy to overlook some of the uses of the Endnote feature. For example, in a document such as a brief, the Endnote feature can be used to automatically number supporting exhibits and create an exhibit list. There are three steps to using the Endnote feature in this manner:

➤ Changing the default settings in Endnote options

- Placing the Endnote code at each reference to an exhibit in your document
- Preparing the Exhibit List page

Step 1: Change endnote options

> *Whenever you wish to do anything against the law, Cicely, always consult a good solicitor first.*
> — George Bernard Shaw [1856–1950]
> *Sir Howard, Captain Brassbound's Conversion.*

As in WordPerfect's Footnote feature, the user has extensive control over how he or she wishes the endnotes to appear in a document. However, for our purposes, WordPerfect's defaults should be retained except for Endnote Options 3 (Style for Numbers in Text) and 4 (Style for Numbers in Note).

1. Press [Home], [Home], [↑] to move the cursor to the beginning of your brief.

2. Press [Ctrl][F7], [2] for **E**ndnote, [4] for **O**ptions.

3. Choose [3] for **T**ext and at the prompt, type [Exhibit, press [Spacebar], press [Ctrl][F7], [2], [2] (to insert the [Num Code]), and then type the closing bracket,]. Press [Enter] when done.

■ *The above is a simple, generic example. Use parentheses, punctuation, or whatever format you currently use in your firm.*

4. Insert a similar numbering style for Number in **N**ote by pressing [4] for **N**ote and typing the following at the prompt: Exhibit [space], [Ctrl][F7], [2], [2] (to insert the **[Num Code]**), then type a colon (:). When finished, press [Enter] twice to return to your document.

An [End Opt] code has been inserted.

The completed Endnotes Options screen should look like Figure 5-4.

Step 2: Type the endnotes

1. At the first reference to an exhibit in your brief, press [Ctrl][F7], [2] for **E**ndnote, [1] for **C**reate.

2. Press [F4] to indent, then type the description of the exhibit. Notice that the "Style for Number in Note" that you chose in step 1 appears in the footnote editing window.

3. When finished, press [F7] to return to your document.

■ *You do not have to place a hard return at the end of your description to put a space between endnotes. This is handled by the endnote option*

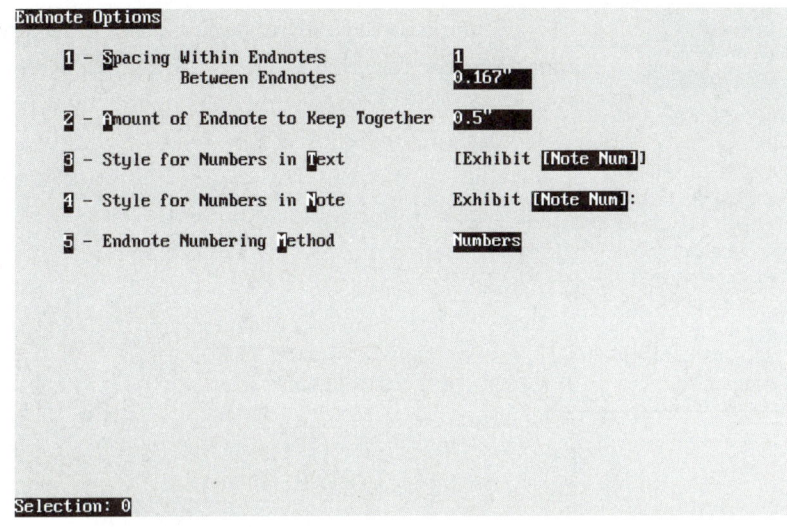

FIGURE 5-4

The Endnote Options screen shows the style used to number exhibits in the text and in the endnote.

"Spacing Between Endnotes," which automatically places a blank line between each endnote.

4. Repeat this process for each new exhibit in your brief.

Step 3: Create a separate Exhibit List page

1. Press [Home], [Home], [↓] to move to the end of the document, then press [Ctrl][Enter] to place a hard page break.

2. Center and type EXHIBIT LIST as your page heading. That's it! WordPerfect's endnote feature has automatically created the exhibit list. To see your handiwork, press [Shift][F7], [6] (Print Preview). Or, better yet, use our [Alt][V] macro.

■ *Remember that, like footnotes, endnotes are codes and cannot be seen from the editing screen.*

5.2.5 THE COMMENT FEATURE

The Comment feature is another one of the more obscure WordPerfect features that can be of tremendous use to any legal professional who has to do extensive writing or editing. Comments are text—displayed on screen with a box around it—that will not be printed with the document. (This is also known as Hidden Text.) In essence, it serves as an electronic version of a sticky tag by allowing the user to make editorial or other remarks in the text that nevertheless will *not* be printed with the document.

SOFTWARE

VoiceOver from Rational Data Systems allows you to insert spoken comments into WP5.1, turning your PC into a dictaphone. Voice comments are stored as WP comments. Call 800-743-3054 for information.

Comments have many possible uses in legal work. For example, it is often the case that the task of writing a brief is split among various associates in a firm, with final review by a partner. In this type of scenario, Comments can be used to highlight a question, problem, or anything else the user wishes to point out to someone else who will be reviewing the same document. Comments are also equally useful as personal reminders or as bookmarks to highlight items for later review.

Creating a comment

1. Press [Ctrl][F5] (Text In/Out).
2. Choose [4] (**WP5.1**) or [5] for **Comment**.
3. Choose [1] for **Create a Comment**. A double-lined box appears on the screen.
4. Type the text for the comment.
5. Press [F7] (Exit) to return to the document.

A [Comment] code is inserted.

MACRO

Use the [Ctrl][C] macro to quickly create comments. To edit a comment, use the [Ctrl][E] (edit a code) macro. To do so, Reveal Codes, highlight the Comment code with the cursor, and press [Ctrl][E].

Creating a comment from previously entered text

1. Block out the text you wish to change into a comment by pressing [Alt][F4] or [F12] (Block).
2. Press [Ctrl][F5] (Text In/Out). WordPerfect will prompt you with "Create a comment? No (Yes)."
3. Type [Y] to convert the block into a comment.

Deleting a comment

1. Press [F11] or [Alt][F3] (Reveal Codes) to locate the [Comment] code.
2. Place the cursor on the code and press [Del].
3. **WP5.1** WordPerfect will prompt you with "Delete [Comment]? No (Yes)." Type [Y] to delete the comment.

Editing a comment

1. Press [Ctrl][F5].
2. Select [4] (**WP5.1**) or [5] for **Comment**.
3. Select [2] for **Edit**. See Figure 5-5.

FIGURE 5-5

The screen shows text with a sample comment.

```
Supreme Court's holding in Bankers Trust, procedural problems
concerning the separate document rule have persisted in this
─────────────────────────────────────────────────────────────
circuit and others.
┌─────────────────────────────────────────────────────────────┐
│ Check to see if Kanematsu was denied Cert.                  │
└─────────────────────────────────────────────────────────────┘
                    In Kanematsu-Gosho, Ltd. v. M/T Mesiniaki
Aigli, 805 F.2d 47 (2d Cir. 1986), this court categorically
stated in clear and direct language how Rule 58 would be applied
in this circuit. The case concerned a motion to dismiss as
untimely an appeal that was filed later than thirty days after a
separate order filed by the court. Rejecting the position that a
document denominated an order can be a judgment that satisfies
C:\WP51\MANUAL\BRIEF.TST                      Doc 2 Pg 5 Ln 1" Pos 2.9"
```

TIP

Use the Search feature to quickly find comments in your text.

■ *When selecting Edit, you will be placed in the last comment box above the cursor. Remember, WordPerfect works in a linear fashion; therefore, until you create another comment box, the last one takes precedence.*

Turning comments into text

1. Move the cursor to the immediate right of the comment code, select Comment (`Ctrl` `F5`).

2. Press `4` (**WP5.1**) or `5` and then `3` for "convert to text." This operation will involve less guesswork if you Reveal Codes first.

5.2.6 THE SEARCH, EXTENDED SEARCH, AND SEARCH AND REPLACE FEATURES

The Search feature and the Search and Replace feature are two of the most useful features in WordPerfect and can save hours of time when text or formatting codes have to be found or changes made to long documents. These features illustrate one of the basic maxims about using a computer program wisely—let the computer do the grunt work whenever possible.

As an example, let's say you're reviewing a 50-page brief on your trusty PC and you want to check the spelling of a certain word or case. By using the Search feature, you can instantly find every occurrence of that word in the brief. And, with the Search and Replace feature, you can instantly change the spelling of each occurrence. Without these features, you'd be forced to find and change each misspelling manually, a tedious process that could take hours with lengthy documents.

Familiarize yourself thoroughly with this feature. We're sure you'll find many uses for it as you become more and more proficient with WordPerfect.

Using Search and Extended Search to search for text

> **TIP**
>
> Use Extended Search to find text in footnotes, endnotes, headers, and footers as well as the body of the brief.

1. Press [F2] (Search), [Shift][F2] (reverse search), or [Home], [F2] (Extended Search, which searches within footnotes, headers and footers as well as in the body of the text). The "->Srch:" or "->Extended Srch:" prompt should appear at the bottom of the screen.

2. Enter the text you wish WordPerfect to search for.

3. Press [F2] (Search) or [Shift][F2] (reverse search) to have WordPerfect initiate the search.

> **TIP**
>
> To change your search direction, start your search by pressing [F2], then press . Note how that little arrow changed directions.

4. To continue a normal search after the first occurrence of the text string has been found, press [F2] (or [Shift][F2] for reverse search). If you wish to continue an Extended Search, you *must* press [Home], [F2] or [Home], [Shift][F2] again.

■ *While it may be tempting, do not press* [Enter] *to start the search. This merely tells WordPerfect to search for the [HRt] code. If you do insert a [HRt] into the search, use* [Backspace] *to delete the [HRt] code, then press* [F2].

> **TIP**
>
> You can use the Search Feature [F2] to search for a file while in the List Files [F5] menu. For more information on how to use List Files, refer to Appendix B.

■ *When typed in lowercase, searches are not case-sensitive. In other words, all occurrences of the text will be found. However, if you enter the search string in uppercase letters, only uppercase occurrences will be found.*

Using Search and Extended Search to search for codes

This feature works much like the text search, except that you must enter the keystrokes necessary to insert the specific code. The following example uses the footnote code [Footnote].

1. Press [F2] (Search), [Shift][F2] (reverse search), or [Home], [F2] (Extended Search). The "->Srch:" or "->Extended Srch:" prompt will appear at the bottom of the screen.

2. Enter the keystrokes necessary to insert the proper code. For example, to insert the footnote code [Footnote], press [Ctrl][F7] (Foot-

note), then choose [1] for **Footnote**, [1] for **Note**. The [Footnote] code should appear next to the "->Srch:" prompt.

3. Press [F2] (Search) or [Shift][F2] (reverse search) to have WordPerfect initiate the search. To continue the search after the first occurrence of the text string has been found, press [F2], [Shift][F2], [Home], [F2], or [Home], [Shift][F2].

■ *To search for a code, you must have WordPerfect properly insert the code. You cannot type a copy of the code at the Search prompt.*

Using Search and Replace

1. Press [Alt][F2] (Replace) or [Home], [Alt][F2] (Extended Replace).
2. Press [N] or [Y] at the "w/Confirm?" prompt. If you answer [Y], WordPerfect will stop and ask for a confirmation before replacing the "hit" each time it finds it.
3. At the "->Srch:" prompt, type the text you wish to replace. If you want to change a code, enter the keystrokes necessary to insert the code. (For example, if you wish to replace the footnote code, press [Ctrl][F7] [Footnote], [1], [1])
4. Press [F2] again.
5. At the "Replace with:" prompt, enter the new text or codes you wish to use.
6. Press [F2] (Search) again to execute the search and replace.

■ *We just performed a forward search and replace; you can also perform a reverse search and replace by pressing [↑] at the "->Srch:" prompt to make the little arrow change direction.*

7. Type [Y] at the "w/Confirm" prompt that appears again, to indicate that you want to make the change, or [N] to skip it.

TIP

If you wish to use the Search and Replace feature to quickly and automatically delete text or codes, do not type any text or codes at the "Replace with:" prompt. Simply continue the search and replace by pressing [F2] (Replace) or [Home], [F2] (Extended Replace).

5.2.7 USING SEARCH AND REPLACE TO CLEAN UP DOWNLOADED TEXT

After downloading documents from on-line services like WESTLAW, you may frequently find it useful to replace hard-return codes with soft-return codes so that the document can be cleaned up and formatted properly. To do so, follow these steps:

1. Press [Alt][F2] (Replace) or [Home], [Alt][F2] (extended replace).
2. Press [N] or [Y] at the "w/Confirm?" prompt. If you answer [Y], WordPerfect will stop and ask for a confirmation before replacing.

3. At the "- Srch:" prompt, press `Enter` to insert the hard-return code ([HRt]).

4. Press `F2` or `Shift`-`F2`.

5. At the "Replace with:" prompt, press `Ctrl`-`V` (compose) then `Ctrl`-`M` to insert the soft return code ([SRt]).

6. Press `F2` (Search) or `Shift`-`F2` (reverse search) again to execute the search and replace.

Bringing downloaded text from WESTLAW and other on-line services into WordPerfect

> **TIP**
>
> WESTLAW gives you the option of downloading documents to disk in WordPerfect 5.0/5.1 format, so that your documents are ready to use without converting from text. Just follow these simple steps:
> 1. Type `options` at any WESTLAW screen.
> 2. Type `14` to bring up the Downloaded Format menu.
> 3. Choose either `1` for WordPerfect 5.0/5.1 format or `2` for WordPerfect 5.0/5.1 format with search terms highlighted. WESTLAW will retain this download format for all of your subsequent downloads. See Appendix B.3 for more information.

Without a doubt, the development of powerful on-line services that can be accessed from any PC equipped with a modem—such as WESTLAW, CompuServe, and Dialog—has transformed the way lawyers work. We've already touched on the subject of downloading. (To "download" means to store data available from a central database on your computer.) This seems like a good spot to talk about some of the WordPerfect techniques you can use to bring research from such services into your legal documents.

When a file from an on-line service such as WESTLAW is downloaded onto your computer's hard disk, it is stored in a format known as *ASCII*. (For the curious, ASCII stands for American Standard Code for Information Interchange.) ASCII text is completely generic and thus can be read by virtually any program that runs on a PC. It does not contain any hidden codes or special formatting. However, each line ends with a carriage return (i.e., a hard return) and a line feed. Therefore, before you can easily use ASCII text in WordPerfect, you'll need to convert the hard returns ([HRt]) into soft returns ([SRt]). Then you'll need to clean up the file by getting rid of extraneous characters. Fortunately, WordPerfect makes short work of these operations through the use of the Text In/Out function.

Step 1: Use Text In/Out to convert hard returns and line feeds into soft returns

Because downloaded text does not come set with left/right margins, the trick to successfully retrieving an ASCII file is to first set your left and right margins to 0" or as far as they'll go. (This depends on the printer you are using.)

1. Press `Shift`-`F8`, `1` for **L**ine, `7` for **M**argins, then enter 0 as your left and right margins.

2. Press `Ctrl`-`F5` (Text In/Out), `1` for **D**os Text.

3. Press [3] for **Retrieve** (CR/LF to [SFt] in Hzone).

   ■ *This means, as you've probably already guessed, that the carriage returns and line feeds will be converted to soft returns in the hyphenation zone.*

4. At the "Document to be Retrieved:" prompt, type the file name of the document you wish to retrieve and press [Enter]. If it is located in another directory, you must give the full path name (e.g., `C:\WP51\RESEARCH\LIABILIT.WL`).

Presto! Your research will appear, ready to be whipped into shape by WordPerfect's powerful formatting features. Be sure to use the Search and the Search and Replace features to quickly get rid of unwanted hard page codes ([HPg]) and extraneous text.

   ■ *If you are already a WESTLAW user, using WESTLAW's Word-Perfect Download Format option will spare you this bit of tedium. See tip on previous page and Appendix B.3 for more information.*

5.2.8 USING THE COMPOSE FEATURE TO INSERT SPECIAL CHARACTERS

The Compose feature of WordPerfect allows for the use of special characters that are not available via the keyboard. The most common special characters used in legal work are the Section (§) and Paragraph (¶) symbols, although there are many others available as well, including Trademark (™), Copyright (©), Registered Trademark (®), etc.

WordPerfect special characters are available through "Character Sets," 12 of which come with the program. (Refer to the Appendix in your WordPerfect reference manual entitled *WordPerfect Characters*.) To insert special characters into a document, you need to know the character set it belongs to, as well as its number within the character set. The following examples all come from character set 4 (Typographic Symbols).

MACRO

Use the [Alt][K] macro to quickly insert the most commonly used legal special characters.

Inserting a § and ¶ symbol

1. Press [Ctrl][V] (Compose).

   ■ *[Ctrl][2] can also be used, but it does not provide the user with a prompt.*

FIGURE 5-6

This example shows how WordPerfect displays certain special characters. Here, the Copyright symbol is shown in the edit mode as ■. In the Print Preview mode it will display as ©.

2. At the "Key =" prompt, type 4,5 for the ¶ symbol and press [Enter] (this symbol is the fifth character in the fourth character set), or 4,6 for the § symbol (this symbol is the sixth character in the fourth character set).

Inserting a © and ™ symbol

1. Press [Ctrl][V] (Compose).
2. At the "Key =" prompt, type 4,23 for the © symbol (this symbol is the 23rd character in the fourth character set), or 4,41 for the ™ symbol. See Figure 5-6.

■ *Most special characters do not display on the regular editing screen. Instead, they appear as small boxes (■). However, they should print properly. (There may be certain limitations on printing, depending on your printer.) To view your characters, use Print Preview ([Shift][F7], [6]) or the [Alt][V] macro that comes with this book.*

5.2.9 TECHNIQUES FOR KEEPING LINES OF TEXT TOGETHER

The following WordPerfect functions are used to ensure that your document does not have stray lines of text. These functions may seem purely cosmetic, but they can make an important difference in the intelligibility of the document.

The system of private property is the most important guaranty of freedom, not only for those who own property, but scarcely less for those who do not.

Friedrich August von Hayek
The Road to Serfdom [1944]

The Widow/Orphan feature

This feature is found in the Format Line menu [Shift][F8], [1]. Saying yes to this option assures you that you'll never have one line in a paragraph hanging out alone at the beginning of a page or at the end of a page. You might even put this code in your initial settings ([Shift][F1], [4], [5] [[5], [4] in **WP5.0**]) so you won't have to insert it at the beginning of every document you create. (See Appendix A for a description of initial settings.) The only drawback to this feature is that you'll sometimes encounter a block of white space at the bottom of a page as WordPerfect forces a line or two of text to the next page to avoid an instance of an orphan. If you find this circumstance unacceptable, then don't use this feature.

Block protection

Block protection is used when you want a block of text, say a small table or a list of names, kept together at all times. Simply block the desired text ([Alt][F4], or [F12]), press [Shift][F8], and answer yes to the prompt "Protect block?"

[Block Pro:On] and [Block Pro:Off] codes surround the designated text to make sure it will always be kept together.

Conditional end of page

"Conditional End of Page" is similar to Block Protect, but should be used to keep headings with the text that follows. For example, let's say you've just printed out your document only to find a heading at the bottom of page 16 floating in limbo, bereft of any of the text that follows it. Intolerable, right? Here's how to remedy the situation using the Conditional End of Page feature.

1. Place your cursor at the very beginning of the line immediately above the heading. Count the number of lines you want kept together, e.g., 1: the heading itself; 2: the line separating it from the text; 3: the first line of text itself; 4: the line separating that first line of text from the next, if the document is double-spaced; and 5: the second line of text after the heading.

2. Press [Shift][F8], [4], for **O**ther, and [2] for Conditional End of Page. In response to the prompt "Number of Lines to Keep Together," type 5, or whatever is appropriate in your situation. If five lines is insufficient, try six lines. See Figure 5-7.

FIGURE 5-7

A [Cnd|EOP:13] code above the "Questions Presented" heading ensures that the heading and questions I and II remain together on a page.

```
                         Questions Presented¶
    I.   Whether the 2nd Circuit Court of Appeals has jurisdiction
    over this appeal when the Appellant complied with Rule 4(a) of
    FRAP by filing within 30 days after date of entry of final
    judgement.¶
    ¶
    II.  Whether the district court erred in denying a preliminary
    injunction by finding that the display of the cross, the menorah
    and religious scriptures on a municipally owned electronic
    billboard located on the front lawn of the Smallville municipal
    building did not violate the establishment clause of the first
    amendment.  ¶
    ¶
    C:\WP51\MANUAL\BRIEF.TST                    Doc 2 Pg 1 Ln 3.17" Pos 1"
    ▲▲▲▲▲▲▲▲▲▲▲▲▲▲▲▲▲▲▲▲▲▲▲▲▲▲
    {   ▲    ▲   ▲    ▲   ▲   ▲    ▲   ▲   ▲   ▲   }   ▲   ▲
    jurisdiction to hear this appeal.[HRt]
    [Cndl EOP:13][HRt]
    [Center][BOLD]Questions Presented[bold][HRt]
    I.[Tab]Whether the 2nd Circuit Court of Appeals has jurisdiction[Ln Spacing:1][S
    Rt]
    over this appeal when the Appellant complied with Rule 4(a) of[SRt]
    FRAP by filing within 30 days after date of entry of final[SRt]

    Press Reveal Codes to restore screen
```

▲▲▲▲▲▲▲▲▲▲▲▲▲▲▲▲▲▲▲▲▲▲▲▲▲▲▲▲▲▲▲▲▲▲▲▲▲

A [Cnd] EOP:#] code is inserted. Try to keep this code on the line immediately above the heading when performing revisions to the document in order to ensure its continued effectiveness. If any extra lines of text are placed between the code and the heading, it will impair the code's effectiveness and you'll have to place it again.

5.2.10 USING HYPHENATION TO IMPROVE THE APPEARANCE OF YOUR DOCUMENT

A good way to make your documents look better is to use hyphenation. Documents that are right-justified tend to have large, unsightly spaces between some words. Hyphenation will make the interword spacing more even, giving the document a professional look. In documents that are left-justified, hyphenation can make the right margin look less "ragged," so there will be fewer large gaps.

It's easy to apply hyphenation; simply move your cursor to the point in the document where you want hyphenation to begin (usually the very beginning), press [Shift][F8], [1] for Line, [1] for Hyphenation, [Y], and Exit until you return to the editing screen. A [Hyph On] code will be inserted. As you move [↓], any words that fall into the Hyphenation Zone will be hyphenated. "Hyphenation Zone? What's that," you may very well ask. Obviously, there are a few other things you should know.

First, let's look at the Setup menu. Press [Shift][F1] and [3] for Environment. There are three settings here that directly apply to hyphenation. The first, [F7] **P**rompt for Hyphenation, has three settings: [1] for **N**ever, [2] **W**hen Required, and [3] for **A**lways. In the interest of succinctness, we'll recommend that you opt for number [2] if it's not already selected. This setting instructs WordPerfect to prompt you with the "Position Hyphen, Press ESC" message when it can't find the word in the dictionary.

The second setting, [6] for **Hy**phenation, gives you two options for the dictionary that WordPerfect will be using to determine hyphenation. The External Dictionary (the first choice) is much larger than the internal one and takes up more disk space, but it has many more words. We recommend it, unless you have severe hard disk space constraints.

Last is [2], **B**eep Options, [2] Beep on **Hy**phenation. If you answer [Y] you'll hear what you might find to be an annoying beep each time WordPerfect prompts you to "Position Hyphen; Press ESC." If you answer [N] there will be no beep. The choice is yours. When WordPerfect gives you that prompt, move your [→] or [←] to determine the place you want the word to be hyphenated and press [Esc]. Sometimes you won't be able to move the hyphen as far as you'd like; that's a function of the Hyphenation Zone, which we'll get to in a moment. If you don't want the word hyphenated at all, press Cancel ([F1]). Don't worry, that won't cancel the operation.

Just a few more things: if, after you hyphenate your document, you find a few words with hyphens that you want to eliminate, place your cursor in front of the word, press [Home], then type a slash (/). Then place your cursor on the hyphen and delete it. If you find a word that hasn't been hyphenated and you want to manually place a hyphen in it, place your cursor at the point where you want the hyphen to appear and press [Ctrl][-]. Finally, if you want to turn off hyphenation temporarily during spell-checking or a scrolling procedure, press [F7] (Exit) at the first "Position Hyphen; Press ESC" prompt. Of course, if you want to eliminate hyphenation completely in a document, all you need to do is find the [Hyph On] code and delete it.

We promised you an explanation of Hyphenation Zone. Well, we're going to cheat a little, because you don't really need to know much. In fact, all you really need to know is that if you increase the zone percent, either right or left, fewer words will be hyphenated, while if you decrease the zone, more words will be hyphenated. So, if you want to make your right margin less ragged (if your document is left-justified) or you want a more even spacing between words (if your document is full-justified), and you don't mind those extra hyphens (some people hate them), you can reduce the hyphenation zone sizes. Play around with it. Here's how:

I have a dream that my four little children will one day live in a nation where they will not be judged by the color of their skin, but by the content of their character.

*Martin Luther King, Jr.
Speech at Civil Rights March on Washington
[August 28, 1963]*

Press [Shift][F8], then select [1] for Line. Select [2] for Hyphenation Zone. Enter the left and right hyphenation zone settings and press Exit to return to document.

5.3 ADVANCED WORDPERFECT BRIEF WRITING SKILLS

5.3.1 USING MACROS TO AUTOMATE FREQUENTLY PERFORMED TASKS

> *The most stringent protection of free speech would not protect a man in falsely shouting fire in a theatre and causing a panic . . . The question in every case is whether the words used are used in such circumstances and are of such a nature as to create a clear and present danger. . . .*
>
> — Justice Oliver Wendell Holmes, Jr., *Schenck v. United States*, 249 U.S. 47, 52 [1919]

As we mentioned in Chapter 2, creating and using macros is essential if you wish to harness the true power of WordPerfect. (It is for that reason that this book comes with so many of them.) Macros can be simple and straightforward, or complex and extremely sophisticated, depending upon how far the user is willing to explore the WordPerfect macro language (a computer programming language), which is built into WordPerfect. Examples of simple macros include inserting address and signature blocks into correspondence, while a more complicated macro might present the user with a menu system for using boilerplate documents. (Examples of both kinds of macros can be found in Appendix C. You can also order these and many more WordPerfect macros on disk, as well as sample documents, for a minimum fee, using the order form at the back of the book.) Many simple macros may only save the user one or two keystrokes when using a common function, such as Print Preview ([Shift][F7], [6]). But even those few keystrokes over time can lead to thousands of keystrokes and many hours saved.

Because most legal WordPerfect users will not have the time or inclination to learn advanced macro programming techniques, we have left that discussion to Appendix C. However, every user should know how to create and use simple macros. What follows, then, is a quick overview of the different types of macros you can use in WordPerfect and some examples of how they can help you write a brief. Don't worry if they don't immediately make sense to you in the grand scheme of things. That will come when we explore each type individually.

WordPerfect allows the user to create four kinds of macros:

[Alt] key macros

The [Alt] key is used in conjunction with a letter key to name and play back the macro. Because these are mnemonic devices and hence the easiest to use, they should be assigned to the most commonly used functions and editing tasks.

[Alt] key macros are the easiest to use—simply hold down the [Alt] key while pressing a letter to play back the macro. The disadvantage of [Alt] key macros is that you are limited to the 26 letters of the alphabet. (Numbers cannot be used, because they are reserved for the temporary macros, explained below.) Therefore, [Alt] key macros should be reserved for the most common functions used by law offices.

> **TIP**
>
> Define Macro, [Ctrl][F10], is a toggle function. To begin and end macro definition, you use [Ctrl][F10].

Named macros

A named macro uses up to eight letters as its name. The macro is then played back by pressing [Alt][F10] (Macro), typing the name of the macro, then pressing [Enter]. These are best used for less common or more individual tasks.

Temporary macros

Temporary macros are created by pressing [Ctrl][PgUp] and assigning up to 80 characters to a number from 1 to 9, including spaces. The macro is then played back by pressing the [Alt] key together with a number from 1 to 9. These macros disappear when you exit WordPerfect, making them useful for automating repetitive keystrokes in a single document.

Keyboard macros

Keyboard macros are used via a keyboard layout, where the user defines how certain keys are to be mapped. (See Figure 5-11.) Although they work in a similar fashion to [Alt] key macros, keyboard macros are more flexible because they can include [Alt] and [Ctrl] key combinations and even function keys ([F1] through [F12]). Furthermore, the user can create many different keyboard layouts and switch between them, allowing for a much greater number of possible letter combinations. However, macro keyboards an advanced feature of WordPerfect and therefore correspondingly more difficult to learn. The macros described in this book are designed to be used as keyboard macros and come that way if ordered on disk. Don't worry, we've done the hard work for you by creating the macros. You can just key them in or order them from us (and get hundreds of other macros not described in this book) by sending away for the disk as described on the card in the back of this book. Then all you have to do is figure out how and when they can best help you automate various procedures. And even there we've done most of the work by suggesting throughout the book where particular macros are best implemented.

> **TIP**
>
> All macros created by WordPerfect are saved as a file in the macros directory specified under Setup and given the three-letter extension .WPM. For example, an [Alt][Z] macro might be saved as: C:\WP51\-MACROS\ALTZ.WPM. By pressing [F5] (List Files) and viewing the directory where macros are kept (usually C:\WP51\MACROS), then highlighting the file and pressing [Enter], you can see the description for each macro. You can also use List Files to rename the macro.

Creating [Alt] key and named macros

The procedure for creating [Alt] key macros is the same as creating named macros, except that [Alt] key macros are named by holding down the [Alt] key and pressing a letter, instead of typing a name.

IMPORTANT: If you are using our macro keyboard layouts, only [Alt][W] through [Alt][Z] are available unless you deactivate the keyboard.

1. Press [Ctrl][F10] (Define Macro) to turn on the macro definition process (i.e., turn on the keystroke recorder).
2. Name the macro. (When creating an [Alt] key macro, hold the [Alt] key down and press a letter. Otherwise, type out a name of up to eight characters, no spaces.)
3. Describe the macro, then press [Enter].
4. Record the keystrokes.
5. Press [Ctrl][F10] again to turn off the keystroke recorder.

Editing macros with the WordPerfect macro editor

> **SOFTWARE**
>
> WordPerfect Office comes with a powerful macro editor that is far superior to WordPerfect's native editor. The program also has other programs including a calendar and flat-file database.

If you made a mistake while defining the above macro, or if you should decide to change or edit a macro, you can use WordPerfect's built-in macro editor to do the job. We discussed how to use the macro editor in depth in Chapter 1 so we won't repeat everything here again. However, we will review the basic keystrokes so that you don't have to go flipping frenziedly through the book to find what you need. But for detailed information on how to insert advanced macro codes and other neat tricks using the macro editor, see Chapter 1.

1. Press [Ctrl][F10] (Define Macro) to turn on the macro definition process (i.e., turn on the keystroke recorder).
2. At the "Define Macro:" prompt, type the name or press [Alt] and the letter of a macro that already exists.
3. At the "Macro already exists:" prompt, choose [2] for Edit.

EXERCISE: CREATING AN [Alt] [Z] MACRO TO CHANGE LINE SPACING FOR QUOTES

Cindy has just finished giving Linda an overview of macros and their various uses similar to the one you just read. Naturally, Linda must prove she's assimilated the information by completing an exercise Cindy has devised.

"You're constantly switching from double to single spacing and left/right indenting twice to start a long quote, right?" she asks Linda. "Might you not take advantage of WordPerfect's macro feature to automate these routine tasks, hmmmm?" Linda, being a capable, resourceful person, immediately picks up on this suggestion. "This is beginning to get pretty interesting," she thinks.

Setting up a long quote is a rather routine task, but it can be done more efficiently with a macro. Linda decides to create an [Alt] key macro, which she names [Alt][Z]. Here's how:

1. Press [Ctrl][F10] (Define Macro) to turn on the macro definition process. (i.e., turn on the keystroke recorder).

2. At the "Define Macro:" prompt, name the macro [Alt][Z] by holding down the [Alt] key, then pressing the letter [Z].

3. At the "Description:" prompt, type Set up long quote and press [Enter]. The "Macro Def" prompt should now be flashing, indicating that any keystroke you enter will now be recorded by WordPerfect.

4. Enter the following keystrokes:

[Shift][F8] (Format), [1], [6], [1], [Enter], [F7], [Enter], [Enter], [Shift][F4], [Shift][F4].

5. Press [Ctrl][F10] (Define Macro) to turn off the macro recorder.

To play back the macro, simply hold down the [Alt] key and press [Z].

▲▲▲▲▲▲▲▲▲▲▲

This macro will automatically insert a [Ln Spacing:1] code, several hard returns, and two [-indent-] codes.

Entering codes in the macro editor

In the macro editor, when you press a key such as [Enter], [Del], or [→], [←], [↓] or [↑], it performs its regular editing function. However, when editing a macro you may sometimes want to have the macro insert an actual hard return [Hrt], [Del], [Up], or [Down] code. To do so, you must switch to the WordPerfect commands mode. There are two ways to do this, depending on how many codes you need to insert:

➢ Type [Ctrl][V] (Compose) before pressing the desired key, or

➢ Type [Ctrl][F10] (Macro Define) to toggle back and forth between the default editing mode and the WordPerfect commands mode.

In addition, if you want to access the advanced macro language codes, press [Ctrl][PgUp] while in the macro editor, highlight the code you wish to use, and press [Enter]. (For examples, see the section in Chapter 1 on how to insert advanced macro codes using the macro editor. Also see Figure 5.8.)

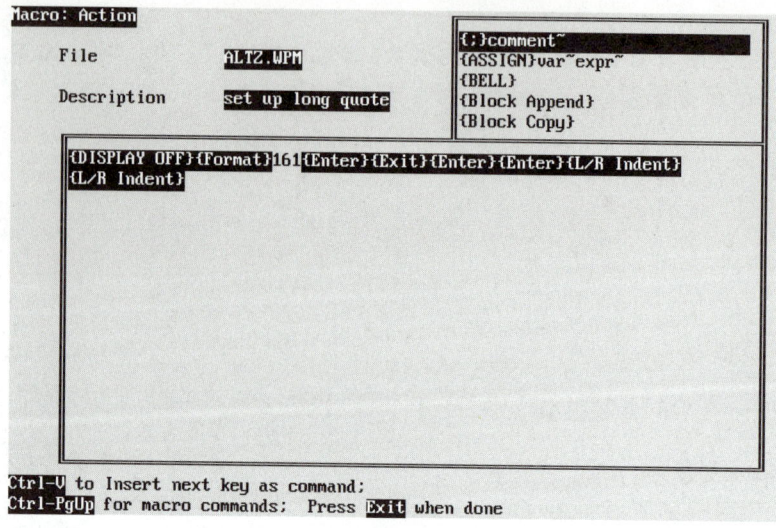

FIGURE 5-8

The WordPerfect Macro editor displays the [Alt][Z] macro. The advanced WordPerfect macro codes displayed in the upper right-hand corner are accessed by pressing [Ctrl][PgUp].

WordPerfect temporary macros

Temporary macros are strings of text that are temporarily assigned to a variable and recalled by pressing the [Alt] key and a number from 1 to 9. When the user exits WordPerfect, the variables are cleared. Temporary macros can come in rather handy in the writing of legal documents where you will, as you are probably all too aware, often find repeating phrases, words, and case names that are long and difficult to type. To create temporary macros, execute the following steps:

1. Press [Ctrl][PgUp].

2. At the "Variable:" prompt, choose a number from 1 to 9 and press [Enter].

3. At the "Value:" prompt, type the text you wish to use and press [Enter]. You may enter up to 80 characters.

To play back the temporary macro:

4. Hold down the [Alt] key and press the number you chose for the variable. What could be simpler? Admit it, you flinched the first time we mentioned macros.

5.3.2 WORDPERFECT KEYBOARD MACROS

WordPerfect 5.1 and 5.0 permit users to create Keyboard layouts that allow keys and key combinations to be assigned virtually any value. Each keyboard layout can be made up of many different [Alt] and [Ctrl] key macros. There are advantages to using keyboard layouts

EXERCISE: CREATING A TEMPORARY MACRO FOR FED. R. CIV. P.

"You know, Linda, once you become a power user of WordPerfect—and you're well on your way—you should always be looking for shortcuts that will automate the document creation process," says Cindy. ("Now if I could only find an artificial intelligence program that actually wrote my memos and briefs," thinks Linda.)

"While working on the various drafts of your briefs, you're going to realize that you are constantly having to retype certain such unwieldy words and phrases as "Fed. R. Civ. P.," declares Cindy. "Naturally, you'd like to eliminate as many of these keystrokes as possible, but you don't want to use valuable [Alt] key macros to do so. Fortunately for you, I am going to let you in on the little-known but highly useful temporary macro feature that is perfectly suited to this task. Boy, are you ever getting your money's worth, Linda—you're probably the only attorney I'd ever considering doing this for. As a matter of fact, I feel quite confident that you'll soon be a patron of the performance art scene."

1. Press [Ctrl][PgUp].

2. At the "Variable:" prompt, type [2] then press [Enter].

You can pick any number from 1 to 9.

3. At the "Value:" prompt, type `Fed. R. Civ. P.` and press [Enter].

To play back the temporary macro:

1. Hold down the [Alt] key and press [2].

---

instead of regular macros created by using the Macro Define function ([Ctrl][F10]). The benefits of this flexibility include:

- The ability to assign macros to the [Ctrl] key as well as the [Alt] key. This allows up to 52 different "one-press" macros *per keyboard*, as opposed to just 26 when using the [Alt] key.

- The ability to remap (in effect, relocate) function keys. For example, you can remap the [F3] key (Help) to the [F1] key so that, as in many other programs, pressing [F1] brings up help. This feature also allows you to define macros with the use of the [Alt], [Shift], and [Ctrl] keys in combination with the [F11] and [F12] keys (on extended keyboards only), which are not otherwise used.

- The ability to assign permanent [Alt] key macros to numbers from 1 to 9. (Without using a keyboard layout, you can only use the numbers in conjunction with the [Alt] key to create temporary macros. See above for details on how to use temporary macros.)

- The ability to temporarily disable keyboard macros by deselecting the keyboard layout.

- The ability to use the same key or key combinations for many different macros, as long as they exist in different keyboard layouts. For example, the WordPerfect 5.1 keyboard SHORT-

CUT.WPK that comes with the program uses an [Alt][E] macro to "Edit a Code" (a highly useful and powerful macro), while the WordPerfect keyboard MACROS.WPK uses [Alt][E] to "Return User to Main Editing Screen."

We know what you're thinking: "Wow, keyboard macros are one of the most powerful and advanced features of WordPerfect 5.X." That's why we stress them so highly. If you can get comfortable with creating and using keyboard macros, you will be well on your way towards becoming a true WordPerfect power user.

Let's quickly review the material you've been exposed to so far in this chapter concerning macros. After a quick overview of the four types of macros, you learned about the simple [Alt] key macro where you hold down the [Alt] key and press a letter to play back the macro. It's used for mundane office tasks like saving a document. You also learned about temporary macros used for repeating pain-in-the-neck-to-type phrases. These are accessed by pressing the [Alt] key and a number from 1 to 9. Unfortunately, they are evanescent and disappear from memory (literally) when you exit WordPerfect. You also got a quick look at the macro editor, which is discussed in greater depth in Chapter 2.

Now back to our show.

> [W]hen men have realized that time has upset many fighting faiths, they may come to believe . . . that the ultimate good desired is better reached by free trade in ideas—that the best test of truth is the power of the thought to get itself accepted in the competition of the market. . . .
>
> Justice Oliver Wendell Holmes, Jr., dissenting, Abrams v. United States, 250 U.S. 616, 630 [1919]

Using a keyboard layout

1. Press [Shift][F1] (setup), [5] (**WP5.1**) or [6] for **K**eyboard layout.
2. Highlight the keyboard you want to use (such as Enhanced) and press [1] for **S**elect.

■ *WordPerfect will only find keyboards that are in the directory specified in Location of Files under Setup for Keyboard/macro files. If you are unsure about how to configure WordPerfect to use macros and keyboard layouts, refer to Appendix A.*

IMPORTANT: Once a keyboard layout has been selected, it takes precedence over other macros. For example, if you have created an [Alt][S] macro through the Macro Define feature ([Ctrl][F10]) and you have a keyboard layout that includes [Alt][S] as a mapped keyboard macro, the keyboard macro will take effect when you press [Alt][S], not the [Alt] key macro. You must disable the keyboard layout for the regular [Alt] key macro to work again.

FIGURE 5-9

These macros in the recommended keyboard layout are discussed in Appendix C.

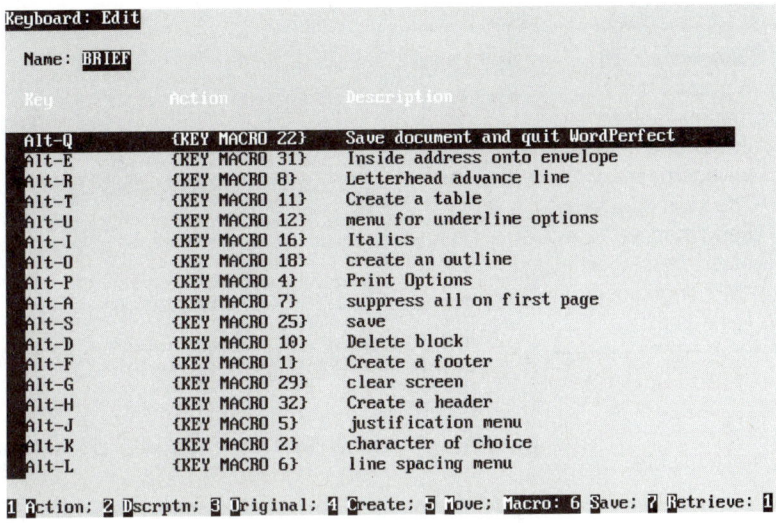

Viewing and editing the contents of a keyboard layout

Now that we've piqued your curiosity about keyboard layouts, you may be eager to become familiar with techniques to view and edit their contents, that is, the macros they contain. WordPerfect 5.0 gives you only one way to edit a keyboard. WordPerfect 5.1 gives you two different ways to get an overview of a keyboard layout: Edit and Map.

Editing a keyboard layout

1. Press [Shift][F1] (Setup), [5] (**WP5.1**) or [6] for **K**eyboard layout.

2. Highlight the keyboard layout you wish to edit, press [7] (**WP5.1**) or [5] for Edit. This will present you with a list of every key macro available in that layout. See Figure 5-9.

3. Highlight the specific macro you wish to edit, then choose [1] for Action (**WP5.1**) or **E**dit to edit the key macro. This will take you into the WordPerfect macro editor, which you may have seen before. From here, you can add or delete additional keystrokes and macro codes. See above and Chapter 2 for more information on how to use the macro editor.

WP5.1 Viewing a map of a keyboard layout

The Keyboard Map feature of WordPerfect 5.1 is an alternative means of viewing and editing the contents of a keyboard layout. It displays which keys have been mapped as macros and, as in the Edit

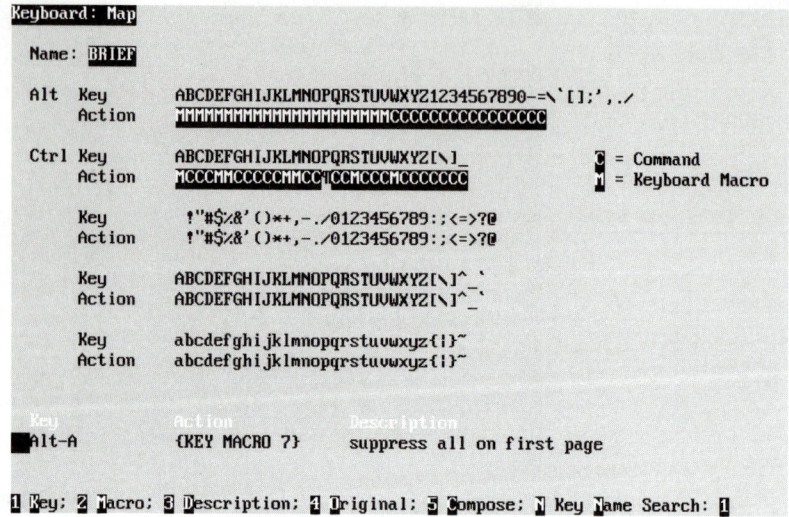

FIGURE 5-10

A map of the macros is shown in the Brief keyboard layout. The keys that have been mapped to a macro display an "M"; unmapped keys display a "C."

mode described above, allows you to edit, delete, and move the macros as you see fit.

1. Press [Shift][F1] (Setup), [5] for **K**eyboard layout.
2. Highlight the keyboard layout you wish to edit and press [8] for **M**ap. This will present you with a map of the keyboard and show which keys have been mapped to macros.

■ *"M" stands for macros, "C" for commands (which is what you'll see before you map any macros to the keyboard). Once you map macros to the keyboard, an "M" will appear beneath the key that has been mapped.*

3. To view the contents of a specific macro, position the cursor on a specific [Alt] or [Ctrl] key and press [2] for **M**acro. (Note that when you move the cursor, the Key, Action, and (**WP5.1**) Description fields below change appropriately.) See Figure 5-10.

Deleting a keyboard macro

1. Press [Shift][F1] (Setup), [5] (**WP5.1**) or [6] for **K**eyboard layout.
2. Highlight the keyboard layout you wish to edit and press [7] (**WP5.1**) or [5] for **E**dit. This will present you with a list of every key macro available in that layout.
3. Highlight the specific macro you wish to delete and press the [Del] key. (Pressing [2] in **WP5.0** and [3] in **WP5.1** have the same effect.)

Alternatively, you can delete a macro from within the Map function:

1. Press [Shift][F1] (Setup), [5] for **K**eyboard layout.
2. Highlight the keyboard layout you wish to edit and press [8] for **M**ap. This will present you with a map of the keyboard and reveal which keys have been mapped to macros.
3. Move the cursor to the macro you wish to delete, then choose [4] for **O**riginal, [Y] to delete the key macro, or press the [Del] key.

■ *WordPerfect 5.1 uses the term "Original" instead of delete here because you are restoring the value of that key to its original state.*

Moving a keyboard macro

1. Press [Shift][F1] (Setup), [5] (**WP5.1**) or [6] for **K**eyboard layout.
2. Highlight the keyboard layout you wish to edit and press [7] (**WP5.1**) or [5] for **E**dit. This will present you with a list of every key macro available in that layout.
3. Highlight the specific macro you wish to move, choose [5] for **M**ove.
4. At the "Key:" prompt, hold down the [Alt] or [Ctrl] key and press the letter you wish to move it to.

WP5.1 Copying a keyboard layout

This function will copy all the macros from a keyboard that already exists to a new keyboard. Then, you can edit the new keyboard as you see fit.

1. Press [Shift][F1] (Setup), [5] for **K**eyboard layout.
2. Highlight the keyboard layout you wish to copy and press [5] for **C**opy.
3. At the "Keyboard Filename=" prompt, type a name for the new keyboard layout you wish to create. The name can be up to eight characters long.

Deleting a keyboard layout

1. Press [Shift][F1], [5] (**WP5.1**) or [6] for **K**eyboard.
2. Press [2] for **D**elete or press the [Del] key, then press [Y].

EXERCISE: CREATING A KEYBOARD MACRO

The easiest way to create a keyboard macro is to create a named macro using the Macro Define function and then import that macro into a keyboard layout. This may sound difficult, but it's actually very easy once you get the hang of it. In the following exercises, we will map a Signature block macro to a keyboard and show you how to use the Compose feature to map a special character such as the § to a keyboard.

Mapping a named macro to a keyboard

1. On a blank screen, press [Ctrl][F10] and define a macro called SIGBLOCK. Give it a description such as "Signature Block." (If you already created this macro when going through Chapter 2, you can skip this step and proceed directly to step 3.)

2. With the "Macro Def" prompt flashing, type your signature block. When finished, press [Ctrl][F10] to turn off the macro recorder. You have now created a named macro called SIGBLOCK.

3. Press [Shift][F1] (Setup), [5] **WP5.1** or [6] for **K**eyboard layout, [4] for **C**reate. At the "Keyboard Filename:" prompt, type TEST. This will add a new file to your list of available keyboards. Press [Enter].

4. **WP5.1** Highlight the Test keyboard, and press [7] for **E**dit. Because the keyboard is new, no keys or macros have been mapped yet.

5. Press [7] (**WP5.0**) or [6] for "Retrieve." (This allows you to retrieve a named or [Alt] key macro into your keyboard.)

6. At the "Key:" prompt, hold down the [Ctrl] key and press [S]. This will map our macro to [Ctrl][S] on this keyboard.

7. At the "Macro:" prompt, type SIGBLOCK (or whatever you named your macro). You'll now see that [Ctrl][S] has been added as a key. If you want to view the contents of the macro, press [1] for **A**ction (**WP5.1**) or **E**dit.

8. To invoke this keyboard macro, select the "TEST" keyboard, [Shift][F1], [5], for **K**eyboard Layout, highlight "TEST," and press [1] for **S**elect. Press [F7] (**E**xit). Now press [Ctrl][S]. There's your signature block.

Disabling a keyboard layout

Disabling a keyboard does not delete the keyboard layout and its macros, it just turns the keyboard "off." This can be handy if you wish to use a regular [Alt] key macro that is being overridden by a keyboard macro mapped to the same key.

1. Press [Shift][F1], [5] (**WP5.1**) or [6] for **K**eyboard.

2. Press [6] for **O**riginal. ("Original" means that no keyboard is presently active.)

ERE'S a twist in our narrative: Linda did all the research on this feature herself. She's really become quite a WordPerfect fan. We just want you to know that she was in her office until 2:00 a.m., CPU humming, video display terminal glowing, immersed in the WordPerfect reference manual. Here's an exercise she devised for herself to test her understanding of keyboard macros.

WP5.1 Using Compose to map special characters to a keyboard

Earlier in this chapter, we showed you how to use the Compose feature to insert special characters into documents. The following steps will show you how to use Compose to map the ¶ special character to the [Ctrl][P] key in any keyboard layout, although we'll reference the TEST keyboard from the exercise.

1. Press [Shift][F1] (Setup).

2. Choose [5] for **K**eyboard, highlight the keyboard you wish to use (TEST), then press [8] for **M**ap.

3. Move the cursor until it is under the P in the [Ctrl] keys, then press [5] for **C**ompose. (The Key heading below should say Ctrl-P and the Action heading should say {^P}).

4. At the "Key =" prompt, type 4,5 (the ¶ symbol is the fifth character in the fourth character set) and press [Enter]. (See your WordPerfect reference book on WordPerfect characters.) Notice that the ¶ symbol now appears under the P and that the Action heading now says [:4,5].

5. Press [F7] to exit. If you haven't already done so, select the keyboard by pressing [1] for **S**elect from the Setup: Keyboard Layout screen. See Figure 5-11.

5.3.3 USING THE PARALLEL COLUMNS AND TABLES FEATURES

Y now, most of the hard work of writing the brief has been done. The footnotes are in place, the arguments polished, and the citations checked. However, the exhibit or schedules for the brief must still be assembled. This brief will require an exhibit that lists information in columns and rows. The best way to achieve this result is by using

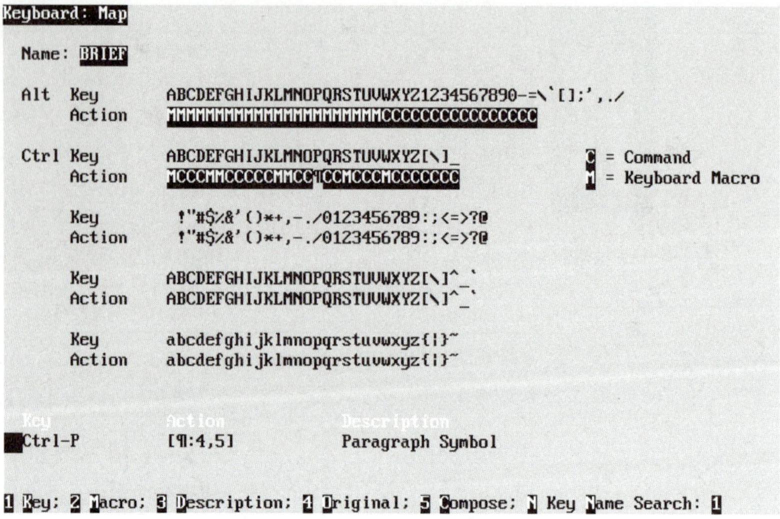

FIGURE 5-11

A keyboard map showing the key Ctrl P mapped to the paragraph symbol (¶) using the Compose feature (see the Action and Description near the bottom of the screen).

either the Parallel Columns feature (available in both WordPerfect 5.0 and 5.1) or, if you are using Word Perfect 5.1, the Tables feature. The Tables feature of WordPerfect 5.1 is probably the best single addition to the program and provides what we believe is a simpler and more elegant alternative to columns (still available in WordPerfect 5.1) for formatting text in columns and rows. In fact, the Tables feature can even be used to create forms and duplicate spreadsheets. Linda does not know if she can afford the time to explore both these options and compare them, but she's having too much fun to care.

WP5.0 Creating parallel columns

Parallel columns can be often used in a legal office environment, as when writing a list or comparison table. With parallel columns, adding or deleting text in one column does not affect text in the others. (This is not true for Newspaper columns.)

But we feel we should be honest about the limitations of parallel columns. The Columns feature inserts [Col On] and [Col Off] and other codes, which if accidently deleted can wreak havoc on your painstakingly created product. If this does happen, trying to piece your columns together again can seem like the word processing equivalent of trying to repair Humpty Dumpty. For this reason, if you're a 5.1 user, stick to using the Tables feature whenever possible instead of Parallel Columns. The Tables feature is easier to use and edit—as well as providing all sorts of other capabilities that we will soon regale you with—and you cannot accidently delete important codes. If you are a 5.0 user, you have no choice (except for upgrading, which we highly encourage) but to use this feature.

Those who won our independence believed that the final end of the state was to make men free to develop their faculties. . . . They valued liberty both as an end and as a means. They believed . . . that the greatest menace to freedom is an inert people; that public discussion is a political duty; and that this should be a fundamental principle of the American government.

Justice Louis Dembitz Brandeis, concurring, Whitney v. California, 274 U.S. 357, 375 [1927]

That being said, here are the steps for creating parallel columns in WordPerfect 5.0.

1. Press [Alt][F7] (Math/Columns).
2. Select [4] for **C**olumn Define.
3. Select [1] for **T**ype, then select [2] for **P**arallel columns.
4. WordPerfect defaults to two columns. If you want more, choose [2] or **N**umber. Based on the number of columns you choose, WordPerfect automatically creates equal-sized columns as well as gutters (the distance between columns, which defaults to .5"). If you want to alter these settings, choose [3] **D**istance and [4] **M**argins. When finished defining the columns, press [F7] (Exit) to return to the document.
5. Choose [3] for **C**olumn On/Off to turn on the columns mode. (Notice now that the bottom right of the screen now says "Col 1.")

Entering text in columns

1. Enter the text as you normally would in a document. The text will automatically wrap at the column edge.
2. Once you reach the end of one column and want to start the next column, press Hard Page ([Ctrl][Enter]). (Pressing [Enter] alone will give a hard return within the column.)

■ *Parallel columns can be thought of as virtual pages, each column a page. All of WordPerfect's editing and formatting features can be used within the column as they would in a normal document, including centering, justification, etc.*

Moving between columns

1. Press [Ctrl], [Home], [→] to move to the right column, [Ctrl], [Home], [←] to move to the left column, and [Home], [↑] or [Home], [↓] to move to the first or last parallel column.

Turning columns on and off

Press [Alt][F7] (Math/Columns), [3] for **C**olumns On/Off.

■ *You can turn Columns on and off throughout a document as many times as you like and even have standard text and multiple columns within a document.*

5.3.4 WP5.1 USING THE TABLES FEATURE

The Tables feature, new to WordPerfect 5.1, is, as we said, one of the program's most powerful features and can be used as an alternative to the parallel columns feature of WordPerfect 5.0. But it is actually much more flexible than that, as it can also be used to create a vast diversity of forms, organization charts (or any kind of documents involving boxes), and even calendars. Although it is fairly easy to use, it does include many options, some of which tend to be obscure and confusing. We'll only touch on the basics here, but if you are adventurous and have time, you'll have a solid foundation for trying some of Tables' more esoteric capabilities.

Creating tables

> **MACRO**
>
> You can use the [Alt][T] macro to quickly set up the basic structure of a table.

1. Press [Alt][F7] (Columns/Tables).
2. Choose [2] for **T**ables.
3. Choose [1] for **C**reate.
4. Enter the number of columns you want. (You can have up to 32 columns.)
5. Enter the number of rows. (You can have up to 32,767 rows.)
6. At this point, the table is created and a menu appears at the bottom of the screen. You can use the options on this menu to format the table or press [F7] (Exit) to leave the menu and begin entering text.

Entering text

You can use any WordPerfect editing or formatting function in a cell such as [F6] (Bold), [Shift][F6] (Center), and [F8] (Font). As you enter text, the height of a cell increases according to the number of lines entered. However, if, for instance, the cell increases in height several lines and you move to the next cell in the table, you must start inputting text at the first line of that cell. The other lines in the cell aren't available for text input until you get to them when typing.

Moving between cells

Press [Alt][→] to move to the right cell, [Alt][←] to move to the left cell and [Alt][↑] or [Alt][↓] to move up and down within a table. You can also use the [Tab] key to move between cells. If you would like to include an actual tab in a cell, press [Home], [Tab].

Editing a table

Adding/Deleting Rows and Columns: There are two methods for adding and deleting rows and columns.

METHOD 1:

1. Move the cursor into the table and press [Alt][F7] (Columns/Tables).
2. Choose [1] for **S**ize.
3. Choose [1] for **R**ows or [2] for **C**olumns. The current number of rows or columns is displayed.
4. Enter the total number of columns or rows you want. If the total number is less you will be prompted "Cells will be deleted, continue?" Type [Y] to delete.

METHOD 2:

1. Move the cursor into the table and press [Alt][F7] (Columns/Tables).
2. Press [Ins] or [Del], then choose [1] for **R**ows or [2] for **C**olumns.
3. Enter the number of rows or columns to be added or deleted.

TIP

If you have already created a table and want to save it permanently, block out the entire table, press [F10] to save and name the block. This will ensure that you have a prior version of the table.

TIP

If you want to insert a row or rows at the very bottom of your table, the only way to do so is (in table edit mode) [1] for **S**ize, [1] for **R**ows, and type the desired number of rows. This also works for **C**olumns, [2], which will be added to the right side of your table.

Lines and Shading

TO ADD SHADING TO CELLS:

1. Move the cursor into the table and press [Alt][F7] (Columns/Tables).
2. Block out the cells you want shaded [F12].
3. Press [3] for **L**ines, then [8] for **S**hade, and [1] for **O**n.
4. Exit the tables edit mode by pressing [F7].

TO CHANGE THE APPEARANCE OF LINES IN THE TABLE:

1. Move the cursor into the table and press [Alt][F7] (Columns/Tables).
2. Block out the cells you want changed [F12].
3. Press [3] for **L**ines, then choose the option for the lines you wish to change (e.g., [1] for **L**eft for the lines on the left of the cells, etc.).
4. Select the style of line you desire, e.g., [3] for **D**ouble or [4] for **D**ashed.
5. Exit the tables edit mode by pressing [F7].

Using the Tables feature to recreate parallel columns

As we mentioned earlier, we recommend using the Tables feature rather than the Parallel Columns feature because of its flexibility and ease of use. "But," you say, "suppose I don't want the lines that appear

> **TIP**
>
> A fast way to move text from one row to another is to use the Undelete feature. In table edit mode turn on Block [F12] or [Alt][F4], press [End] and then [Backspace]. In answer to the question "Delete Block?" type [Y]. Now move your cursor to the beginning of the row you want your text to appear in and press [F1]. In answer to the question "Undelete Block?" answer [Y]. This also works for moving text from one column to another. Make sure your cursor is in the first cell of the column you want your text to appear in.

in a table?" Well, one of the options in the Lines menu discussed above is "none." In other words, you can turn off all the lines in a table. Here's how:

1. Create the table you wish and enter your text as desired.

   ■ *It is easier to write the text first before you remove the lines.*

2. Move the cursor into the table and press [Alt][F7] (Columns/Tables).
3. Block out the entire table using [F12].
4. Press [3] or Lines, [7] for All, then [1] for None.
5. Exit the tables edit mode by pressing [F7]. See Figure 5-12.

These are some of the basics of the Tables feature. We're going to let you have a little fun now by allowing you to create your own table (complete with shading and line effects). While you're involved with this task, we'll painlessly introduce some more information you will find useful.

5.3.5 TABLE FORMATTING OPTIONS

Now that we've given you a chance to have fun, we'd like to discuss a few more of the table features that haven't been covered yet, but that we feel may come in handy.

One option you may very well find useful is a method of changing the defaults on the thickness of the various types of lines you can draw in the table mode. Now you can determine exactly how thick "extra thick" should be.

Go into the format menu, [Shift][F8], and then press "other" and [8] for border options. As you can see, that's not the only line attribute you can effect. This might seem like an obscure feature not worth mentioning, but if you do numerous forms or simple organization charts it may come in handy.

You can take tables that have already been created with tabs or parallel columns and turn them into the kind of tables we've been discussing. Simply block the text, press [Alt][F7], then [T], [C]. If you created the table with tabs, choose tabs; if you created it with parallel columns, choose parallel columns. If you created your chart or table with tabs, be sure there is only one tab between the items in each column or else you will be dismayed by the result.

If you want to edit a table in table edit mode and you're somewhere else in the document, press [Alt][F7] then [T], [E], and WordPerfect will search backwards for the last table in the document. If there is none,

> *We are dealing now with the liability of the manufacturer. . . . If he is negligent, where danger is to be forseen, a liability will follow. . . . We have put aside the notion that the duty to safeguard life and limb . . . grows out of contract and nothing else. . . . We have put its source in the law.*
>
> *J. Benjamin Nathan Cardozo, MacPherson v. Buick Motor Co., 217 N.Y. 382, 389, III N. E. 1050, 1053 [1916]*

FIGURE 5-12

Use a table to create parallel columns. All the lines in a table can be turned off in the table edit mode. Note the [Tbl Def] code indicating that this is a table.

```
Exhibit Number:¶            Exhibit Description:¶
1.¶                         Accident Report of Officer Greenwald¶
2.¶                         Insurance Report¶
3.¶                         Hospital bills¶


                                              Cell B1 Doc 2 Pg 1 Ln 1.1" Pos 5.05"
{    ▲    ▲    ▲    ▲   ]{  ▲    ▲    ▲    ▲    ▲    ▲    ▲    ]
[Tbl Def:I;2,2.5",4"]
[Row][Cell][BOLD]Exhibit Number:[bold][Cell][BOLD]Exhibit Description:[bold]
[Row][Cell]1.[Cell]Accident Report of Officer Greenwald
[Row][Cell]2.[Cell]Insurance Report
[Row][Cell]3.[Cell]Hospital bills
[Tbl Off]

Press Reveal Codes to restore screen
```

EXERCISE: CREATING A TABLE

Firm Operating Expenses for Second Half of 1992			
Expense	**3rd Quarter**	**4th Quarter**	**Totals**
Payroll	$99,837.35	$102,234.34	$202,071.69
Rent	$12,349.36	$3,325.37	$15,674.73
Equipment	$19,934.35	$2,343.33	$22,277.68
Benefits	$2,343.38	$23,432.23	$25,775.61

Let's create a table 4 columns across by 5 rows down. Press [Alt][F7], [2] for Tables, [1] for Create, [4], [Enter], [5], [Enter].

"Voilà, un table," as the French might say. As you can see if you look at your status line, you are in cell A1. Columns are designated by letter, rows by numbers. You can use this knowledge, in fact, to navigate through a table in another manner. Say you're in the first cell, A1, and you want to go to the third row, fourth column. Press [Ctrl][Home] and type C4, press [Enter] and presto, you are there.

Now, let's highlight the entire first row of cells. Turn block on and press [End]. Let's also join them to make one large cell ([7] for Join, [Y]). (You can reverse this process by selecting split, columns, and [4].) Enter a heading here. OK, we'll provide you with our own selection: "Firm Operating Expenses for Second Half of 1990." Remember to press [F7] (Exit) first to enter text and then type the text as it appears above. We'll format it later.

Move to cell A2 and type Expense, A3 Payroll, A4 Rent, and A5 Equipment.

Let's create one more row to include the category of Equipment. Press [Alt][F7] to return to Table Edit mode. Select size (1), rows, and [6]. Now return to text edit and type Benefits.

In B2 type 3rd Quarter, C2 4th Quarter, and D2 Totals. Now type in some numbers under each year, using decimal points.

Now for some fun. Go into table editing mode and place your cursor anywhere in column 4. While holding down [Ctrl], press [←] 3 times. Wow, the column got smaller! (Note, if you tried to enlarge it by pressing the [→] key, it wouldn't work because the table is already page-wide.)

Move the cursor into the B column and press [Ctrl][→] a few times and do the same in the C column. These two will grow because there is now room on the page. Adjust the column sizes until you're satisfied.

Let's do something about our heading. While in table edit mode, place your cursor in cell A1 and choose [2] for format and [1] for cell, [3] for justify, and [2] for center. Press format and cell again, [2] for Attributes, [2] for Appearance, and [1] for bold. You've centered, bolded, and enlarged your heading. Go into view mode to see the results.

Let's get slick and shade cell A1 as well. Choose [3] for lines, [8] for shading, [1] for on. Once again, you'll have to look in view mode to see the effect. You can control the degree of shading by going into options, pressing [8], choosing [4], and indicating the desired percent. Don't select any more than 20 unless you have a high-resolution printer (600 dpi or more). The other options in this menu are pretty much self-explanatory.

Next, place your cursor in column A, select format, [2] for column, [2] for Attributes, [2] for Appearance, [1] for bold. You could have chosen any of the other attributes. If, instead of selecting attributes, you had selected justify, you could have changed the position of the text in each cell by selecting center, left, etc. Block the second row and bold the headings in the same fashion, choosing cell instead of column.

Now, let's align those numbers you were supposed to have placed in the table. All right, we'll give you another chance. We're waiting. . . . OK.

Go into table edit mode, move your cursor to cell B3, and turn on block. Block the rest of the column. Now go into format and choose cell or column (it works with either). Press justify and then decimal align. As you'd expect, all the numbers in the column are aligned by their decimal points.

If you choose column, you also have the option of indicating a certain number of digits to the right of the decimal point. The default is 2, but if you opt for a larger number, say 5, the numbers would move left while retaining their alignment on the decimal point. Although you only have two numbers to the right of the decimal point, WordPerfect thinks you have five and responds accordingly. Do the same with the other columns.

You could also center- or right-align all the numbers simultaneously using the same method if you were so inclined, as well as text. Center the column headings in the second row.

As you can see, the line defaults for a table gives you a double line around the border of the table and single lines between cells. That's easy to alter. You could remove all the lines in a table by blocking the entire table in the table edit mode, choosing lines, and then selecting all and then none; but don't do that, please.

You should be in table edit mode now. Move your cursor to cell A2 (Expense), turn on block, and press [End] to block the entire row. Select lines, bottom, and thick. Go into view mode and check out your handiwork. Nice effect, right? By the way, there is still a single line there (the top line of the row below row A) as well, although it's obscured by the thick line. If you'd like to remove it, go to the next row and repeat the procedure, but select top and none.

Good. Go ahead, be adventurous now. Try some of the funkier effects, like dotted and dashed lines. Make the lines between cells double; see how thick "extra thick" is. Try removing various lines within cells. Use some more shading effects.

We're certain you can come up with many ways these features might be used to create all sorts of forms in your office.

it will search forward. When it finds it, you will be automatically placed in table edit mode.

In the event that your table is more than one page (although it usually shouldn't take up that much room), you can easily create a repeating header. In our sample table, if we wanted to make the row beginning with "Expense" our header, we would go into table edit mode, block that row, and select  for header. We would then be asked for the number of rows. We would select [1], because we only want this one row to repeat on the following page or pages.

Well, there you have it, the humble little Tables feature. As we stated, there are other aspects of this powerful tool that we decided to skip out of a sense of compassion for you (and ourselves). But you probably will be able to make sense of all them with a little trial and error, now that you've read our lucid exposition and created a masterpiece yourself.

5.3.6 CREATING THE TABLE OF CONTENTS AND THE TABLE OF AUTHORITIES—OVERVIEW

> *Instead, therefore, of saying that the liability for negligence should be co-extensive with the judgement of each individual . . . we ought rather to adhere to the rule which requires in all cases a regard to caution such as a man of ordinary prudence would observe.*
>
> Chief Justice Tindal, Vaughan v. Menlove, 132 Eng. Rep 490 [1837]

LINDA is so delighted with herself and the progress she's made that she can't resist the temptation to call Cindy and crow. Big mistake. "I'll be over right after my temp assignment is finished," announces Cindy. "I've got some stuff I have to show you that will blow your mind—automatic table of authorities and table of contents generation. Actually, they're not quite that automatic, but they'll save you a lot of time in the long run, trust me. Oh, and don't worry, Linda, there won't be any tests. As far as I'm concerned, you've earned your WordPerfect diploma with honors."

Creating a table of contents and a table of authorities is one of the most complicated tasks to be done in a legal office using WordPerfect, and it takes a little practice to get it right. It can also take some time, especially in a long brief. However, the table of authorities feature can save hours of time if the brief goes through many revisions (and which brief doesn't?), because once the cites are properly marked and defined, the table can be instantly regenerated. Here, then, are Cindy's detailed instructions to Linda to create tables of contents and authorities. The following exercises are based on the BRIEF.DOC file that comes on the supplementary disks. However, if you have not purchased the disks, you should (hopefully!) be able to extrapolate from our lucid description as you work through your own brief.

Basic steps

Both tables of contents and tables of authorities are generated by following these five steps:

➤ Define the table format.

➤ Renumber the brief pages.

➤ Mark the text to be included as entries in the table.

➤ Generate the table.

➤ Touch up the generated table.

A table of contents or a table of authorities generated in WordPerfect can consist of up to five levels. Once the necessary text is marked in the document as entries, new tables can be generated as needed. For example, when text in a document that appears as an entry in a table of contents is edited, the current table must be regenerated to reflect those changes.

5.3.7 CREATING A TABLE OF AUTHORITIES

Step 1: Define a table of authorities

The first step in defining a table of authorities is to determine the sections that will be used. For the Smallville brief, we will use these three sections: (1) Cases, (2) Rules of Civil Procedures, and (3) Miscellaneous. To define a table of authorities, follow these steps:

SHAREWARE

The LEGMAC.EXE file, available as shareware on the supplementary disks, contains sophisticated macros for automatically marking tables of authorities.

1. Press [Home], [Home], [↑] to move the cursor to the very beginning of the brief.

2. Press [Ctrl][Enter] (Hard Return) to create a new page.

3. Move the cursor up to the line on the new page on which the title for the table of authorities will appear and type Table of Authorities. You may also skip a line or two after that and type Cases at the left margin and [Alt][F6] (Flush Right) Pages at the right margin.

4. Press [Enter] several times to move the cursor to the line where you'd like your table of authorities to begin.

5. Press [Alt][F5] (Mark Text).
6. Choose [5] for **D**efine.
7. Choose [4] for Define Table of **A**uthorities.
8. Enter the number of the section being defined. For example, the Cases section would be number 1 (if you want them to appear first in the table).
9. Choose the options to be used for that section. Generally, underlining of cases and dot leaders are used in tables of authorities. Type [Y] for **U**nderlining Allowed if you want cases to be underlined in the table. If you want case names not to appear with underlines in the table of authorities, leave the default, [N].

▪ *If your case names are italicized in the brief, and you want them to appear italicized in the table of authorities, include the italics codes when marking cites in the brief. (See the section "Step 3: Mark authorities (cites) for the table of authorities.") If the cites aren't italicized in the brief and you want them italicized in the table of authorities, you're going to have to do that manually (or develop an elegant macro to do the job).*

▪ *Remember that all sections are defined separately, and each section can have its own options.*

10. Press [F7] (Exit) to return to the document.

The code [Def Mark:ToA,1] has been inserted.

11. Repeat steps 5 through 10 for the other sections in the table.

▪ *You can preformat the table a bit by doing the same thing for each section that you did for Cases—that is, type the heading, press [Enter] two or three times, and then put in your define code for that section. When the table of authorities is generated, your headings will appear separated by one or two lines from the authorities cited.*

Step 2: Renumber the brief pages

The next step is to renumber the pages in our brief to ensure the page accuracy of the cases listed in the table of authorities. Because a new page has been added for the table of authorities, we must ensure that the table is given a Roman numeral page number and that page 1 of the brief begins where the body of the document starts, not at the table of authorities.

Now we think the proper rule in such a case as the present is this: Where two parties have made a contract which one of them has broken, the damages which the other party ought to receive in respect of such breach of contract should be such as may fairly and reasonably be considered either arising naturally . . . from such breach . . . or such as may reasonably be supposed to have been in the contemplation of both parties, at the time they made the contract. . . .

Judge Alderson
Hadley v. Baxendale,
156 Eng. Rep. 145
[1854]

FIGURE 5-13

The Page Numbering screen is used to renumber the table of authorities and table of contents pages to lowercase Roman numerals. It is also used to start the actual text of a brief at page 1.

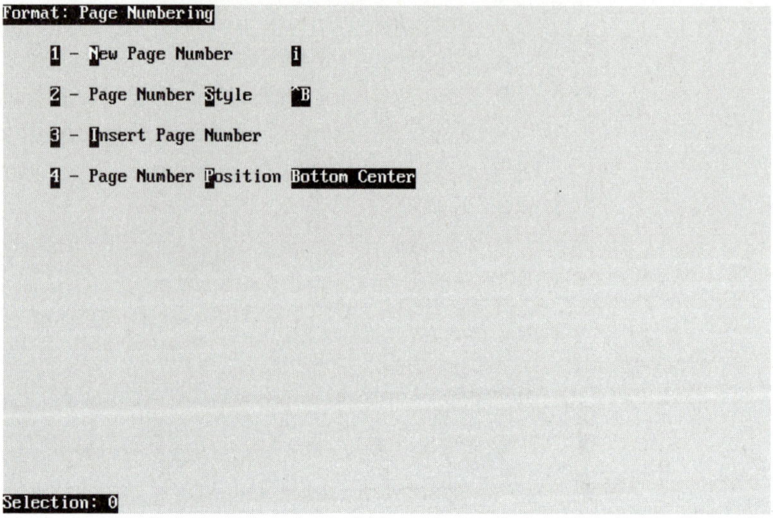

```
Format: Page Numbering

    1 - New Page Number          i

    2 - Page Number Style        ^B

    3 - Insert Page Number

    4 - Page Number Position     Bottom Center









Selection: 0
```

WP5.1 Giving the tables of authorities Roman numeral page numbers

1. Press [Home], [Home], [↑] to move the cursor to the beginning of the table of authorities.
2. Press [Shift][F8] (Format).
3. Choose [2] for **P**age.
4. Choose [6] for page **N**umbering.
5. Choose [4] for Page Number **P**osition, then [6] for bottom center.
6. Choose [1] for New Page **N**umber.
7. Type i, then press [Enter].
8. Press [F7] (Exit) to return to the document. See Figure 5-13.

The code [Pg Num:i] has been inserted.

WP5.0 Giving the tables of authorities Roman numeral page numbers

1. Press [Home], [Home], [↑] to move the cursor to the beginning of the table of authorities.
2. Press [Shift][F8] (Format).
3. Choose [2] for **P**age.
4. Choose [6] for **N**ew Page Numbering, type i, and press [Enter].
5. Choose [7] for **P**age Numbering, then [6] for bottom center.
6. Choose [1] for New Page **N**umber.

7. Press [F7] (Exit) to return to the document. See Figure 5-13.

▲▲▲▲▲▲▲▲▲▲▲▲▲▲▲▲▲▲▲▲▲▲▲▲▲▲▲▲▲▲▲▲

The codes [Pg Num:i] [Pg Numbering: Bottom Center] have been inserted.

WP5.1 Starting the text of the brief on page 1

1. Move the cursor to the beginning of the page where the actual text of the brief begins.
2. Press [Shift][F8] (Format).
3. Choose [2] for **P**age.
4. Choose [6] for page **N**umbering.
5. Choose [1] for **N**ew Page Number.
6. Type [1] and press [Enter].
7. Press [F7] (Exit) to return to the document.

■ *A [Pg num:1] code should now be inserted. Also note that the page indicator on the status line on the bottom right of the screen should now properly indicate 1. If you neglect this step, you will see a message informing you that a new page number was not found when the table was generated. Insert the new page number and generate the table again.*

WP5.0 Starting the text of the brief on page 1

1. Move the cursor to the beginning of the page where the actual text of the brief begins.
2. Press [Shift][F8] (Format).
3. Choose [2] for **P**age.
4. Choose [6] for **N**ew Page Numbering, type 1, and press [Enter].
5. Press [F7] (Exit) to return to the document.

■ *A [Pg num:1] code should now be inserted. Also note that the page indicator on the status line on the bottom right of the screen should now properly indicate 1. If you neglect this step, you will see a message informing you that a new page number was not found when the table was generated. Insert the new page number and generate the table again.*

Step 3: Mark authorities (cites) for the table of authorities

When you mark an item for the first time, you will be asked to specify the section number in the table of authorities and the full form of the cite, i.e., what will actually appear in the table after it is generated. The full form of the cite is generally the form used when a case is cited for the first time in a brief. You will also be asked for the short form (a nickname for the full form). The short form is used to reference cites once a long form has been defined; when you mark an item again, you need specify only the short form.

■ *If you want your case cites to appear with underlines in the table of authorities, perform the marking procedure with Reveal Codes on so that you can include the underline codes.*

Entering a long form

1. Move the cursor to the beginning of the first authority in your brief. If you are using our sample brief, move the cursor to *Lemon v. Kurtzman*, 403 U.S. 602 (1971), which should be on page 3.

2. Press [F12] or [Alt][F4] (block options) to turn on the block function and highlight the entire authority. If you want underlining included in the generated table of authorities, remember to include the underlining codes when you highlight. Again, this procedure should be done with Reveal Codes on (the moral: "Turn on those Reveal Codes or pay the price").

3. Press [Alt][F5] (Mark Text) to access the Marking Options menu.

4. Choose [4] for ToA.

5. At the "ToA Section Number:" prompt, type the section number of the table of authorities this cite will belong to. Our first example is a case and will therefore get a section number designation of 1.

6. The full-form cite is placed in a separate editing screen. You can now edit the cite the way you wish it to appear in the table of authorities. For example, you can use bold, underlining, italics, etc. If you've opted not to include underlining (in the Define Table of Authorities menu), you do not have to manually delete it. You might find it easier, if you do want your cases to be underlined in the finished table of authorities, to include the underline codes when you block the entire authority.

■ *An option in the Definition menu deletes underlining when the table is generated if you've included the underlining codes when you blocked the cite.*

The flag is constant in expressing beliefs Americans share, beliefs in law and peace and that freedom which sustains the human spirit. . . . It is poignant but fundamental that the flag protects those who hold it in contempt.

— Justice Anthony M. Kennedy, concurring, Texas v. Johnson, 491 U.S. 397, 421 [1989]

7. Press `F7` (Exit) when you have finished editing the full form. You will now see a "Short Form:" prompt followed by the case name.

> The long form code looks like [ToA:# of level;short form name;Full Form].

Entering a short form

The short form is an abbreviated form used to mark subsequent entries. WordPerfect will automatically use up to the first 40 characters of the highlighted block as a short form, but this can be very confusing. We strongly recommend that you use your own nickname (for example, each case Plaintiff's name) for each cite. Just make sure that each nickname is short and unique to that particular cite (this will speed up the marking process) and that you remain consistent in your use of the nickname.

1. Edit the short form and press `Enter`. For example, a good short form for *Lemon v. Kurtzman*, 403 U.S. 602 (1971) would be *Lemon*.

> The short form code looks like [ToA:;*short form name*;].

Marking the remaining authorities

Now that a long and short form have been defined for the cite, you must search through the rest of the brief to find recurrences of the cite. Remember to use the same short form each time you mark the cite.

1. Press `Home`, `F2` (extended search), then type the name or part of the name of the cite you wish to find and press `Home`, `F2` again. For example, to find other instances of *Lemon v. Kurtzman*, use Lemon.
2. Place your cursor in front of the cite. You do not need to highlight it as you did with the long form. Again, if you want the underlines included in the generated TOA, make sure to include the underline code by placing your cursor on it before marking the cite with the short form name. Let us remind you again that you also have to indicate `Y` to underline in the Define Table of Authorities menu.
3. Press `Alt`-`F5` (Mark Text) to access the Marking Options menu.
4. Choose `4` for ToA Short Form.
5. "Lemon" (or whatever short form you're searching for) will appear at the "Short form:" prompt; you don't have to rekey it. Press `Enter`.

FIGURE 5-14

An example of a Table of Authorities long and short forms. The top portion shows the long form for *Everson v. Board of Ed*, the bottom portion a short form that could be used.

```
See Everson v. Board of Education, 330 U.S. 1 (1947)










ToA Full Form: Press Exit when done                    Ln 1" Pos 4.91"
Jefferson's Crumbling Wall-A comment on Lynch v.  , 1984 Duke L.J.
770, 771. See Everson v. Board of Educ., 330 U.S. 1, 14-15
(1947); In Lemon v. Kurtzman, 403 U.S. 602 (1971), the Supreme
Court adopted the following three prong approach ("Lemon test")
to determine whether government has impermissibly involved itself
in matters of religion:¶
          First, the statute must have a secular
          legislative purpose; second, its principal or
          primary effect must be one that neither
          advances nor inhibits religion...finally, the
          statute must not foster "an excessive
          government entanglement with religion."¶
¶
Lemon v. Kurtzman, 403 U.S. 602, 612-13 (1970) (quoting Walz v.
Tax Commission, 397 U.S. 664, 674 (1970)).¶
     In recognition of the inherent difficulty of drawing the
Short Form: Everson
```

IMPORTANT: Be sure always to use the same short form for each occurrence of the cite, and don't use the same short form for different cites.

▲▲▲▲▲▲▲▲▲▲▲▲▲▲▲▲▲▲▲▲▲▲▲▲▲▲▲▲▲▲▲

The case that has been marked with the short form should have the following code: [ToA:;short form;].

6. Repeat the above steps until every reoccurrence of the cite has been properly marked with the short form.

7. Press [Home], [Home], [↑] to move to the beginning of the brief, and repeat the process for all the other case cites, rules, and authorities used in the brief. Remember to indicate the correct table of authori-

ties section number for rules and authorities when you enter them as long forms.

Step 4: Generate a table of authorities

TIP

Because the process of generating and cleaning up a table of authorities can be time consuming, it is better to make minor changes to the table manually. We also recommend saving a copy of the table as a separate document by blocking it out, pressing [F10] to save the table, and naming the block. That way you'll have a copy of the table if something disastrous happens.

Once all of the cites have been marked, the table needs to be generated. If a prior table already exists for that brief, the generation process will delete the old table and replace it with a new one.

1. Press [Alt][F5] (Mark Text) from anywhere in the document.
2. Choose [6] for **G**enerate.
3. Choose [5] to **G**enerate Table, Indexes, etc.
4. Type [Y] at the "Existing tables, lists and indexes will be replaced. Continue?" prompt.

■ *WordPerfect generates all tables, indexes, etc., at the same time. Once the generation process has begun, a counter will be displayed showing the progress being made. WordPerfect makes several passes through the entire document before generating the document. Therefore, if it is a long document and you have a slow machine, the process can take some time.*

■ *WP5.1 If you have decided to enhance the default page numbering style in the Page Numbering menu of your brief, e.g., -#-, that style will be included with the page numbers of the cites when the table is generated. In other words, if the page number style is -^B-, the page numbers of the cites will appear in the table of authorities as -1-, -2-, and so on. If you don't want this format for the page numbers in your generated table of authorities, simply perform a search and replace beginning at the TOA for a "hard hyphen" (-), replacing it with nothing. A hard hyphen is created by pressing [Home] in combination with the hyphen key rather than pressing the hyphen key alone.*

5.3.8 PUTTING A GENERATED TABLE OF AUTHORITIES IN ALPHABETICAL ORDER

"Hey," you exclaim, "the cases in my generated table of authorities are not in alphabetical order the way I like them. What gives?" The TOA feature does not sort automatically, but that's easily rectified by using WordPerfect's powerful Sort feature.

1. Highlight all the cases using [Alt][F4] or [F12].

2. With the cases highlighted, press [Ctrl][F9] for Sort, [7] for Type, [3] for **P**aragraph.

3. Press [1] for perform action. Presto, instantaneous alphabetized cases.

Error messages

Because creating and generating a table of authorities is a complex process, you may see the following error messages:

Not Enough Memory: WordPerfect uses Document 2 to generate tables, lists, etc. Document 1 is allotted twice as much memory as Document 2. Therefore, if you are running out of memory, retrieve the brief into Document 2. The table can then be generated using the additional memory available in Document 1.

No [DefMark] Found: The [DefMark] code is created when you first define the tables of authorities. If you forgot to define the location and format of the table, WordPerfect will be unable to generate the table. Follow the steps used to define a table, and regenerate.

Can't Find End of Table of Contents, Lists or Index Text: This message generally means that the [EndDef] code was deleted accidently. The [EndDef] code is created when you first generate a table and is found at the end of each section in the table. (Each [DefMark] code has a corresponding [EndDef] code). If WordPerfect can't find an [EndDef] code, that section will be generated again, without deleting the first table. Therefore, you have two options: delete the prior duplicate table once you have regenerated or, if possible, copy an existing [DefMark] code from another section of the table to the section that's missing it.

New Page Num Not Found: WordPerfect kindly generates this message to warn you that the page count of your table will be wrong because you have not inserted a new page number at the beginning of the text of the brief. Use the steps outlined above to start the text of your brief on page 1, then regenerate the table.

Non Unique Short Forms Found: This message warns you that you have used the same short form for two different cites or that you have used a short form that has not been assigned to a full form. The table will still be generated, but asterisks will appear instead of page numbers in the entries affected. To fix this problem, be sure that the

To find that the President has "inherent power" to halt the publication of news by resort to the courts would wipe out the First Amendment and destroy the fundamental liberty and security of the very people the Government hopes to make "secure." . . . [I]t was injuctions like those sought here that Madison and his collaborators intended to outlaw in this Nation for all times.

Justice Hugo LaFayette Black, concurring, New York Times Company v. United States, 403 U.S. 713, 719 [1971]

affected cites have a long form and a unique short form, then regenerate the table.

Step 5: Clean up a generated table of authorities

> **TIP**
>
> You can manually create flush right dot leaders by pressing [Alt][F6] twice. This also works for creating center dot leaders by pressing [Shift][F6] twice.

We have never once in our experience seen WordPerfect generate a flawless table of authorities or table of contents the very first time. Therefore, once the table has been generated, you will have to clean it up to make sure that the page numbers are properly aligned and the dot leaders not out of place. Sometimes removing a [Margin Release] code can do the trick. Be sure to use Reveal Codes for this task.

If the cite runs to several lines and you want to truncate each line in a specific place or indent each line several spaces, you'll have to do that manually.

The completed table of authorities for our sample brief should look something like Figure 5-16.

See Figure 5-15 for an illustration of the fully formatted and printed table of authorities, with its cases, rules of civil procedure, and miscellaneous.

5.3.9 CREATING A TABLE OF CONTENTS

Like the tables of authorities, tables of contents are generated by following these five steps. However, you'll be glad to know that it is considerably easier to generate a table of contents because, unlike a table of authorities, there are no reoccurring cites throughout the brief that have to be marked. The steps to generate a table of contents are:

- Define the table.
- Renumber the brief pages.
- Mark the text to be included as entries in the table.
- Generate the table.
- Touch up the generated table.

A table of contents in WordPerfect can consist of up to five levels. Once the necessary text is marked in the document as entries, new tables can be generated as needed.

FIGURE 5-16

A generated Table of Authorities for the BRIEF.DOC file is shown. Yours may differ somewhat, depending on the particular cites you marked.

```
                    TABLE OF AUTHORITIES¶
¶
CASES:                                              PAGE:¶
¶
Bankers Trust Co. v. Mallis, 435 U.S. 381 (1978) . . . . . . . .4¶
¶
Committee for Public Education & Religious Liberty v. Nyquist,
413 U.S. 756 (1973), aff'd mem., 471 U.S. 83 (1985). . 10, 12, 14¶
¶
County of Allegheny v. American Civil Liberties Union, 57
U.S.L.W. 5045 (U.S. June 27, 1989), 109 S. Ct. 3086 (1989), 106
L. Ed. 2d 472 (1989) . . . . . . . . . . . . . . . . . . . . .11¶
¶
Everson v. Board of Educ., 330 U.S. 1 (1947) . . . . . . . .9, 13¶
¶
Fox v. City of Los Angeles, 22 Cal. 3d 792, 587 P.2d 663, 150
Cal. Rptr. 867 (1978). . . . . . . . . . . . . . . . . . .11, 13¶
¶
Kanematsu-Gosho, Ltd. v. M/T Mesiniaki Aigli, 805 F.2d 47 (2d
Cir. 1986) . . . . . . . . . . . . . . . . . . . . . . . .4, 5, 7¶
¶
Lemon v. Kurtzman, 403 U.S. 602 (1971) . . . . .3, 9, 10, 12-14¶
¶
C:\WP51\CONLAW\BRIEF.TOA                     Doc 1 Pg 1 Ln 1" Pos 1"
```

FIGURE 5-15

The Table of Authorities is complete and alphabetized.

TABLE OF AUTHORITIES

CASES: **PAGE:**

Bankers Trust Co. v. Mallis, 435 U.S. 381 (1978) 4

Committee for Public Education & Religious Liberty v. Nyquist, 413 U.S. 756 (1973), aff'd mem., 471 U.S. 83 (1985) 10, 12, 14

Everson v. Board of Educ., 330 U.S. 1 (1947) 9, 13

Fox v. City of Los Angeles, 22 Cal. 3d 792, 587 P.2d 663 (1978) 11, 13

Kanematsu-Gosho, Ltd. v. M/T Mesiniaki Aigli, 805 F.2d 47 (2d Cir. 1986) 4, 5, 7

Lemon v. Kurtzman, 403 U.S. 602 (1971) 3, 9, 10, 12-14

Lynch v. Donnelly, 465 U.S. 668, reh'g denied, 466 U.S. 994 (1984) 10, 14

Stone v. Graham, 449 U.S. 39 (1980) 9

Wallace v. Jaffree, 472 U.S. 38 (1985) 9

Walz v. Tax Commission, 397 U.S. 664 (1970) 9

RULES OF CIVIL PROCEDURE:

Federal Rule of Appellate Procedure 4(a) 1, 4, 5, 8

Federal Rule of Civil Procedure 77(d) 7

Federal Rule of Civil Procedure 79 4

Federal Rule of Civil Procedure 84 6

MISCELLANEOUS:

28 U.S.C. § 1331 (1950) 3

Moore, Handbook on Federal Rules of Civil Procedure 707 (1989). 6

U.S. CONSTITUTION amend. I. 8

Van Alstyne, Trends in the Supreme Court: Mr. Jefferson's Crumbling Wall-A comment on Lynch v. Donnelly, 1984 Duke L.J. 770, 771. 9

i

How to Use WordPerfect 5.0/5.1 in the Law Office
§5.3

Step 1: Define a table of contents

The table of contents for our sample brief (BRIEF.DOC) contains the following major headings: the table of authorities, the introduction, the argument, and the conclusion. Under the argument section, a second level or subheading will be created within each major part of the argument. Therefore, this table of contents will consist of two levels.

When the table of contents is generated, each successive level will be indented to the next tab stop. In our case, since we have only two levels, only the second level will be indented.

To define a table of contents with this structure, follow these steps:

1. Press [Home], [Home], [↑] to move the cursor to the very beginning of the brief.
2. Press [Ctrl][Enter] (Hard Return) to create a new page.
3. Move the cursor up to the line at which the title for the table of contents will appear and type `Table of Contents`.

■ *You may, as in the table of authorities, press another return or two and type* `Page` *at the right margin using the* [Alt][F6] *(Flush Right) key combination.*

4. Press [Enter] several times to move the cursor to the line at which the first line of the table of contents will appear.
5. Press [Alt][F5] (Mark Text).
6. Choose [5] for **D**efine.
7. Choose [1] for **D**efine table of contents.
8. Choose [1] for **N**umber of Levels that will be included in the table of contents, then type `2`. The other options will be left at their default settings ("no" for Display Last Level in Wrapped Format and Flush Right with leader for both levels).

■ *WordPerfect allows a number of different listing styles for tables of contents. Although our fictional firm uses mostly the Flush Right Page Numbers with Leaders style, the following example shows the other listing styles available:*

No Page Numbers
    Page Numbers Follow Entries: `1;5;7`
    (Page Numbers) Follow Entries: `(1);(5);(7)`
    Flush Right Page Numbers: `1,5,7`
    Flush Right Page Numbers with Leaders: . . . .`1,5,7`

FIGURE 5-17

This Table of Contents Definition screen shows choices for a two-level table with flush-right leaders.

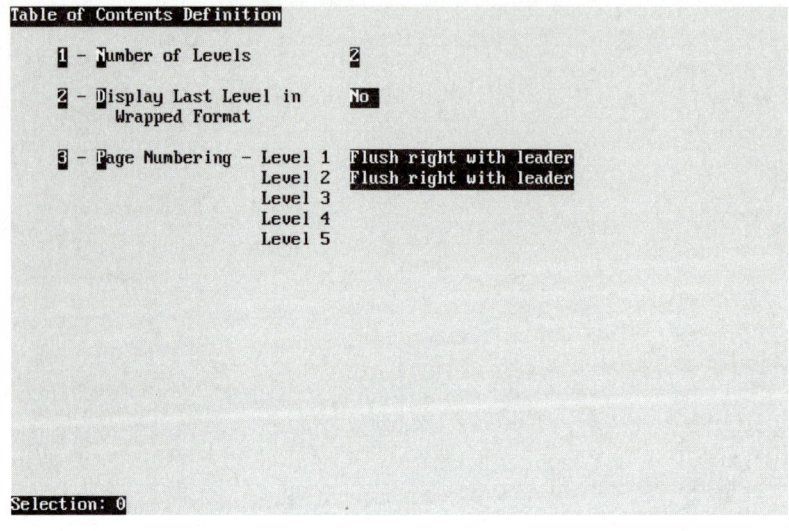

9. Press [F7] (Exit) to return to the document screen. See Figure 5-17.

The code [Def Mark: ToC, 2:5, 5] means that you have defined a table of contents with 2 out of 5 possible levels.

Step 2: Renumber the brief pages

Again, as in the table of authorities, there are two important steps that must now be taken to ensure the page accuracy of the table of contents. Because new pages have been added for the table of contents and the table of authorities, we must ensure that both tables are given Roman numeral page numbers and that page 1 of the brief begins at the start of the text, not at the table of contents.

Giving the table of contents Roman numeral page numbers

IMPORTANT: If you already performed this step for the table of authorities, you must delete the [Pg Num: i] code that you inserted previously for the table of authorities in order for WordPerfect to number the pages properly. Otherwise, both the table of contents and the table of authorities will be numbered "i." Use the Search feature to search for the [Pg Num] code.

WP5.1

1. Press [Home], [Home], [↑] to move the cursor to the beginning of the table of contents.

2. Press [Shift][F8] (Format).
3. Choose [2] for **P**age.
4. Choose [6] for Page **N**umbering.
5. Choose [4] for Page Number **P**osition, then [6] for bottom center.
6. Choose [1] for New Page **N**umber.
7. Type i, then press [Enter].
8. Press [F7] (Exit) to return to the document.

WP5.0

1. Press [Home], [Home], [↑] to move the cursor to the beginning of the table of contents.
2. Press [Shift][F8] (Format).
3. Choose [2] for **P**age.
4. Choose [6] for **N**ew Page Numbering, type i, and press [Enter].
5. Choose [7] for **P**age Numbering, [6] for bottom center.
6. Press [F7] (Exit) to return to the document.

A [Pg num:i] [Pg Numbering: Bottom Center] code should now be inserted.

> *We are now forming a republican government. Real liberty is neither found in despotism or the extremes of democracy, but in moderate governments.*
> Alexander Hamilton
> Debates of the Federal Convention
> [May 14–September 17, 1787].
> June 26, 1787

Starting the text at page 1

■ *This step is unnecessary if done previously for the table of authorities.*

WP5.1

1. Move the cursor to the beginning of the page where the actual text of the brief begins.
2. Press [Shift][F8] (Format).
3. Choose [2] for **P**age.
4. Choose [6] for Page **N**umbering.
5. Choose [1] for **N**ew Page **N**umber.
6. Type 1 and press [Enter].
7. Press [F7] (Exit) to return to the document.

A [Pg num:1] code has been inserted. Also note that the page indicator on the status line on the bottom right of the screen should now properly indicate 1.

WP5.0

1. Move the cursor to the beginning of the page where the actual text of the brief begins.
2. Press [Shift][F8] (Format).

3. Choose [2] for **P**age.
4. Choose [6] for **N**ew Page Numbering, type 1, and press [Enter].
5. Press [F7] (Exit) to return to the document.

A [Pg num:1] code has been inserted. Also note that the page indicator on the status line on the bottom right of the screen should now properly indicate **1**.

Step 3: Mark text for the table of contents

Now that the table has been defined, each heading to appear on the table must be marked.

1. Move the cursor to one end of the heading to be included in the table of contents, press [F12] or [Alt][F4] (Block), and block out the text. In our case, the first item we want to include in the table of contents is Preliminary Statement on page 1.

> *Any codes that are included in the block, such as bold, underline, etc., will appear in the generated table. To ensure that as few extraneous codes as possible are included, turn on Reveal Codes [F11] or [Alt][F3].*

2. Press [Alt][F5] (Mark Text).
3. Choose [1] for To**C**.
4. Enter the number of the table of contents level to which this heading will be assigned. For example, *Preliminary Statement*, as a major heading, would be on level 1 of our table of contents.
5. Repeat the above steps for the other headings and subheadings that will appear in the table of contents. See Figure 5-18.

TIP

A fast way to go from one heading to another is to use the Search [F2] feature to find the text of each heading.

Step 4: Generate a table of contents:

Now that the necessary text has been marked, the pages properly numbered, and the table defined, all that remains is to generate and touch up the table.

1. Press [Alt][F5] (Mark Text).
2. Choose [6] for **G**enerate, [5] for **G**enerate Tables, Indexes, etc.
3. At the "Existing tables, lists, and indexes will be replaced. Continue?" prompt, type [Y] to tell WordPerfect to generate the table. Remember, this will delete any prior versions of both the tables of contents and tables of authorities that you may have created for this file.

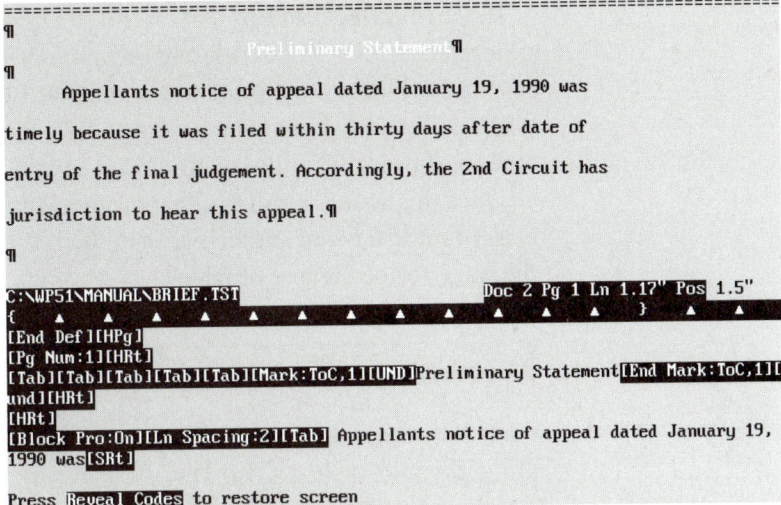

FIGURE 5-18

The heading "Preliminary Statement" is marked as a first-level head for a Table of Contents.

■ *During generation, the following message appears in the status line: "Generation in progress. Pass #, Page #." WordPerfect will make a number of passes through the entire document. Depending on the size of the brief, this may take a while.*

4. Press [Home], [Home], [↑] to move the cursor to the top of the document to view the table.

Error messages

Because creating and generating a table is a complex process, you may see the following error messages:

Not Enough Memory: WordPerfect uses Document 2 to generate tables, lists, etc. If Document 2 is in use, WordPerfect will use Document 3. Document 1 is allotted twice as much memory as Document 2. Therefore, if you are running out of memory, retrieve the brief into Document 2. The table of contents feature can then use the additional memory available in Document 1.

No [DefMark] Found: The [DefMark] code is created when you first define the table of contents. If you forgot to define the location and format of the table, WordPerfect will be unable to generate the table. Follow the steps used to define a table and regenerate.

Can't Find End of Table of Contents, Lists or Index Text: This message generally means that the [EndDef] code was deleted accidentally. The [EndDef] code is created when you first generate a table and is found at the end of each section in the table. (Each [DefMark] code has a corresponding [EndDef] code.)

If WordPerfect can't find an [EndDef] code, that section will be generated again, without deleting the first table. Therefore, you have two options: delete the prior duplicate table once you have regenerated or, if possible, copy an existing [DefMark] code from another section of the table to the section that's missing it.

Does this sound familiar? That's right, we're simply repeating the text from the table of authorities section. The potential problems are the same for both types of tables.

Touching up the finished table of contents

TIP

You can manually create flush-right dot leaders by pressing [Alt][F6] twice. This also works for creating center dot leaders; press [Shift][F6] twice.

As with the table of authorities, you will probably have to touch up the generated table of contents. Use Reveal Codes to delete any extraneous codes and align the flush-right dot leaders.

The completed table of contents for the Smallville brief should look on screen something like Figure 5-19.

Figure 5-20 shows the finished product—a fully formatted, printed table of contents. The table of contents is finished.

Printing documents from disk with several sections, each beginning with a new number

If your document is divided into more than one section, each beginning with a new number, you must take that into account when printing selected pages from disk.

Let's use the purely hypothetical example of a document that consists of the following sections:

```
Table of Contents i-iv
1st part of the body of the document 1-25
2nd part of the body of the document 1-30
Exhibit i-iv
```

To indicate the numbers of individual pages at the Print From Disk menu ([Shift][F7]), select [3] for **Document on Disk**, then type in the file name of the document. At the "Page(s)" prompt, type the appropriate section number first, followed by a colon, then the desired pages in that particular section. Let's see how this might be done:

You must enter `1:ii` to print the second page of the table of contents (or simply `ii`, because it is the first instance of the Roman numeral ii).

FIGURE 5-19

A generated Table of Contents for the BRIEF.DOC file is shown. Yours may differ somewhat, depending on the particular headings you marked.

```
                        TABLE OF CONTENTS¶
¶                                                            PAGE:¶
¶
¶
ARGUMENT:. . . . . . . . . . . . . . . . . . . . . . . . . . . .4¶
¶
  I.  THE DISTRICT COURT ERRED IN REFUSING TO GRANT¶
      APPELLANT'S MOTION FOR ENTRY OF JUDGMENT. . . . . . . . 4¶
¶
 II.  THE DISTRICT COURT ERRED IN DENYING APPELLANTS¶
      MOTION FOR A PRELIMINARY INJUNCTION TO PREVENT¶
      THE DISPLAY OF THE CROSS AND THE MENORAH ON¶
      THE SMALLVILLE SENTINEL IN VIOLATION OF THE¶
      ESTABLISHMENT CLAUSE OF THE FIRST AMENDMENT.. . . . . . 8¶
¶
      A.  Appellee violated the  "Primary Effect" prong of
          the Lemon test by endorsing Christianity and
          Judaism as opposed to merely observing a national
          holiday. . . . . . . . . . . . . . . . . . . . . . 9¶
¶
      B.  Appellee violated the "Excessive Entanglement"
          prong of the Lemon test because of the potential
          political divisiveness of the display. . . . . . .12¶
C:\WP51\CONLAW\BRIEF.TOC              Doc 1 Pg 1 Ln 4.83" Pos 2.9"
```

FIGURE 5-20

The Table of Contents for the BRIEF.DOC file is finished.

```
                          TABLE OF CONTENTS

                                                              PAGE:


        ARGUMENT: ................................................ 4

          I.    THE DISTRICT COURT ERRED IN REFUSING TO GRANT
                APPELLANT'S MOTION FOR ENTRY OF JUDGMENT ........... 4

         II.    THE DISTRICT COURT ERRED IN DENYING APPELLANTS
                MOTION FOR A PRELIMINARY INJUNCTION TO PREVENT
                THE DISPLAY OF THE CROSS AND THE MENORAH ON
                THE SMALLVILLE SENTINEL IN VIOLATION OF THE
                ESTABLISHMENT CLAUSE OF THE FIRST AMENDMENT. ....... 8

                A.   Appellee violated the  "Primary Effect" prong of the Lemon
                     test by endorsing Christianity and Judaism as opposed to
                     merely observing a national holiday. ........................ 9

                B.   Appellee violated the "Excessive Entanglement" prong
                     of the Lemon test because of the potential political
                     divisiveness of the display  ................................ 12


                Conclusion ........................................ 14
```

Enter 2:18 to print page 18 of the first part of the body of the document (or simply 18, because it is the first instance of the Arabic numeral 18).

Enter 2:iii to print the third page of the Exhibit, because it is the second instance of the Roman numeral iii.

Enter 2:16 to print page 16 of the second part of the body of the document, because it is the second instance of the Arabic numeral 16. If you wanted to print page 29 of the second part of the body of the document, all you'd have to do would be to enter the number 29, because it is the first instance of the Arabic number 29 in the document.

5.4 COMMAND REVIEW

Centering text

[Shift][F6]

Changing line spacing

[Shift][F8], [1] for **Line**, [6] for **Line Spacing**, [1] for single spacing, [2] for double spacing, etc.

Indenting (left/right)

[Shift][F4]

Underlining words only (not the spaces between)

[Shift][F8], [4] for **Other**, [7] for **Underline**. Press [N]

Using text attributes, e.g., double underlining, italicizing

[Ctrl][F8], [2] for **Appearance**

Using the outling function to organize ideas

`Shift`+`F5` (Date/Outline), `4` for **Outline**, `1` for **On**, `Enter` for a new level, `Tab` for next sublevel number/letter. To turn off outline: `Shift`+`F5`, `4` for **Outline**, `2` for **Off**

Selecting the legal outline style

`Shift`+`F5` (Date/Outline), `6` for **Define**, `4` for **Legal**, `F7`, `4` for **Outline**, `1` for **On**

Inserting footnotes and endnotes

`Ctrl`+`F7` (Footnote), `1` for **Footnote**, `2` for **Endnote**, `1` for **Create**

Editing a footnote

`Ctrl`+`F7`, `1` for **Footnote**, `2` for **Edit**. Enter the # of the footnote and press `Enter`

Deleting a footnote

Place cursor on the footnote number and press `Del`

Changing footnote and endnote appearance

`Ctrl`+`F7` (Footnote), `1` or `2`, `4` for **Options**

Search and Extended Search

`F2` or `Shift`+`F2`, `Home`, `Shift`+`F2`, type text or the function keys for codes, `F2` again

Search and Extended Search and Replace

`Alt`+`F2` or `Home`, `Alt`+`F2`, `Y` or `N` to confirm, type text or press the function keys to insert the codes to be replaced, `F2` again, type the new text or insert the new codes, `F2` to execute the replace

Using Compose to insert a special character

[Ctrl][V], "character set," "character" (e.g., 4,5 for the ¶ symbol)

Keeping text together

Widow/Orphan: [Shift][F8], [1], [9], [Y]
Block protection: [F12], [Shift][F8], [Y]
Conditional End of Page: [Shift][F8], [4], [2]

Inserting comments into text

[Ctrl][F5] (Text In/Out), **(WP5.1)** [4] for **Comment**, **(WP5.0)** [5] for **Comment**, [1] for **Create**

Creating macros to automate tasks

[Ctrl][F10] (Define Macro) to turn on macro recorder, type name of new macro or press a letter while holding down the [Alt] key, type description, perform the desired keystrokes, press [Ctrl][F10] (Define Macro) to turn off macro recorder

Using macros

[Alt][F10] (Start Macro), type name of macro or press the proper letter while holding down the [Alt] key

Creating temporary macros

[Ctrl][PgUp], press [1] through [9], type variable

Using temporary macros

[Alt] + number of variable

Using a Keyboard macro layout

[Shift][F1], **(WP5.1)** [5], **(WP5.0)** [6]

Creating a table

[Alt][F7] (Columns/Tables), [2] for **T**ables, [1] for **C**reate, enter number of columns and rows, edit and format cells, [F7] (Exit)

Creating parallel columns

[Alt][F7] (Columns/Tables), [1] for **C**olumns, [3] for **D**efine, enter number of columns, margins, etc., [1] for **O**n

Defining a table of contents

[Alt][F5] (Mark Text), [5] for **D**efine, [1] for Define Table of **C**ontents, select **N**umber of levels and **P**age numbering style

Creating a table of contents (must be defined first—see above)

[Alt][F4] or [F12] (Block options), block appropriate text, [Alt][F5] (Mark Text), choose [1] for To**C**, enter number of the ToC level

Generating a table of contents (must be created first—see above)

[Alt][F5] (Mark Text), [6] for **G**enerate, [5] for Generate **T**ables, [Y]

Defining a table of authorities

1. [Home], [Home], [↑], then [Ctrl][Enter] (Hard Page), enter title and section heading (example: Cases, Statutes), [Alt][F5] (Mark Text), [5] for **D**efine, [4] for Define Table of **A**uthorities, enter appropriate section number (1–16), choose formatting options, repeat for each section

2. Press [Ctrl][Enter] (Hard Page) after table to start text on separate page, on first page of text press [Shift][F8] (Format), [2] for **P**age, [6] for Page **N**umbering, and [1] for **N**ew Page Number

Creating a table of authorities (must be defined first—see above)

1. [Alt][F4] or [F12] (Block options), block the full form of the cite, [Alt][F5] (Mark Text), choose [4] for ToA, enter number of the section in the table, edit full form, and press [F7] (Exit), enter short form to be used to mark subsequent cites (must always be the same)

2. [F2] (Search) or [Home], [F2] (extended search) to find next occurence of cite, [Alt][F5] (Mark Text), choose [4] for ToA, type in name of short form for the cite, and press [Enter]

Generating a table of authorities (must be created first—see above)

[Alt][F5] (Mark Text), [6] for **G**enerate, [5] for **G**enerate Tables, [Y]

Desktop Publishing Corporate Documents in WordPerfect

FUNCTIONS USED
- The basic principles of typography §6.1
- Choosing a base font §6.2.1
- Creating lines with Graphic Line Draw §6.2.2
- Using a figure box to insert graphics and clip art §6.2.3
- Rotating text with the user box §6.2.4
- Changing the size of text §6.2.5
- Using paired styles to format text §6.2.6
- Creating tables with WordPerfect 5.1 Tables feature §6.2.7
- Placing a border on a page §6.2.8

SUBJECT TO COMPLETION, DATED DECEMBER 3, 1991

PROSPECTUS

3,400,000 Shares

SAM'S LEGAL SUPPLIES

Common Stock

Of the shares of Common Stock, par value $.01 per share (the "Common Stock"), offered hereby, 3,000,000 shares are being offered by Sam's Legal Supplies ("Sam's" or the "Company") and 400,000 shares are being offered by two stockholders of the Company (the "Selling Stockholders"). See "Selling Stockholders". See "Selling Stockholders". The Common Stock is quoted on the National Association of Securities Dealers Automated Quotation National Market System (the "NASDAQ-NMS") under the symbol "LEGL". On December 2, 1991, the last sale price of the Common Stock, as reported by NASDAQ-NMS, was $10.50 per share. See "Price Range of Common Stock."

THESE SECURITIES INVOLVE A HIGH DEGREE OF RISK. SEE "RISK FACTORS".

THESE SECURITIES HAVE NOT BE APPROVED OR DISAPPROVED BY THE SECURITIES AND EXCHANGE COMMISSION OR ANY STATE SECURITIES COMMISSION NOR HAS THE SECURITIES AND EXCHANGE COMMISSION OR ANY STATE SECURITIES COMMISSION PASSED UPON THE ACCURACY OR ADEQUACY OF THIS PROSPECTUS. ANY REPRESENTATION TO THE CONTRARY IS A CRIMINAL OFFENSE.

	Price to Public	Underwriting Discount(1)	Proceeds to Company(2)	Proceeds to Selling Stockholders
Per Share	$	$	$	$
Total(3)	$	$	$	$

(1) The Company amd the Selling Stockholders have agreed to indemnify the Underwriters against certain liabilities. See "Underwriting".
(2) Before deducting expenses payable by the Company estimated to be $
(3) The Company has granted the Underwriters a 45-day option to purchase up to 510,000 additional shares of Common Stock on the same terms and conditions as set forth above to cover over-allotments, if any. If the over-allotment option is . . .

The shares of Common Stock are being offered by the Underwriters, subject to prior sale, when, as, and if delivered to and accepted by the Underwriters, and subject to their right to reject orders in whole or in part. It is expected that delivery of the shares of Common Stock will be made in New York, New York on or about   , 1992.

The date of this Prospectus is   , 1992

A summation "a la Demosthenes."

OVERVIEW

Attorneys involved in corporate law regularly produce documents with such exotic appellations as 10-Q, 8-K, and 4-K, as well as prospectuses and registration statements. Many of these become elaborate tomes, undergoing numerous revisions before they finally end up at the printer. Unfortunately, too many of these revisions occur while the document is already at the printer and wind up costing much more money than necessary.

Before the advent of such sophisticated word processing software as WordPerfect, the printer would do all the typesetting. Now law firms can take advantage of WordPerfect's desktop publishing features to create documents with that typeset look, making them "camera ready" for the printer and impressing the clients—and perhaps saving everybody some money. (Actually, a few law firms have taken the process a step further and do all their printing in-house, a trend that's sure to grow as firms realize how much money this can save them.)

This chapter will cover many of the fundamentals of WordPerfect's desktop publishing features. While these features are particularly useful when laying out sophisticated corporate documents, they can be used by anyone who wants to turn out more attractive documents in-house, including newsletters and forms.

However, before exploring the brave new world of desktop publishing with WordPerfect, it is important to have a firm grasp of some of the essential principles of layout and typography. For this reason, the chapter will be split into two parts. The first half will cover some of the basic principles of typography, and the second half will demonstrate how to use WordPerfect's many advanced desktop publishing features to create a prospectus cover page. We hope that this practical exercise will not only teach you the procedures but also throw into sharp relief some of the principles covered in the first half.

A word of caution, however, for beginning users of WordPerfect. The concepts and features covered in this chapter are, apart from advanced macro programming, the most difficult to master. Consequently, we recommend reading this chapter only after you have a very firm grip on using WordPerfect. Most importantly, you must be very comfortable with using Reveal Codes to see what is going on in the background of your document.

This chapter is organized as follows:

Part 1: Understanding the basic principles of typography

- Some basics on typefaces and fonts
- Desktop publishing do's and don'ts
- Understanding leading and kerning

Part 2: Using WordPerfect's desktop publishing features to create a sample prospectus cover page

- Using Graphic Line Draw
- Using Paired styles to quickly format headings
- Using text and figure boxes to rotate text and insert graphics
- Tables features

WE'D now like to introduce you to Larry Blackstone, who will be your tour guide for this chapter. Larry is an aspiring bon-vivant. A fine arts major in college, he is a something of an aesthete.

It should come as no surprise then that Larry wants his documents to look impeccable. Fortunately, he knows more than a little about page layout and graphic design, because he's had a lot of experience using a popular (if somewhat user-unfriendly) page layout program.

You see, he used to publish a wine newsletter in college—can you believe it?

"Learning WordPerfect's page layout and graphics features is going to be a breeze for me," thinks our modest hero. "I'll just peruse the WordPerfect reference manual for an hour or two."

As a matter of fact, it's not going to be very difficult for you to understand WordPerfect's desktop publishing features, due to WordPerfect's ease of use and Larry's lucid exposition. However, before you and Larry tackle the prospectus cover page, there are some basic principles of layout and typography that are important to understand. Fortunately, Larry's got a small library on the subject of layout, design, and typography. (A list of some of them can be found at the end of Section 6.1.9.) He's culled for us what he believes to be the essentials for our purposes.

6.1 THE BASIC PRINCIPLES OF TYPOGRAPHY

Typography at its most basic is simply the selection and arrangement of typefaces, sizes, and spacing on the printed page. For graphic designers, this means giving a page a certain personality (formal, modern, classic) and feeling (dense, open, light). Most of us take for granted the importance of typography and graphic design in conveying information in our society. Imagine, for example, if *Time* magazine or *Rolling Stone* used only the basic Courier typeface (the one that comes standard on Hewlett-Packard Series II and compatible laser printers) for their articles. Would you be more or less willing to read it? What about advertisements? With the sheer volume of written information competing for the attention of our eyes, designers must constantly come up with new ways of arranging type on a page so that it is inviting and easy to read.

Fortunately for those in the legal profession, the task is a great deal easier. The inherently conservative nature of legal documents means that lawyers do not have to worry too much about the intricacies of type design and layout. This fact notwithstanding, a basic and practical knowledge of the principles of typography can be put to use by any law firm to make its documents more distinctive looking and easier to read. After all, if the work product of a law firm is documents, why not make them as attractive to look at as possible?

Let's begin, then, with a few important definitions.

6.1.1 TYPEFACES VS. FONTS

These two terms are often used interchangeably, and that can be misleading. In fact, a *typeface* is a family of letters and symbols of a particular design, such as Helvetica or Times Roman. A *font* is a full assortment of characters in a particular typeface at a specific size, e.g., Times Roman 12-point bold.

Proportional and monospaced typefaces

> *Why has government been instituted at all? Because the passions of men will not conform to the dictates of reason and justice, without constraint.*
> — Alexander Hamilton
> *The Federalist*
> [1787–1788]

With monospaced typefaces, each letter has the same width on a page (e.g., "I" takes up the same amount of space as "M")—as in the Letter Gothic face used in this book to show words you type. Chances are, your firm is using a monospaced typeface right now, Courier, which is standard on typewriters and the HP Series II laser printer. To be frank, Courier is an uninspired and characterless typeface. The only choice you might have is the *pitch* of the type—the number of letters per inch. Ten pitch means 10 characters per inch (cpi), 12 pitch means 12 characters per inch.

With the advent of sophisticated software such as WordPerfect and equally sophisticated hardware such as PostScript printers (more on these in a moment), things have gotten a lot more exciting and a lot more confusing. Now it's possible to choose, depending on what kind of printer and software you have, from any number of typeface families. Typeface families include established classics such as Times, Helvetica, Palatino, Avant Garde, and Futura, as well as much more specialized typefaces like Benguiat, Zapf Chancery, Hobo, etc. Most of these typefaces are *proportional*, that is, each letter has a different width on a page. Proportionally spaced type improves the appearance of the type and makes it easier to read. The body text in this book is set in Adobe Janson and the headings and display text are from the Franklin Gothic family.

Do not confuse pitch (cpi) with point size. *Point size* is a measure of the height of the text. (We'll talk about point size a little later.) With the advent of proportionally spaced typefaces, the question of pitch is not really relevant anymore. There is such a variation in the amount of space the same letters take up in different typefaces (not to mention different letters in the same typeface) that pitch is fast becoming an obsolete term. Take a look at the following two paragraphs.

Here are several lines of type. The first paragraph is in Times Roman, a classic serif typeface designed in England in the last century specifically to be used by the Times of London. It has since become something of an industry standard.

Here are several lines of type. The first paragraph is in Times Roman, a classic serif typeface designed in England in the last century specifically to be used by the Times of London. It has since become something of an industry standard.

The paragraph above is actually set in Palatino, another popular serif typeface. Notice that despite the fact the text is exactly the same and the point size is 12 in both (take our word for it), the text actually takes up half a line more. This is because the width of the letters in Palatino is greater than in Times Roman. This is the reason Times Roman is ideal for newspapers—more text can comfortably fit into narrow columns. It is also incredibly legible, making it even more ideal.

6.1.2 THE "COLOR" OF TYPE AND BODY VS. DISPLAY TEXT

The *color* of a typeface refers to the overall tone or texture of the type, which includes its lightness and darkness on a page and the evenness of the type as determined by the spacing. To put it simply, different typefaces make different statements; they have different connotations. Times, a popular typeface for body text, connotes solidity and substantiality, at least to us. Palatino is more graceful and stately. In short, most typefaces have personality. By the way, Adobe (the world's leading purveyor of computer fonts) at last count claims to have 3,210 typefaces in its type library.

Serifs and sans-serif typefaces

One of the major factors influencing the color of a typeface is whether the type is serif or sans-serif. Wait, we think we hear you asking, "What on earth is a serif?" Well, it's those little doo-dads on the ends of letters . . . "I think I deserve a somewhat more precise explanation," you rejoin. OK, the typographic definition of a serif is a finishing stroke or curve projecting from the end of a letterform. (For the history buffs out there, serif typefaces are also frequently referred to as roman, because the serif derived from the marks made chiseling letters into Roman monuments.) Some serif typefaces include Times and Palatino, as well as Bembo and Bookman. A sans-serif typeface does not have this finishing stroke (from the French "sans" for "without").

Serif typefaces have been proven easier to read—the serifs lead the reader fluidly from letter to letter, word to word, and the eye recognizes the shapes faster. Thus, they are more appropriate for large blocks of text. Other factors also influence legibility such as the space between lines (*leading*) and the length of lines (*measure*).

Sans-serif typefaces, such as Helvetica, are better for headings where there are few words in a row. They are usually made to stand out by being enlarged or bolded or set off with rules of varying widths above or below.

We've already used the terms *body text* and *display text*. Body text, as you've probably gathered, comprises the "body" of the document. Headings and subheadings are display text. To oversimplify matters somewhat, typefaces with serifs often comprise body text and those without are used for display text. It's a good rule to follow in the law office even if it doesn't always apply.

It's said, "a picture is worth a thousand words." See below for a sample of serif and sans-serif typefaces.

Serif	Sans Serif
Times Roman	Helvetica
Palatino	Avant Garde
Janson	Franklin Gothic
Bodoni	Gill Sans

6.1.3 STYLE

In desktop publishing, *style* refers to attributes such as bold, underline, italics, and special effects such as shadow. The samples shown here are available from the appearance menu under Font ().

Bold	Underline	*Italic*
Outline	Double Underline	SMALL CAP
Redline	Strikeout	Shadow

Not to complicate matters too much, some typeface families, such as the classic sans-serif Helvetica, have their own italic and small cap character sets, as well as character sets with different weights such as bold, black, and extra bold. Each of these are technically different typefaces in that each is designed differently.

6.1.4 MEASURING TYPE

Points: Type is measured by its vertical height, with that height expressed in "points." There are 72 points to an inch so a point is pretty small. But the difference in a 50-page document between using 11-point and 12-point type can be several pages. Remember the difference between point size and pitch: point size is a measure of the height of the letters; pitch measures characters per inch and only relates to monospaced typefaces like Courier.

WordPerfect, being the sophisticated program that it is, recognizes points and will automatically convert them into inches if that is your default system of measurement. Try this little exercise. Use the Advance Down Feature ([Shift][F8], [4], [1], [2]) and type 72p (for "points"). Then, Reveal Codes. WordPerfect has inserted an [AdvDn:1] code.

> ■ *Typefaces like Times and Helvetica are proportionally spaced typefaces; each letter takes up a different amount of space on the line. Therefore, the concept of pitch (characters per inch) is no longer relevant. If you are using a proportionately spaced typeface (and we hope you are), you should concern yourself with the height of the letters or their "point size."*

Picas: Pica is a unit of horizontal measure used to measure line lengths. A "pica" is 12 points, and there are 6 picas in an inch. Two and a half picas is 30 points. If you want to be one of the typographic cognoscenti, you'll use picas and points instead of inches for all your page design measurements.

We've discussed point size and measure (the length of lines). Try to make sure they work together. For instance, you don't want lines with too many words too tightly spaced or you'll risk the possibility of your deathless prose going unread.

Here's a helpful little formula we've seen: The line length should be (in picas) one to three times your point size—ideally 2½ times. If your body text is 12-point type, then your optimal line length should be 30 picas or 5 inches. That's why newspapers, with their small point sizes, have narrow columns—for greater readability.

If the end be clearly comprehended within any of the specified powers, and if the measure have an obvious relation to that end, and is not forbidden by any particular provision of the Constitution, it may safely be deemed to come within the compass of the national authority.
Alexander Hamilton
Opinion on the Constitutionality of the Bank [February 23, 1791]

6.1.5 BASELINE

The *baseline* is the imaginary line on which the text sits. Falling below it are the *descenders*, the g's, y's, and p's, etc—those letters that descend below the baseline. See below for an illustration of this and a few other concepts.

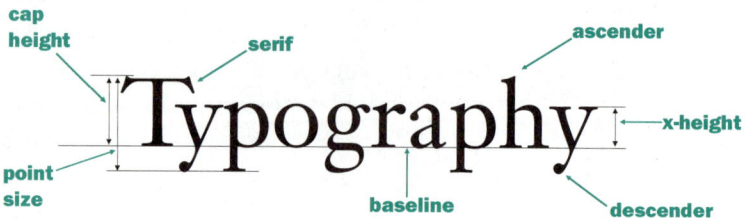

■ *As you may be able to see in this figure, point size is not measured from the tip of a particular typeface's ascenders to the bottom of its descenders. If you really want to accurately measure point size, you need a "pica stick." They're dirt cheap and often obtainable for free. (One comes with CorelDraw, a graphics program.)*

6.1.6 LEADING

Leading is defined as the vertical space between lines of type. WordPerfect's default is 120% of your point size. In WordPerfect, if you're using 10-point type, your leading will automatically be 12 points. You don't need to tamper with that setting. However, things change with display type in larger point sizes and the leading has to be tightened up somewhat.

Here's a heading of two lines (you usually don't want to make headings or subheadings any more than two lines, if possible):

This is the first line
This is the second line

The point size is 24 and you'll probably notice—with your already well-honed typographic sense—that there's too much space between the lines. The automatic leading that WordPerfect applied to your body text doesn't look good when applied to text this size.

Here's the same heading with the leading adjusted:

This is the first line
This is the second line

Here's how we adjusted the above leading in WordPerfect 5.1 (this feature is not available in 5.0).

1. With the cursor at the beginning of the first line, press [Shift][F8] (Format), [4], [6], [6], [Enter] so that the cursor is in the In Secondary - [HRt] field.

■ *Because there is a [HRt] between the two lines we chose the second option.*

2. Type `-6p` (negative 6p) to reduce the leading by 6p, i.e., 6 points.

A [Leading Adj:0", –0.083"] has been inserted.

You can, of course, experiment with this number—the more you reduce the leading, the smaller the space between the two lines. (A positive number will increase the leading, obviously.) You may change the leading of your body type as well in this manner. Simply change the setting on the first line—Primary - [SRt]—in the same fashion. You probably don't want to fool around with that setting for body text, though. WordPerfect's default is fine. By the way, remember to change the Leading adjustment back to 0 for the body text that follows or there will be some strange-looking leading in between paragraphs.

There is a homely adage which runs, "Speak softly and carry a big stick; you will go far." If the American nation will speak softly and yet build and keep at a pitch of the highest training a thoroughly efficient navy, the Monroe Doctrine will go far.
Theodore Roosevelt
Speech at Minnesota State Fair [Sept. 2, 1901]

6.1.7 KERNING

You've probably heard the term *kerning*. It is a black art that typesetters practice to get the space between characters just right. WordPerfect's PTR program, which allows you to customize your printer driver (a file that ends with the .PRS extension), also allows you to adjust kerning pairs, but this arcane skill is something we don't think any law firm needs to worry about, so we're not going to talk about it here.

If you want WordPerfect to kern your letter pairs, press [Shift][F8], [4], [6], [1] and just say "yes." It will be done automatically if your printer's .PRS file has the necessary information. If it doesn't, no harm is done.

6.1.8 PORTRAIT VS. LANDSCAPE PAPER ORIENTATION

Most of the time you'll be producing documents in portrait mode (8.5" x 11"), the way a business letter is typed. However, there will be occasions where you'll want to switch the paper orientation (11" x 8.5") sideways to print a chart or a long table, for instance. The latter paper orientation is known as landscape. To change the default orientation (portrait) to landscape perform the following steps:

WP5.1

1. Press [Shift][F8], [2] for **P**age.
2. Press [7] for **S**ize and select Landscape if available from the Paper Size/Type menu. If not, you'll have to add it. To do so:
3. Press [2] for **A**dd, [9] for **O**ther.
4. At the "Other Paper Type:" prompt, type Landscape.
5. At the Edit Paper Definition screen, press [1] for **S**ize, [2] for Standard Landscape.
6. Press [Enter]. You should now see the Landscape (Wide) paper size you just added on the Paper Size/Type menu (see Figure 6-1).

■ *You add other paper sizes and types in the same manner, i.e., legal size in portrait and landscape modes, as well as 8.5" x 14" in portrait and landscape.*

WP5.0

1. Press [Shift][F8], [2] for **P**age.
2. Press [8] for **S**ize.

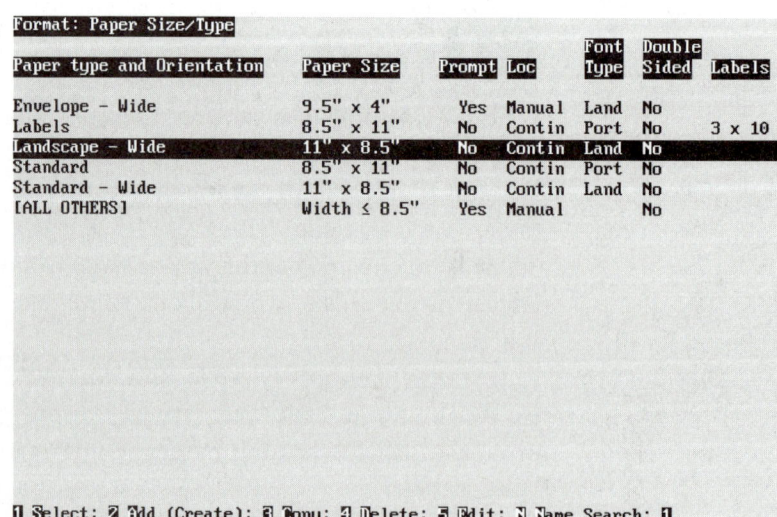

FIGURE 6-1

The Paper Size menu for WordPerfect 5.0. Note that 11" X 8.5" Landscape paper is referred to here as Standard Landscape.

FIGURE 6-2

The Paper Size menu for WordPerfect 5.0. Note that 11" x 8.5" Landscape paper is referred to here as Standard Landscape.

```
Format: Paper Size              Width  Height

     1 - Standard               (8.5" x 11")
     2 - Standard Landscape     (11" x 8.5")
     3 - Legal                  (8.5" x 14")
     4 - Legal Landscape        (14" x 8.5")
     5 - Envelope               (9.5" x 4")
     6 - Half Sheet             (5.5" x 8.5")
     7 - US Government          (8" x 11")
     8 - A4                     (210mm x 297mm)
     9 - A4 Landscape           (297mm x 210mm)
     0 - Other

Selection: 1
```

3. Select 2 for Standard Landscape, 3 for Legal, and 4 for Legal Landscape (see Figure 6-2).

▲▼▲▼▲▼▲▼▲▼▲▼▲▼▲▼▲▼▲▼▲▼▲▼▲▼▲▼▲▼▲▼▲▼▲▼▲▼

A [Paper Sz/Typ:11" x 8.5", Landscape] code has been added.

6.1.9 SOME BASIC TYPESETTING DO'S AND DONT'S

Indulge us just a little longer—come on, admit it, you love this. Much of this might seem a bit abstruse, but if you really care about the appearance of your documents, you'll bear with us.

TIP

To make documents, whether fully justified or left-justified, look better, use hyphenation. To turn hyphenation on, press Shift F8, 1 for Line, 1 for Hyphenation, and type Y. For more about this feature, see Chapter 5.

Use one space after periods for proportionally spaced typefaces!

Since you're now following our suggestion and using proportionally spaced typefaces, don't put two spaces between sentences—one is sufficient. Take our word for it; it will make your typeset documents look better.

Use italics instead of underlines

When using a proportional typeface such as Times, use italics instead of underlining for case citations. In addition to refraining from underlining, abstain from relying on bold for emphasizing text.

Use italics instead, as it is more aesthetically pleasing in that it's a closer match to the "color" of the regular text.

Emphasize display type

Emphasize display type by using a different typeface. You can also achieve a similar effect by increasing the point size, bolding, and using ruling lines of varying thicknesses and color above and below. There are many other more creative methods as well.

Using typographical special characters

> *The following tips use WordPerfect's Compose feature to insert special characters. If you plan to use any of these tips, you should map the special characters to a keyboard using the Compose feature. Refer to Chapter 5 for a detailed discussion of the Compose feature and details on how to map special characters to a keyboard.*

> *Your success in printing various special characters will depend on the particular printer you're using and the version of WordPerfect you own. Print out the CHARACTER.DOC file (it's a large one) on your printer to see what characters it supports. The CHARACTER.DOC file also serves as a handy reference. To produce a character in any character set, press* [Ctrl][V]*, the character set number, e.g., Character Set 4 (Typographic Symbols), and the character number, e.g., 61 for the British pound symbol.*

If we would guide by the light of reason, we must let our minds be bold.

Justice Louis Dembitz Brandeis, dissenting, New State Ice Co. v. Liebmann, 285 U.S. 262, 311 [1932]

Quotation marks

Don't use the " key on your keyboard for quotation marks. Use [Ctrl][V] (Compose) 4,31 for closing quotation marks and [Ctrl][V] 4,32 for opening quotation marks for the real thing. Ditto for '. Use [Ctrl][V] 4,28 and 4,29. And while we're at it, use [Ctrl][V] 4,28 for apostrophes as well.

Hyphens

Use an en dash ([Ctrl][V] 4,33) instead of the hyphen key in instances such as 1:00 a.m.–3:00 p.m. or 1933–1935. And use an em dash ([Ctrl][V] 4,34) instead of two hyphens for setting off a parenthetical phrase or clause in a sentence as in the following.

"We cooed in admiration—while suppressing the urge to giggle—as the dedicated follower of fashion modeled his newly-acquired wardrobe for us."

▪ *An em dash is equivalent in size to an em space, which is a typographic unit of measurement equal to the point size of the type being used. An en dash is half that size. The em dash in a document with 12-point Times Roman body text will be 12 points in size, the en dash 6 points.*

Fractions

Instead of creating fractions by simply typing the two numbers separated by a backslash to simulate the symbol, create the real thing. An easy way to do this for the fractions ½ and ¼ is to type [Ctrl][V] then /2 or [Ctrl][V] /4. The following lists some other common fractions and the keystrokes needed to create them.

⅓	–	[Ctrl][V] 4,64
⅔	–	[Ctrl][V] 4,65
⅛	–	[Ctrl][V] 4,66
⅜	–	[Ctrl][V] 4,67
⅝	–	[Ctrl][V] 4,68

These five fractions, when created, will show up on your screen as a little black box. Do not be alarmed; just go into Print Preview and they will appear in their natural states.

Don't hyphenate more than two subsequent lines

Limit the number of subsequent lines ending with hyphenation to two if possible, certainly no more than three. Don't hyphenate display text, i.e., headings and subheadings. To turn hyphenation off in WordPerfect, press [Shift][F8] (Format), [1], [1], [N].

Create ellipses with the period and hard space key

We know this is getting a little nitpicky, but if you've read this far you might be interested in this tip. Your ellipses (yes, that's the plural) should be hand-crafted—don't use [Ctrl][V] 4,56 or the ASCII character, because the dots are too close. Instead, type three dots with hard spaces between each ([Home][Spacebar]) so they'll stay together. Make sure

---

TIP

Some other symbols that can be created using mnemonic shortcuts like /2 and /4 for the two fractions are [Ctrl][V] followed by two hyphens for the em dash, [Ctrl][V] followed by tm for the trademark symbol, [Ctrl][V] followed by ro or RO for the registration symbol, [Ctrl][V] co for the copyright symbol, [Ctrl][V] L- for the pound symbol, [Ctrl][V] c/ for cents, [Ctrl][V] n~ for an n with a tilde, and [Ctrl][V] *., **, *o and, *0 for the following bullet types: •, ●, °, ○.

there's a space after the word preceding the ellipsis and before the word following it. If the ellipsis ends a sentence, make the ellipsis four dots (one extra for the period) with hard spaces between each dot. Finally, if the ellipsis ends a sentence, attach it to the word preceding it with a hard space so it won't end up orphaned on a line. An orphaned ellipsis is just too pathetic for words.

Additional reading

Needless to say, we've merely scratched the surface of an immensely involved subject. Typography, page layout, and design are art forms as well as crafts and can only be touched upon in a few paragraphs. If you wish to delve deeper into this often fascinating subject, here are a few of the many excellent books available:

Desktop Publishing by Design, by Ronnie Shushan and Don Wright (Microsoft Press). Written by two of the premier desktop publishers in the country, these books are meant both as an inspirational guide and as a manual for those who use either the PageMaker or Ventura Publisher programs. However, both books are chock full of useful information about layout and design—apart from being models of good design in and of themselves. Both books include many examples by professional designers.

Font and Function (Adobe Systems). Available free from Adobe, this oversize type catalog is full of information and ideas about using type.

Using Type Right—121 Basic No-Nonsense Rules for Working with Type, by Philip Brady (North Light Books). This is an easy-to-read, graphically imaginative and very informative introduction to, well, the basics of type.

Aldus Magazine, which comes free every month if you are a licensed owner of one of Aldus's products like PageMaker, Freehand, or Persuasion. (They are all very fine products.) There's lots of interesting stuff about page layout, graphics, type, and presentations, presented in a lively and readable manner. It's also laid out (as you might expect) in a lively and attractive fashion.

Looking Good in Print, by Roger C. Parker (Ventana Press). This is a wonderful introduction to the basics of page layout. Very lucid and commonsensical, it also contains many pages with extremely helpful before- and after-examples.

Of course, all this incredibly valuable advice is of no use if your printer can't support these features, or if you don't know how to use your printer to take advantage of them.

> *Our Government is the potent, the omnipresent teacher. For good or for ill, it teaches the whole people by its example.*
> Justice Louis Dembitz Brandeis, Olmstead v. United States, 277 U.S. 438, 485 [1928]

6.1.10 SCALABLE TYPEFACES

Scalable typefaces are the cream of computer fonts. With a scalable typeface, the user can change the point size of the typeface (the height of the letters), thus allowing for an almost unlimited number of available fonts. For example, with a scalable Times typeface, you could make the title of a contract 36 points and the proverbial "fine print" 8 points in size. This font magic is possible because of sophisticated mathematical formulae that generate an ideal "outline" of the specific font. This outline is then rasterized or converted into a *bitmap* font of the proper size and printed.

PostScript "scalable" typefaces

For years, a company called Adobe had a virtual monopoly on scalable typefaces in the PC market. Back in the early 1980s, Adobe developed a highly sophisticated Page Description Language (PDL) called PostScript, which used the Adobe Type 1 font format. Until recently, you could only use Type 1 fonts on PostScript printers, because Type 1 was a trade secret. However, you can now change a laser printer like a Hewlett-Packard into a PostScript printer by adding a PostScript cartridge. (In the same way, Hewlett-Packard's Printer Control Language [PCL] bitmap fonts work only with Laser-Jets and other printers that use HP's PCL—see "Upgrading your Hewlett-Packard Series II laser printer.") PostScript laser printers were considerably more expensive than the standard HP II Series laser printers, so few of them found their way into law firms.

Because of the quality of Type 1 typefaces, major type houses, such as Adobe, Agfa Compugraphic, Linotype Hell, and Monotype, have provided an unparalleled range of typefaces for use on PostScript printers. Furthermore, Type 1 is supported on every major platform as well as by all the *service bureaus*. For example, if you're designing a brochure for your firm and you want to send it to a service bureau to have it printed at a very high resolution (1200 dots per inch or higher), you should use a Type 1 typeface.

Other scalable typeface formats

Today, thanks to the productive wonders of capitalism, there are now several different scalable-type formats that compete with Adobe's Type 1. Companies such as Bitstream, with its Speedo format, Agfa Division with its Intellifont format (used on the latest generation Hewlett-Packard Series III printers), and Apple Computer and Microsoft's joint TrueType format (built into Microsoft's popular Windows 3.1 program) have sparked a price revolution. Today, scalable font technology is more affordable than ever and easily within the reach of any law firm. And, thanks to this good old fashioned capitalist competition, PostScript printers have now come down in price to the point where they are almost the same price as Hewlett-Packard laser printers.

6.1.11 SOME PRACTICAL BUYING TIPS

If the above discussion has whetted your appetite, here are a few practical tips for getting scalable typefaces into your law office. You'll be glad to know that WordPerfect for DOS's support of scalable typefaces rivals that of programs such as Windows, and that there are all kinds of options for WordPerfect users.

Upgrading your Hewlett-Packard Series II laser printer

The HP Series II is a true workhorse laser printer and has rightfully earned a place of honor in many law firms because of its dependability and reliability. The good news is that you can easily upgrade a Series II printer so that it can use Adobe's PostScript language. To do so, you must add some memory to the printer and purchase a cartridge that contains the PostScript Interpreter. Generally, you'll need to add at least 1MB of memory, because most PostScript cartridges require at least 1.5MB of memory and the HP Series II comes standard with 512K.

The major manufacturers of PostScript cartridges are Hewlett-Packard (3000 Hanover Street, Palo Alto, CA 94304; [800] 752-0900), Pacific Page Products (9125 Rehco Road, San Diego, CA 92121; [619] 552-0880) and of course Adobe Systems, (P. O. Box 7900, 1585 Charleston Road, Mountain View, CA 94039; [800] 833-6687). These cartridges generally retail for $500 (the street price might be considerably less), although keep in mind that the additional memory must ordinarily be purchased separately. The exception to this is the PacificPage II, which combines a PostScript cartridge and a 2MB memory module for about $499.

Some technical considerations: Printing in PostScript can be notoriously slow. Depending on the complexity of your document, it can

---

Where justice is denied, where poverty is enforced, where ignorance prevails, and where any one class is made to feel that society is in an organized conspiracy to oppress, rob, and degrade them, neither persons nor property will be safe.
  Frederick Douglass Speech on the 24th anniversary of Emancipation in the District of Columbia, Washington, D.C. [April 1886]

more than double the time it takes to print your work. Also, once you make the PostScript cartridge the primary font source, all files will be printed with PostScript until you remove the cartridge. This can cause problems for programs like Timeslips that do not support PostScript. (The ability to switch between PostScript and the Hewlett-Packard Page Control Language from within an application didn't come along until the release of the HP LaserJet III.) Finally, if you have one of the many laser printers that emulate the HP Series II printer but are not actually made by Hewlett-Packard, the above cartridges won't work. Don't despair. The software solution discussed below will take care of your problem.

Using the LaserJet Series III or 4 printer

If your firm is using a HP Series III or 4 printer, you already have a printer with built-in scalable fonts. The Series III comes with scalable versions of CG Times and Univers (similar to Helvetica) developed by Agfa. The Series 4 comes with 35 scalable fonts. You can, of course, buy the PostScript cartridges mentioned above, but buying scalable font cartridges that support PCL5 will give you speedier performance. The best deal for HP Series III users is a program called Fonts-on-the-Fly, by LaserTools Corporation ([800] 767-8004), discussed below. If you've got the Series 4, we envy you.

Software font scalers for WordPerfect

As mentioned, WordPerfect for DOS supports more font scalers than just about any other program. The beauty of the software solution is that it gives any user access to many scalable typefaces at a fraction of the cost of a hardware solution such as a new cartridge or PostScript printer, with only a slight penalty on speed. Best of all, these font scalers can print to virtually *any* printer, including dot-matrix, inkjet, and any brand of laser printer. Below are the font scalers for the major scalable formats. Once you choose one of these programs, you can use any of the typefaces available in that format with WordPerfect.

Type 1 format (Adobe): Primetype for WordPerfect from LaserTools Corporation ([800] 767-8004) is an on-the-fly font scaler that works with WordPerfect for both DOS and Windows. Once it's installed, you can use Type 1 fonts from Adobe and other Type 1 vendors.

Intellifonts (Agfa and HP III): Fonts-on-the-Fly, also from LaserTools Corporation, works similarly with Intellifonts from Agfa.

Speedo (Bitstream): Facelift for WordPerfect provides scalable Speedo fonts, available from Bitstream.

TrueType (Apple and Microsoft): TrueType ([800] 522-FONT) for DOS from MicroLogic Software ([800] 888-9078) gives you 36 scalable fonts plus access to TrueType fonts from other vendors.

6.2 CREATING A PROSPECTUS COVER PAGE USING WORDPERFECT'S DESKTOP PUBLISHING FEATURES

Now that we've covered the basics of typography, it's time to apply our new-found knowledge to construct the cover page for the sample prospectus. The prospectus is for a company called Sam's Legal Supplies that Larry has represented since he wrote its certificate of incorporation years ago while at his former firm (see the sample document at the beginning of the chapter). Now, thanks to his good legal advice, the company is going public and wants Holmes, Cardozo to write the prospectus for the offering. Fortunately, Larry's desktop publishing skills in WordPerfect will make short work of this tricky assignment. Here are the different functions he used:

6.2.1 CHOOSE A PROPORTIONALLY SPACED SERIF BASE FONT

The first thing to do is select the proper base font for the body text—which you now know should be a serif typeface. Because Larry insisted that the firm get a PostScript printer, he has access to Palatino, Times Roman, and others. Chances are, however, that your firm is using an HP or compatible laser printer. If you have a Hewlett-Packard Series III printer, you can select CG Times, which is a knock-off of Times Roman. If you have a PostScript Cartridge in the printer or a PostScript printer, you have Times Roman. Here's how you select it:

1. [Shift][F8] (**Format**).
2. Press [3] for **D**ocument.
3. Press [3] for **I**nitial Base Font.
4. Highlight the font you wish to use and press [1] to Select. Don't select italic, bold, or bold italic, otherwise your entire document will be italic or bold or bold italic.

5. If you've chosen Times Roman or CG Times and you have scalable typefaces, enter the point size and press [Enter]. Eleven or 12 is a pretty good choice for body text. (The SEC says text size must be at least 10 points.)

6.2.2 ADDING GRAPHIC LINES

Our sample prospectus cover page is framed on the top and bottom by double lines extending from the left to right margin, the outer one of the two lines being a little thicker than the inner. Actually, the lines normally appear on the Form S-3 Registration Statement cover page, but for the purposes of this exercise, we thought we'd take the liberty of putting as many graphic elements on one page as we could. See the sample prospectus cover at the beginning of the chapter. These lines are easily produced with the aid of the Graphic Line Draw option.

WP5.1

1. Press [Alt][F9].
2. Press [5] for Line.
3. Press [1] to create a horizontal line
4. Leave the default settings and press [Enter].
5. Go into view mode to see what you have wrought.

The line extends across the page. The default width of the line is a stout .013".

A [Hline:Full,Baseline,6.5",0.013",100%] code has been inserted. "Full" refers to the fact that the line extends from left margin to right, making it 6.5" in length. It is .013" in width and 100% shaded (meaning it's black). You can make the line lighter by indicating a lower percentage.

Figure 6-3 illustrates three different types of lines produced using WordPerfect's Graphic Line Draw feature.

Let's create our thick line.

1. Press [Alt][F9].
2. Press [5] for Line.
3. Press [1] to create a horizontal line.
4. Select [2] for Vertical position and [2] again to set the position. You'll notice the default is 1", which is the top margin. Let's make it .95" so that it's a bit above the first line.
5. Select option [4] to change the width and type .020.
6. Go into View Document mode and take a look. Gorgeous.

> **TIP**
> If your printer does not have any typefaces for you to experiment with, don't despair. Simply install and select the WordPerfect printer driver for a PostScript printer such as the Apple Laserwriter Plus. You'll be able to see how scalable fonts work on the screen by using the View Document mode, but you obviously won't be able to print the document on your printer. See Appendix A on how to install additional drivers.

> **MACRO**
> Use the [Alt][G] macro to add horizontal and vertical graphic lines.

FIGURE 6-3

A selection of line styles (figure reduced to fit page).

This line has a Horizontal position of Right, a Vertical position of "Baseline," a Length of 2", a Width of .3", and a Gray Shading of 100%.

This line has a Horizontal position of Left, a Vertical position of 1.5", a Length of 3.5", a Width of .5", and a Gray Shading of 60%.

This line has a Horizontal position of Full, a Vertical position of 3", a Length of 6.5", a Width of .05", and a Gray Shading of 10%.

MACRO

Use the [Alt][V] macro to quickly go into View Document mode.

Now set up the bottom two lines, repeating the previous steps.

We're not going to bore you by repeating the steps. Suffice it to say that our vertical position for the thin line (.013") is 10", which puts it 1" from the bottom of the page. And the vertical position of the thicker line (.020") is 10.05", which places it a bit below the thin line. Take a look at your creation in View Document mode at 100% so that you can see the difference in the dimensions of the two lines. Press [↓] until you can view the bottom two lines. Now return to full page mode by pressing [3] to see how they look in relation to each other. We're sure you'll be delighted by the results.

You can edit your horizontal (or vertical lines) by selecting the edit horizontal or vertical line option. If you do select it, you'll find yourself placed in the horizontal or vertical line menu of whatever line precedes your present cursor position.

The other options (Horizontal Position, Length of Line, and Gray Shading [% of black]) are self-explanatory. One thing worth noting: if you select for your horizontal position anything but full, option [3] (length of line) becomes activated, allowing you to determine the length of your line.

You can also draw vertical lines. The principles are the same. The only difference is that one of the options for horizontal position is "between columns." If you've created columns using the column feature, you can use this option to put vertical lines between columns. Select it and you'll be asked which column you want the vertical line

If you once forfeit the confidence of your fellow citizens, you can never regain their respect and esteem. It is true that you may fool all the people some of the time; you can even fool some of the people all the time; but you can't fool all of the people all the time.
— Abraham Lincoln
To a caller at the White House.
From Alexander K. McClure, Lincoln's Yarns and Stories [1904]

placed to the right of. If your page is two columns and you select "place line to the right of column" 1, you'll get a lovely vertical line right between the two columns. Perfect for that in-house firm newsletter you've been dying to create.

One last consideration—the concept of vertical position in the vertical line menu. This is how that perhaps paradoxical menu choice works. If you choose any option but full, you can determine where the line begins relative to the top or bottom margin and how long it is. Let's say you select top for vertical position and indicate a length of 5". You'll get a line 5 inches in length, extending from the top margin at the left margin of the page. (Left is the default.) Indicate a horizontal position of 4", and that line will begin 4 inches from the left margin.

WP5.0

The horizontal line feature in WP 5.0 is not nearly as flexible as in WP 5.1, because you don't have nearly as much control over the positioning of the lines.

1. Press [Alt][F9].
2. Press [5] for **Lines**.
3. Press [1] for **Horizontal**.
4. For option [1], Horizontal Position, choose [2] for **Right**.
5. Finally, for option [3], **W**idth of Line, select whatever size is appropriate for your purposes.

The problem at this point is that you don't have any control over the vertical positioning of the line (or lines) within the Graphic Line feature. In order to position the horizontal lines you've created with this feature on the page precisely, you're going to have to use the Advance feature in the Format-Other menu. (See Chapter 2 for a description of this feature.) It's not so difficult, but it is somewhat cumbersome and awkward.

6.2.3 INSERTING GRAPHICS INTO TEXT USING A FIGURE BOX

Our sample prospectus for Sam's Legal Supplies incorporates the company's logo—a gavel. (Actually, this gavel is one of the graphic images that comes with WordPerfect.) WordPerfect's figure box feature allows you to drop images into your documents and edit them as well. Although you may think that you'll have little use for inserting graphics into text—think again. Besides corporate logos and the like, you can use this feature to incorporate scanned images of attorney signatures for use in mass mailings, or to incorporate clip art for spicing up documents. And even if you never have any use for it, playing with this feature is still more fun than you're likely to have with your computer in the foreseeable future.

WP5.1 If you're a 5.1 user, make sure that you indicate in Setup the location of your graphic files. WordPerfect's sample clip art files all end with the extension .WPG.

1. Press [Shift][F1].
2. **WP5.1** Type [6] for Location of Files.
3. Select [6] for Graphic Files.
4. Type `c:\wp51` (assuming the graphic files are there with the rest of the program files—you may wish to move them to a separate directory).
5. Exit to return to the document.

Make sure your cursor is at the top of the page. Let's return to the Graphics menu.

1. Press [Alt][F9].
2. This time select [1] for **F**igure and [1] for **C**reate.
3. Press [1] for **F**ile Name, then either type `GAVEL.WPG` or press [F5] (List Files), highlight GAVEL.WPG, and retrieve it into the box.
4. Press [4] for **A**nchor Type, select [2] for **P**age, [0] pages to skip. Once again, we want this item to remain in a specific place on this page.
5. Press [5] for **V**ertical Position, [5] for **S**et Position, and enter `2"` as the "Offset from top of page."
6. Press [6] for **H**orizontal Position, [3] for **S**et Position, and type `2.75"`.
7. Press [7] for **S**ize, select [1] for Set **W**idth/Auto Height, and make the graphic 3" wide. This will automatically give you a height of 2.26". (Larry does it this way so that the proportions of the graphic will remain constant and the graphic does not become distorted.) The completed screen should look like Figure 6-4.

A [Fig Box:1;GAVEL.WPG;] code has been inserted.

Editing a graphic image

If you go into view mode, you'll notice an outline around the graphic. If you don't want it there (and you probably don't), you have to change the Figure box Options. Here's how.

FIGURE 6-4

Larry's completed Figure Definition screen will place the Gavel image exactly where he wants it on the cover of the prospectus.

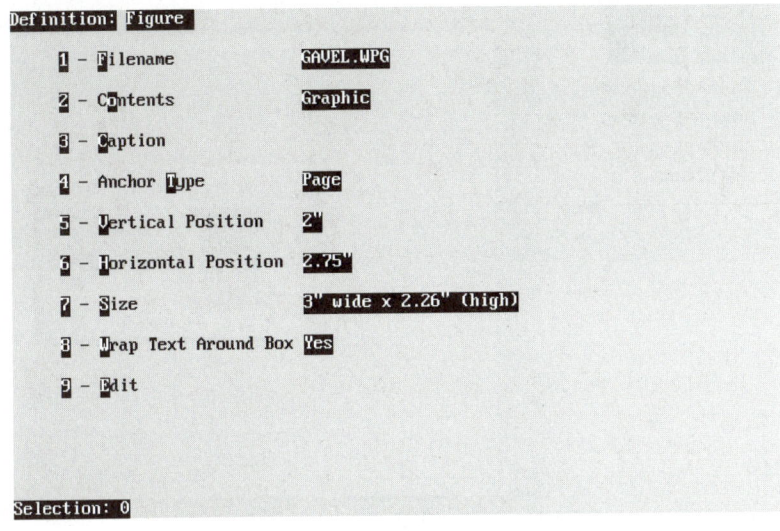

1. With Reveal Codes on, put your cursor on the figure box code and press [Alt][F9], [1] and [4] for options.

2. As you'll see, in [1] for **B**order Style, the default is a single line on all sides of the figure box. Choose [1] and press [1] for **N**one for each. All gone (see Figure 6-5).

MACRO

Use the [Alt][V] macro to quickly go into View Document mode.

A [Fig Opt] [Fig Box:1;GAVEL.WPG;] code has been inserted.

3. View it again—pretty nice, right? Bet you had no idea Word-Perfect could do this kind of thing. Don't worry, there's a lot more fun to come. For example, try out this cool effect. Select [1] for **B**order Style and type 2,7,2,7. This should give you a drop shadow. (See Figure 6.6.)

FIGURE 6-5

The Gavel image is shown without a border around it.

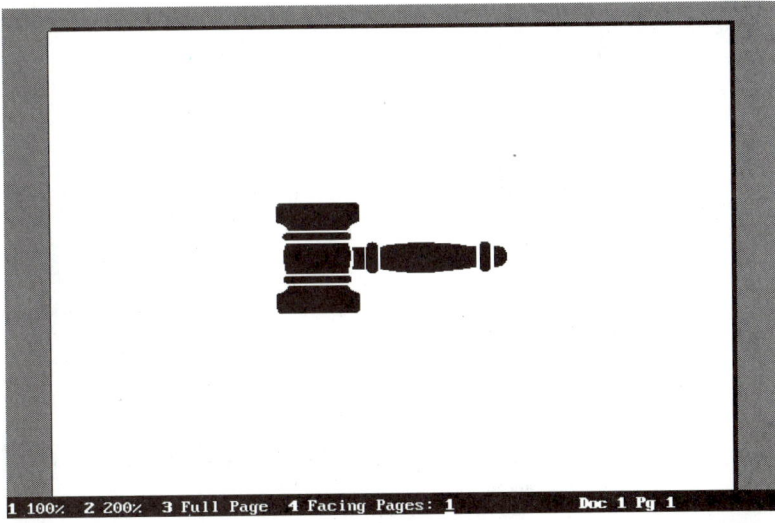

FIGURE 6-6

The Gavel image now has a drop shadow, giving it a 3-D effect.

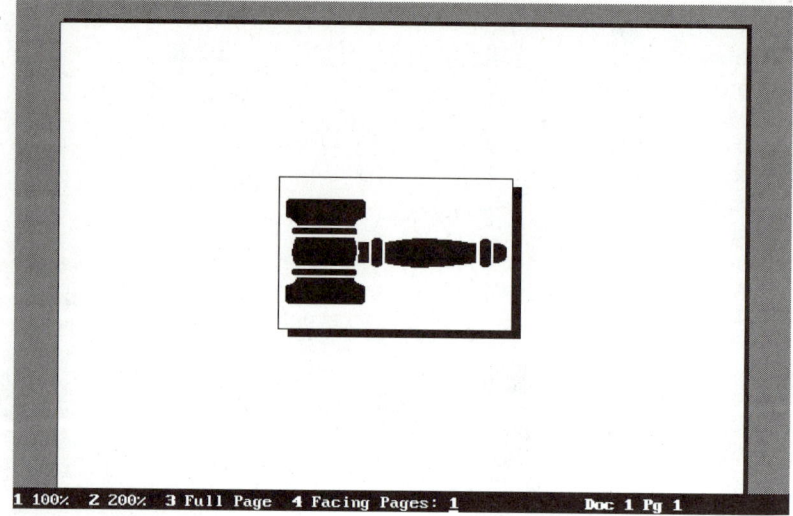

Not impressed? Try this. Press [Alt][F9], [1] for Figure, [2] for Edit. Press [Enter] to edit Figure 6.5—the gavel. Now press [9] for Edit ([8] in **WP5.0**). You should now be in the graphic edit screen.

Press the left and right arrows and watch the image move left and right. Press [Ctrl][Home] to revert to the original. Press [PgUp] and the picture will get 10% larger. Press [PgUp] again and the image will increase in size by another 10%. [PgDn] does the opposite. Rotate the image 10% or (45 degrees) counterclockwise by pressing the + (plus) key *on the numeric keyboard*. (If you have an old keyboard, turn [NumLock] on.) The - (minus) key *on the numeric keyboard* does the opposite. Or use the menu at the bottom of the screen for more precise measurements. Press [Ins] to change the percentage in the lower-right-hand corner of the screen. Remember, [Ctrl][Home] erases all of these changes. See Figure 6-7.

FIGURE 6-7

A slightly enlarged, slightly rotated gavel is now shown without a border.

When you finally decide on a look, exit the screen and return to your document. When you print the document or view it in the View Document mode, it will look exactly as you modified it in the graphic edit screen.

6.2.4 ROTATING TEXT USING A USER BOX

WordPerfect offers other graphic boxes besides the Figure box, including a text, table (in **WP5.1**), and user box. Actually, these boxes are all interchangeable except that their default appearances are different. For example, you could place a graphic image in the text box or text in the graphic box.

For our sample prospectus cover page, Larry is going to put the text rotation feature of these boxes to good use. "This should be perfect for the Red Herring!" he exclaims out loud. Linda glances towards his office, a look of concern passing over her countenance.

What Larry is referring to is not an hors d'oeuvre but the vertical block of text running the length of the left side of the prospectus. Naturally, in order to achieve this somewhat contorted state of being, it has to be rotated 90 degrees.

Here's how we do it. This is going to be fun; trust us.

Starting at the very top of the page (or else it will end up on the next page):

1. Press [Alt][F9] to go into the graphics menu.
2. Choose [4] for User box.

■ *You could use the text box or the graphic box as well, but the User box defaults better suit our purpose.*

3. Press [1] for **Create**.
4. You can input the text at this point or import a file already created. If you choose the latter option ([1]), don't forget to give the full path name. Otherwise, press [9] for **Edit** ([8] in **WP 5.0**).

Red Herring Text:

```
Information contained herein is subject to
completion or amendment. A registration statement
relating to these securities has been filed with the
Securities and Exchange Commission. These securities
may not be sold nor may offers to buy be accepted
prior to the time the registration statement becomes
effective. This prospectus shall not constitute an
```

It is rather for us to be here dedicated to the great task remaining before us—that from these honored dead we take increased devotion to that cause for which they gave the last full measure of devotion; that we here highly resolve that these dead shall not have died in vain; that this nation, under God, shall have a new birth of freedom; and that government of the people, by the people, for the people, shall not perish from the earth.

Abraham Lincoln Address at Gettysburg [November 19, 1863]

```
            offer to sell or the solicitation of an offer to buy
            nor shall there be any sale of these securities in
            any State in which such offer, solicitation, or sale
            would be unlawful prior to registration or
            qualification under the securities laws of any such
            State.
```

5. Before inputting the text, press [Ctrl][F8], [4] for Base **F**ont and select Helvetica Narrow bold, 9-point, if you have it. If not, select another sans-serif font in bold. Yes, you can format and edit this text as you would regular text in a document.

6. Now comes the fun part. Press [Alt][F9] (Graphics) and choose [2] to rotate the test 90 degrees.

7. Exit when done. You should now have returned to the Definition: User Box screen.

We're know you're just dying to see your creation, but show a little more patience—we've got to perform a few more changes to make it perfect.

In the Definition: User Box menu choose the following options:

8. Press [4] for **A**nchor type, choose **P**age. (Choosing this option ensures that the box always remains with this page, as opposed to a particular paragraph.) At the prompt "Number of pages to skip:," press [Enter] to accept the default of 0. If you enter [1], the User Box (and its contents) will appear on the following page when you print the document; enter [2] and the Box will appear two pages from the page it was placed on. This option exists for all the various types of graphics (in the [Alt][F9] menu in WordPerfect 5.1), except for graphic lines.

WP5.0 Press [3] for **T**ype, and choose **P**age.

9. Press [5] ([4] in **WP 5.0**) for **V**ertical position and [5] for set position, and 1" to conform with your top margin (if you're using WordPerfect's default).

10. Press [6] ([5] in **WP 5.0**) for **H**orizontal position, [1] for margin, [1] for left.

11. Press [7] ([6] in **WP 5.0**) for **S**ize, [3] for set both. Make it 1" by 9.5". WordPerfect will make the length a little smaller, because there is a .25" non-printable area on all four sides when you print a page to a laser printer. (What do you want? Printer technology has still got a ways to go.) WordPerfect takes this into account.

> ■ *You must perform this sizing procedure after you input your text (or import the file) and rotate it. Why? We don't know, but it won't work otherwise. We found that out after hours of frustration by calling the ever-helpful WordPerfect hotline.*

FIGURE 6-8

The Main Document screen with a representation of the User Box. To see the actual box with the text, press [Shift][F7], [6].

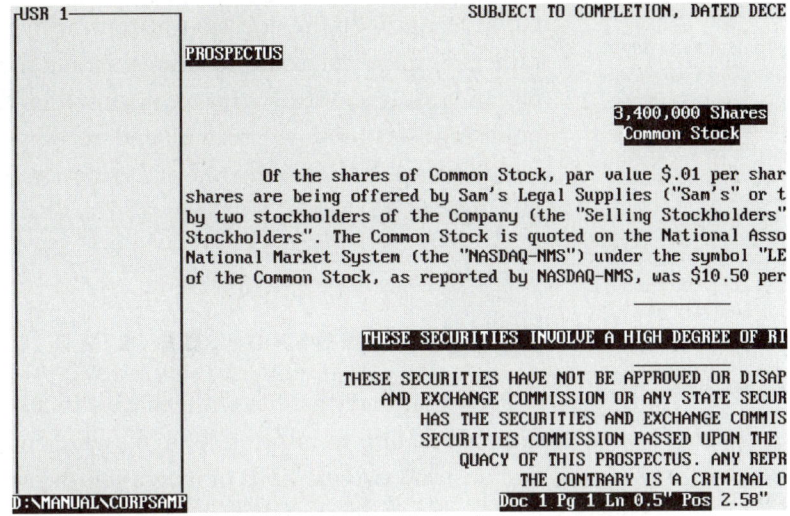

12. Exit this menu to return to the main document. You won't actually see the text box. WordPerfect will represent it as seen in Figure 6-8.

MACRO

Use the [Alt][V] macro to quickly go into View Document mode.

13. Now the moment of truth is at hand. Go into the View Document mode ([Shift][F7], [6]). Pretty nice, yes?

Graphics options

Now you can tweak your masterpiece a little to achieve complete perfection by playing with the options available in the Options menu ([Alt][F9], [4], [4]). Here are some of the more important ones:

Number 2—Outside borders is pretty self-explanatory. If you want less space between the text in the box and the rest of the text on the page (and you might very well), reduce the space on the right. You'll notice that this option also allows for space at the top and bottom of the box, which is why when we chose 9½" for the length of the box, we got 9.3".

Number 3—Inside borders refers to the space between the text in the box and the (imaginary borders) of the box.

The others we haven't gotten to can probably be ignored. Several of them deal with the automatic caption numbering features and other esoterica. We feel confident that if you're curious enough to experiment with them you'll be able to figure them out.

There's much more to the graphic feature. We didn't even begin to discuss table boxes, which allow you to put tables inside boxes and place them within columns (think of the possibilities—sort of like a

"A house divided against itself cannot stand." I believe this government cannot endure permanently half slave and half free. I do not expect the Union to be dissolved—I do not expect the house to fall—but I do expect it will cease to be divided. It will become all one thing, or all the other. Either the opponents of slavery will arrest the further spread of it, and place it where the public mind shall rest in the belief that it is in the course of ultimate extinction; or its advocates will push it forward till it shall become alike lawful in all the states, old as well as new, North as well as South.

Abraham Lincoln Speech at the Republican State Convention, Springfield, Illinois [June 16, 1858]

Chinese Egg), or the equation feature, which allows you to create rather complex and exotic equations, should the urge ever strike you, or captions. If you truly want to master all of WordPerfect's desktop publishing features, we recommend reading Daniel Will-Harris's book *Desktop Publishing in Style*, or *Desktop Publishing with WordPerfect* by Roger C. Parker.

6.2.5 CHANGING THE SIZE OF TEXT

Now that Larry has licked the more difficult problems of using the Graphic feature to insert graphic files and rotate text, he's going to demonstrate two methods of increasing the size of your letters (enlarging the point size). Either of these two techniques will come in handy here because the words "Common Stock" under the graphic are larger than the body text.

The first method is a bit more involved than the second—at least initially; however, it might prove ultimately to be the more efficient. We'll let you decide.

Method 1: Size attribute

1. Block the text—"Common Stock."
2. Press [Ctrl][F8] (Font).
3. Select [1] for **S**ize.
4. Now choose either [5] for large, [6] for Very large, or [7] for Extra large.

"Wait a minute," you exclaim. "These are rather vague terms. How large is very large, for example?" That's a legitimate question. Our answer is, "It all depends." That's a rather unsatisfying answer, we admit, but we will elucidate.

It all depends on the setting in the following menu:

1. Press [Shift][F1] (Setup).
2. Choose [4] for **I**nitial settings.
3. Choose [8] for **P**rint options.
4. Choose [6] for **S**ize attribute ratios.

Note that "Large" is 120%, "Very Large" is 150%, and "Extra Large" is 200%. Sorry, there is no Jumbo.

A little arithmetic will tell us that if our Initial Base Font is 10-point, "Large" will be 12-point, "Very Large" 15-point, and "Extra Large" 20-point. Naturally, these settings can be changed. Once they are changed to your satisfaction for a particular document, you need do nothing more to change your point size than block and select the appropriate size. You will not, in all probability, need more than four point sizes in a document. Any more may be confusing.

> A [LARGE], [VRY LARGE], or [EXT LARGE] (the same applies to small and very fine) code will be placed in front of and at the end of the text. Place your cursor on the first code, and it will tell you how large the font is.

You can use the same method to make text small or fine. This will come in handy on the Form S-3 Registration Statement cover page to recreate the fine print, i.e., "(Exact name of registrant as specified in its charter)" under the name of the corporation.

Method 2: Base font

We promised you a second method. Here it is.
1. Place your cursor in front of the text you want to change.
2. Press [Ctrl][F8].
3. Press [4] for Base Font.
4. Select a typeface.
5. Indicate a point size.

Yes, it's basically the same method as the one for choosing an Initial Base Font.

One advantage to changing size by using the first method (the size attribute) is that the attributes are relative; if you change your base font, all the text you selected throughout the document in this manner will also change relative to the new base-font size. For example, if we change our base font from 10- to 12-point, text that has been assigned a large size attribute (120% in this example) will increase from 12 to 14.4 points.

Another advantage to using the size attribute method is that if you change the body text typeface, from Times Roman to Palatino for example, text sizes will reflect this change. It's easier than continually changing your base font whenever you want to modify your text size and cluttering up your document with these codes.

6.2.6 USING PAIRED STYLES TO FORMAT TEXT

Styles are the smartest way to insert text that require sophisticated formatting. Once a style is defined, you can instantly insert numerous

Government of limited power need not be anemic government. Assurance that rights are secure tends to diminish fear and jealousy of strong government, and by making us feel safe to live under it makes for its better support.

Justice Robert H. Jackson, West Virginia State Board of Education v. Barnette, 319 U.S. 624, 636 [1943]

sophisticated formatting codes and text simply by turning a style on. In Chapter 2, we introduced you to the philosophy behind styles and showed you how to use the Open style feature for formatting a letter. Here, Paired styles come in very handy.

Coincidentally, that's just what Larry is thinking as he mulls over the best way to facilitate the process of inserting the two center, bold, all caps, boilerplate paragraphs that come after the description of the common stock: "If these two boilerplate paragraphs are always center-justified and use the small caps, Times Roman 12-point bold typeface, and if this particular format occurs on all prospectus cover pages—and perhaps on other corporate forms of this type—then maybe, just *maybe*, creating a style for this format that I can easily access might be a solution."

Let's give Larry a little credit here for his innovative approach to this problem. And let's stop talking and show you how this might be done.

1. Press [Alt][F8] (Styles) to take you to the style menu. You may already have some sample styles there, depending on which version of WordPerfect you're using.

2. Press [3] to **C**reate a new style.

3. Select [1] to give it a name. We'll call it `Larry` in honor of our hero; you might want to be a bit more descriptive when you name your own styles.

4. Leave Paired as the type. Type `Prospectus boilerplate Display Type` for your description.

▪ *A paired style allows you to place text between formatting codes. Paired styles are often used for formatting display type such as headlines. Open styles are used for inserting global formatting commands that apply throughout a document. For an example of how to use Open styles, see Chapter 2.*

5. Press [4] for **C**odes to create the style.

The first thing you'll probably notice in this screen is the message in the comment box: "Place Style On Codes Above, and Style Off Codes Below." If it's not already apparent to you—and don't feel inadequate if it's not, since this Paired style business can be a little confusing—codes entered before the Comment code affect the text you've tagged with a particular style, while codes after the Comment code affect the text that comes after the style off code (as in open styles). With codes that toggle, such as the text attributes bold and underline, you need to place the code before *and* after the Comment code in order to turn the bolding or underlining off. If you don't, the

FIGURE 6-9

Larry's paired style, when applied, makes text Times Roman 14-point, small caps.

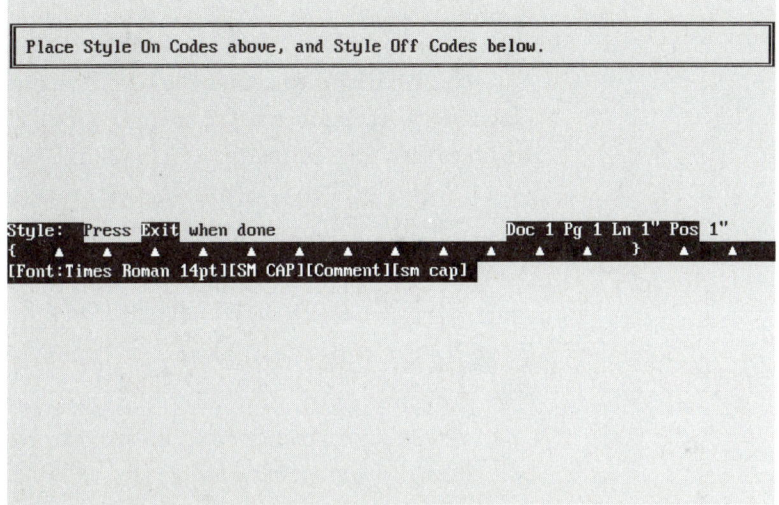

rest of the document will be underlined or bolded. We'll see how this works with the small caps text attribute.

1. Press `Ctrl`+`F8` and select `4` for Base Font.
2. Select a serif typeface if you have one—Times Roman Bold or CG Times Bold—and choose 12 for Point size.

■ *Remember, you can always use the printer driver of a printer with scalable fonts such as the HP Series III or a PostScript printer to view your work, even if you can't print it.*

3. Press `Ctrl`+`F8` again, `2` for Appearance, and choose `7` for Sm Cap.
4. Now move the cursor past the comment code and press `Ctrl`+`F8`, `2`, `7` again to place another [sm cap] at the end of the style. This turns off small caps so that the rest of the document doesn't have this attribute.
5. Press `F7` three times to return to your document. Your screen in Reveal Codes should look something like Figure 6-9.
6. Now, if you haven't already typed `these securities involve a high degree of risk. See "risk factors"`, take a moment to do so.

■ *You can type the text in lowercase.*

7. Block the text and press `Alt`+`F8`.
8. If Larry's style isn't already highlighted, do so and select `1` for On.
9. Go into view mode to see what it looks like.

Editing a style

Oops, we forgot to center the text. No, don't center it here in the document—remember, we're creating a style we want to use again and again to save time formatting. Let's put the center code in our style.

1. Press [Alt][F8] to return to the style menu.

2. Highlight Larry's style and press [4] to Edit and then [4] for Codes.

3. Press [Shift][F6] to insert a center code.

■ *We didn't place the center code after the Comment code because it wasn't necessary. Remember, in WordPerfect, when you press a hard return after a centered line you are returned to the left margin. The Center feature is not a toggle.*

4. Exit styles and return to your document. Take a look at your text now. It should be centered.

This little exercise illustrates one of the best assets of the Style feature. All you need to do is change a code or codes in the style, and all the text that you've tagged with that style in all your documents will change automatically.

Let's take a moment to look at the codes WordPerfect has placed in your document. Turn on Reveal Codes and place your cursor on the Style On code. Did you see how it magically expanded to reveal everything contained in that style? You are informed that the style name is "Larry's Style" and shown what all the codes in the style are. Place your cursor on the Style Off code, and it too will expand to reveal the style name and the codes you entered after the Comment box. See Figure 6-10.

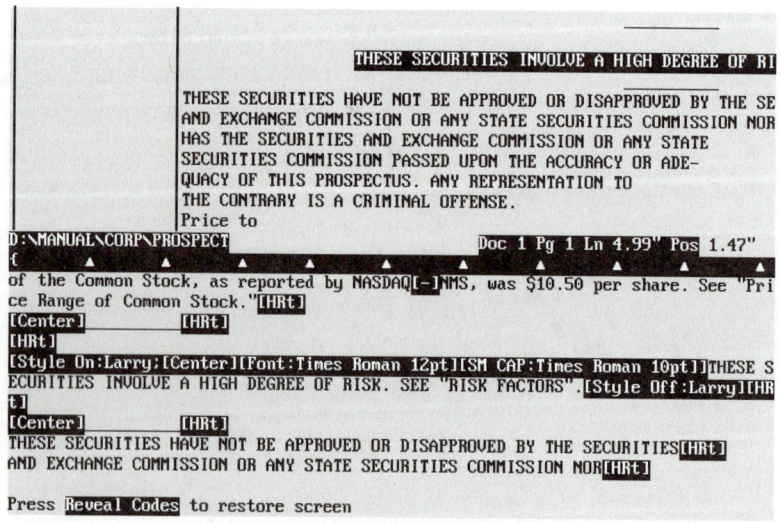

FIGURE 6-10

Larry's paired style is applied to text on the prospectus cover page. Note that the cursor is on the code, revealing the formatting attributes of the style.

Saving styles for use in other documents

■ *Once you've saved the style library, press* [8] *for* **Update** *if you don't see the name of your new style.*

Without a doubt, one of the most confusing aspects about Styles is saving and updating your Style library so that your styles become available in every new document you create. You will recall that styles are stored in one file called a style library (WordPerfect's default style library is called LIBRARY.STY). Currently, our Larry style is available only in the current document we're creating because it has not been permanently saved in the style library. (This can have its uses because certain documents—such as a prospectus—might have styles not needed anywhere else. Therefore, you'd have access to them only when you retrieved the prospectus.) To save a new style permanently to the style library, follow these steps:

1. Press [Alt][F8] to return to the Style menu.
2. Press [6] to **S**ave.
3. At the "Filename:" prompt, type `library.sty` (the default), [Enter], [Y] to replace the old file with the new. If you wish, you can create a new style library now. Just be sure to use the .STY extension (e.g., PROSPECT.STY).

Other style options

Naturally, you can create infinitely more complex styles with all kinds of graphics features if you're ambitious. To aid you in that endeavor, we're going to discuss a few of the other features to be found in the menus you've just seen. Some of them are confusing and are probably entirely dispensable. We and Larry are going to try to make this as painless as possible.

Deleting styles

Just as you can create styles, you can delete them. An obvious way to do this in a single instance in a document is to simply delete the style code. Presto, your text returns to its prior state. But suppose you'd like to delete that same style throughout your document or documents. Here's how:

1. Go into your style menu ([Alt][F8]) and choose [5].
2. You are given three options. The middle one, option [2] for Including Codes, eliminates both the style and the codes. This is what you'd generally use.

Option 1 for Leaving Codes: Lets you delete the style from the list of styles while retaining the formatting codes for that style in the document. For example, the Larry style above would disappear from the style list, but your document would still retain the center, small caps, etc., codes of the style.

Option 3 for Definition: Deletes the style from the menu but leaves the style codes intact. Then, when you retrieve the document, those style codes will be added again to the Style list. Yes, this is a bit esoteric. The idea is that this feature may be useful if you have a long list of styles and you just want to use the styles that come with your document. If you can find a good use for this feature, congratulations. You have definitely entered into the pantheon of WordPerfect power users.

Using the [Enter] key with Paired styles

There are a few more things you should know. For example, the different uses of the [Enter] key with Paired styles. We saved it for last because it's probably the most confusing concept in styles. We're going to simplify it by ignoring certain aspects. Don't worry, you won't be missing anything critical.

If you're not already in the Styles: Edit screen, please go into it ([Alt][F8], [4]). Option [5] is Enter. Select it and you're given three choices.

1 Hrt: If you opt for this choice, when you press [Enter] after a style, a regular old return will be inserted and your style will remain on. We think this is the way to go; no muss, no fuss—if you want to turn your style off, you can select [2] for **Off** in the styles menu. The other two options complicate matters.

2 Off: The second Enter option turns the style off. Pressing [Enter] again will bring you to a new line. This option gives you less flexibility to insert new text between the style codes.

3 On/Off: Worse still is the third option. Theoretically, it allows you to turn off a style and then turn it back on again. But it can be more trouble than it's worth.

6.2.7 USING WORDPERFECT 5.1'S TABLES FEATURE

> You may ask what then will become of the fundamental principles of equity and fair play which our constitutions enshrine; and whether I seriously believe that unsupported they will serve merely as counsels of moderation. I do not think that anyone can say what will be left of those principles; I do not know whether they will serve only as counsels; but this much I think I do know—that a society so riven that the spirit of moderation is gone, no court can save; that a society where that spirit flourishes, no court need save; that in a society which evades its responsibility by thrusting upon the courts the nurture of that spirit, that spirit in the end will perish.
> — Learned Hand
> *The Contribution of an Independent Judiciary to Civilization* [1942]

Well, Larry has solved every tricky layout problem on the prospectus cover page except the table, using a variety of sophisticated WordPerfect features. But Larry is supremely confident. "I'll make short work of this problem with WordPerfect 5.1's powerful Tables feature," he exclaims. "After all, I'll be working with data in this form more often than I'd care to think about."

We have no quarrel with that assessment. WordPerfect's Tables feature gives you the formatting flexibility to create virtually any kind of table you want. Fortunately, Larry takes notes as he works so that he can share his discoveries with his partners at the firm. Here's what he writes:

1. Press [Alt][F7], [2], [1] and create a table of five columns and three rows.

2. Turn block on and block out cells A1 through A3 by pressing [↓].

3. Press [3] for **L**ines, [1] for **L**eft, and [1] for **N**one to delete the double lines on the left side of the table. Repeat this procedure for the right side as well.

Centering, bolding, and reducing the size of the headings and aligning the numbers

1. In the Table Edit mode, block out the first row (cells A1–E1).

2. Press [2] for **F**ormat, [1] for **C**ell, [3] for **J**ustify, and finally [2] for **C**enter.

3. Block the cells again and press [2] for **F**ormat, [1] for **C**ell, [2] for **A**ttributes, [2] for **A**ppearance, and [1] for **B**old.

4. Bear with us. Block the cells once again and press [2] for **F**ormat, [1] for **C**ell, [2] for **A**ttributes, [1] for **S**ize, and either [3] for **F**ine or [4] for **S**mall, depending on your preference.

Now we'll line up the numbers. Remember, you should still be in Table Edit mode.

5. Block out the eight cells that contain numbers (B2 through E3).

6. Press [2] for **F**ormat, [1] for **C**ell, [3] for **J**ustify, and finally [5] for **D**ecimal Alignment.

Adjusting column width

1. While still in the Table Edit mode, put your cursor in the first row and press [Ctrl][→] until the column has been properly enlarged.

You might have to experiment with the size of the other columns in the same manner (using the [Ctrl][→] and [Ctrl][←] combinations to get the table just the way you want it). Go into view mode periodically (you have to exit Table Edit mode first) to see how the table really looks, because appearances often are deceiving.

2. When finished, press [F7] to exit Table Edit. You are now ready to input text into the table.

Inputting text into the table

You can use any WordPerfect editing or formatting function in a cell such as bold, underline, and fonts. For example, the table headlines should be a Times Roman bold 8-point font or equivalent. Note that, as you enter text, the text will automatically wrap within the cell and the height of the cell will automatically adjust.

To move from cell to cell, press the cursor keys or the [Tab] key.

When in a cell that has been formatted using Decimal Align, type the numbers and then press the period (.) to end Decimal Alignment.

6.2.8 PLACING A BORDER ON A PAGE

Before we leave Larry, he wants to demonstrate one last trick—putting a border around the text on a page. This may sometimes be necessary in a prospectus summary. As you might have expected, Larry's prospectus contains this effect. The following shows how, after a little trial and error, he achieved it.

First of all, before anything else, start a new page by striking [Ctrl] and [Enter] in combination. Now we're going to change our page margins to give us some space between border and text.

1. Press [Shift][F8] and select [1] for **L**ine.
2. Select [7] for margins and make both left and right 0.5 inches.
3. Now select [2] for **P**age from the Format menu.
4. Select [5] for Top and Bottom Margins and make both .75 inches. Press [Enter] twice.

Congratulations, you've completed step 1. Now, we're going to create a header and place a graphic figure box in it so that it will print on as many consecutive pages as you need it to. You won't even know it's there while you input.

1. Press [Shift][F8].
2. Select [2] for **P**age.
3. Select [3] for **H**eader.
4. Choose [1] for Header **A**.
5. Choose [2] for Every **P**age.

Right. You're going to place a graphic figure box in that header now. First let's enter an option code.

1. Press [Alt][F9].
2. Select [1] for **F**igure.
3. Select [4] for **O**ptions.
4. If you want to change the border style from the default single, do so here. Don't worry about any of those other settings.
5. Press [Enter].

A [Fig Opt] code has been inserted.

Last, we'll create the graphic figure.

1. Press [Alt][F9] (Graphics).
2. Select [1] for **F**igure and [1] for **C**reate.
3. Select [4] for **A**nchor **T**ype, select [2] for **P**age, and press [Enter] to skip 0 pages.

(Select [3] for **T**ype, [2] for **P**age, in **WP 5.0**.)

4. Select [5] ([4] in **WP 5.0**) and make the Vertical Position Full Page.
5. Select [8] ([7] in **WP 5.0**), [N] for text wraparound. (This is so that the graphic won't displace the text on the page by forcing it to wrap around itself.)
6. Press [F7] three times and return to the Format Line menu screen ([Shift][F8], [1]). Revert to the old left and right margins—one inch left and one inch right (if you're using the defaults). This is to ensure that there will some space between the border and the text you input.
7. Use View Document mode to check your work. See Figure 6-11.

■ *When you no longer want the border to appear, go back to the header menu and discontinue Header A. You should also restore your old top and bottom margins.*

FIGURE 6-11

The border you so painstakingly labored over is shown in Print View mode. Good work!

6.2.9 CREATING CHECK BOXES

Now, you want to know how to create those neat little check boxes found on the cover of the Form S-3 Registration Statement, as in the following: "If the only securities being registered on this Form are being offered pursuant to dividend or interest reinvestment plans, please check the following box. ☐ " Fortunately, it's quite easy—in fact, you might have figured it out for yourself already if you have read this chapter thoroughly.

1. Press [Alt][F9] for Graphics, [1] for Figure, and [1] for Create.

2. Set the Anchor Type to Character. The Vertical Position will automatically change to Bottom. Don't change that setting.

3. You can experiment with the following settings, but start with .15" x .15" for the size of the box. To do that, press [7] for Size, [3] for Set Both, and Width = .15", Height = .15".

4. Press [F7] to return to the document. Once again you'll have to go into view mode to see your creation. The neat part is that the character box always stays with the text that precedes it or follows.

Though he never doubted himself for an instant, Larry has mastered WordPerfect's desktop publishing features in a single day. (It might take you a *little* longer.) If he had one, he'd be smoking a victory cigar right now à la Red Auerbach. Fortunately for Linda and his other colleagues at the firm, he doesn't indulge. But he decides to give himself the rest of the day off to go to his favorite wine store and indulge himself with the purchase of a bottle of vintage port.

Chances are that your firm doesn't create many prospectuses for public offering, but we hope we've given you an idea of WordPerfect's many desktop publishing features. Now, the rest is up to you. Good luck!

6.3 COMMAND REVIEW

Choosing a different font (i.e., a scalable one)

[Shift][F8], [3] for **D**ocument, [3] for **I**nitial **B**ase **F**ont. Highlight the desired font and press [1] to select. If you've chosen a scalable font, type the desired point size

5.1 Adding graphic lines

[Alt][F9], [5] for **L**ines, [1] for **H**orizontal ([2] for **V**ertical). In the Graphics: Horizontal/Vertical Line menu, enter the correct settings, e.g., line thickness and position

5.0 [Alt][F9], [5] for **L**ine, [1] for **H**orizontal, [2] for **R**ight, [3] for **W**idth of Line, and indicate width. (Use Advance feature to position lines vertically)

Inserting graphics into your document

1. Make sure you indicate the location of your graphic files in Setup—[Shift][F1], [6] for **L**ocation of Files, [6] for **G**raphic Files. Enter the correct path

2. Go to the top of the document. [Alt][F9], [1] for **F**igure, [1] for **C**reate

3. [1] for **F**ilename and type the name of the file or use [F5] to locate it

4. [4] for **A**nchor Type and enter appropriate type (usually [2] for **P**age, [0] pages to skip)

5. Assign the other settings, e.g., [5] for **V**ertical Position and [7] for **S**ize

6. If you want to change any of the options, for instance border style of the box surrounding the graphic or degree of shading of the box, place your cursor on the figure box code, [Alt][F9], [1], [4] and change the settings

Rotating text in a user box (creating the Red Herring)

1. [Alt][F9], [4] for **User Box**, [1] for **Create**, and input the desired text [9] for **Edit** ([8] in **WP5.0**) (or import a file already created). (Before inputting you may change the Base Font—[Ctrl][F8], [4] for **Base Font**)

2. [Alt][F9], [2] to rotate the text 90 degrees, [F7] (Exit)

3. In the Definition: User Box menu choose [4] for **Anchor** type, choose **Page** ([3] in **WP5.0**)

4. Set appropriate **Vertical** position ([5] for **Set Position**, 1") ([4] in **WP 5.0**)

5. Set appropriate **Horizontal** position ([6], [1] for margin, [1] for left) ([5] in **WP 5.0**)

6. Set **Size** ([7], [3] and 1" x 9.5"), [F7], [Shift][F7] to view the result ([6] in **WP 5.0**)

Changing the size of text

1. Block the text, [Ctrl][F8], [1] for **Size**, choose [5] for **Large**, [6] for **Vry Large**, [7] for **Ext Large**. (To change these settings [Shift][F1], [4] for **Initial Settings**, [8] for **Print** options, [6] for **Size Attribute Ratios**)

2. Place cursor in front of the text, [Ctrl][F8], [4] for **Base Font**, select a typeface and indicate a point size

Using paired styles to format text

1. [Alt][F8], [3] for **Create**, [1], name and describe the style
2. [4] for **Codes** to create style
3. Place the codes before and after the Comment code, if necessary, so the rest of the document won't be affected by the style
4. To edit the style, [Alt][F8], highlight the style, [4] for **Edit**, [4] for **Codes**
5. To delete the style, [Alt][F8], highlight the style, [5] for **Delete**, [2] for **Including Codes**

Creating a table

[Alt][F7] (Columns/Tables), [2] for **Tables**, [1] for **Create**, enter number of columns and rows, edit and format cells, [F7] (Exit)

Placing a border on a page

1. [Shift][F8], [1] for **L**ine, [7] for **M**argins (make both .5"), [Spacebar], [2] for **P**age, [5] for **T**op and Bottom **M**argins (make both .75")

2. [Shift][F8], [2] for **P**age, [3] for **H**eader, [1] for Header **A**, [2] for **E**very **P**age

3. [Alt][F9], [1] for **F**igure, [4] for **O**ptions

4. [Alt][F9], [1] for **F**igure, [1] for **C**reate, [4] for Anchor **T**ype (select **P**age, 0 pages), [5] for **V**ertical Position (Full Page), [8] and [N] for **W**rap Text Around Box

WP5.0   [3] for **T**ype, [2] for **P**age, [4] for **V**ertical Position, [7] for **W**rap Text

5. Return to the Format Line menu, [Shift][F8], [1] and revert to the original left and right margins. [Shift][F7] to see border

APPENDIX A: CONFIGURING WORDPERFECT FOR THE LEGAL OFFICE

FUNCTIONS USED

➤ *Essentials of installing WordPerfect 5.1 on a network* §A.1

➤ *Installing additional printers* §A.2

➤ *Properly configuring WordPerfect for macros* §A.3

➤ *Editing the Master Setup file to create a global macro subdirectory* §A.4

➤ *Initial codes* §A.5

➤ *Document summary/management options* §A.6

➤ *Document backup options* §A.7

OVERVIEW

WordPerfect allows the user to easily customize and change the default configurations for the program. These are mostly found under the Setup menu (Shift F1). This appendix will discuss the most important configuration options, including:

➤ Installing WordPerfect on a network

➤ The location of files for macro, keyboard layouts, and styles

➤ Using Initial Codes to insert global formatting codes

➤ Installing additional printers

➤ Document summary and document management options

A.1 THE ESSENTIALS OF INSTALLING WORDPERFECT 5.1 ON A NETWORK

One of the many changes made to WordPerfect 5.1 was the network installation procedure. Prior to version 5.1, you were required to buy a separate network version. However, because of the rapid proliferation of networks, WordPerfect wisely decided to make one version of the program that could be installed either stand-alone or as network-ready. Now, when you install WordPerfect 5.1, you merely have to choose Network Installation for WordPerfect to have your system be properly configured for network use.

As you might expect, WordPerfect 5.1 is one of the most savvy programs on the market when it comes to working on networks, and the program supports every major network operating system. If you have a solid, basic understanding of DOS, you can easily configure WordPerfect 5.1 yourself without the help of expensive consultants.

Appendix R of the WordPerfect 5.1 reference manual goes into depth on the different options for installing on a network, as well as network administration techniques. So, instead of repeating the reference book, we'll highlight the salient points for network installation and give you a few tips.

A.1.1 UNDERSTANDING PERSONAL AND MASTER SETUP FILES

When WordPerfect 5.1 is used on a network, it must be able to support different simultaneous users. Each user might want WordPerfect 5.1 configured differently. For example, User A might want to print to a laser printer and use the Long Document Names feature, while User B might need to print to a dot-matrix printer and use only short document names. WordPerfect 5.1 handles these different user configurations by creating personal setup files every time the user enters WordPerfect. (That's why WordPerfect 5.1 prompts for three letter initials upon startup—these initials go into the setup files called WPXXX}.SET, where the X's are the user initials.)

As a network administrator, then, you want all of these setup files in one place, in case you need to quickly make changes to them. We recommend creating a subdirectory under WP51 called SETUP to store all these files. (Example: F:\WP51\SETUP.) You then indicate the name of this directory in the .ENV file using the /ps= option. (See below for details.) Furthermore, as the administrator, you want to set up the defaults and store them in the master setup file before people start using WordPerfect and creating their own personal setup files (which copy the master settings until the individual user changes them). If, later, you wish to change the personal setup files, you can use the NWPSETUP.EXE utility that comes with WordPerfect 5.1.

A.1.2 CHANGING THE MASTER SETTINGS

1. At the DOS prompt, start WordPerfect 5.1 using the Supervisor's initials, {WP. Example: `wp /u={wp` (the /u means "user").

2. Go into Setup ([Shift][F1]) and make the necessary changes, especially for the location of macros, styles, and keyboard layouts. (See "Creating a global macros directory on a network" in Section A.3, below.) Also, install and configure the network printers (see below).

3. Exit WordPerfect. Now, when a new user logs on, his or her personal setup file will have the master settings.

A.1.3 RUNNING NWPSETUP.EXE TO UPDATE PERSONAL SETUP FILES

Every time a new user logs on to WordPerfect 5.1 on the network, a personal setup file is created. (These files are named WPXXX}.SET, where XXX is the user's initials.) But suppose you've changed the master settings after all the personal setup files have been created. How do you quickly update them to reflect the new settings? Use the NWPSETUP.EXE utility. Here's how:

1. At the DOS prompt, change to the specific directory where the individual user setup files are located, as defined by the /ps startup option.

2. Type `nwpsetup` and press [Enter]. The Network Setup Maintenance Utility should appear. (See Figure A-1.)

3. At the "Update Auxilliary File Locations?" prompt, type [Y]. If you are using one of our keyboard layouts or one of your own keyboard layouts as a default, type [Y] at the "Keyboard Map?" prompt.

4. Enter [Y] or [N] at the "Update Setup Initial Codes" and "Update Network Printers" prompts. A message should appear, telling you how many user setup files have been updated.

> Our constitution is named a democracy, because it is in the hands not of the few but of the many. But our laws secure equal justice for all in their private disputes, and our public opinion welcomes and honors talent in every branch of achievement, not for any sectional reason but on grounds of excellence alone. And as we give free play to all in our public life, so we carry the same spirit into our daily relations with one another. . . . Open and friendly in our private intercourse, in our public acts we keep strictly within the control of law. We acknowledge the restraint of reverence; we are obedient to whomsoever is set in authority, and to the laws, more especially to those which offer protection to the oppressed and those unwritten ordinances whose transgression brings admitted shame.
>
> — Thucydides
> *The History of the Peloponnesian War*
> [431–413 B.C.]

FIGURE A-1

The NWPSETUP.EXE utility, which comes with WordPerfect 5.1, is used to update user setup files on a network. It is run from the DOS prompt.

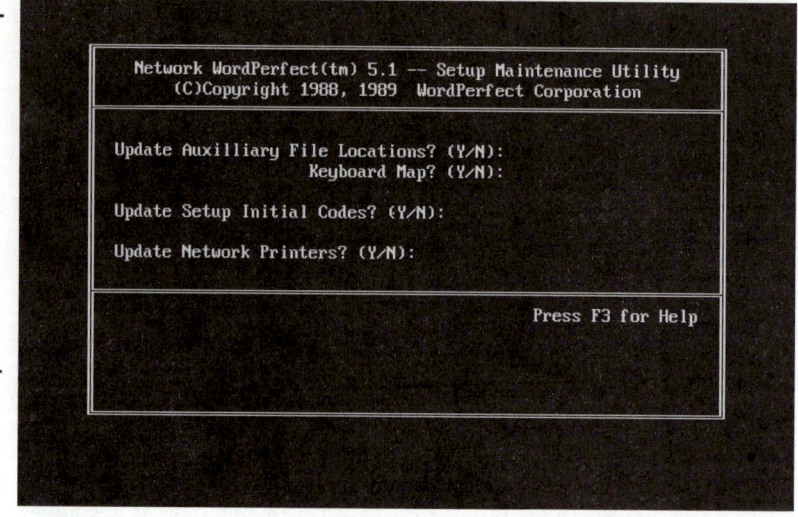

A.1.4 THE WP{WP}.ENV FILE

When you choose to install WordPerfect 5.1 on a network, WordPerfect will create a file call WP{WP}.ENV that contains the essential information about your network. It is an ASCII file, which means it can be edited by a text editor (for example, the EDIT program that comes with DOS 5.0). *This file is the switch that turns on WordPerfect's network capabilities—get comfortable with it!*

There are two essential startup options in the ENV file:

/nt=#: This tells WordPerfect what network systems you are using. For example, /nt=1 is for Novell NetWare, /nt=8 is for a Lantastic network.

/ps=setup directory path name: This tells WordPerfect where to store the personal setup files. We recommend a separate directory called SETUP.

The following is a sample .ENV file for a Novell network:

```
/nt=1
/ps=f:\wp51\setup
```

For a list of other startup options, see Appendix R in the WordPerfect reference manual.

A.1.5 THE AUTOEXEC.BAT FILE

As you probably know, the AUTOEXEC.BAT file, located in the root directory, is one of the key configuration files on a PC (the other being CONFIG.SYS). Use the SET WP /U=XXX line in each user's AUTOEXEC.BAT to bypass the user log-in prompt, where X is a user initial. That way, entering WordPerfect on a network is transparent and each user will always use the same personal setup file.

Sample AUTOEXEC.BAT for Novell and DOS 5 users:

```
REM THIS IS A SAMPLE AUTOEXEC.BAT FOR USER GUY
SPEC=C:\DOS\COMMAND.COM
PATH=C:\;C:\DOS;

SET TEMP=C:\TEMP
SET WP /U=GUY
PROMPT $P$G
C:\IPX
LOADHIGH C:\NET5
F:
LOGIN
```

■ *Some users have reported problems with the keyboard's locking up when using WordPerfect on a Novell LAN running DOS 5. WordPerfect Corporation recommends using the following DOS variable in the AUTOEXEC.BAT file to get around this problem:* SET WP=/NC/NK/NH/NE. *Be aware that this will disable function keys* [F11] *and* [F12] *on an extended keyboard. Call WordPerfect network support at (800) 321-3389 for more information.*

A.1.6 INSTALLING NETWORK PRINTERS

For certain network operating systems such as Novell, print jobs are sent to queues, rather than parallel ports. (This is not true for DOS-based peer-to-peer network systems such as Lantastic and NetWare Lite.) For most programs, assigning print queues can be a difficult task. But once again, WordPerfect Corporation has done its homework—all you have to do is edit the WordPerfect printer definition:

1. Press [Shift][F7], press [S] for **S**elect Printer, and highlight the printer you wish to use.

2. Press [3] for **E**dit.

> **TIP**
>
> You can easily setup different drivers for different print queues by using the Copy command in the Select Printer menu.

3. Press [2] for **P**ort, then [8] for **O**ther.

4. At the "Device or Filename:" prompt type the name of the network print queue, then press [Y] for Network printer. That's all there is to it!

NOTE: An example of a Novell print queue might be PRINTQ_1. Peer-to-peer networks such as Lantastic do not generally use print queues. Refer to your network's documentation for more information.

A.2 INSTALLING ADDITIONAL PRINTERS

WordPerfect 5.0 printer drivers may be installed by merely copying files off the installation disk. However, WordPerfect 5.1 files come compressed on the disk and you must use the installation program to unarchive them. These steps assume that you are installing new printer drivers from drive A:.

WP5.1

1. At the DOS prompt, type `install` and answer [Y] to all the prompts until you get to the Installation menu.
2. Press [4] for **P**rinters.
3. Insert the Master Printer Diskette into drive A: and press [Enter]. When the list of printer names appears, use Name search or [PgDn] to find the printer you wish to install, type the appropriate number, and type [Y].

WP5.0

1. Press [Shift][F7], [S] for **S**elect Printer.
2. Press [2] for **A**dditional Printer, [2] for **O**ther Disk.
3. At the "Directory for other printer files" prompt, type `a:` and press [Enter].
4. Highlight the new printer you wish to use and press [1] for **S**elect.

A.3 PROPERLY CONFIGURING WORDPERFECT FOR MACROS

Before creating and using macros, you must make sure that WordPerfect is configured so that all macros and keyboard layouts are saved in a specific directory as indicated in the Setup menu. For example, if WordPerfect has been stored in a directory called C:\WP51, we recommend that the macros be stored in a separate subdirectory called C:\WP51\MACROS. This accomplishes two things: first, it tells WordPerfect to store every macro you create in that directory, ensuring that they are kept in one place for easy maintenance; and second, by telling WordPerfect where all your macros are stored, you can use your macros globally, i.e., in any document in any subdirectory on the computer. The default location for styles is C:\WP51\LIBRARY.STY. We can find no good reason to change this.

■ *If the term "directory" is confusing you, we strongly recommend that you review Appendix B or your DOS manual.*

To ensure that WordPerfect is properly configured, follow these steps:

Step 1: Create a MACROS subdirectory

Use one of the two following methods to create a new MACROS subdirectory:

Exit WordPerfect and create the new subdirectory at the DOS prompt by using the MD (Make Directory) command. (Example: `MD\WP51\MACROS` creates a MACROS subdirectory of \WP51, assuming that a directory named \WP51 already exists.)

– OR –

1. Press [F5] (List Files), then [Enter].
2. Press [7] for **O**ther Directory.
3. At the "New Directory:" prompt, type `C:\WP51\MACROS` (assuming that WordPerfect is stored on drive C:) and press [Enter].
4. At the "Create C:\WP51\MACROS?" prompt, type [Y].

Step 2: Tell WordPerfect the location of files for macros

1. Press [Shift][F1] (Setup) to access the Setup menu.
2. Choose [6] (**WP5.1**) or [7] for **L**ocation of Files.

It is the highest impertinence and presumption, therefore, in kings and ministers to pretend to watch over the economy of private people, and to restrain their expense. . . . They are themselves always, and without any exception, the greatest spendthrifts in the society. Let them look well after their own expense, and they may safely trust private people with theirs.

Adam Smith
Wealth of Nations
[1776]

3. Choose [2] (**WP5.1**) or [3] for **K**eyboard/Macro file, then insert the name of the directory where you wish the macros to be stored (e.g., `C:\WP51\MACROS`).

4. Press [F7] (Exit) to return to your document.

■ *If you get the message "Error: invalid drive/path specification," you have either not created the new MACROS subdirectory or mistyped it. To create a new directory, follow the steps in the "Step 1" section above.*

WP5.1 Creating a global macros directory on a network

As mentioned previously, the master and personal setup files contain the information on the location of macros and keyboard layouts. The Master Setup File should be defined *before* users start to use WordPerfect on the network. Then, when a user starts WordPerfect for the first time, the Master Setup File is copied to that user's setup file. The user can then edit his or her own setup file using the [Shift][F1] (Setup) command.

A.4 EDITING THE MASTER SETUP FILE TO CREATE A GLOBAL MACROS SUBDIRECTORY

TIP

If an individual user wishes to use macros different from those available on the network, he or she simply has to change the location of files for keyboard and macro files under Setup ([Shift][F1]). Remember that this new information will be stored in that user's setup file, so the user must always use the same three user initials when starting up WordPerfect on the network.

Step 1: Create a MACROS subdirectory on the network drive

1. Exit WordPerfect and create the new subdirectory at the DOS prompt by using the MD (Make Directory) command. (Example: `MD\WP51\MACROS` creates a MACROS subdirectory of F:\WP51, assuming that a directory named F:\WP51 already exists on your network drive.)

– OR –

1. Press [F5] (List Files), then [Enter].
2. Press [7] for **O**ther Directory.
3. At the "New Directory:" prompt, type `F:\WP51\MACROS` (assuming that WordPerfect is stored on the network's drive F: in the \WP51 directory). For Novell and most other networks, network drive letters generally start at F: and go up to Z:.
4. At the "Create F:\WP51\MACROS?" prompt, type .

Step 2: Start WordPerfect as Supervisor

At the DOS prompt, start WordPerfect with the special Supervisor user initials:

1. At the F:\WP51> prompt, type `WP /U={WP`
2. Press [Shift][F1] (Setup) to access the Setup menu.
3. Choose [6] for **L**ocation of Files.
4. Choose [2] for **K**eyboard/Macro file, then insert the name of the directory where you wish the macros to be stored (e.g., `f:\wp51\macros`).
5. Exit WordPerfect.

A.5 INITIAL CODES

WordPerfect has two Initial Codes features, one under Setup ([Shift][F1], [4] **[WP5.1]** or [5]) and one under Format ([Shift][F8], [3]). The Initial Codes option in Setup applies to all documents, while the one in Format applies to that specific document only.

This option is useful for inserting global or document-wide formatting codes that won't be changed. For example, if you wanted to change the default justification for all of your WordPerfect documents from full- to left-justified, inserting a left-justification code ([Shift][F8], [1], [3]) in the Setup Initial Codes screen will make all documents default to left-justified. Other useful initial codes are font codes, margin codes, widow/orphan codes, and underlining options.

A.6 DOCUMENT SUMMARY/ MANAGEMENT OPTIONS

Both WordPerfect 5.1 and 5.0 have a helpful document summary option, which allows users to include additional information about the document, including Subject, Author, Keywords, Account, Typist, and Abstract in a document summary. If you turn the option on, a summary will be created automatically whenever a document is saved or exited. You can then view and search through document summaries in List Files, as well as print them. Document summaries may prove very useful for law firms that want to keep closer track of their documents.

FIGURE A-2

The Long Document Names feature permits users up to 26 characters to name a file.

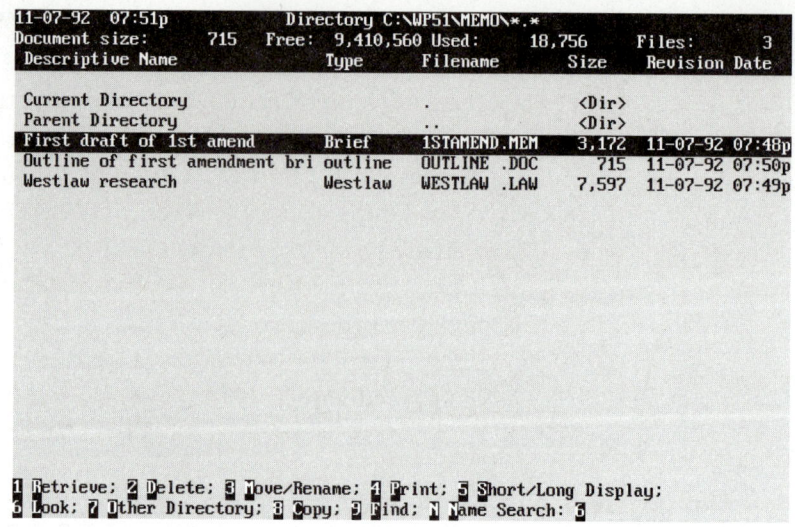

In addition, WordPerfect 5.1 has the Long Document Names feature, which allows users to give a document a standard English descriptive name as well as the more cryptic eight-letter DOS file name. (See Figure A-2.) There is a downside to the Long Document Names feature, however. If you have a slow computer or network and a great many files in your directories, it takes considerably longer for List Files to display. We recommend using Long Document Names, but only if you don't have to lose precious time.

Document Summary

WP5.1 Press [Shift][F1], [5], [3], [1], [Y].
WP5.0 Press [Shift][F1], [3], [4], [1], [Y].

■ *To Edit a Document Summary once it has been created, press* [Shift][F8], [3], [5].

WP5.1 Long Document Names Feature

Press [Shift][F1], [3], [4], [3], [Y].

■ *The Long Document Type refers to part of the Long Document Names. The default is Memo but can be changed by pressing* [Shift][F1], [3], [4], [4].

A.7 DOCUMENT BACKUP OPTIONS

WordPerfect has two backup options: Timed and Original. The timed backup will create a temporary backup of the document at a regular interval (we recommend 15 minutes); the backup copy will disappear when you exit WordPerfect properly. The Original Backup feature will make a copy of your original with the file extension .BK!

Using the Original Backup feature is clearly the most cautious choice, but we don't recommend its use. Unless you are diligent about deleting your backup files, your hard disk will soon be cluttered with them. The best way to ensure that you never lose your work is first to save frequently to disk, next to make permanent backups of your hard disk on floppy disks or tapes on a regular basis.

WP5.1 Press [Shift][F1], [3], [1].
WP5.0 Press [Shift][F1], [1].

Restoring a lost file

The purpose of the Timed Backup feature is to allow you to retrieve work that hasn't been properly saved to disk, should something go awry (e.g., the network server shuts down, the computer "crashes," the computer is turned off before exiting WordPerfect). Here's how it works:

1. When you try to use WordPerfect again after an improper exit (i.e., a "crash"), WordPerfect will prompt you with: "Are other copies of WordPerfect running? (Y/N)." Answer [N].

2. WordPerfect will then say that an old backup file exists. Press [1] to Rename the temporary backup file. You can then retrieve it using List Files.

■ *Renamed temporary backup files may be kept in the \WP5X directory.*

APPENDIX B: DOCUMENT MANAGEMENT TECHNIQUES

FUNCTIONS USED

➤ *Using List Files to understand DOS functions* §B.1

➤ *Basic DOS concepts* §B.1

➤ *How to get the most out of the List Files feature* §B.1

➤ *File management tips and techniques—installing a network* §B.2

➤ *Creating a directory structure that matches your practice* §B.2

➤ *WESTMATE downloading format options* §B.3

OVERVIEW

The importance of good document management in law firms cannot be overemphasized. With the computer's ability to create new files comes a concomitant need to organize these files for easy retrieval and use. This is especially true in law firms on local area networks (LANs). This appendix will discuss the basic DOS concepts that are critical to understanding both how a computer is organized and how List Files can be used to perform basic DOS file-management tasks. It concludes with a brief discussion of various file-management techniques and ideas.

B.1 USING LIST FILES TO UNDERSTAND DOS FUNCTIONS

> *We are all Republicans—we are all Federalists. If there be any among us who would wish to dissolve this Union or to change its republican form, let them stand undisturbed as monuments of the safety with which error of opinion may be tolerated where reason is left free to combat it.*
>
> Thomas Jefferson
> First Inaugural Address [March 4, 1801]

The simple truth for anyone who uses an IBM-compatible PC is that you will never really understand how to manage your files until you've learned some of the basics about DOS, the disk operating system. Why? Since DOS is your PCs librarian, it lays down all the rules about how to name documents and where to store them. Every piece of software on your PC must abide by the DOS rules. When you become familiar with the all-important List Files feature, keep in mind that it is really performing DOS functions, albeit in an easier and more elegant manner than performing DOS functions from the plain old DOS prompt.

Are you despairing already? You shouldn't. The little secret about DOS is that there are only a few concepts you have to become familiar with to do 99% of your work on the computer. We'll cover those concepts in conjunction with the List Files feature. Once you learn these few basic rules, you're well on your way towards taming the beast.

B.1.1 BASIC DOS CONCEPTS

Changing drives

A drive name in DOS consists of a drive letter and a colon. Floppy drives are either A: or B:, your local hard drive is generally C:, and your network drive (if applicable) is F: or higher.

> ■ *DOS follows the same rules on either floppy or hard disks. The only difference is the speed and size of the disk itself.*

There are two ways of changing drives in WordPerfect:

➢ Press [F5] once, then type a: (or b:, etc.), and press [Enter].

➢ Press [F5] twice, press [7] for **O**ther directory, then type a: (or b:, etc.), and press [Enter].

File and directory names

In DOS, file and directory names are made up of two parts, the file name itself and the extension. These two parts are separated by a period. The name can have up to eight characters, the extension up to three characters. Two general rules when naming files in WordPerfect: always use extensions, and be consistent in your use of extension. For example, all letters might end with the extension .LET (e.g., RETAINER.LET), all templates with the extension .TEM (LASTWILL.TEM), and all memos with the extension .MEM (1STAMEND.MEM). Enforcing this simple rule will make finding and filtering files with the List Files feature dramatically easier.

■ *You can use the underscore to separate items in a name, but there can be no gaps. For example, MON_TUES.DOC is acceptable, but MON TUES.DOC is not.*

You create a new file in WordPerfect by pressing the save key ([F10]). Then, at the document name prompt, you enter the file name and extension.

WP 5.1 The Long Document Names feature

One of the useful features of WordPerfect 5.1 is the Long Document Names feature, which allows you to use a regular descriptive name of up to 26 characters to identify a document as well as a regular DOS file name. (Example: First Amendment Brief vs. 1STAMEND.BRF.) This feature is a boon to anyone who has struggled with the infamously cryptic DOS file name when trying to find a file. There are two disadvantages of the Long Document Names feature. The first is that it takes a considerably longer amount of time for List Files to display the files, depending on the number of files in the directory and the speed of your computer. The second is that when the Long Document Names feature is on, WordPerfect will list only valid WordPerfect files, and not files saved in a different format such as ASCII. However, you can switch back and forth between long and short document names by pressing [5] in List Files. See Figure B-1.

To turn on Long Document Names: Press [Shift][F1] (Setup), [3], [4], [3], [Y].

FIGURE B-1

The Long Document Names feature of WordPerfect 5.1 allows users up to 26 characters to name a file.

```
11-07-92  07:51p              Directory C:\WP51\MEMO\*.*
Document size:      715   Free:  9,410,560 Used:     18,756   Files:        3
Descriptive Name                 Type        Filename         Size    Revision Date

Current Directory                            .                <Dir>
Parent Directory                             ..               <Dir>
First draft of 1st amend         Brief       1STAMEND .MEM    3,172   11-07-92 07:48p
Outline of first amendment bri   outline     OUTLINE  .DOC      715   11-07-92 07:50p
Westlaw research                 Westlaw     WESTLAW  .LAW    7,597   11-07-92 07:49p




















1 Retrieve; 2 Delete; 3 Move/Rename; 4 Print; 5 Short/Long Display;
6 Look; 7 Other Directory; 8 Copy; 9 Find; N Name Search: 5
```

Understanding the DOS wild card (*)

The asterisk (*) in DOS is a *wild card*. In other words, just like the joker in cards, it can be used to represent any character(s). A DOS file name is made up of two parts, the name and the extension, separated by a period. Therefore, `*.*` means all files in the current directory. One of the major uses of the wild card is to *filter* files to help you find certain ones. This function highlights the importance of using consistent extensions. For example, `*.let` in List Files would show only those files that end with the .LET extension. Conversely, `brief*.*` would show only those files whose names begin with BRIEF. To use the wild card feature, insert the * *before* executing the List Files command.

To illustrate these concepts, try the following exercise:

1. Press [F5] once. The "DIR" prompt should appear on the bottom left of the screen.

2. Depending on what directory you are currently in, move the cursor and delete any extra characters so that the prompt looks as follows: `C:\WP51\*.WPG`. (This tells DOS that you want to see only the files that end with the .WPG extension in the C:\WP51 directory. This example assumes that you are using WordPerfect 5.1 and that the files are stored in a directory called WP51.)

3. Press [Enter] or [F5] again. You will be in List Files and only the files with the .WPG extension will be shown on the screen. Note that the top center of the screen gives the full path. See Figure B-2.

4. To clear the filter, press [Enter] twice on the Current Directory listing.

FIGURE B-2

The DOS wild card (*) can be used to filter files in a directory. In this instance, *.wpg shows just the files with the .WPG extension. This illustrates the importance of using consistent extensions when naming files.

```
11-09-92  07:37p              Directory C:\WP51\*.WPG
Document size:         0  Free:  9,279,488 Used:     100,055  Files:        30

.          Current   <Dir>          | ..        Parent    <Dir>
AIRPLANE.WPG    8,486  01-03-89 11:00a | AND     .WPG    1,980  01-03-89 11:00a
ANNOUNCE.WPG    5,390  01-03-89 11:00a | APPLAUSE.WPG   1,524  01-03-89 11:00a
ARROW1  .WPG      368  01-03-89 11:00a | ARROW2  .WPG     740  01-03-89 11:00a
AWARD   .WPG    1,748  01-03-89 11:00a | BADNEWS .WPG   3,752  01-03-89 11:00a
BOOK    .WPG    1,802  01-03-89 11:00a | BORDER  .WPG  13,520  01-03-89 11:00a
CHECK   .WPG    1,076  01-03-89 11:00a | CLOCK   .WPG   6,236  01-03-89 11:00a
CONFIDEN.WPG    3,228  01-03-89 11:00a | FLAG    .WPG     730  01-03-89 11:00a
GAVEL   .WPG      887  11-06-89 12:00p | GOODNEWS.WPG   4,244  01-03-89 11:00a
HAND    .WPG    1,056  01-03-89 11:00a | HOURGLAS.WPG   1,836  01-03-89 11:00a
KEY     .WPG    1,580  01-03-89 11:00a | MAPSYMBL.WPG   2,452  01-03-89 11:00a
NEWSPAPR.WPG    1,390  01-03-89 11:00a | NO1     .WPG   3,236  01-03-89 11:00a
PC      .WPG    2,588  01-03-89 11:00a | PENCIL  .WPG   3,512  01-03-89 11:00a
PHONE   .WPG    4,182  01-03-89 11:00a | PRESENT .WPG   1,432  01-03-89 11:00a
QUILL   .WPG    1,312  01-03-89 11:00a | RPTCARD .WPG   6,056  01-03-89 11:00a
THINKER .WPG    4,628  01-03-89 11:00a | USAMAP  .WPG   9,084  01-03-89 11:00a

1 Retrieve; 2 Delete; 3 Move/Rename; 4 Print; 5 Short/Long Display;
6 Look; 7 Other Directory; 8 Copy; 9 Find; N Name Search: 6
```

Creating new directories

Think of files as documents, your work product. Files are stored in directories. Everything on your computer is either a file or a directory. To use the traditional filing system analogy, files are pieces of paper, and directories are the folders in which they are stored.

Just as you can create new files, you can create new directories. In fact, you must understand how to create new directories if you're ever going to organize your hard disk. You would never put all of your different clients' documents in one folder and, likewise, you would never store all of your files in one directory.

The key point to remember is this: nothing is more fundamental to managing your documents than understanding how to create new directories for new clients, projects, etc.

■ *Networks often do not allow the flexibility to create new directories at will, because of the concept of user "rights." Only the network supervisor generally has the "right" to make new directories at will.*

To create a new directory in WordPerfect, follow these steps:

1. Press [F5] twice to bring up the List Files screen.

2. Press [7] for **O**ther Directory, type the path name of a subdirectory under the WordPerfect directory with your new directory name (e.g., C:\WP51\ALICE), and press [Enter].

3. At the "Create?" prompt, type [Y].

Understanding DOS's hierarchical structure and decoding a "PATH" name

So far, we've used the analogy of documents and folders when talking about files and directories. Now, we'll introduce another analogy—the *upside down tree*—when talking about DOS's hierarchical structure. Why "upside down tree"? Because all disks (floppy and hard) start with a root directory. Directories and subdirectories then "branch" off the root directory. To take this analogy even further, you can then think of files as the "leaves" on a particular "branch."

The root directory is symbolized by a drive letter and a backslash (e.g., C:\). The confusing thing about DOS is that the backslash is also used as a *delimiter* to separate one directory from another. For example, C:\WP51\LETTERS\RETAINER.LET says that the file RETAINER.LET is stored in the directory called LETTERS, which is a subdirectory (one level beneath) a directory called WP51. Finally, the WP51 directory is a subdirectory of the root directory of the C: drive. This is known as the *path name*, i.e., the full name of a file or directory. It shows the file name, the directory the file is in, and the drive that is being used. See the illustration below for a diagram representing this path.

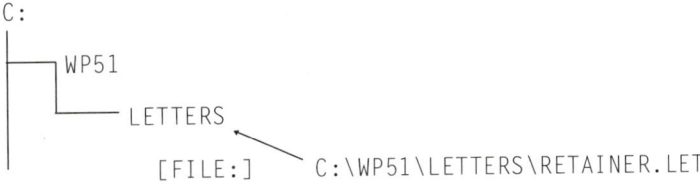

To illustrate this concept, press F5 once. You will see on the bottom left of the screen the current path name of the directory you are currently in. Also, if you retrieve a file that you've previously saved, you'll see that file's path name at the bottom left of the screen.

If your computer uses DOS 4 or 5, you can use the DOSSHELL command to get a visual "tree" of all your directories and subdirectories. To do so, exit WordPerfect to the DOS prompt, and type DOSSHELL.

> In no country perhaps in the world is law so general a study [as in America]. . . . This study renders men acute, inquisitive, dexterous, prompt in attack, ready in defence, full of resources. . . . They augur misgovernment at a distance; and sniff the approach of tyranny in every tainted breeze.
>
> Edmund Burke
> Second Speech on Conciliation with America. The Thirteen Resolutions [March 22, 1775]

B.1.2 HOW TO GET THE MOST OUT OF THE LIST FILES FEATURE

Quick navigating

Use [Home], [Home], [↑] or [↓] to navigate through a long list of files.

Using tags to work with multiple files

As we've already seen, the List Files feature is WordPerfect's way of allowing you to use basic DOS functions. These include changing drives, creating directories, and using DOS wild cards to find files. Other basic DOS functions available in List Files are copying, deleting, renaming, and printing. To use these functions, you highlight the file with the cursor and press the appropriate number or letter. This can be a slow process, however, if you have a lot of files you want to copy/delete/move. When you need to manipulate more than one file in List Files, tag the file first with the asterisk (*) ([Shift][8]), press the appropriate number or letter to perform the file function, and answer [Y] to the prompt. To tag all files instantly, press [Alt][F5].

■ *The * tag is a toggle. In other words, to untag a file, press* [Shift][8] *after it has been tagged.*

Finding files

It happens at some point to anyone who uses a computer. You'll forget the name or location of a file. The List Files feature comes to the rescue with several powerful ways of finding files. Once you learn these, you'll never fear losing a file again.

Use the DOS wild card to list only specified files: If you know part of the file name you wish to use, insert it *before* executing the List Files command. Doing so will list only the files that include the name, saving time and simplifying operations. Example: suppose you wish List Files to list only those files that have the word CLAUSE as part of the file name. There are two ways of doing this:

METHOD 1:

1. Press [F5] (List Files) once to get the path of your current directory.

2. Press the [End] key to move the cursor past the asterisks (*.*). (The asterisk is a DOS wild card. In other words, it can stand for any character or group of characters.)

3. Cursor left to the first asterisk and enter the word `Clause` so that the command looks like this: `Clause*.*`.

4. Press [Enter]. Only the file names that start with "clause" will be listed.

METHOD 2:

1. Press [F5] twice to enter List Files.

2. Press [Enter] once on the "Current <DIR>" listing to get the path of your current directory.

3. Press the [End] key to move the cursor past the asterisks.

4. Cursor left to the first asterisk and enter the word `Clause` so that the command looks like this: `Clause*.*`.

5. Press [Enter]. Only the file names that start with "clause" will be listed.

WP5.1 Turning the Long Document feature on and off in List Files: If you normally use the Long Document Names feature and you can't find a file, turn off Long Document Names by pressing [5], then [1] for **S**hort Display, [2] for **L**ong Display.

Using Name Search: If you know the first few letters of your file, press [N] for **N**ame Search, and type the letters. The highlight will move automatically to files beginning with that letter. To clear name search, press [Enter].

Using the Search function: The Search function ([F2]) can be used in List Files to find any occurrence of a text string in a long or short file name. To use, simply press [F2] (Search), type the text that comprises part of the file name(s) you wish WordPerfect to find, and press [F2] again.

Using the (WP5.1) Find and (WP5.0) Word Search features: If all else has failed, List Files lets you do full text searches through all of the documents in your directory. (This feature, called Find in WP5.1 and Word Search in WP5.0, is used by pressing [9] in List Files.) For example, if you have no idea what the file's name is but you know that it contains the plaintiff's name, you can have WordPerfect search through all the files for that particular string of text. WordPerfect 5.1 has improved upon this function considerably by allowing you to set very specific search conditions and to specify which part of the files the program should look through to locate the text you are looking for.

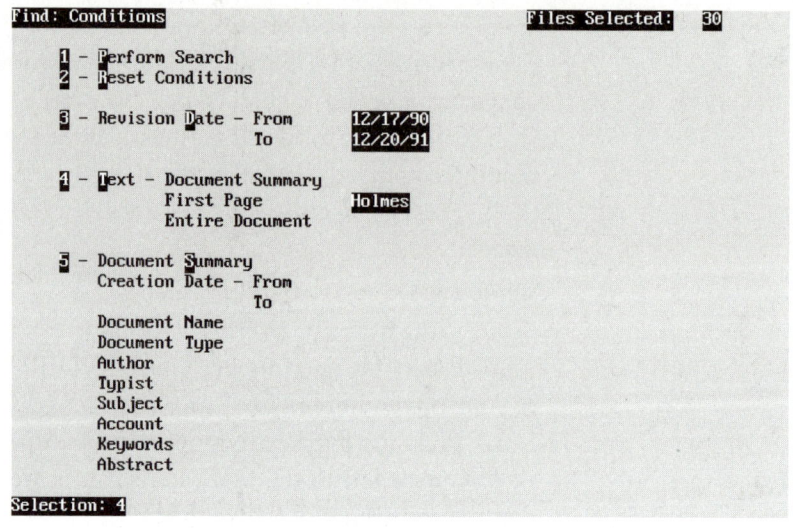

FIGURE B-3

WordPerfect 5.1's sophisticated Find feature can be used to locate files using a variety of different conditions.

WordPerfect provides the following options:

[1] for **N**ame: Will search for an occurrence of text in the file name.

CAUTION: In WP5.1, when the Long Document Names option is turned off, it will only search the short file name, the same as Search [F2]. This is the fastest search option.

[2] for **D**oc Summary: Will search through document summaries if this feature has been turned on. (See Appendix A for more information on the Document Summary option.) This feature can also be used to search through Long Document Names feature, even when the Long Document Names feature has been turned off.

[3] for First **P**g: Searches through the first page of every file in the current directory.

[4] for **E**ntire Doc: Searches through every page of every document. This is the slowest search method and can take a considerable amount of time if there are many files in the current directory. If you are a WP5.1 user, try to narrow this search using the [5] Conditions function described below.

WP5.1 [5] Conditions: Lets you change the conditions of the search. To use, press the number for the condition, enter the condition, press [F7], then [1] for **P**erform Search. For example, in Figure B-3 the search has been narrowed to files that were created between the date range of 12/17/90 and 12/20/91 that had the word Holmes in the first page.

WP5.1 [6] for **U**ndo: Allows you to "undo" the last "find," returning the previous list of files before the last search.

B.2 FILE MANAGEMENT SUGGESTIONS AND TECHNIQUES—INSTALL A NETWORK

The smartest thing, bar none, that a law firm can do is install a network. This applies to the solo practitioner with one secretary as well as to the megafirm with 300+ lawyers. A network allows users to share files and expensive peripherals such as laser printers and CD-ROM drives. Most importantly, networks enable lawyers and their staff to share important information. For example, besides facilitating the sharing of WordPerfect files, a network allows staff to communicate and send files using E-mail, as well as to share access to time and billing software, case management software, client databases, and any other software your firm might be using.

B.2.1 PEER-TO-PEER VS. DEDICATED NETWORKS

It used to be that installing a network was an expensive and complicated proposition. You had to buy the network software, a dedicated server, and other hardware such as network cards. The whole system had to be set up by expensive consultants and, once installed, it required an administrator. For small firms these costs, which could be $10,000 or more, were often prohibitive. However, there is an inexpensive and effective solution—peer-to-peer networks. These networks are DOS based and very simple to install and use. Best of all, for small offices, they can do everything that the dedicated networks do, at a fraction of the cost. If you're comfortable with opening up your computer and you know the basics about DOS, chances are you could install one yourself in a couple of hours.

The most popular peer-to-peer networks for DOS are Lantastic by Artisoft ([602] 293-6363) and NetWare Lite by Novell ([800] 526-5463). If you have the hardware to run Windows, you'll want to look at Workgroup for Windows by Microsoft Corporation ([800]-227-4679). These network systems start at around $600 for the software and hardware to hook up two computers. You'll need to buy additional network cards for additional computers.

B.2.2 FILE MANAGEMENT TIPS AND TECHNIQUES—CREATE A DIRECTORY STRUCTURE THAT MATCHES YOUR PRACTICE

Think very carefully about the structure of your practice. Do you have many short-term clients (e.g., personal bankruptcies, real estate closings) or a few long-term clients (e.g., complex civil litigation, class action suits)? Do you write numerous different kinds of documents for your clients? Do a number of lawyers work on the same cases? Does your firm have a widely used form book? Does your current file system work well? How could it be improved? Once you've thought about these issues, you should translate these questions into a workable directory system. Then, *everybody* in the firm must become intimately familiar with the system. That means—believe it or not— that everyone has to be comfortable with the basic DOS concepts outlined above.

What follows are a few ideas to get you thinking.

SCENARIO 1: SMALL FIRM PRACTICE, MANY SHORT-TERM CLIENTS, REPETITIVE USE OF SIMILAR FORMS AND LETTERS

Keep only active clients on the computer; archive all other files onto floppy disks that are kept in the client file. Create a directory for each active client (with subdirectories if necessary) and a separate directory for standard forms and correspondence. See the sample structure below.

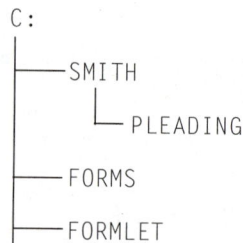

SCENARIO 2: LARGER FIRM PRACTICE, LARGE CASES WORKED ON BY DIFFERENT ATTORNEYS

Create directories based on the client/matter number, with the extension used as the matter number if possible. If there is extensive correspondence, create a correspondence subdirectory under each matter number. Use a separate network drive or server for documents that should be added to a firm-wide forms library. (These could be divided between corporate and litigation, for example.) See the sample structure below. Use sophisticated text retrieval software such as Zyindex from Zylab ([800] 544-6339), Folio Views from Folio Corporation ([800] 543-6546), or Isys from Odyssey Development ([800] 992-4797) to make the firm's work product available to all PC users.

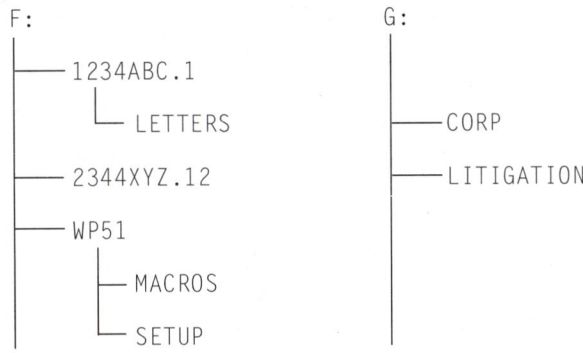

B.2.3 FILE MANAGEMENT TIPS AND TECHNIQUES—MANAGEMENT MUST GET INVOLVED

The managing partner, or whoever is in charge of day-to-day operations, must ensure that everyone is thoroughly trained in the system and understands its uses and potential. *Yes, this includes the lawyers*. In fact, they have the most to gain. Imagine the freedom of no longer being dependent on the support staff to find and edit documents, etc. However, too many attorneys still resist automation. Therefore, it is imperative that management make it perfectly clear that all attorneys must learn to use the firm technology. Also, large firms should create a technology committee that includes attorneys who are interested in computers as well as the technical support staff. The biggest snafus occur when the lawyers aren't talking to the technical staff about their needs and problems.

B.2.4 COMPUTERS CAN GIVE YOUR FIRM A COMPETITIVE EDGE

PCs are changing the world—even the legal profession! Courts are now starting to automate, and large firms are switching from their old proprietary systems to PCs running on LANs. If you're a small firm, you have the advantage of moving to the latest hardware and software without being forced to throw out tens of thousands of dollars in outdated technology. The simple fact is that any lawyer or any member of a firm's legal support staff who is computer literate can do the work of several people doing things the old-fashioned way. Today, tools such as notebook computers, electronic research (whether on-line or on CD-ROM), and sophisticated software that can do everything from litigation support to time and billing all make it possible to gain a competitive edge over the technically illiterate.

If you want to educate yourself on the possibilities, we suggest getting subscriptions to at least one major computer magazine such as *PC Magazine* as well as a subscription to a magazine like *Law Office Computing* that is dedicated just to the legal profession. You should also explore on-line legal databases, including the ABA Net and LAWSIG on CompuServe. (See Appendix E for listings.) These can be a tremendous source of ideas, legal shareware, and contacts with other lawyers around the country. Finally, our supplementary disks have a variety of legal shareware, including hundreds of WordPerfect macros and a variety of software demos, and includes a booklet on how to use and explore shareware. (Use the order form at the back of this book.) We hope they will give you ideas and access to software you might not otherwise be aware of. One word of warning: Once you get bitten by the technology bug, you may become addicted. But at least it's in the name of increasing productivity!

B.3 WESTMATE DOWNLOADING FORMAT OPTIONS*

If you use WESTMATE to access WESTLAW and you want to download WESTLAW information, you can choose from several downloading formats:

Standard (default)

If you have never changed your downloading format, the format will be automatically set to *Standard*. The Standard format is the option you should use if you plan to view or print your downloaded WESTLAW information using the browse feature in WESTMATE.

---

* SOURCE: WESTMATE Downloading Format Options, by Elizabeth A. Funke (Copyright 1992 by West Publishing Company).

Word processing

If you select this option, your WESTLAW information will be downloaded in ASCII text format, allowing you to easily incorporate the information into a word-processing document. This format removes the hard carriage returns from the end of each line, and text that was previously centered becomes flush left. Select this option if you want to incorporate your downloaded text into word-processing software.

Word Perfect 5.0/5.1 or WordPerfect 4.2

If you are using WESTMATE for Windows, IBM WESTMATE version 4.8, or WESTMATE for the DEC VAX version 4.0, selet one of these options if you want to use your downloaded WESTLAW information in a WordPerfect word-processing document. If you select this option, WESTLAW will automatically download your WESTLAW information in the desired WordPerfect format. You can then work with the downloaded text just as you would work with any other WordPerfect document. If you use WordPerfect version 5.0 or 5.1, select "WordPerfect 5.0/5.1." If you use WordPerfect version 4.1, select "WordPerfect 4.2."

WordPerfect 5.0/5.1 or WordPerfect 4.2 with highlighted search terms

If you are using WESTMATE for Windows, IBM WESTMATE version 4.8, or WESTMATE for the DEC VAX version 4.0, select one of these options if you want to use your downloaded WESTLAW information in WordPerfect and you want your search terms to appear in boldface type. If you use WordPerfect version 5.0 or 5.1 and you want your search terms highlighted, select "WordPerfect 5.0/5.1 with highlighted terms." If you use WordPerfect version 4.2 and you want your search terms highlighted, select "WordPerfect 4.2 with highlighted terms."

To select any of the downloading formats, display the WESTLAW Options Directory by typing opt, type the number corresponding to the "Assign your downloading format" option, and then select one of the options listed.

If you are not sure which downloading format you should select, call West Customer Service at (800) WESTLAW ([800] 937-8529).

APPENDIX C: CREATING MACROS FOR AN ADVANCED KEYBOARD LAYOUT

OVERVIEW

So, you're an adventurous soul. You've decided to delve into the mysteries of advanced macro programming—specifically how to create the macros suggested throughout this book and perhaps even to write some yourself. Well, your courage will be rewarded. While writing advanced macros is far more intellectually challenging than just about anything else you can do in WordPerfect, with a little practice, you'll soon see that creating advanced macros is really quite easy. And, besides the fact that it will impress your friends and co-workers, being able to adapt our macros or create your own will give you and your firm unprecedented control over WordPerfect. Along with creating your styles and templates, the ability to create your own advanced macros turns WordPerfect from a standard (albeit excellent) "off the shelf" package into a customized word processing environment tailored to your firm's specific needs.

This appendix, then, will show you the programming code necessary to create the macros we suggest. It will also discuss our philosophy for how to best create and use macros in the legal environment.

Supplementary disks

If you don't have the time or the inclination to create the macros described in this appendix, you can order them, as well as hundreds of other WordPerfect shareware macros and legal shareware programs, on disk for a nominal fee from the authors. See the order form at the back of this book.

C.1 WRITING AND EDITING ADVANCED MACROS

The best way to learn how to create advanced macros is to closely examine how other macros have been written. With this in mind, we have described (where appropriate) some of the special programming techniques we've used. And, to give you an idea of how to create macro menus, we have broken down the [Ctrl][M] (Main Menu) macro into its component parts, with a detailed explanation of the structure and codes. These parts, when joined together, create the macro "engine." Once you learn the basic structure you'll find it easy to modify for your own needs.

One word of warning: you must pay extremely close attention to every code and keystroke in your macros. Writing an advanced macro is actually a simple form of computer programming, and, as with all computer programs, one missing code or keystroke can prevent the macro from working properly. Since you've embarked on this ambitious path, you should be prepared (like all programmers) to spend some time "debugging" (checking and correcting for syntax errors) your work. One other word of warning: once you get past the initial hurdles, writing and debugging advanced macros can be such challenging fun that you may not want to return to your normal legal work. Don't say we didn't warn you!

C.2 USING THE MACRO EDITOR

There are two methods of editing WordPerfect macros. You can use the WordPerfect macro editor that is built into the program or, better yet, you can use the WordPerfect Office 3.X Editor (ED.EXE). WordPerfect's editor is fine for editing simple keystroke macros, but if you plan to write or edit any advanced macros (such as the macros we cover in this appendix), we strongly advise that you use the Office 3.X Editor. It allows you to write and edit macros in a very similar fashion to writing and editing a regular document, with many of the keystrokes and functions that you already know from using WordPerfect.

The editor available in WordPerfect Library, the predecessor to WordPerfect Office, does *not* have the ability to edit WordPerfect macros. You must have WordPerfect Office 3.0 or higher.

Retrieving a macro into the editor

The WordPerfect Editor

1. Press [Ctrl][F10] (Define Macro) to define a macro (i.e., turn on the keystroke recorder).

2. At the "Define Macro:" prompt, type the name of the macro you wish to edit and press [E].

3. At the "Macro already exists:" prompt, choose [2] for **E**dit. The cursor will automatically be placed inside the macro editing screen.

Office 3.X Editor

1. Press [Shift][F10] (Retrieve) and type the name of the macro or press [F5] (List Files), [1] for **R**etrieve.

> **TIP**
>
> If most or all of your macros are in one directory, you can use the Location of Files feature in the Office Editor to specify where they can be found. Press [Shift][F1], [4], [2].

Moving within the macro editor

Cursor movement is the same in the macro editor as in the normal WordPerfect editing screen. For example, pressing [Home], [Home], [↓] will take you to the bottom of the macro. You can also use the [Tab] and [Enter] keys, but these keys are used to format macros (i.e., make them easier to read). They do not insert a [Tab] or [HRt] code as part of the macro unless they are inserted as codes. (See below.)

Inserting programming codes

Once in the macro editor, you use [Ctrl][PgUp] to access the advanced macro codes. Press the first letter of the code you wish to use (e.g., [V] for {VARIABLE}) to quickly scroll down the list, then press [Enter] to place the code in the macro. If the programming code uses a tilde (~), be sure that it is properly inserted at the end of the statement.

Inserting editing keys and function keys as codes

When writing or editing macros, it is often necessary to switch between the regular macro editing mode and the "WordPerfect Commands" mode, which allows you to place editing, function keys, and cursor movement keys in the macro. You can use either of the following:

[Ctrl][V] (Compose) toggles to the WordPerfect Commands mode for one keystroke. (For example, pressing [Ctrl][V], then [Enter] will insert an {Enter} code in the macro.)

> **TIP**
>
> If while in the Macro editor you press a key and it responds in a strange manner, it is possible that an active keyboard is getting in the way. You can quickly turn off a keyboard layout from anywhere in WordPerfect by pressing [Ctrl][6].

– OR –

[Ctrl][F10] toggles to the Commands mode for every keystroke. (You must press [Ctrl][F10] to return to the editing mode again.)

Differences between the WordPerfect 5.0 and 5.1 macro language

While the changes in the macro language between versions 5.0 and 5.1 are not nearly as substantial as the changes in the merge language, there are some key differences. A few commands are new, for example, the {SYSTEM} command. We have used it in the [Alt][B] macro (below), which automatically inserts a footer with file and path name, and Alan Kaplan has used it in his sophisticated Print Envelope macro. However, most macros don't use this command.

The {VARIABLE} command

A key difference between versions 5.0 and 5.1 is in the use of the **{VARIABLE}** code. Many of our macros, especially those that present the user with a menu of some sort, use the following codes: variables **{VARIABLE}**, labels **{LABEL}** and character **{CHAR}**. With WordPerfect 5.1, you can assign variable names of up to seven characters (make sure that there are no spaces or gaps in the name) *or* you can assign a number. If you are using WordPerfect 5.0, you can only assign numbers to variables, not names. Therefore, you are limited to 1 through 9 in 5.0.

To insert a variable code in WordPerfect 5.1, simply press [Ctrl][PgUp] and access it from the list of available codes. To insert a variable code in WordPerfect 5.0, press [Ctrl][V] and then press the [Alt] key and the variable number, such as [1] or [2]. Many of our macros use the **{VARIABLE}** code, and we have used the 5.1 method of giving the variable names. If you are a 5.0 user, you will have to substitute numbers for the names.

WP5.1

```
{VARIABLE}firstname~         NO
{VARIABLE}first name~        NO
{VARIABLE}1stname~           YES
{VARIABLE}1~                 YES
```

WP5.0

```
{VAR 1}                      YES
{VAR}1stname~                NO
```

The {CHAR} command

Because the purpose of the **{CHAR}** command is to retrieve input from a user and store it in a variable, you can only use numbers in WordPerfect 5.0. In WordPerfect 5.1, you can use either names or numbers.

WP5.1

{CHAR}options~	YES
{CHAR}1~	YES

WP5.0

{CHAR}1~	YES
{CHAR}one~	NO

C.3 MACRO KEYBOARDS

As we've mentioned in the book, the smartest way to use macros in WordPerfect 5.X is in a macro keyboard layout. The major advantages to this are:

- You have use of the [Ctrl] as well as the [Alt] key for macros

- You gain much greater flexibility. You could have one keyboard with macros just for writing briefs and another just for contracts. You can also use the Compose feature to replace keys such as quotation marks (") with the (") [4,31] special character to give your documents that "typeset" look. And, with keyboard layouts, you can switch from one set of macros to another or disable them completely in just a few keystrokes.

- Your becoming familiar with using keyboard macros takes a little work, but the extra time spent will be amply rewarded.

That said, we have found from experience that the smartest way to use keyboard layouts is to use [Alt][A] through [Z] and [Ctrl][A] through [Z] for the most common editing tasks such as copying, deleting, printing, etc. When assigning keys to macros, try to make your macros mnemonic so that they'll be easier to remember. And, to call up more esoteric, complex, or specialized macros, use a Main Menu macro. (See [Ctrl][M], below.) Using a menu that branches to a named macro has several advantages: it makes it easier for users to call up named macros, and it helps to cut down on the memory requirements of keyboards, especially for large, complex macros.

On this and the following pages are lists of the macros and the keys they have been assigned to on our keyboard. They are meant purely as a starting point, since no doubt you will want to use your own macros in place of some of ours.

SAMPLE KEYBOARD LAYOUT

ALT KEY MACROS (press [Alt] key with letter)

A	Suppress All on Page 1	N	Bottom Center page number
B	Footer B with Path\Filename	O	ASCII Margin fix (for Westlaw, etc.)
C	Copy Block	P	Print menu
D	Delete Block	Q	Save Document and Quit WP
E	Print address on envelope	R	Letterhead advance macro
F	Create a Footer	S	Save document
G	Graphic Line Draw	T	Make a Table
H	Create a Header	U	Underline menu
I	Italics on/off	V	View document
J	Justification menu	W	(User defined)
K	Character of choice	X	(User defined)
L	Line spacing menu	Y	(User defined)
M	Move block	Z	(User defined)

ENHANCED KEYBOARD USERS ONLY

[Alt][F11]	Tab set screen
[Alt][F12]	Make Parallel Columns
[Shift][F11]	Reset standard tabs
[Shift][F12]	Make Newspaper Columns

CONTROL KEY MACROS (press [Ctrl] key with letter)

- C Insert text Comment
- E Edit a code (use the [Alt][E] macro that comes with WordPerfect 5,1 keyboard layout SHORTCUT.WPK)
- F HP III fonts menu
- L Outline On/off
- M Main macro menu
- N Page Numbering Options
- P View Printer control

Named Macros

COVER.WPM: This macro merges a template called COVER.TEM. The COVER.TEM template then chains to a macro called COVERMEN.WPM, which presents the user with different options for the Pleading Cover.

TOCTITLE.WPM: Sets up Title Page for a Table of Contents.

TABLECAP.WPM: Creates a caption for a pleading document using the WordPerfect 5.1 Tables feature.

51COLCAP.WPM: Creates a caption for a pleading document using the WordPerfect Newspaper Columns feature

51MANAGE.WPM (WP5.1): Document Management Options.

LABELS.WPM: Avery and 3M Label macro. (This, again, is a macro that comes with WordPerfect 5.1. See Chapter 2 for more details.)

Inserting macros into a keyboard

There are two methods for inserting macros into a keyboard layout. You can create a named macro using [Ctrl][F10] and then retrieve the macro into the keyboard or you can enter the code directly into the keyboard itself. For detailed instructions on how to use keyboards, refer to Chapter 5.

C.4 DISSECTING THE [Ctrl][M] MACRO

To help reveal the mysteries of the WordPerfect programming language, we have broken down the [Ctrl][M] (MAINMENU) macro into its component parts and described its logic and structure. Why this macro? Because its structure is similar to most of the macros that call up a menu system for the user. In this case, the [Ctrl][M] macro presents the user with a menu of available "named" macros. Using a menu makes it much easier to use named macros, and furthermore it helps in maintaining uniformity in the office, especially if you are running WordPerfect on a network.

Basic structure

The MAINMENU macro that we will discuss uses a structure known as *conditional branching*. Although there are many ways to create conditional branches in macros, the most straightforward approach is through the use of the {CASE} command. Here's the basic structure of the MAINMENU macro:

1. Display menu using {CHAR} and wait for input (1 keystroke).
2. Use {CASE} to test the result of user input.
3. Branch to indicated label with a named macro for each of the possible choices of the menu.

Keeping in mind this basic structure, we can now look at the MAINMENU.WPM macro. Its principal parts are as follows:

```
1. {DISPLAY ON}
{LABEL}top~
{CHAR}1~{Del to EOP}
{^P}¶{^A}{^]}{^R}NAMED MACRO MENU (CtrlM){^S}{^\}
{^P}¶♥<{^]}1{^\}>Table of Contents Title Page
{^P}¶♦<{^]}2{^\}>Labels Macro
{^P}¶♣<{^]}3{^\}>Caption Headings
{^P}¶♠<{^]}4{^\}>Pleading Cover
{^P}¶•<{^]}5{^\}>Document Management Options
{;}{^P}¶{Home}<{^]}6{^\}>Your macro here!~
{;}{^P}¶{Tab}<{^]}7{^\}>Your macro here!~
{^P}¶{Enter}<{^]}Q{^\}<uit this menu{Enter}
{^P}¶{^V}Enter your selection =~
{IF}"{VARIABLE}options~"="{Enter}"~{GO}top~{END IF}
2. {CASE}{VARIABLE}options~
~1~mac1~2~mac2~3~mac3~4~mac4~5~mac5~6~mac6~7~
mac7~q~end~Q~end~~
{GO}top~

3. {LABEL}mac1~
{NEST}toctitle.wpm~
{GO}end~
{LABEL}mac2~
{NEST}labels.wpm~
{GO}end~
{LABEL}mac3~
{NEST}tablecap.wpm~
{GO}end~
{LABEL}mac4~
{NEST}cover.wpm~
{GO}end~
{LABEL}mac5~
{NEST}wpmanage.wpm
{GO}end~
{LABEL}mac6~
{NEST}~
```

Column and row position — (points to the `{^P}¶{^A}{^]}{^R}NAMED MACRO MENU...` line)

Comment — (points to the `{;}{^P}¶{Home}...` line)

Traps the Enter key press — (points to the `{IF}"{VARIABLE}options~"="{Enter}"~{GO}top~{END IF}` line)

Case structure assigns a keypress to a label — (points to the `{CASE}{VARIABLE}options~` line)

Each label branches off (nests) to another named macro — (points to `{LABEL}mac2~`)

```
{GO}end~
{LABEL}mac7~
{NEST}~
{GO}end~
{LABEL}end~
{DISPLAY OFF}{PROMPT}{Del to EOP}
This concludes the Main Macro Menu!{Enter}{Enter}
Come back soon!
{WAIT}7~
{QUIT}
```

Part 1: Several different functions are used here: the **{CHAR}** code to display the menu, the **{^P}** code to position the menu choices on the screen, and the **{IF}**, **{GO}** and **{LABEL}** statements to trap errors.

a. The **{CHAR}**options~ command displays the menu, with the user's response (1 keystroke only) captured in the variable *options*.

b. The **{^P}** code, in conjunction with different ASCII codes (see table), is used to position the different menu options at specific coordinates on the screen. The **{^P}** code is always followed by two ASCII codes that represent the row and column on which you wish to position your text. For example, the standard screen is 80 columns wide by 25 lines high. Therefore, to start the menu ¼ of the way across the screen, the column position should be 20, which is represented by ¶ in ASCII. Because each menu item must be on a different row, the corresponding ASCII code for that row must then be used. For example, the first menu item is on line 3, which is represented by the ♥ code.

To insert these codes while in either macro editor, do the following:

For the **{^P}** code, press [Ctrl][V] (Compose), then press [Ctrl][P]. Alternatively, toggle to the WordPerfect Commands mode by pressing [Ctrl][F10], then press [Ctrl][P].

For ASCII Symbols, hold down the [Alt] key, type the number for the ASCII symbol on the *numeric keypad*, then release the [Alt] key.

c. The **{^]}** and **{^\}** codes turn bold on/off. The **{^R}** and **{^S}** codes turn the color red on/off. These codes are inserted in the same way as the **{^P}** code.

d. The statement **{IF}**"**{VARIABLE}**options~"="**{Enter}**"~**{GO}** top~ **{END IF}** tells the macro to loop back to the "top" label at the beginning of the macro if the [Enter] key is pressed (this has the effect of running the macro again). When trapping a keystroke such as [Enter], be sure to use quotations marks around **{VARIABLE}** statements in the **{IF}** instructions. Otherwise, they will not be recognized by the **{IF}** statement. (A key press is a nonnumeric string.)

Also, be sure that you use quotes in pairs, as shown above. Finally, all **{IF}** statements must end with an **{END IF}**.

e. The **{;}** code allows text and codes to be placed in the macro as comments without being executed by WordPerfect. For example, deleting the **{;}** codes and accompanying tildes (~) for menu choices 6 and 7 would then display them on the screen. When adding your own comments, be sure to end them with a tilde (~).

Part 2: This is the **{CASE}** structure. The **{CASE}** command looks at the contents of the **{VARIABLE}**options~ and compares it with the 6 possible options (1 to 5 and [Q] for quit). It then branches to the appropriate label. For example, if you enter a 1, the case statement will branch the macro to the "mac1" label, which then executes the FORMMENU.WPM macro. When using a letter as a menu option, be sure to include both the lowercase and uppercase characters in the case statement.

The **{GO}**top~ statement is used to trap erroneous keystrokes. In other words, if any key outside of 1 through 5, q and Q are pressed, the macro will loop back to the "top" label and begin again. (However, an **{IF}** statement as described above, must be used when trapping the [Enter] key.)

Part 3: This part contains the labels that execute the subroutine for the different menu choices. In the case of the MAINMENU macro, each of these subroutines nests in another macro. When the nested macro finishes executing, the **{GO}**end~ command makes the MAINMENU macro go to the "end" label, which then displays the message on the screen. If you prefer, you can use the **{CHAIN}** code instead to pass control directly to another macro without returning to the "end" label.

{DISPLAY OFF}{PROMPT}{Del to EOP} clears the screen and displays the message at the top of the screen. The **{WAIT}7~** flashes the message on the screen for $7/10$'s of a second. The **{QUIT}** command terminates the macro.

C.5 SAMPLE MACROS

NOTE: The following macros were written in the WordPerfect 5.1 macro language. Many of these macros can be used, without any change, in WordPerfect 5.0. However, if you are a WordPerfect 5.0 user, you will have to change the keystrokes for some of the more involved macros.

[Alt][A] (Suppress All on page 1)

USE: Suppress All on Page 1 (page numbers, headers, and footers).

```
{DISPLAY OFF}{home}{home}{Up}{format}281{exit}
```

[Alt][B] (Inserts footer B with path\filename)

USE: Works only in WordPerfect 5.1, and the document must be saved first before using the macro.

NOTES: The {SYSTEM} code is new to WordPerfect 5.1 and very powerful. It returns the value of the given system variable, which makes it possible for a macro or merge to be aware of the current state of WordPerfect. See Appendix T in the WordPerfect reference manual for a detailed list of all the value tables for {SYSTEM}.

Returns the value of the system variable "path" →

```
{DISPLAY OFF}{home}{home}{Up}
{format}pfbp
{SYSTEM}path~{SYSTEM}name~
{exit}{exit}
```

[Alt][C] (Copy block)

USE: Press twice, once to turn the block on and again to copy the block.

NOTES: The **{STATE}** code returns a number representing the current operational state of WordPerfect. For example, **{STATE}**&4 represents the Normal Editing Screen, **{STATE}**&128 represents Block Active. The **{STATE}** code lets your macros test WordPerfect's operational state before executing the macro. Also, each **{IF}** statement must be followed by an **{END IF}**.

{If} statement tests whether block is on. If yes, copy is performed. Otherwise, block is turned on →

```
{IF}{STATE}&4~                                  {;}Editing screen~
    {IF}{STATE}&128~                            {;}Block on~
        {DISPLAY ON}
        {Move}12
        {DISPLAY ON}
    {ELSE}
        {Block}
    {END IF}
{END IF}
```

[Alt][D] (Delete block)

USE: Press twice, once to turn the block on and again to delete the block.

NOTES: Same structure as Copy and Move Block macros.

```
{IF}{STATE}&4~                              {;}Editing screen~
    {IF}{STATE}&128~                        {;}Block on~
        {DISPLAY ON}
        {Del}y
        {DISPLAY ON}
    {ELSE}
        {Block}
    {END IF}
{END IF}
```

[Alt][E] (Print address on envelope) Copyright by Alan M. Kaplan. Used with permission of the author.

USE: You must have the cursor at the left margin on the line above the inside address and two hard returns after the address block. Follow the directions from your printer's manufacturer regarding loading envelopes. If you have a dot-matrix or daisy-wheel printer, make sure the envelope is inserted the same way as for regular paper. If the document requires regeneration ([Alt][F5], [G], [G]), it will do this automatically prior to printing. You may have to send a GO to print. This macro works with laser printers, if the printer has a properly defined envelope form.

NOTES: This is one of several hundred WordPerfect macros available as shareware from Alan Kaplan, Esq. His current version, WPMAC51 version 6, is available on the supplementary disks as shareware, as are prior versions of WordPerfect 5.0 macros. (You can also download them from the WPUSERS SIG on CompuServe.)

```
{;}copyright 1991, Kaplan~
{DISPLAY ON}
{IF}{STATE}&512~                    {;}turn off reveal codes~
    {Reveal Codes}
{END IF}
{PROMPT}* Printing Envelope *~
{HPg}                               {;}create new page~
{Search}{Enter}{Enter}{Search}{HPg}    {;}page ends
                                       after two HRT's~
{Search Left}{HPg}{Search}
```

```
{format}pua{Enter}{Enter}                    {;}turn off
                                             headers/footers~
psn
env                         {;}select form begining with 'env'~
{Enter}s{Enter}
1m40u{Enter}0u{Enter}
0oad6u{Enter}
{Enter}
{Enter}
{Print}p
{LABEL}test~
        {IF}{STATE}&1024~
        y
{END IF}
{LABEL}cleanup~
        {Down}

{Search}{Enter}{Enter}{HPg}{Search}{Backspace}
        {Search Left}{format}oa{Search}
        {Block}{Search Left}{HPg}{Search}{Left}
        {Del}y
{IF}{SYSTEM}print~&8~        {;}give a "Go" if needed~
        {WAIT}10~
        {Print}
        4g{exit}
{END IF}
```

[Alt][F] (Create footer A)

USE: Inserts a Footer A.

```
{DISPLAY OFF}
{format}PFAP
{DISPLAY ON}
```

[Alt][G] (Insert a horizontal or vertical Graphic Line)

USE: Gives user the choice of creating either a vertical or horizontal graphic line, then steps the user through each line draw option.

NOTES: The **{^R}** and **{^S}** turn red highlighting on/off; and the **{^]}** and **{^\}** codes turn bold on/off. For a detailed explanation on the **{CASE}**, **{CHAR}**, and **{VARIABLE}** codes, see the [Ctrl][M] Main Menu described above. The **{PAUSE}** command allows user input from the keyboard before executing the macro.

```
                {LABEL}start~
                {CHAR}option~
                  {^R}GRAPHIC LINES{^S}: {^]}1 H{^\}orizontal {^]}2
                V{^\}ertical~
                {DISPLAY OFF}
                {CASE}{VARIABLE}option~~
                        1~one~H~one~h~one~
                        2~two~V~two~v~two~~
                                        {;}direct possible choices~

                {GO}start~
                                {;}Keystrokes for horizontal lines~
                {LABEL}one~
                {DISPLAY ON}
                {Graphics}511
                5{PAUSE}{Enter}
                22{PAUSE}{Enter}
                3{PAUSE}{Enter}
                4{PAUSE}{Enter}
                {TEXT}1~Enter the percentage of shading:~
                5{VARIABLE}1~{Enter}
                {Exit}
                {QUIT}

                                {;}keystrokes for vertical lines~
                {LABEL}two~
                {DISPLAY ON}
                {Graphics}52
                14{PAUSE}{Enter}
                25{PAUSE}{Enter}
                3{PAUSE}{Enter}
                4{PAUSE}{Enter}
                {TEXT}1~Enter the percentage of shading.~
                5{VARIABLE}1~{Enter}
                {Exit}
                {QUIT}
```

{^R} turns red background on → (annotation for `{^R}GRAPHIC LINES` line)

[Alt][H] (Create header A)

USE: Inserts a Header A.

```
{DISPLAY OFF}
{format}PHAP
{DISPLAY ON}
```

[Alt][I] (Italics on/off)

USE: Block out text and press [Alt][I] or press [Alt][I] to toggle italics on/off.

```
{IF}!{STATE}&4~              {;}Check to see if at Normal
                                         Editing screen~
        {RETURN}
{END IF}
{DISPLAY OFF}
{Font}24                     {;}Keystrokes for Italics~
```

[Alt][J] (Justification menu)

USE: Allows user to change to Left, Full, Center, or Right Justification.

```
{DISPLAY ON}
{LABEL}start~
{CHAR}just~
{^R}JUSTIFICATION:{^S} {^]}1 L{^\}eft {^]}2
C{^\}enter{^]} 3 R{^\}ight {^]}4 F{^\}ull ~
{CASE}{VARIABLE}just~~
        1~left~L~left~l~left~
        2~center~C~center~c~center~
        3~right~R~right~r~right~
        4~full~F~full~f~full~~
{GO}start~
{LABEL}left~{format}1j1{exit}{GO}end~
{LABEL}center~{format}1j2{exit}{GO}end~
{LABEL}right~{format}1j3{exit}{GO}end~
{LABEL}full~{format}1j4{exit}{GO}end~
{LABEL}end~
{QUIT}
```

[Alt][K] (Character of choice menu)

USE: Presents users with a number of the most commonly used special characters.

NOTES: Characters that cannot be displayed on the screen are spelled out. For a detailed explanation of the menu structure, see the [Ctrl][M] macro reference above. Many of these special characters may not be supported if you are a WordPerfect 5.0 user.

```
{LABEL}start~{DISPLAY OFF}{CHAR}choice~
{^]}S{^\}   §  {^]}P{^\}  ¶  {^]}R{^\}  Registered
{^]}C{^\}  Copyright   {^]}T{^\}  Trademark
{^]}A{^\}  •  {^]}B{^\}      {^]} L{^\}   {Enter}
{^]}M{^\}  ¢  {^]}D{^\}  Dagger   {^]}G{^\}  Double
Dagger   {^]}H{^\}  ½  {^]}O{^\}  ¼  {^]}Q{^\}  Three
quarters~
                              {;}print menu and take choice~
{CASE}{VARIABLE}choice~~
                  S~s~s~s~
                  P~p~p~p~
                  R~r~r~r~
                  C~c~c~c~
                  T~t~t~t~
                  A~a~a~a~
                  B~b~b~b~
                  L~l~l~l~
                  K~k~k~k~
                  L~l~l~l~
                  M~m~m~m~
                  D~d~d~d~
                  G~g~g~g~
                  H~h~h~h~
                  O~o~o~o~
                  Q~q~q~q~~
                                    {;}direct menu choices~
{DISPLAY OFF}{DISPLAY OFF}
{GO}start~              {;}send back for valid choice~
{LABEL}s~
§                                            {;}4,6~
{QUIT}
{LABEL}p~
¶                                            {;}4,5~
{QUIT}
{LABEL}r~
®                                            {;}4,22~
{QUIT}
{LABEL}c~
©                                            {;}4,23~
{QUIT}
{LABEL}t~
™                                            {;}4,41~
{QUIT}
{LABEL}a~
○                                            {;}4,45~
{QUIT}
```

```
{LABEL}b~
 •                                                    {;}4,3~
{QUIT}
{LABEL}l~
 •                                                    {;}4,0~
{QUIT}
{LABEL}m~
 ¢                                                    {;}4,19~
{QUIT}
{LABEL}d~
 †                                                    {;}4,39~
{QUIT}
{LABEL}h~
 ½                                                    {;}4,17~
{QUIT}
{LABEL}o~
 ¼                                                    {;}4,18~
{QUIT}
{LABEL}q~
 ¾                                                    {;}4,25~
{QUIT}
{LABEL}g~
 ‡                                                    {;}4,40~
{QUIT}
```

[Alt][L] (Line spacing menu)

USE: Presents user with the option of single, double, or triple line spacing, or of a user-defined line spacing.

NOTES: For a detailed explanation of the menu structure, see the [Ctrl][M] macro reference above.

```
{LABEL}start~
{CHAR}option~
{^R}LINE SPACING{^S}:  {^]}1 S{^\}ingle {^]}2
D{^\}ouble {^]}3 T{^\}riple {^]}4{^\} One and a
{^]}H{^\}alf {^]}5 O{^\}ther~        {;}menu on bottom~
{DISPLAY OFF}
{CASE}{VARIABLE}option~~
        1~one~S~one~s~one~
        2~two~D~two~d~two~
        3~three~T~three~t~three~
        4~four~H~four~h~four~
        5~five~O~five~o~five~~
{GO}start~
```

```
{LABEL}one~
{format}ls1{Enter}              {;}single line spacing~
{exit}{QUIT}
{LABEL}two~
{format}ls2{Enter}              {;}double line spacing~
{exit}{QUIT}
{LABEL}three~
{format}ls3{Enter}              {;}triple line spacing~
{exit}{QUIT}
{LABEL}four~
{format}ls1.5{Enter}    {;}1 and a half line spacing~
{exit}{QUIT}
{LABEL}five~
{DISPLAY ON}{format}ls          {;}leave user at menu~
{QUIT}
```

[Alt][M] (Move block)

USE: Move block macro. Press twice, once to turn the block on and again to move the block.

NOTES: Similar to Copy ([Alt][C]) and Delete ([Alt][D]) block macros. See Copy Block macro above for more details.

```
{IF}{STATE}&4~                          {;}Editing screen~
        {IF}{STATE}&128~                        {;}Block on~
                {DISPLAY OFF}
                {Move}11
                {DISPLAY ON}
        {ELSE}
                {Block}
        {END IF}
{END IF}
```

[Alt][N] (Insert bottom centered page number -#-)

NOTES: Automatically inserts the page number style code and number code on the first page. Use the the [Alt][A] (Supress All) macro if you wish to suppress it on the first page.

```
{DISPLAY OFF}
{home}{home}{Up}{format}pns-{^B}-{Enter}
p6{Enter}
{Enter}
{Enter}
```

[Alt][O] (ASCII margins)

USE: Reduce left/right and top/bottom margins as close to zero as possible. (Used when importing ASCII text from Westlaw and other on-line services.)

```
{DISPLAY OFF}
{home}{home}{home}{Up}
{format}170{Enter}0{Enter}{Enter}
250{Enter}0{Enter}
{Enter}
{Enter}
```

[Alt][P] (Print menu) Copyright by Alan M. Kaplan. Used with permission of the author.

USE: Allows user to print current page, all pages, or a selected range.

NOTES: This is one of several hundred WordPerfect macros available as shareware from Alan Kaplan. His current version, WPMAC517 (version 7), is available on the supplementary disks as shareware for a fee of $25 per user.

```
{DISPLAY OFF}
{IF}{STATE}&512~
        {Reveal Codes}
{END IF}
{ON CANCEL}
        {GO}end~~
{ON ERROR}
        {GO}end~~
{LABEL}menu~
{CHAR}choice~
        {^R}PRINT OPTIONS:{^S} {^]}1 A{^\}11  {^]}2 P{^\}age {^]}3 R{^\}ange of pages  {^]}4 E{^\}xit~
                        {;}menu for print options~
{CASE}{VARIABLE}choice~~
        1~one~A~one~a~one~
        2~two~P~two~p~two~
        3~three~R~three~r~three~
4~end~E~end~e~end~{exit}~end~{Esc}~end~
                        {;}direct choices to labels~
{GO}menu~
{LABEL}one~
{ASSIGN}choice~1~
```

```
{Print}1{WAIT}10~
        {IF}{STATE}&1024~
        y
{END IF}
{GO}end~
{LABEL}two~
{ASSIGN}choice~2~
{Print}p{WAIT}10~
        {IF}{STATE}&1024~y
{END IF}
{GO}end~
{LABEL}three~
{ASSIGN}choice~3~
{DISPLAY OFF}
{Screen}{Screen}
{TEXT}1~{Del to EOL}What page do you want to begin
printing?  ~
{TEXT}2~{Del to EOL}What is the last page to print?
([RETURN] is thru end):~
{LABEL}print~
{Print}m
{VAR 1}-{VAR 2}
{Enter}
{IF}{STATE}&1024~y
{END IF}
{GO}end~
{LABEL}end~
{ASSIGN}1~~
```

[Alt][Q] (Save document and quit WordPerfect)

NOTES: Can be used whether WP 5.1 Long Document Names are on or not.

```
{exit}y{Enter}{Enter}{Enter}yy
```

[Alt][R] (Turn on a Letterhead Style and insert the date as text)

USE: Create a style that calls up your firm letterhead or formatting. Use the Letterhead style below as an example. Then execute the macro. This macro assumes that the Letterhead style is the first style on the Styles list and that you are using the CG Times font available on the HP III LaserJet printer. Please modify this to conform with your Style List and your printer/font selection.

NOTES: A benefit to using this macro with a paired style is that you can evoke the Date Text function with the macro. In a style, the Date Text function will not work properly (you'll always have the date you created the Style), and you generally don't want to use the Date Code feature in case you need to reference the date of the correspondence sometime in the future. Note, also, that the Styles feature does not have a Name Search function. Therefore, you have to specify the number of keystrokes needed to highlight the style. In general, if a name search function is available (as in finding keyboard layouts, for example), always use it instead of the cursor keystrokes to find a file. This will guarantee that the macro will always work, even if you make changes in the future.

```
{DISPLAY OFF}{Style}{Down}1{Date/Outline}1

Sample Letter Head Paired style (Codes and text)
[Center][Font:CG Times (Scalable) 14pt][SM CAP:CG
Times (Scalable) 12pt]
Marshall, Hand, Holmes, Cardozo & Blackstone[sm
cap][Hrt]
[Center]123 Fifth Avenue[Hrt]
[Center]Suite 1800[Hrt]
[Center]New York, New York 10014[Hrt]
[Center]Tel: (212) 123-4567  Fax: (212) 123-4568[Hrt]
[Hrt]
[Hrt]
[Hrt]
[Hrt]
[Hrt]
[Hrt]
[Tab][Tab][Tab][Tab][Tab][Tab][Tab]
```

[Alt][S] (Save document—perhaps the most important macro of all!)

NOTES: Can be used with either long or short documents.

```
{DISPLAY OFF}{Save}{Enter}{Enter}{Enter}y
```

[Alt][T] **WP5.1** (Create a Table)

USE: User is prompted for the number of rows and columns and then left in the Table Edit mode.

NOTES: The **{TEXT}** code stores a variable that is retrieved by the **{VARIABLE}**~ code

{Text} stores the user's input in a variable, which can be retrieved with the {variable} code

```
{TEXT}1~Enter the number of columns:~
{TEXT}2~Enter the number of rows:~
{LABEL}table~
{DISPLAY OFF}
{Columns/Tables}21
{VARIABLE}1~{Enter}
{VARIABLE}2~{Enter}
{exit}
{DISPLAY ON}{Columns/Tables}
```

[Alt][U] (Underline options menu)

USE: Allows user to choose whether or not to single- or double-underline spaces and tabs between words.

```
{IF}!{STATE}&4~
        {RETURN}
{END IF}
{IF}{STATE}&128~        {;}Checks to see if block is on.
                            If yes, block is turned off~
{Block}
{END IF}
{LABEL}start~
{CHAR}choice~
{^R}UNDERLINE OPTIONS:{^S} SINGLE WORDS/TABS:
{^]}Y{^\}es {^]}N{^\}o {^]}DOUBLE WORDS/TABS:{^\}
Y{^]}e{^\}s  N{^]}o{^]}~
                        {;}menu for underline options~
{DISPLAY OFF}
{CASE}{VARIABLE}choice~~
        1~one~Y~one~y~one~
        2~two~N~two~n~two~
        3~three~E~three~e~three~
        4~four~O~four~o~four~~
{GO}start~
{LABEL}one~
{format}47yy{exit}      {;}underline words and tabs~
{DISPLAY OFF}
{Underline}
{QUIT}                  {;}Keystrokes for underline~
{LABEL}two~
{format}47nn{exit}
{Underline}
```

```
{QUIT}
{LABEL}three~
{format}47yy{exit}            {;}underline words and tabs~
{DISPLAY OFF}
{Font}23              {;}Keystrokes for double underline~
{QUIT}
{LABEL}four~
{format}47nn{exit}
{DISPLAY OFF}
{Font}23              {;}Keystrokes for double underline~
{QUIT}
```

[Alt][V] (View document)

```
{DISPLAY OFF}
{Print}6
```

[Alt][F11] (Tab set)

USE: Takes user to Tab set screen. Once Exit is pressed, user is returned to normal editing screen.

NOTES: The **{PAUSE KEY}** feature in WordPerfect 5.1 pauses the macro until the designated key (here, [F7]) is pressed. **{PAUSE KEY}** can be used with any key or function key.

```
{IF}{STATE}&4~   {;}Check to see if at editing screen~
{format}1t
{PAUSE KEY}{exit}~      {;}F7 key press takes user
                              back to editing screen~
{exit}{exit}
{END IF}
```

Here, the Pause key is [F7]

[Shift][F11] (Reset Tabs to the default)

USE: Use to clear current tab settings and return to tab stops every .5".

NOTES: The **{Del to EOL}** code is inserted by pressing [Ctrl][End] while in the WordPerfect Command mode.

```
{DISPLAY OFF}
{format}1t
{home}{Left}{Del to EOL} {;}Deletes current tab stops~
t2
-0.5{Enter}-1.0{Enter}1{Enter}0.5{Enter}1{Enter}1.5
{Enter}2{Enter}2.5{Enter}3{Enter}3.5{Enter}4{Enter}
```

```
4.5{Enter}5{Enter}5.5{Enter}6{Enter}6.5{Enter}7{Enter}
7.5{Enter}
{exit}
{exit}
```

[Alt][F12] **WP5.1** (Make parallel columns)

USE: At each prompt, enter the appropriate number and press [Enter]. The standard size for distance between columns is .25".

NOTES: This macro will create equal-sized parallel columns, with or without block protect. Block protect is used to keep a block of text from being split between two pages. If possible, we recommend using the WP5.1 Tables feature instead of the Parallel Columns feature for arranging text in columns and rows.

```
{TEXT}1~Enter the number of parallel columns:~
{TEXT}2~Enter the distance between columns:~
{TEXT}3~Select {^]}2{^\}-Parallel;
{^]}3{^\}-Parallel with Block Protect:~
{LABEL}columns~
{DISPLAY OFF}
{Columns/Tables}131
{IF}{VAR 3}=2~{GO}parallel~
        {ELSE}
{IF}{VAR 3}=3~{GO}block~
{END IF}{END IF}
{LABEL}parallel~
2
{GO}definition~
{LABEL}block~
3
{GO}definition~
{LABEL}definition~
2{VAR 1}{Enter}
3{VAR 2}{Enter}
{exit}
1
```

[Shift][F12] **WP5.1** (Create newspaper columns)

USE: At each prompt, enter the appropriate number and press [Enter]. The standard size for distance between columns is .25".

NOTES: This macro will create equal-sized newspaper columns.

```
{TEXT}1~Enter the number of newspaper columns:~
{TEXT}2~Enter the distance between columns:~
{LABEL}columns~
{DISPLAY OFF}
{Columns/Tables}1311
{GO}definition~
{LABEL}definition~
2{VAR 1}{Enter}
3{VAR 2}{Enter}
{exit}
1
```

[Ctrl][C] (Insert a comment)

USE: Use comments anywhere you want to annotate text.

{DISPLAY OFF}{Text In/Out}4{DISPLAY ON}1

[Ctrl][E] (Edit a code)

USE: Reveal Codes, place cursor on the code to be edited, and press [Ctrl][E]. Works with most formatting and attribute codes.

NOTES: The code for this macro is not displayed because it is very long and complex. However, this macro is very powerful and its use is highly recommended. You'll find the macro as [Alt][E] in the WordPerfect 5.1 keyboard SHORTCUT.WPK. Save the keyboard macro as CODEDIT.WPM, then import it into your own keyboard. For help on this procedure, refer to Chapter 5, on using keyboard layouts.

[Ctrl][F] (HP III Fonts menu)

```
{DISPLAY OFF}
{LABEL}start~
{CHAR}pitch~{^R}{^]}FONTS:{^S} 1 {^\}Cour 10 {^]}2
{^\}Cour 12 {^]}3 {^\}Times {^]}4 {^\}Times Italics
{^]}5 {^\}Univers {^]}6{^\} Univers Italic~
{CASE}{VARIABLE}pitch~~
        1~10 Pitch~
        2~12 Pitch~
        3~Times~
        4~Times Italics~
        5~Univers~
        6~Univers Italic~~
```

```
{GO}start~
{LABEL}10 Pitch~{Font}4nCourier 10cpi{Enter}1{GO}end~
{LABEL}12 Pitch~{Font}4nCourier 12cpi{Enter}1{GO}end~
{LABEL}Times~{Font}4ncg times {Enter}{DISPLAY
ON}1{QUIT}
{LABEL}Times Italics~{Font}4ncg times
italic{Enter}{DISPLAY ON}1{QUIT}
{LABEL}Univers~{Font}4nUnivers{Enter}{DISPLAY
ON}1{QUIT}
{LABEL}Univers Italic~{Font}4nUnivers
italic{Enter}{DISPLAY ON}1{QUIT}
```

[Ctrl][L] (Outline options)

USE: Present the user with the option to turn the outline feature on/off and to use the legal outline.

```
{LABEL}start~
{CHAR}option~
{^R}OUTLINE OPTIONS{^S}:  {^]}1 O{^\}n {^]}2{^\}
O{^]}f{^\}f {^]}3 L{^\}egal outline style on~
{DISPLAY OFF}
{CASE}{VARIABLE}option~~
        1~one~O~one~o~one~
        2~two~F~two~f~two~
        3~three~L~three~l~~
{GO}start~
{LABEL}one~{;}Outline On~
{Date/Outline}41
{QUIT}
{LABEL}two~
{Date/Outline}42{;}Outline Off~
{QUIT}
{LABEL}three~
{Date/Outline}64{exit}41{;}Legal outline style on~
{QUIT}
```

[Ctrl][M] (Main menu macro)

See beginning of appendix for a detailed explanation of the code for this macro.

[Ctrl][N] (Page numbering options)

USE: Presents the user with the option of inserting a Roman numeral i as the page number (useful for table of contents and authorities) and starting the current page at number 1 (used before generating tables).

```
{LABEL}start~
{CHAR}option~
{^R}PAGE NUMBERING OPTIONS{^S}:   {^]}1 R{^\}oman
numeral i {^]}2 S{^\}tart at 1~
{DISPLAY OFF}
{CASE}{VARIABLE}option~~
        1~one~R~one~r~one~
        2~two~S~two~s~two~~
{GO}start~
{LABEL}one~{;}insert roman numeral i~
{format}261i{Enter}46{exit}
{QUIT}
{LABEL}two~{;}start page numbering at 1~
{format}2611{Enter}46{exit}
{QUIT}
```

[Ctrl][P] (View printer control)

USE: Useful when checking the status of a print job or to see if there is a problem with printing.

```
{Print}C
```

C.6 NAMED MACROS TO BE CALLED FROM THE [Ctrl][M] MAIN MENU MACRO

TABLECAP (Create a case caption for pleading using the WP5.1 Tables feature)

USE: The user will be prompted to fill in the name of the parties, case number, and name of the pleading.

NOTES: The {Pause Key} function will temporarily pause the macro until the [F7] key is pressed. This macro will have to be edited to conform to the pleading format of your jurisdiction.

```
{IF}!{STATE}&4~{;}check to make sure block is not on~
        {RETURN}
{END IF}
{IF}{STATE}&128~
{Block}
{END IF}
{DISPLAY OFF}              {;}Hide keystrokes~
{Enter}{Enter}             {;}put in two hard returns
                                     before caption~
{Columns/Tables}212{Enter} {;}Create table~
{Enter}
372311{Right}371           {;}keystrokes for single
                                     lines on table~
{Word Right}{Word Right}{Word Right}
{exit}
{Up}
{DISPLAY ON}               {;}Show keystrokes and prompts~
{PROMPT}Type in name of court, press [F9] to
continue~
{PAUSE KEY}{exit}~         {;}Use Pause Key and [F9] key
                                     for user prompts~
{Right}{Right}
{PROMPT}Type in name of Plaintiff(s), press [F9] to
continue~
{PAUSE KEY}{exit}~         {;}Use Pause Key and [F9] key
                                     for user prompts~
{Enter}{Enter}
{home}{Tab}{home}{Tab}Plaintiff(s),    {;}tab stops
                                              in table~
{Enter}{Enter}{Enter}
{Center}v.
{Enter}{Enter}{Enter}
{PROMPT}Type in name of Defendant(s), press [F9] to
continue~
{PAUSE KEY}{exit}~         {;}Use Pause Key and F9 key
                                     for user prompts~
{Enter}{Enter}
{home}{Tab}{home}{Tab}Defendant(s),
{Tab}                      {;}Move to next cell in table~
{Enter}{Enter}
CASE NO:{PROMPT}Type in Docket Number, press [F9] to
continue~
{PAUSE KEY}{exit}~
{Enter}{Enter}{Enter}
{PROMPT}Enter name of pleading, press [F9] to
continue~
```

```
{PAUSE KEY}{exit}~
{Down}                                        {;}Exit table~
```

50COLCAP (Create case caption for pleading using WP5.0 newspaper columns)

USE: This macro creates three newspaper columns automatically and uses line draw to draw the caption. The user will be prompted to fill in the names of the parties, docket number, and title of pleading. Pressing [Enter] will resume the operation of the macro. (WP5.0 does not offer the better {PAUSE KEY} command.)

```
{DISPLAY OFF}                   {;}Turn off keystrokes~
{Enter}{Enter}
{Columns/Tables}423{Enter}      {;}Define 3 columns~
4{Enter}5.4{Enter}
5.4{Enter}5.5{Enter}
5.7{Enter}7.9{Enter}
{DISPLAY ON}         {;}Display keystrokes and prompts~
{exit}3
{Up}
{PROMPT}Type in name of court, press [enter] to
continue~{PAUSE}{Enter}
{Typeover}{Screen}21{Esc}43{Right}      {;}Single Line
                                             Draw right~
6{Esc}10{Down}                  {;}moving Line Draw~
1{Esc}43{Left}{exit}            {;}Line draw left~
{Esc}9{Up}
{PROMPT}type in name of Plaintiff(s), press [enter]
to continue~{PAUSE}
{Down}{home}{Left}{Esc}5{Tab}Plaintiff(s),
{Down}{Down}{home}{Left}{Esc}4{Tab}v.{Down}{Down}
{home}{Left}
{PROMPT}type in name of Defendant(s), press [enter]
to continue~{PAUSE}
{Down}{home}{Left}{Esc}5{Tab}Defendant(s),
{home}{home}{Down}{HPg}         {;}Move to next column~
{Esc}9                          {;}Insert right parentheses~
{HPg}                           {;}Move to 3rd column~
{Enter}
{Enter}
CASE NO: {PROMPT}Enter case number, [enter] to
continue~{PAUSE}
{Enter}
{Enter}
```

```
{PROMPT}Enter title of pleading, [enter] to
continue~{PAUSE}
{Columns/Tables}3{Enter}{Enter}{Typeover} {;}Turn off
                                                columns~
```

51COLCAP (Create case caption for pleading using WP5.1 newspaper columns)

USE: This macro creates three newspaper columns automatically and uses line draw to draw the caption. The user will be prompted to fill in the names of the parties, docket number, and title of pleading. Pressing [F7] will resume the operation of the macro.

NOTES: Using the {PAUSE KEY} feature allows the user to press [Enter] without resuming the macro. This allows for multiple line entries.

```
{DISPLAY OFF}               {;}Turn off keystrokes~
{Enter}{Enter}
{Columns/Tables}1323{Enter}    {;}Define 3 columns~
4{Enter}5.4{Enter}
5.4{Enter}5.5{Enter}
5.7{Enter}7.9{Enter}
{DISPLAY ON}      {;}Display keystrokes and prompts~
{exit}1{PROMPT}Type in name of court, press [F9] to
continue~
{PAUSE KEY}{exit}~ {;}User prompt with [F9] pause key~
{Enter}{Typeover}{Screen}21{Esc}45{Right}
                             {;}Single Line Draw right~
6{Esc}10{Down}{Enter}          {;}moving Line Draw~
1{Esc}45{Left}{exit}            {;}Line draw left~
{Esc}9{Up}
{PROMPT}type in name of Plaintiff(s), press [F9] to
continue~{PAUSE KEY}{exit}~
{Down}{home}{Left}{Esc}6{Tab}Plaintiff(s),
{Down}{Down}{home}{Left}{Esc}4{Tab}v.{Down}{Down}
{home}{Left}{PROMPT}type in name of Defendant(s),
press [F7] to continue~{PAUSE KEY}{exit}~
{Down}{home}{Left}{Esc}6{Tab}Defendant(s),
{home}{home}{Down}{HPg}{Enter} {;}Move to next column~
{Esc}11)              {;}Insert right parentheses~
{HPg}                     {;}Move to 3rd column~
{Enter}
{Enter}
CASE NO: {PROMPT}Enter case number, [F9] to
continue~{PAUSE KEY}{exit}
~{Enter}
```

```
{Enter}
{PROMPT}Enter title of pleading, [F9] to
continue~{PAUSE KEY}{exit}~
{Columns/Tables}12{Enter}{Enter}{Typeover}
                              {;}Turn off columns~
```

51MANAGE (WP5.1 Document management options)

USE: Presents a menu that gives the user the option to turn Document Summaries and the Long Document Name feature on/off.

NOTES: Menu structure very similar to the [Ctrl][M] Main Menu described at the beginning of this appendix.

```
{LABEL}top~
{DISPLAY OFF}
{CHAR}choose~{Del to EOP}{^]}
{^P}
{^P}¶{^A}{^]}{^R}WP 5.1 Document Management
Options{^S}{^\}
{^P}¶♥<{^]}1{^\}> Document Summary Screens - ON
{^P}¶♦<{^]}2{^\}> Document Summary Screens - OFF
{^P}¶♣<{^]}3{^\}> Long Document Names - ON
{^P}¶♠<{^]}4{^\}> Long Document Names - OFF
{^P}¶{Tab}<{^]}Q{^\}>uit this menu
{^P}¶{^V}Enter your selection =~
{IF}"{VARIABLE}1~"="{Enter}"~{GO}top~{END IF}
{CASE}{VARIABLE}choose~~1~sumon~2~sumoff~3~longon~4~
longoff~q~quit~Q~quit~~
{GO}top~
{exit}ny{QUIT}{RETURN}
{LABEL}sumon~
{Setup}341y{exit}
{QUIT}
{LABEL}sumoff~
{Setup}341n{exit}
{QUIT}
{LABEL}longon~
{Setup}343y{exit}
{QUIT}
{LABEL}longoff~
{Setup}343n{exit}
{QUIT}
{LABEL}quit~
{QUIT}
```

TOCTITLE (Sets up title page for a table of contents)

USE: Start this macro at the beginning of your document. It will automatically renumber the pages and insert a table definition code for five levels. After the page has been set up, the user will be asked whether or not to generate the table.

```
{DISPLAY OFF}
{HPg}
{format}pnn1{exit}{exit}{;}set page numbering to one.~
{Up}{format}pnni{Enter}46{exit} {;}set page
numbering to i, bottom center~
{Center}{Underline}TABLE OF CONTENTS        {;}centered
                                             title for table~
{Enter}{Enter}
{Enter}{Enter}
{Flush Right}
Page{Underline}{Enter}
{Enter}                                {;}put in "page"~
{Mark Text}dcn5{Enter}                 {;}put in toc define
                                          code for 5 levels~
{DISPLAY ON}
{CHAR}choice~
{^R}DO YOU WISH TO GENERATE THE TABLE?{^S}
{^]}Y{^\}es  {^]} N{^\}o~
{CASE}{VARIABLE}choice~~
       Y~gen~y~gen~
       N~end~n~end~~
{GO}start~     {;}send back for appropriate response~
{LABEL}gen~
{Mark Text}ggy{Enter}   {;}generate table of contents~
{GO}end~
{LABEL}end~                              {;}end macro~
{QUIT}
```

COVER (Executes a merge template for a pleading cover)

USE: Create a pleading cover as a merge template. To add power to your template, see the COVERMEN.WPM macro below, which can be called up during the merge process by using the **{NEST MACRO}** code. (See Chapter 4 if you're not sure about this procedure.) Then use the following macro to execute the merge.

```
{DISPLAY OFF}
{Merge/Sort}1cover.tem{Enter}{Enter}
```

COVERMEN (Menu options for pleading cover)

USE: This macro presents the user with the choice of including a Notice of Entry, Notice of Settlement, or Affidavit of Service to a pleading cover. Edit the text to conform the macro to your practice.

NOTES: This macro looks more complicated than it actually is. Like the other macros, it presents the user with a menu for inserting a Notice of Entry, Notice of Settlement, and Affidavit of Service into a pleading cover. Each menu option branches to a label that contains the actual text. The {PAUSE KEY} command is used to allow user input from the keyboard. When finished, the macro then inserts the name and address of the firm and opposing counsel. Use this macro in conjunction with the **{NEST MACRO}** merge code at the end of a Pleading Cover template. For more information on creating merge templates using advanced merge codes, see Chapter 4.

```
                              {;}Menu for special options to be included
                                                on the pleading cover~
{DISPLAY ON}
{LABEL}top~
{CHAR}1~{Del to EOP}
{^P}¶{^A}{^]}{^R}SPECIAL OPTIONS SELECT AS
NEEDED{^S}{^\}
{^P}¶♥<{^]}1{^\}> Notice of Entry
{^P}¶♦<{^]}2{^\}> Notice of Settlement
{^P}¶♣<{^]}3{^\}> Skip to Affidavit of service
{^P}¶♠<{^]}Q{^\}>uit this menu
{^P}¶{^V}Enter your selection =~

{IF}"{VARIABLE}1~"="{Enter}"~{GO}top~{END IF}
{CASE}{VARIABLE}
1~~1~mac1~2~mac2~3~mac3~q~end~Q~end~~
{GO}top~
{exit}ny{QUIT}{RETURN}

                                   {;}sample notice of entry~
{LABEL}mac1~
{Enter}{Enter}PLEASE TAKE NOTICE{Enter}{Enter}
That the within is a (certified) true copy of a
{DISPLAY ON}{PROMPT}
INSERT NAME OF PLEADING, [F7] TO CONTINUE~{PAUSE
KEY}{exit}~
entered in the office of the clerk of the
```

Menu for pleading cover options — points to the menu block above.

Notice of entry macro — points to the {LABEL}mac1~ block.

within named Court on {DISPLAY ON}{PROMPT}INSERT
DATE OF ENTRY,
[F7] TO CONTINUE~{PAUSE KEY}{exit}~.
{GO}end~

Notice of settlement macro →

{;}sample notice of settlement~
{LABEL}mac2~
{Enter}{Enter}PLEASE TAKE NOTICE
{Enter}{Enter}That an Order of which the within is a
true copy will be presented for settlement to the
Hon. {PROMPT}INSERT NAME OF JUDGE, [F7] TO
CONTINUE~{PAUSE KEY}{exit}~ one of the judges of the
within named Court, at {PROMPT}INSERT NAME OF COURT,

{PROMPT} code with user prompt →

JUDGE OR PART, [F7] TO CONTINUE~{PAUSE KEY}{exit}~
on {PROMPT}INSERT DATE FOR NOTICE OF SETTLEMENT,
[F7] TO CONTINUE~{PAUSE KEY}{exit}~ at 9:30
A.M.{GO}end~

Affidavit of service macro →

{;}sample affidavit of service~
{LABEL}mac3~
{Enter}{Enter}{Center}AFFIDAVIT OF SERVICE BY
MAIL{Enter}{Enter}STATE OF {PROMPT}ENTER NAME OF
STATE, [F7] TO CONTINUE~{PAUSE KEY}{exit}~{Enter}
{Enter}COUNTY OF {PROMPT}ENTER NAME OF COUNTY, [F7]
TO CONTINUE~{PAUSE KEY}{exit}~{Enter}{Enter}

Store name of person making the affidavit in a variable called "affname" →

{TEXT}affname~INSERT NAME OF PERSON MAKING
AFFIDAVIT, [ENTER] TO CONTINUE:
~{VARIABLE}affname~{LABEL}iam~ ,being sworn
says:{Enter}{Enter}{Enter} I am not a party to the
action, am over 18 years of age and reside in the
State of {PROMPT}INSERT STATE OF RESIDENCE, [F7] TO
CONTINUE~{PAUSE KEY}{exit}~.
On {Date/Outline}1, I served a true copy of the
annexed {PROMPT}INSERT NAME OF PLEADING, [F7] TO
CONTINUE~{PAUSE KEY}{exit}~ by mailing the same in a
sealed envelope, with postage prepaid thereon, in a
post-office or official depository of the United
States Postal Service within the State of
{PROMPT}INSERT STATE, [F7] TO CONTINUE~{PAUSE
KEY}{exit}~ , addressed to the last address of the
addressee(s) as indicated
below:{Enter}{Enter}{PROMPT}INSERT NAME OF ADDRESSEE
OR FIRM NAME, [F7] TO CONTINUE~{PAUSE KEY}{exit}~
{Enter}{PROMPT}INSERT STREET ADDRESS, [F7] TO
CONTINUE~{PAUSE KEY}{exit}~{Enter}{PROMPT}INSERT

```
                        CITY, STATE & ZIP, [F7] TO CONTINUE~{PAUSE
                        KEY}{exit}~{Enter}{Enter}{Enter}{Enter}{Enter}
                        {Esc}7{Tab}{Esc}28_{Enter}
                        {Esc}8{Tab}{VARIABLE}affname~
```
Text in the variable "affname" is retrieved here ───────▶
```
                        {Enter}{Enter}{Enter}{DISPLAY OFF}Sworn to before me
                        this {Date/Outline}3
                        {Del}{Del}{Right}{Del}{Del}{Del}{Enter}
                        1{Enter} day of {Date/Outline}33, 4{Enter}
                        1.{Date/Outline}3{Right} 1{Enter}{exit}{Enter}
                        {Enter}{Enter}{Enter}{Enter}
                        {Esc}32_{Enter}
                        {Tab}NOTARY PUBLIC{QUIT}
                        {GO}end~

                                   {;}End of macro—inserts firm name and name
                                              and address of opposing counsel~
                        {LABEL}end~
                        {Enter}{Enter}Dated:
                        {Tab}{Date/Outline}1{Enter}{Esc}7{Tab}
                        MARSHALL, CARDOZO, HAND, HOLMES & BLACKSTONE
                        {Enter}{Esc}7{Tab}123 Fifth Avenue - Suite 1800
                        {Enter}{Esc}7{Tab}
                        New York, N.Y. 10014
                        {Enter}{Enter}To:{Tab}{PROMPT}INSERT NAME OF
                        ATTORNEY FOR OTHER SIDE, [F7] TO CONTINUE~{PAUSE
                        KEY}{exit}~
                        {Enter}{Tab}{PROMPT}INSERT ADDRESS, [F7] TO
                        CONTINUE~{PAUSE KEY}
                        {exit}~{Enter}
                        {Tab}{PROMPT}INSERT CITY STATE & ZIP, [F7] TO
                        CONTINUE~
                        {PAUSE KEY}{exit}~
```

APPENDIX D: SUPPLEMENTAL DISK CONTENTS

This book has two supplementary floppy disks that you can order from the authors. On these disks, you will find all of the WordPerfect macros discussed in this book, as well as many WordPerfect and legal-related shareware programs and utilities. In this appendix, you'll find a listing of the disks' contents, plus a brief description of the different "shareware" programs and utilities.

D.1 A FEW WORDS ABOUT SHAREWARE

Most of the programs you use on your computer, such as WordPerfect, are commercial programs. With such programs, you have to buy a copy before you can use it. With *shareware*, however, you can try out the application first to see if you like it and if it is of practical use to your office. If it is, you pay a registration fee to the author for the program and for receiving updates and technical support.

There are several advantages to shareware. First, shareware is less expensive than commercial applications because there is no advertising or promotional cost to the developer, nor are there generally costs associated with packaging the product. In general, shareware costs less than $50, but you shouldn't take this to mean that shareware is inferior to commercial software. On the contrary, many shareware applications are as good as similar commercial applications—and some of the best commercial programs began as modest shareware.

The second great advantage of shareware is that it gives you, the consumer, a much bigger choice of possible programs that you can use to increase your productivity—with little risk. For example, writing sophisticated WordPerfect macros can take many, many hours of expensive time. But with shareware, you get the benefit of hundreds of hours of WordPerfect macro programming for $25 or less. The developer benefits as well since the macros are something he or she could probably not market successfully as a commercial product.

There is one catch. This wonderful system (which exists surely in the personal computer market, as far as we know) will only continue to work if you, the user, register and pay the shareware fee if you continue to use the product. Shareware developers rely on your honesty and conscience to register (not to mention the fact that, as legal professionals, you shouldn't be breaking the copyright laws of the United States!). When you register, you receive program updates and technical support. Shareware registration helps everyone—it supports the shareware developer's ability to continue to update the product and produce new ones, and it provides you with a better product and more choices.

You'll also find some *freeware* applications on the supplementary disks. The developers retain the copyright to the program, but you can use them without a fee. The only restrictions on freeware are related to copyright—you must not violate it by selling the freeware.

A final note: if your computer has a modem that you use to access WESTLAW and other legal research services, consider subscribing as well to information services such as CompuServe. For example, the LAWSIG on CompuServe is chock full of information for the legal profession, and includes many different libraries of shareware and freeware that you can download. There are also electronic bulletin boards or "BBSs" that exist just for the legal profession. See Appendix E for a partial listing.

D.2 DISK CONTENTS

D.2.1 DISK 1: BOOK AND SHAREWARE WORDPERFECT MACROS AND WORDPERFECT-RELATED SHAREWARE

The floppy disk contains the following directories: /BOOKMACS, /WPMACROS, and /WPSHARE

/BOOKMACS contains all of the macros mentioned in this book, for both 5.0 and 5.1 users. These macros are available on keyboards and by themselves.

/WPMACROS contains both shareware and freeware WordPerfect macros for both version 5.0 and 5.1. These macros include:

ADDBK.ZIP (Shareware) Address book macro and supporting documents. Author: Rex Goulding

ADDRS2.ZIP (Freeware) Macro to retrieve addresses for letters. By Ken Chestek, Esq.

ANSWER.ZIP (Freeware) WP5.0/5.1 macro used to automate the preparation of answers to complaints. Author: Edwin Peck, Esq.

BREEF.ZIP (Shareware) Brief writing tools and a template. Author: William D. Marvin, Esq.

CAPDOS.ZIP (Freeware) A macro to create, store, and retrieve a pleading caption. By Ken Chestek, Esq.

CITER2.ZIP (Shareware) A sophisticated WP5.1 macro system designed to produce citation formats for every jurisdiction from its database of bluebook forms. Completely menu driven. Author: William D. Marvin, Esq.

DBM.ZIP (Shareware) Macro to manage secondary file as database. Author: Abbot Koloff

DEPNOT.ZIP (Freeware) Merge file for depositions and subpoenas; must be modified for your use. Author: Edward Still, Esq.

DOC.EXE (Freeware) Document Assembly macro

FACMAC.EXE (Shareware) A collection of over 80 powerful WordPerfect 5.1 macros for office productivity and general use. Author: Ken Fackler, WordPerfect Certified Resource

FEDS51.ZIP (Freeware) Sophisticated WP5.1 merge for Federal Service of Process Forms; must be modified for your district court. Author: Edward Still, Esq.

LEGMAC.EXE (Shareware) Legal Cite marking macros for Table of Authorities version 1.1

LTRHEAD.EXE (Shareware) *The* Letterhead Kit/*DOS version 2.0* for WP5.1, these sophisticated macros will create a letterhead, combine it with fax forms and invoices, and create enlarged print on any printer. Also includes over 30 graphical business messages, such as "Confidential" and "Next Day Air," that can be printed on any document. Author: Jerry Stern, member of the Association of Shareware Professionals, WordPerfect Certified Resource

RULENO.ZIP (Shareware) Sophisticated style sheets for both WP5.0 and 5.1 that allows the printing of legal pleadings in a ruled and numbered format at the same time as the word processing document; eliminates the need to purchase expensive pleading paper

RULENO2.ZIP (Shareware) The companion style sheet to RULENO.ZIP used in creating pleading paper

WLCLN.ZIP (Freeware) A WP5.1 macro system to clean up the formatting of Court Opinions downloaded from Westlaw, as well as result files from WestCheck. Author: William D. Marvin, Esq.

WPMAC517.ZIP (Shareware) Over 115 powerful WP5.1 macros from programmer/lawyer Alan Kaplan, Esq. This is version 7 and contains macros for both general and legal use

WPMAC509.ZIP (Shareware) Over 100 powerful WP5.0 macros from programmer/lawyer Alan Kaplan, Esq.

/WPSHARE includes demos and shareware related to WordPerfect Corporation products.

AUTNUM.EXE (Shareware) A stand-alone program that converts all paragraph, section, and article numbers to WordPerfect automatic paragraph number codes. Optionally, it can insert table-of-contents codes around each section heading. Each replacement may be confirmed, modified, or rejected by the user. Author: Flying Buttress Software

COMPARE.ZIP (Shareware) A stand-alone program that performs word-for-word comparison of WordPerfect documents for "legislation-style" document comparison. Author: James White

CLX version 2.1 (Shareware) A Clause Cross Referencer for WP5.1 designed specifically for the legal profession. Analyzes a document, identifies clause numbers, and produces a report listing references in the text to these clause numbers. Author: Andrew McBurnie

PIPERF.EXE (Demonstration version) A Personal Injury Case Management database program for personal injury attorneys. Runs under DataPerfect from WordPerfect Corporation. Author: Julian Goldstein

D.2.2 DISK 2: LEGAL SHAREWARE AND DEMOS

BLKBOOK.ZIP (Shareware) A powerful and easy-to-use client database/Rolodex program. Autodials, mail merges with WordPerfect. Keystroke compatible with WordPerfect. Author: CIDEX Computer Systems

HUDDEM.EXE (Demonstration version) HUD Form Assistant Software; performs all the calculations for a real estate closing and prints out a complete HUD form. Author: Tom Witt

LEGBIL.EXE (Demonstration version) An integrated time and billing program for lawyers and law firms. Supports networks at no additional cost. Author: FrostByte Software

PROPIM.EXE (Shareware) A Personal Information Manager for attorneys; works both as a stand-alone program and as a TSR; network compatible. Author: Ward Moody

TBANK.ZIP (Demonstration version) The Total Bankruptcy program version 2.0 for Chapters 7, 11, and 13 bankruptcies; updated for the new forms. Author: Bit Legal Software

To order these supplementary disks, use the order card at the back of the book, or contact:

> CIDEX Computer Systems
> 2 Willow Terrace
> Hoboken, NJ 07030
> Tel: (201) 653-5105
> Fax: (201) 653-8507

APPENDIX E PRODUCT INFORMATION

PRODUCTS/SERVICES

The following products/services are mentioned in this book. The manufacturer's or distributor's name is included here for those desiring additional information.

WEST PUBLISHING COMPANY
610 Opperman Dr.
P.O. Box 64526
St. Paul, MN 55164-0526
(612) 687-7000
(800) 328-WEST (9377)
Customer Service (800) 937-8529

WESTLAW
Subscription information: (800) 329-0109
Customer service (800) 328-9833
West's Reference Attorneys (800) 688-6363
WESTfax (800) 562-2329

WEST DISK PRODUCTS
WESTMATE and WESTCHECK
    Black's Law Dictionary—
        Electronic Edition
    Black's Legal Speller—
        Electronic Edition
    Express Forms—California
        Litigation and Arbitration
        (other states will become available
        soon)
    (800) 328-9352

WORDPERFECT CORPORATION
1555 N. Technology Way
Orem, UT 84057
Orders/upgrades: (800) 321-4566
WP5.1 support numbers:
Installation: (800) 533-9605
Laser printers: (800) 541-5170
Macros, merges, and labels: (800) 541-5129
Graphics and tables: (800) 322-3383

Other features: (800) 541-5096
Networks: (800) 321-3389

Gordon McComb: *WordPerfect 5.1 Macros and Template*
Includes two disks with over 400 macros and templates
BANTAM BOOKS
666 Fifth Ave.
New York, NY 10103

Ronnie Shushan and Don Wright: *Desktop Publishing by Design*
MICROSOFT PRESS
One Microsoft Way
Redmond, WA 98052

Phillip Brady: *Using Type Right*
NORTHLIGHT BOOKS
1507 Dana Ave.
Cincinatti, OH 45207

ARTISOFT (Manufacturer of Lantastic, a peer-to-peer network)
ARTISOFT Plaza
575 E. River Rd.
Tucson, AZ 85704
(602) 293-6363

NOVELL (Manufacturer of NetWare and NetWare Lite networking software)
(800) NET-WARE
122 E. 1700 South
Provo, UT 84606

MICROSOFT CORPORATION (Networking and application software)
One Microsoft Way
Redmond, WA 98052
(800) 426-9400

HEWLETT-PACKARD
(Printer, scanners, and computers)
16399 W. Bernardo Dr.
San Diego, CA 92127
(619) 592-4522

ADOBE SYSTEMS (PostScript fonts)
1585 Charleston Rd.
Mountain View, CA 94042
(415) 961-4400

RATIONAL DATA SYSTEMS (Voice Over voice annotation for WordPerfect 5.1)
1050 Northgate Drive
San Rafael, CA 94903
(415) 499-3354

LASERTOOLS CORP. (PostScript fonts for WordPerfect)
1250 45th St., Suite 100
Emeryville, CA 94608
(510) 420-8777

PACIFIC DATA PRODUCTS (Font cartridges and printer add-ons)
9125 Rehco Rd.
San Diego, CA 92121
(619) 552-0880

ADVANCED SOFTWARE, INC.
(DocuComp 1.1 Redlining Software)
1095 E. Drane Avenue, Suite #103
Sunnyvale, CA 94086
(408) 733-0745

LEGAL BBS

The following are some of the many legal BBSs around the country:

ABA/NET
Chicago, IL
(312) 988-5000 Information
(800) 242-6005, ext. ABA
5501 LBJ Freeway, #1015
Dallas, TX 75240
Features: On-line legal databases, including access to WESTLAW; extensive faxing and E-mail services to machines and mailboxes. Basic fee: $3 per month.

COMPUSERVE
P.O. Box L-477
Columbus, OH 43260
Voice: (800) 848-8199
Features: One of the largest information systems in the world, CompuServe has forums on almost every subject imaginable. For lawyers, there is the LAWSIG, which has libraries for downloading shareware and general legal information, plus forums on many different areas of law.

ERISA BBS
(407) 841-6016
Orlando, FL
Spitfire
Modems: 2400
Type: Unofficial
Sponsor: Law Offices of David Rhett Baker
Features: For employee-benefits attorneys (ERISA, COBRA, pension plans, welfare plans, compliance, or litigation); forum for exchange of public or private messages among attorneys in this practice, and exchange of pattern plans, briefs, legal memoranda, etc.

LAWMUG (Lawyer's Microcomputer User's Group)
(312) 661-1740
(312) 280-8180
Chicago, IL
Modems: 9600 HST
Type: Unofficial
Features: LawMUG newsletter; Automated Legal Forms, hardware and consulting sales; Illinois legal referral; Ill Sup Ct summaries and files for downloading; messages, and echo-mail; Fidonet 1:115/661. Cost is $25 a year.

OFFICIAL UNITED STATES ELECTRONIC COURTS SERVICES

ACES (APPELLATE COURT ELECTRONIC SERVICES)
An electronic bulletin board for rapid dissemination of appellate court information. Allows the public to view and transfer published slip opinions, oral-argument calendars, court rules, notices and reports, and press releases. (Plans are to make ACES and other electronic services available in the remaining federal courts.)

FOURTH CIRCUIT COURT OF APPEALS—VIRGINIA
Computer: (804) 771-2028, -2063
(804) 771-2213—Voice

SIXTH CIRCUIT COURT OF APPEALS—OHIO
Computer: (513) 684-2842
(513) 684-2953—Voice

NINTH CIRCUIT COURT OF APPEALS—SAN FRANCISCO, CA
Computer: (415) 556-8620, -8647, -8648
(415) 556-3493—Voice

INDEX

Absolute tab settings. *See* Tabs and indents
Address
    Printing on envelopes, §2.3.4
    Printing on labels, §2.3.18-2.3.19
    Using named macros to automatically insert client addresses (and names) into a letter, §2.2.3
Advance feature, §2.2.2
Alignment, text. *See* Text alignment and justification
Appearance. *See* Text attributes
Attribute codes. *See* Reveal codes
AUTOEXEC.BAT file, §A.1.5
    See also Installing WP 5.1
Automatic date feature, §2.1.7
    See also Date
Automatic paragraph numbering. *See* Paragraph numbering

Backup options, §A.7
[Backspace] key. *See* Deleting and undeleting text
Base font, §6.2.1, 6.2.5
Baseline. *See* Typography
Blacklining. *See* Redlining
Block protect, §3.1.6, §5.2.9
Block function
    To delete text. *See* Deleting and undeleting
    To move, copy and delete text. *See* Cutting, pasting and copying text
Body text, §6.1.2
    See also Typography
Boilerplate. *See* Keyboard merge

Bolding text, §1.4.11, §2.1.3
    See also Text attributes and formatting
Border (around the page), §6.2.8

Case captions, §4.1.1-4.1.3
    Using tables feature, §4.1.2
    Using newspaper columns and line draw, §4.1.3
Center justification. *See* Justification
Centering text on a line, §1.4.4
Centering text on a page vertically, §2.1.4
Check boxes (creating), §6.2.8
Citations
    Paragraph symbol, §5.2.8
    Section symbol, §5.2.8
    See also Special characters
Clearing the screen, §1.3.2
Codes. *See* Reveal codes
Columns. *See* Parallel columns and Newspaper columns
Comment feature, §5.2.5
Compose key. *See* Special characters
Configuring WordPerfect
    Backup options, §A.7
    For macros, §A.3
    Initial codes, §A.5
    Location of files, §A.3
    Long document features, §B.1.1
Conditional end of page, §3.1.6, §5.2.9
Copying text. *See* Cutting, pasting and copying text
Cursor movement, §1.2.4
Cutting, pasting and copying text, §1.3.2

Date
    Automatic date feature, §2.1.7
    Positioning in a letter, §2.1.6
Default units, §1.1.1
Deleting and undeleting text (using the undelete function), §1.3.1
Deleting codes. *See* Reveal codes
Directory. *See* DOS functions and List files
Display text, §6.1.2
    See also Typefaces
Document assembly
    Merge templates (simple—in correspondence chapter), §2.3.1-2.3.3
    Merge templates (simple and advanced in Contract chapter), §3.2.4-3.2.6
    Merge templates (simple and advanced to automate pleadings), §4.2.1-4.2.3
Document compare. *See* Redlining
Document summary option, §A.6
DOS functions, §B.1, §1.2.3
Dot leader
    Flush right and Center right (manual), §3.2.8, §5.3.8
    In table of authorities and table of contents. *See* Table of contents and Table of authorities)
Double underlining, §5.1.1
    See also Text attributes
Double spacing. *See* Line spacing
Dupe and revise. *See* Simple document assembly

Endnotes, §5.2.4
Entering text (the basics), §1.1.3
Envelopes (printing address block of a letter), §2.3.4
   Defining paper size/type, §2.3.4
[Esc] key
   to repeat, §1.6.1
   to cancel a command, §1.1.1
Exercises
   Block Function, §1.3
   Copying and Printing Text, and Navigating Around a Document, §1.2
   Creating an Advanced Template Using {Variable} and {Text} Codes, §3.2.4
   Creating an [Alt][Z] Macro to Change Line Spacing for Quotes, §5.3.1
   Creating an Envelope Primary Merge Document, §2.3.10
   Creating a Footnote from Previously Entered Text, §5.2.2
   Creating a Keyboard Macro, §5.3.2
   Creating a Named Macro Using the Pause Feature, §2.2.3
   Creating a Table, §5.3.4
   Creating a Temporary Macro for Fed. R. Civ. P., §5.3.1
   Creating a User Defined Legal Paragraph Numbering Style, §3.1.4
   Page Numbering; Headers, Footers, and Footnotes; Using the Spell Checker and Thesaurus, §1.5
   Using List Files to Retrieve Files, Plus Basic Formatting, §1.4
   Using the Outline Feature, §5.2.1
Exit command. *See* Clearing the screen
Extended search. *See* Search

Field names. *See* Merges
File management tips, §B.2
Figure box. *See* Graphic images

Finding files. *See* List files
Flush right, §2.1.6
Fonts. *See* Typefaces
Footers, §1.5.4
   Using footers in a letter, §2.1.5
   Using a macro to create a footer with path/filename, Appendix C
Footnotes, §1.5.4, §5.2.2-5.2.3
   Options, §5.2.3
Formatting (basics)
   Centering text, §1.4.4
   Changing line spacing, §1.4.6, §5.1.1
   Changing margins, §1.4.3
   Changing text justification, §1.4.5
   Page numbering, §1.5.1-1.5.3
   Tabs and Indents, §1.4.7
   Tab settings, §1.4.8
   Underlining, bolding, and italicizing, §1.4.9-1.4.12
Fractions. *See* Typography
Full justification. *See* Justification

Graphic lines. *See* Horizontal and Vertical lines
Graphic images, §6.2.3

Hard return, §1.1.3
Hard space, §3.1.6
Hard page break, §1.2.1
   Using to start a new label, §2.3.19
Headers, §1.5.4
   Using headers in a letter, §2.1.5
Help (using to explain print options), §1.2.2
Horizontal lines, §6.2.2
Hyphenation, §5.2.10
   Hard hyphen, §3.1.6

Indenting (left/right), §5.1.1
Initial codes, §A.5
Installing WordPerfect 5.1 on a network, §A.1
Italics. *See* Text attributes

Justification. *See* Text alignment

Keeping text together. *See* Block protect, Conditional end of page, and Widow/orphan protection
Kerning. *See* Typography
Keyboard merge, §2.3.1-2.3.2

Labels, §2.3.18-2.3.19
Landscape paper orientation, §6.1.8
Leading. *See* Typography
Left justification, §1.4.5
Legal outline. *See* Paragraph numbering
Line spacing, changing, §1.4.6, §5.3.1
Lines. *See* Horizontal and Vertical lines
Line draw (for case captions and pleading covers), §4.1.3
List files, §1.4.1, Appendix B
   Finding files, §B.1.2
   Working with multiple files, §B.1.1
Line numbers. *See* pleading paper
Long document features, §1.4.1 and, §B.1.1

Macros
   [Alt] key, §5.3.1
   Case caption, §4.1.4
   Editing using the macro editor, §2.2.4, §5.3.1
   Keyboard layout (editing and mapping macros to), §5.3.2
   Keyboard macros, §5.3.2
   Mapping to a keyboard, §5.3.2
   Macro editor, §5.3.2, Appendix C
   Named, §2.2.3
   Pause feature, §2.2.3-2.2.4
   Renaming, §2.2.3
   Temporary, §5.3.1
   See also Appendix C
Margins
   Left/right, §1.4.3, §2.1.2
   Top/bottom, §2.1.2
Mass mailings. *See* Merge

Master document feature, §3.2.1-3.2.2
Master setup file, §A.1.1
Measuring type. *See* Typography
Merge template. *See* Document assembly
Merges (for automating mass mailings), §2.3.5-2.3.17
Monospaced typefaces. *See* Typefaces
Moving text. *See* Cutting, copying and pasting text
Multiple pages, printing, §3.2.7, §5.3.9

Navigating through a document. *See* Cursor movement
Nesting and chaining in macros and templates, §4.2.2, Appendix C
Networks
   Creating and editing a master setup file to create a global macros subdirectory, §A.4
   File management on, §B.2.2-B.2.3
   Installing, §A.1, §B.2
Newspaper columns (using to create case captions), §4.1.3
Notebook (in WordPerfect Office), Using as a secondary merge file, §2.3.17

Open style. *See* Styles
Outlining feature, §5.2.1
Outline Style. *See* Styles

Page numbering, §1.5.1-1.5.2
   Suppressing page numbers, §1.5.3
Paired styles, §6.2.6
   See also Styles
Paper size/type. *See* Envelopes, labels, and Landscape and portrait
Paragraph numbering (automatic), §3.1.2-3.1.4
Parallel columns, §5.3.3
Path, directory. *See* Appendix B and List files

Pause feature. *See* Macros, named
Picas, §6.1.4
Pitch. *See* Typography
Pleading paper, §4.2.4
Point size. *See* Typography
Portrait paper orientation, §6.1.8
Postscript. *See* Typography
Previewing a document, §1.4.13
   See also View document
Primary file. *See* Merges
Printers, §6.1.11
   Installing printers, §A.2
   Installing network printers, §A.1.6
Printing a document, §1.2.2
   Labels, §2.3.19
   Multiple pages, §1.2.2
   Pages in different sections of a long document, §3.2.7, §5.3.9
Proportional typefaces. *See* Typography

Red herring. *See* Rotating text
Redlining, §3.2.3
Relative tab settings. *See* Tabs and indents
Replace, §5.2.6
   See also Search feature
Restoring text. *See* Deleting and undeleting text
Restoring a lost file. *See* Backup options
Retrieving ASCII files (*e.g.*, WESTLAW), §5.2.7
Retrieving files
   Using the List files feature, §1.4.1
   Using the Retrieve option, §1.4.1
   See also List files
Retrieving text. *See* Storing and retrieving text in memory
Reveal codes, §1.1.2
   Editing a document by deleting codes, §1.4.14
   Use of the status line to find attribute codes, §1.1.1
   See also Formatting, Changing line spacing
Right justification. *See* Justification
Rotating text, §6.2.4

Sans-serifs. *See* Typography
Saving a document, §1.2.3
Scalable typefaces. *See* Typography
Search feature, §5.2.6
   To clean up downloaded text from Westlaw, §5.2.7
Secondary file. *See* Merges
Selecting (for sorts), §2.3.15
Serifs. *See* Typography
Setup. *See* Configuring WordPerfect
Shading. *See* Tables
Single spacing. *See* Line spacing
Size attribute. *See* Text attributes
Soft return, §1.1.3
Sorting (a secondary merge file), §2.3.12-2.3.15
Special characters, §5.2.8
   Mapping special characters to a keyboard, §5.3.2
   See also Typography do's and dont's
Spell check, §1.5.5
Splitting the screen (to move text from one document to another), §1.6.2-1.6.3
Status line, §1.1.1
Storing and retrieving text in memory, §1.3.2
Strikeout. *See* Redlining
Styles, §2.2.1-2.2.2, §6.2.6
   Deleting styles, §6.2.6
   Editing a style, §6.2.6
   Outline styles, §3.1.5
   Open styles (creating for letterhead), §2.2.2
   Paired styles, §6.2.6
   Pleading open style for pleading paper, §4.2.4
   Saving styles (for use in other documents), §6.2.6
   Using existing codes to create a style, §2.2.2
Subdocuments. *See* Master document
Superscript. *See* Footers
Suppressing headers and footers, §1.5.4
   In a letter, §2.1.5
Suppressing page numbers, §1.5.3
   See also Page numbers
Switch. *See* Status line and Splitting the screen

Index

Table feature, §5.3.4-5.3.5, §6.2.7
    To create case captions, §4.1.2
Table of authorities, §5.3.7-5.3.8
Table of contents, §3.2.7, §5.3.9
    For a contract, §3.2.7
Tabs and indents
    Absolute tab setting, §2.1.2
    Adding, §1.4.7-1.4.8
    Changing tab settings, §1.4.8, §2.1.2
    Relative tab setting, §2.1.2
Templates, §2.3.1-2.3.3, §3.2.4
    Contracts, §3.2.4-3.2.6
    Letters, §2.3.1-2.3.3
    Pleadings, §4.2.1-4.2.3
    See also Document assembly
Text alignment
    Left, full, centered and right, §1.4.5
Text attributes
    An introduction, §1.4.9-1.4.12
    Double underlining, §5.1.1
    Bolding text, §1.4.11, §2.1.3
    Italicizing text, §1.4.12, §2.1.3
    Text size, §6.2.5
    Underlining text, §1.4.10, §2.1.3
    Words only, §5.1.1
Text size. *See* Text attributes

Thesaurus, §1.5.5
Toggle, §1.1.1
    Insert/typeover, §1.2.1
Typeover, §1.12
Typography, §6.1
    Baseline, §6.1.5
    Body text vs. display text, §6.1.2
    Choosing a proportionally spaced serif base font, §6.2.1
    Do's and dont's, §6.1.9
    Fractions, §6.1.9
    Kerning, §6.1.7
    Leading, §6.1.6
    Monospaced typefaces, §6.1.1
    Measuring type, §6.1.4
    Picas, §6.1.4
    Pitch, §6.1.1
    Point size, §6.1.1
    Postscript, §6.1.10
    Proportional typefaces, §6.1.1
    Scalable typefaces, §6.1.10
    Serifs and sans-serifs, §6.13
    Style, §6.1.3
    Typefaces vs. fonts, §6.1.1
    See also Text attributes

Undelete command, §1.21
    See also Deleting and undeleting text
Underlining, §1.4.10, §2.1.3
    Double underling, §5.1.1
    Words only, §5.1.1
    See also Text attributes and Formatting
User defined outline. *See* Paragraph numbering
User box. *See* Rotating text

Variables. *See* Document assembly
Vertical lines, in creating pleading paper, §4.2.4
View document, §1.4.13

WESTLAW
    Cleaning up a downloaded document from, §5.2.7
    Downloading a document in WordPerect format, §1.4.3, §5.2.7
Widows\orphans, §3.1.6, §5.2.9
Wildcard character, §B.1.2
WYSIWYG. *See* View document

To order additional copies of

How to Use

WordPerfect® 5.0/5.1

in the Law Office

This publication is reasonably priced for individual attorneys and staff members. To order additional copies of this Guide, or for quantity pricing information, please contact West Publishing Company.

Call your West Representative
or
800-328-9352

WEST PUBLISHING COMPANY
610 Opperman Drive
P.O. Box 64526
St. Paul, MN 55164-0526

QUICK REFERENCE

Feature	Keystrokes
Adding page numbers	[Shift][F8], [2], [6], [4]
Adding graphic lines	[Alt][F9], [5]
Advance feature to position text	[Shift][F8], [4], [1]
Automatic date feature	[Shift][F5], [1] (text) or [2] (code)
Bolding	[F6] or [Ctrl][F8], [2], [4] or [Ctrl][F8], [2], [1]
Centering text	[Shift][F8] or [F12], [Shift][F6], [Y]
Centering text vertically on a page	[Shift][F8], [2], [1]
Changing left/right margins	[Shift][F8], [1], [7]
Changing footnote and endnote appearance	[Ctrl][F7] ([1] or [2]), [4]
Changing text justification	[Shift][F8], [1], [3]
Changing tab settings	[Shift][F8], [1], [8]
Changing line spacing	[Shift][F8], [1], [6]
Choosing a different font, i.e., a scalable one	[Shift][F8], [3], [3]
Compose to insert special character	[Ctrl][V] (character set, character)
Creating a Table	[Alt][F7], [2], [1], [F7]
Creating parallel columns	[Alt][F7], [1], [3], [1], # of columns
Creating temporary macros	[Ctrl][PgUp] ([1] to [9]) (Text)
Invoking temporary macro	[Alt] ([1] to [9])
Creating Headers and Footers	[Shift][F8], [2], [3], or [4], [1], [2], [F7]
Creating macro to automate tasks	[Ctrl][F10], name it, [Enter], describe it, [Enter], keystrokes, [Ctrl][F10]
Defining a Table of Contents	[Alt][F5], [5], [1]
Creating a TOC	[Alt][F4] or + [Alt][F5], [1] # or the level
Defining a Table of Authorities	[Alt][F5], [5], [4] section #
Creating a TOA	[Alt][F4] or [F12], [Alt][F5], [4] (section #), [Enter], [F7] Enter short form [Enter], [Home], [F2], [Alt][F5], [4] (type short form name) [Enter]
Cutting, pasting, and copying	
Moving a sentence	[Ctrl][F4], [1], [1], [Enter]
Copying a paragraph	[Ctrl][F4], [2], [2], [Enter]
Copying a page	[Ctrl][F4], [3], [2]
Deleting an attribute code	[Alt][F3], [F11], [Del] or [Backspace]

How to Use WordPerfect® 5.0/5.1 in the Law Office. Copyright 1993 by West Publishing Company. 800-328-9352

Feature	Keystrokes
Flush Right to position the date	Alt F6
Hard Hyphen/Spaces	Home -, Home, Spacebar
Indenting (Left/Right)	F4
Inserting comments into text	Ctrl F5, 4 (5 in **WP5.0**), 1
Inserting Footnotes	Ctrl F7, 1, 1, F7
Inserting graphics into your document	Alt F9, 1, 1, 1, (type file name) (Assign settings)
Italicizing text	Ctrl F8, 2, 4
Keeping text together	
Widow/Orphan	Shift F8, 1, 9, Y
Block Protection	F12, Shift F8, Y
Conditional End of Page	Shift F8, 4, 2
Line Draw	Ctrl F3, 2, 1, or 2 (use cursor arrows)
Line Numbering	Shift F8, 1, 5, Y
List Files to find and retrieve a file	F5, Enter, N (type first letters) Enter, 1
Moving text from one document to another using split screen	Ctrl F3, 1 (# of lines) Shift F3, Shift F10 (cut and paste)
Outline function to organize ideas	Shift F5, 4, 1, Enter (for new level) Tab (for next sublevel)
Printing a document	Shift F7, 1
Saving a document	F10, Y or F7, Y, Y (N to remain in WP, Y to exit)
Search and Extended Search	F2 or Shift F2, Home, F2 (Home, Shift F2) F2
Search and Extended Search and Replace	Alt F2 or Home, Alt F2, Y or N to confirm, F2, F2
Selecting the legal outline style	Shift F5, 6, 4, F7, 4, 1
Spell check	Ctrl F2, 3 (select letter)
Storing and retrieving text in memory	Ctrl F4, 2, 1, F1, Ctrl F4, 4, 1
Suppressing page numbers	Ctrl Home, ↑, Shift F8, 2, 8, 4, Y (2, 9, 4, Y in **WP5.0**)
Suppressing Headers/Footers	Ctrl Home, ↑, Shift F8, 2, 8, 5 or 7, Y
Temporary macros	PgUp, (1 to 9), type value To use: Alt + # of variable
Thesaurus	Alt F1, 1, F7
Undelete funtion	F1, 1 or use ↑ to see last 3 deletions
Underlining (words and spaces)	F8 type text → or Ctrl F8, 2, 2
Underlining (words only)	Shift F8, 4, 7, N
Viewing documents	Shift F7, 6